T0408309

THE FINANCE-INNOVATION NEXUS

INTERNATIONAL SYMPOSIA IN ECONOMIC THEORY AND ECONOMETRICS

Series Editor: William A. Barnett

Recent Volumes:

INTERNATIONAL SYMPOSIA IN ECONOMIC THEORY AND ECONOMETRICS   VOLUME 34

THE FINANCE-INNOVATION NEXUS: IMPLICATIONS FOR SOCIO-ECONOMIC DEVELOPMENT

EDITED BY

WILLIAM A. BARNETT

University of Kansas, USA
Center for Financial Stability, USA

and

BRUNO S. SERGI

Harvard University, USA
University of Messina, Italy

United Kingdom – North America – Japan
India – Malaysia – China

Emerald Publishing Limited

Emerald Publishing, Floor 5, Northspring, 21-23 Wellington Street, Leeds LS1 4DL.

First edition 2025

Editorial matter and selection © 2025 William A. Barnett and Bruno S. Sergi.
Published under exclusive licence.
Individual chapters © 2025 Emerald Publishing Limited.

Reprints and permissions service

Contact: www.copyright.com

No part of this book may be reproduced, stored in a retrieval system, transmitted in any form or by any means electronic, mechanical, photocopying, recording or otherwise without either the prior written permission of the publisher or a licence permitting restricted copying issued in the UK by The Copyright Licensing Agency and in the USA by The Copyright Clearance Center. Any opinions expressed in the chapters are those of the authors. Whilst Emerald makes every effort to ensure the quality and accuracy of its content, Emerald makes no representation implied or otherwise, as to the chapters' suitability and application and disclaims any warranties, express or implied, to their use.

British Library Cataloguing in Publication Data

A catalogue record for this book is available from the British Library

ISBN: 978-1-83608-731-1 (Print)
ISBN: 978-1-83608-730-4 (Online)
ISBN: 978-1-83608-732-8 (Epub)

ISSN: 1571-0386 (Series)

INVESTOR IN PEOPLE

CONTENTS

LIST OF FIGURES AND TABLES

Figures

Tables

ABOUT THE EDITORS

William A. Barnett is the Oswald Distinguished Professor of Macroeconomics at the University of Kansas, Director at the Center for Financial Stability in New York City, Founder and First President of the Society for Economic Measurement and Editor of the Cambridge University Press article, *Macroeconomic Dynamics. His Book, Getting It Wrong: How Faulty Monetary Statistics Undermine the Fed, the Financial System, and the Economy*, published by MIT Press, won the American Publishers' Award for Professional and Scholarly Excellence for the best book published in economics in 2012. With Nobel Laureate Paul Samuelson, he also co-authored the book, *Inside the Economist's Mind*, which is translated into seven languages.

Bruno S. Sergi is an Instructor at Harvard University, where he is also a Faculty Affiliate at the Center for International Development and the Institute for Quantitative Social Science and an Associate at the Davis Center for Russian and Eurasian Studies. He is the Series Editor of *Cambridge Elements in the Economics of Emerging Markets* (Cambridge University Press) and *Entrepreneurship and Global Economic Growth* (Emerald Publishing). He teaches political economy and international finance at the University of Messina, Italy. He chairs the Lab for Entrepreneurship and Development (LEAD), a research lab based in Cambridge, USA, to generate and share knowledge about entrepreneurship, development and sustainability.

ABOUT THE CONTRIBUTORS

Drs Untung Alamsah is currently a Student at Business Administration Department, Universitas Padjadjaran, Bandung, Indonesia. He obtained his Bachelor's in Public Administration from Universitas Padjadjaran, Bandung – Indonesia and participated in several high-profile research. In addition, he works a Logistics Consultant in one of private company in Indonesia, and he is a Practitioner Lecturer in Logistics Business Department, Universitas Padjadjaran.

Lina Anatan is a Lecturer and Researcher at the Faculty of Business, Maranatha Christian University Bandung. She earned her Bachelor's degree in Economics from the Faculty of Economics, Airlangga University, and her Master's and Doctorate Degrees in Management from the Faculty of Economics and Business, Gadjah Mada University. Her areas of research interest are manufacturing strategy, supply chain management, knowledge management and strategic alliance.

Dr Sudatta Banerjee is an Associate Professor of Economics in the Department of Economics and Finance at BITS Pilani- Hyderabad Campus, India. She is involved in teaching, research and consultancy for the past 10 years. Her research, publications, talks and sponsored projects involve empirical developmental issues, education, health, gender studies, applied econometrics and behavioural issues.

Vinka Amalia Hasta Barata is an Undergraduate student at the School of Business and Management Institute of Technology Bandung (SBM ITB) with expected graduation in October 2022. Vinka is an awardee of merit-based scholarship from the Central Bank of Indonesia. This research is part of Vinka's undergraduate thesis research that has benefited from the financial support of a research grant program under the Central Bank of Indonesia research institute. Vinka has research interest in finance and economics.

Prawira Fajarindra Belgiawan is a Lecturer at the School of Business and Management, Institut Teknologi Bandung (SBM ITB). He received his Bachelor's degree from the Regional and City Planning Department, Bandung Institute of Technology. He continued his studies and received his Master's and Doctoral degrees from the Department of Urban Management, Kyoto University, Japan. Fajar is now joining the Business Strategy and Marketing research group in the School of Business and Management. Fajar's main research interests are on the application of the stated choice experiments, psychological aspects and the discrete choice model on travel behaviour and marketing.

Sumedha Bhatnagar is a Research Scholar in the Department of Humanities and Social Sciences, Malaviya National Institute of Technology, Jaipur, Rajasthan, India. Bhatnagar's areas of research interest include green finance and investment, sustainable finance, energy sector, public finance, international trade and the Indian economy.

Riky Candra is the Head of the Public Service, Investor, and Institutional Relations Section, Directorate of Government Securities, Ministry of Finance, Republic of Indonesia. He received Master of Public Policy degree from the National Graduate Institute for Policy Studies (GRIPS), Japan in 2015 and Master's in Economic Science at the University of Indonesia in 2016. His current role is managing the communication strategy and institutional relations of government's financing and risk management.

Jae-Hyeok Choi is a Faculty Member in the International Business Management Program at Bina Nusantara University. He received a Ph.D. in research on ESG activities of exporting small- and medium-sized enterprises. His research interests include ESG management, digital leadership, strategic management, and innovation.

Muhammad Ainul Fahmi, S.Si., M.MT., has recently graduated with a Master of Management Technology in Supply Chain Management Studies from the Institut Teknologi Sepuluh Nopember (ITS), Indonesia. He obtained his Bachelor's degree in Science from Institut Teknologi Sepuluh Nopember (ITS), Indonesia, and has participated in several high-profile research projects. In addition to his academic career, Fahmi does research in statistical methods, particularly SEM-PLS, and has written various types of research and books in Green Supply Chain Management and SEM-PLS methods. Currently, Fahmi works as Supply Chain Analyst in Private National Company in Indonesia, Tutor Online in Universitas Terbuka, and Part-Time Lecturer in Institut Teknologi Insan Cendekia Mandiri (ITICM) in Indonesia.

Taufik Faturohman is currently a Lecturer at the School of Business and Management Institute of Technology Bandung (SBM ITB). He received a PhD in Economics and Finance from Curtin Business School, Curtin University of Technology Western Australia. The title of his dissertation is 'An Examination of the Growth of Islamic Banking in Indonesia from 2003–2010'. Taufik obtained his MBA from ITB and graduated with honours (cum laude). He earned a Bachelor's degree in Materials Engineering, also from ITB. Taufik's research interests include Islamic banking, corporate finance, business risk management and economics.

Dr Bincy George is an Assistant Professor at Tata Institute of Social Sciences (TISS) Hyderabad. She holds a PhD in Economics from the Department of Economics and Finance, Birla Institute of Technology and Science (BITS), Pilani – Hyderabad Campus. Her research interests include climate change, gender, vulnerability, and developmental issues.

Yuddy Hendranata is the Head of the Sub-Directorate of Financing Risk Analysis, Directorate of Government Securities, Ministry of Finance, Republic of Indonesia. He completed his Doctoral studies in Financial Economics at Claremont Graduate University, California, USA in 2016. Yuddy started his career at the Ministry of Finance since 1997 and actively teaches courses in finance and is a thesis supervisor at several universities, including Masters in Management at Gadjah Mada University. Currently, he is responsible for the government's financing portfolio and risk management.

Jessica Christella Hidayat is a Graduate student at the School of Business and Management Institute of Technology Bandung (SBM ITB), majoring in Finance. She earned a Bachelor's degree in Mathematics at the Institute of Technology Bandung. Jessica's research interest is financial risk management, and she is currently doing her thesis on debt management.

Andrian Dolfriandra Huruta, Ph.D., is an Assistant Professor in the Department of Economics, Faculty of Economics and Business, Satya Wacana Christian University, Salatiga, Indonesia. His areas of research interests are macroeconomics, microfinance, applied econometrics and international trade.

Su-Jung Hwang is a Professor of the Graduate School of Global Entrepreneurship at Keimyung University and a Director of the Korean Association of Industrial Business Administration. She received a Ph.D. in research topics on technological innovation in small- and medium-sized enterprises. Moreover, she is interested in research fields such as small- and medium-sized enterprises, technological innovation, entrepreneurship, ESG management, and job engagement.

Takayasu Ito has been a Professor of Monetary and Financial Economics at the School of Commerce, Meiji University since April 2014. He started his academic career in April 2003 when he joined the Faculty of Economics at Niigata University as a Professor. Before his academic career, he worked for a major Japanese news agency, where he covered monetary policy, fixed income, interest rate derivatives markets, etc. He holds two Ph.D.s, one in Economics and other in Business Administration. His research interests are central banks, financial markets and Islamic finance.

Min-Sun Kim, Ph.D., is an Assistant Professor in the International Undergraduate Program in Business and Management, Chung Yuan Christian University, Taiwan (R.O.C). Her research area is management and business ethics and social responsibility.

A'ang Kunaifi is currently a Student at Supply Chain Management Department, Institut Teknologi Sepuluh Nopember (ITS), Surabaya, Indonesia. He obtained his Bachelor's in Marine Engineering from Institut Teknologi Sepuluh Nopember (ITS) – Indonesia and participated in several high-profile research. In addition, he works as a logistician in one of the private companies in Indonesia.

Niki Lukviarman is a Professor concentrating in corporate governance, affiliated with the Faculty of Economics and Business at Andalas University in Indonesia. He did post-doctorate work as an Adjunct senior Research Fellow of the Governance and Corporate Social Responsibility Centre (GCSR), Curtin University of Technology, Perth – Australia (2004–2009). Additionally, he served as a Visiting Professor at several universities, including NHL University of Applied Sciences in Leeuwarden, the Netherlands (2013), and Saxion University of Applied Sciences in Deventer, the Netherlands (2017).

Rifaldi Yunus Mahendra is a final year Master of Business Administration Student at the School of Business and Management Institut Teknologi Bandung (SBM ITB), majoring in business risk and finance. He received a Bachelor's degree in Computer Science from Universitas Komputer Indonesia. He is interested in finance, data analytics, business strategy and technology.

Yunieta Anny Nainggolan completed her Ph.D. in 2011 at Queensland University of Technology (QUT). Previously, Nainggolan took a Master of Commerce in Finance from the University of Melbourne and graduated with honours. Nainggolan has research interests in fund management, ethical fund, socially responsible investment, disclosure and reporting, corporate finance and corporate governance. Currently, Nainggolan is joining the Business Risk and Finance Research Group in the School of Business and Management.

Nadia Shakira Nasr pursued her Undergraduate education at the School of Business Management, Bandung Institute of Technology. As a Management student, made her knows more about the business world. With learning experiences during college and organisations, she has become a person who has a high curiosity, a growth mindset and initiative.

Sari Usih Natari, S.TP., M.M., is currently a Lecturer at Business Administration Department, Universitas Padjadjaran, Bandung, Indonesia. She obtained his Master's in Human Resource Management from Universitas Padjadjaran, Bandung – Indonesia and participated in several high-profile research. In addition, she was a former Human Resource Administrator at one of the logistics companies in Indonesia.

Subhan Noor is the Head of the Sub-Directorate of Investor Relations, Directorate of Government Securities, Ministry of Finance, Republic of Indonesia. He completed his Undergraduate degree from the Bandung Institute of Technology in 1998 and earned his Master's degree from Hiroshima University in 2006. He joined the Ministry of Finance, Republic of Indonesia in 1999 and served various positions. In 2019, he was also assigned as Acting Director of Investment for the Education Fund Management Institute.

Dr Harvey T. Ong (with the rank of Full Professor 2) is a Full-time Faculty Member of the Decision Sciences and Innovation Dept, RVR College of Business,

De La Salle University. He was the former Chairperson of the Decision Sciences and Innovation Dept, RVR College of Business, De La Salle University. He was also the former Chairperson of the Business Management Department of De La Salle University. He graduated with the Bachelor's degree of Science in Computer Science specialised in Software Technology (De La Salle University), Master's in Business Administration (De La Salle University) and Doctor of Philosophy in Business (De La Salle University). His expertise includes management information system, system analysis and design, information management, project management, events management, entrepreneurship, business planning and business mathematics.

Taffy Ukhtia Panduputri acquired her Undergraduate degree from Institut Teknologi Bandung in 2018 in the field of Natural Science, more specifically Bachelor's degree in Physics. In 2019, she started her further education in the School of Business and Management ITB with the Magister of Science of Management major. Currently, she is a Member of Decision Making and Strategic Negotiation research interest group.

Ahmad Danu Prasetyo is a Faculty Member at the School of Business and Management, Bandung Institute of Technology (SBM ITB). He obtained a Ph.D. degree from the Graduate School of Economics, Keio University, Japan. Danu earned his Bachelor's in Industrial Engineering from Telkom Institute of Technology, Indonesia and Master of Science in Management from Bandung Institute of Technology, Indonesia. Danu has a wide range of research interest in economics and finance, especially in macroeconomic policy, fiscal policy, monetary policy, public policy, stock and bond market and personal finance.

Wawas Bangun Tegar Sunaryo Putra, S.E., M.I.Kom., has recently graduated with a Master of Arts in Communication Studies from the Institut Komunikasi dan Bisnis LSPR, Indonesia. He obtained his Bachelor's degree in Economics from Universitas Mercu Buana, Indonesia, and has participated in several high-profile research projects. In addition to his academic career, he teaches statistical methods, particularly SEM-PLS, and has launched various types of research training. Currently, he is the Owner, Founder, and CEO of the Indonesian School of Research (a Member of the WRC Group) in Indonesia.

Ayudya Puti Ramadhanty is a final year Magister of Business Administration Student at the School of Business and Management Institut Teknologi Bandung (SBM ITB), majoring Finance. She received a Bachelor's degree in Islamic Economics and Finance from Universitas Pendidikan Indonesia. Currently, she works as an Information Technology Business Analyst Intern at MMS Group Indonesia, one of the coal mining companies in Indonesia. She is interested in corporate finance, investment project analysis, risk management, Islamic finance, business research and economic research.

Grahithaa Sarathy is a Financial Engineering student at the University of California, Berkeley. With a background in Economics and Computer Science, she is keen on addressing challenges in Economics and Finance using computing techniques. Her research interests include development economics, econometrics, corporate finance, and computational finance.

Erna Setiany holds the position of Associate Professor in accounting at the Faculty of Economics and Business, Universitas Mercu Buana, Indonesia. The areas of research that she focusses on are financial accounting and corporate governance. Her most recent publication is *Corporate Governance and Social Disclosure: A Comparative Study of Listed Hospitality Industries in South East Asia.*

Dr Dipti Sharma is Associate Professor and Head of Department of Humanities and Social Sciences, Malaviya National Institute of Technology Jaipur, Rajasthan, India. Sharma's areas of interest are energy economics, energy policies, management and security. Sharma has been engaged in research related to the Indian power sector, reforms and restructuring process and its impact, supply side and demand side management, electricity markets and power trading, solar-based rural electrification in Rajasthan, Indian automotive manufacturing sector, international trade, green transport and green finance, etc. Sharma's research credentials include international and national journals, conferences and book chapter publications of repute in the areas of economics and management.

Ratu Shavira is a Professional in a private corporation. She graduated from the Faculty of Economics and Business at Andalas University in 2020. Her research interests include corporate governance and capital markets.

Sri Putri Siregar is a Senior Analyst in the Public Service, Investor, and Institutional Relations Section, Directorate of Government Securities, Ministry of Finance, Republic of Indonesia. She received a Master of Public Policy from the University of Chicago in 2019. Her current role is managing the communication strategy and narration of government's financing.

Prof A. Suryanarayana is a Former Dean, Faculty of Management and Chairperson, Board of Studies, Department of Business Management, Osmania University, India with over 42 years of teaching, research, training and consulting experience and the recipient of the Lifetime Achievement Award (2020) and 'Best Professor in Management in HRM' Global Award from World Education Congress (2012), IKON HR *Dronacharya* Award (2018) and also FDP-IIM (A), FAGBA, FWBI, and FISM. He has two Westbury (UK) published international text books in HRM area and five international book chapters and has presented over 200 papers in international conferences alone within and outside India.

Renyi Wen is a Senior Undergraduate in Accounting at the College of Business and Public Management at Wenzhou-Kean University.

Chunxiao Xue is an Assistant Professor of Accounting at the College of Business and Public Management and a Co-investigator in the Center for Big Data and Decision-Making Technologies at Wenzhou-Kean University.

Jianing Zhang is an Assistant Professor of Finance at the College of Business and Public Management and a Co-investigator in the Center for Big Data and Decision-Making Technologies at Wenzhou-Kean University. He is enrolled in the 'Pu Jiang Talent Program' in Shanghai. He has published in numerous journals, including the *Journal of Banking & Finance, Financial Review, Finance Research Letters,* and *International Review of Economics & Finance.*

INTRODUCTION

The chapters published in this volume were presented at the SIBR 2023 Tokyo Conference on Interdisciplinary Business and Economic Research organised by the Society of Interdisciplinary Business Research on January 5th–6th January 2023 in Tokyo, Japan. This volume aims to address contemporary issues pertinent to the interplay of financial technologies and social development in Emerging Economies. The authors utilised a large variety of data sources and methods for their research. Topics covered by this volume include, but are not limited to: CEO characteristics and CSR (Chapter 1); women's decision-making capability at the household level (Chapter 2); inventory management strategies and operational performance (Chapter 3); the effects of internal and external learning on manufacturing capability (Chapter 4); green finance and investment in emerging economies (Chapters 5 and 17); behavioural finance (Chapter 6); service quality and customer satisfaction (Chapters 7 and 16); employees' performance outcome (Chapter 8); intellectual capital, MIS and financial performance (Chapters 9, 18 and 20); online media and customer behaviour (Chapters 10 and 15); capital structure during COVID-19 (Chapter 11); and the online search volume index, working capital, stock return, and banks' risk-taking (Chapters 12, 13, 14 and 19). This volume aims to stimulate cross-disciplinary interest in financial technologies and social development in emerging economies. The emergence and development of the above interdisciplinary finance and social issues are well celebrated throughout this volume.

CHAPTER 1

THE RELATIONSHIP BETWEEN CEO CHARACTERISTICS AND CORPORATE SOCIAL RESPONSIBILITY: EVIDENCE FROM CHINA

Renyi Wen[a], Chunxiao Xue[a,b,c] and Jianing Zhang[a,b,c]

[a]College of Business and Public Management, Wenzhou-Kean University, Wenzhou 325060, China
[b]Center for Big Data and Decision-Making Technologies, Wenzhou-Kean University, Wenzhou 325060, China
[c]Quantitative Finance Research Institute, Wenzhou-Kean University, Wenzhou, China

ABSTRACT

The study examines the relationship between CEO characteristics and corporate social responsibility (CSR) in China. Previous studies showed that good CSR behaviour could enhance the firm's financial performance. CEOs are responsible for major decision-making, including CSR policies. This chapter uses all A-share listed firms in China from 2011 to 2020. The authors find that CEO's gender, age, educational background, and career experience have positive relationships with CSR. This chapter enriches the current literature on the effects of CEO characteristics and highlights the important roles of CEO characteristics in CSR activities.

Keywords: CEO; corporate social responsibility; firm performance; upper echelon theory; China

JEL Classifications: G30; G32; G39

The Finance-Innovation Nexus: Implications for Socio-Economic Development
International Symposia in Economic Theory and Econometrics, Volume 34, 1–13
Copyright © 2025 by Emerald Publishing Limited
All rights of reproduction in any form reserved
ISSN: 1571-0386/doi:10.1108/S1571-038620240000034001

1. INTRODUCTION

This chapter focuses on the relationship between CEO characteristics and corporate social responsibility (CSR). The previous study utilised the upper echelon theory to show the impact of CEO characteristics on CSR (Manner, 2010). The previous relevant studies focus more on the narrow part of the relationship between firm performance and one of the CEO characteristics, such as gender, age, and the CEO's multiple identities (Rahman & Fang, 2019). On the other hand, some researchers studied the relationship between firm performance and CSR activity (Kim & Kim, 2020). Few studies have analysed the relationship between CEO characteristics and CSR activity, impacting firm performance.

We choose the Chinese financial market over the last decade to analyse this relationship. This chapter's objective is to test whether a CEO with specific characteristics related to professional experience and personal background can be conducive to a firm's growth. We formulate independent variables of the CEO by contributing the CEO's background and the related career, financial and oversea experiences. Secondly, this chapter proposes two hypotheses: CEO's educational background and gender affect the firm's CSR activities. Thirdly, this chapter contemplates the impact of CEO characteristics on CSR activities through a linear regression model. Fourthly, this chapter adds control variables such as return on assets, firm size, and Tobin's Q to assess their roles in both CEO characteristics and CSR activity. Finally, this chapter performs robustness checks using control variables to confirm two hypotheses.

Our research enriches the prevailing literature on CSR in several ways. Firstly, we broaden the scope of CSR literature by incorporating an executive-level perspective. Existing scholarship contends that external factors and corporate governance collectively influence a company's propensity for CSR engagement (Flammer, 2015; Hendratama & Huang, 2022; Kemper et al., 2013; Kuo et al., 2022). Our investigation uncovers a notable association between CEO characteristics and CSR performance in Chinese listed companies. Secondly, although previous research has explored the impact of executive attributes on CSR initiatives, the influence of CEO gender remains ambiguous due to conflicting evidence (Adams & Ferreira, 2009; Galbreath, 2011; Zou et al., 2018). By analysing a sample of Chinese listed companies, we discover that organisations led by female CEOs demonstrate superior CSR performance. Thirdly, our study offers empirical insights into CSR research within the context of emerging markets. Most CSR literature has focused on developed markets like the United States and Europe. Our research investigates Chinese firms and reveals that those employing female CEOs and CEOs with advanced educational backgrounds, particularly MBA degrees, exhibit enhanced CSR performance. We also find that firms with older CEOs and CEOs with international and financial backgrounds perform better in CSR.

2. LITERATURE REVIEW AND HYPOTHESIS DEVELOPMENT

Research into CSR has been a subject of study for many decades and has encompassed a diverse range of topics. The literature suggests that ownership structure, laws and regulations, project design methods, and board diversity can influence a company's CSR activities (Cook & Glass, 2018; Hendratama & Huang, 2022; Kuo et al., 2022; Shibuya et al., 2023).

Based on Jensen and Meckling (1976) agency theory, Barnea and Rubin (2010) suggest CSR engagement as a principal-agent relation between managers and shareholders. Dean (2003) also points out a discretionary allocation of corporate resources towards improving social welfare that enhances relationships with key stakeholders. Davis (1973) and Vogel (2005) agree that CSR activities bring benefits beyond legal requirements. In other words, enterprises increase their competitiveness through social activities that generate a sense of CSR. Therefore, CSR gradually becomes the primary concern of businesses worldwide (Javeed & Lefen, 2019).

As a pivotal figure, the CEO can orientate the firm towards adopting CSR measurements (Li et al., 2020). Additionally, the previous literature shows that CEO attributes strongly affect firm performance and CSR disclosure (García-Sánchez et al., 2019; Hegde & Mishra, 2019). Guo (2013) also supports that Chinese CEOs should be concerned about long-term corporate development.

Previous studies have examined the relationship between one of the CEO characteristics and CSR activity. Chatterjee and Hambrick (2007) suggest that CEO characteristics can be divided into the CEO's external conditions (age, gender, educational level, and tenure) and internal qualities (narcissism, overconfidence, humility, charisma, self-evaluation, and hubris). However, the executive's complex psychological and cognitive process types cannot be directly observed (Manner, 2010). Although internal qualities could be measured, this will not be attempted in the present study. We focus on the relationship between CEO's external characteristics and CSR activity. In addition, we combine the CEO's career, overseas, and finance experiences to test the relationship. Hence, this chapter summarises the above research and tests to what extent the characteristics of CEOs affect the degree of CSR.

Adams et al. (2007) find that the gender gap exists in executive compensation, with female executives earning 45% less than their male counterparts presumably because female CEOs mainly own small companies. Using the Wharton Research Data Service database, Rekker et al. (2014) examine all companies in one or more years between 1996 and 2010. They conclude that CSR increases the pay of female CEOs compared to male CEOs, indicating that the gender gap in compensation diminishes in high-CSR firms. Likewise, some studies suggest that the gender gap in compensation is narrowing over time (Loury, 1997; Stanley & Jarrell, 1998). The literature above suggests that the female CEO would be more likely to be responsible for CSR activities. We propose the first hypothesis based on CEO gender:

H1. A female CEO engages in more CSR activities.

Previous research shows that executives' decision-making is affected by their educational level. Tyler and Steensma (1998) argue that top executives with a technical education background place more weight on the opportunities the alliance provides than those with other types of education. Bertrand and Schoar (2003) find that CEOs with higher education backgrounds are more aggressive in risk-taking, so their companies have higher liabilities than the counterparties. Karagiannidis (2012) concludes that CEOs graduating from business school have better performance and less risky portfolios than other CEOs.

We argue that CEOs with high education levels will be more cautious and risk-averse, while CEOs with lower education levels tend to be more aggressive. CEOs with higher education levels are more socially responsible and engage more in CSR activities than CEOs with lower education levels. We propose the second hypothesis.

H2. CEO's educational background positively impacts CSR activities.

3. DATA AND METHODOLOGY

3.1. Data

The initial sample consisted of all A-share listed firms on the Shenzhen and Shanghai stock exchanges. We collect data from the China Stock Market and Accounting Research (CSMAR) database from 2011 to 2020. After excluding some missing values, the final sample includes 25,971 firm-year observations.

CSR is the dependent variable. We retrieve CSR activities from the CSMAR database. We record fourteen CSR activities, as shown in Table 1.1. CSR disclosure dummies are created.

The summation of dummies is normalised to measure the amount of CSR activities:

$$CSRR_{i,t} = \frac{\sum_{i=1}^{N} Z_{pi,t}}{N} \tag{1}$$

Table 1.1. CSR Disclosure Index.

Attribute		Measurement
1.	Whether an independent director	No=0;Yes=1
2.	Whether to concurrently serve as chairman and CEO	No=0;Yes=1
3.	Whether a supervisor or not	No=0;Yes=1
4.	Whether to concurrently serve in the shareholder unit	No=0;Yes=1
5.	Whether a member of the executive team	No=0;Yes=1
6.	Whether to disclose environmental protection	No=0;Yes=1
7.	Whether to disclose public relations	No=0;Yes=1
8.	whether to disclose work safety	No=0;Yes=1
9.	whether to disclose deficiency	No=0;Yes=1
10.	whether to disclose mandatory disclose	No=0;Yes=1
11.	whether the external audit comes from the big four	No=0;Yes=1
12.	whether certified by the third party	No=0;Yes=1
13.	Whether to refer to GRI	No=0;Yes=1
14.	Whether a board member	No=0;Yes=1

where i denotes the sample firm and t denotes the year in the sample period. $Z_{pi,t}$ denotes different properties for firm i at time t. N equals 14 measures in this case.

CEO characteristics are the independent variables. Previous research shows that CEO characteristics affect CSR activities (Manner, 2010; Li et al., 2020). Besides, prior studies commonly highlight CEO's age, gender, and educational background (Manner, 2010; Li et al., 2020; Rahman & Fang, 2019). In addition to these CEO's background independent variables, this study adds CEO's multiple identities, finance experience, career experience, and overseas experience as explanatory variables.

For the CEO's background, we selected listed companies in China from 2011 to 2020, which matches the previous CSR observations. We create a gender dummy for the CEO: zero represents a male, and one represents a female. Besides, we express CEO's multiple identities following Equation (2). Six aspects in Table 1.2 measure the CEO's multiple identities.

$$\text{CEO's Multiple Identities}_{i,t} = \frac{\sum_{i=1}^{N} Z_{mi,t}}{N} \tag{2}$$

where $Z_{mi,t}$ denotes CEO's multiple identities for firm i at time t. N equals six measurements in Table 1.2.

Moreover, we add CEO's educational background, overseas background, finance experience, and career experience as other explanatory variables. For educational background, the number one to five represents the educational degree from lower than junior college to Ph.D. degree. However, MBA is singled out as a separate dummy because it is practitioner-oriented. For overseas and finance experiences, dummy variables equal one for related experience and zero otherwise. We describe career experience using three dummy variables: shareholder, general, and stakeholder dummies. The dummy equals one if the CEO has this career type's function in the past and zero otherwise. Table 1.3 gives a more detailed explanation of independent variables.

Following previous studies on CEO characteristics and CSR (Jian & Lee, 2015; Wei et al., 2018), we choose the control variables, including ROA (net profit divided by average asset), leverage (total liability/total asset), Tobin's Q (market

Table 1.2. CEO's Multiple Identities.

Attribute		Measurement
1.	Whether an independent director	No=0;Yes=1
2.	Whether to concurrently serve as chairman and CEO	No=0;Yes=1
3.	Whether a supervisor or not	No=0;Yes=1
4.	Whether to concurrently serve in the shareholder unit	No=0;Yes=1
5.	Whether a member of the executive team	No=0;Yes=1
6.	Whether a board member	No=0;Yes=1

Table 1.3.   Variable Definitions.

Variable	Symbolic Representation	Evaluation Method and Score Basis
CSR Disclose Index	CSRR	CSR ratio through calculating related formula
Age	Age '	CEO's age
Gender	Gender	1 represents female
		0 represents male
Educational Degree	Degree	0 represents unknown CEO's educational degree
		1 represents under junior college degree
		2 represents a junior college degree
		3 represents a bachelor's degree
		4 represents a master's degree
		5 represent Ph.D. degree
MBA	MBA	1 represents MBA degree, otherwise give 0
Career experience – Shareholder function	Shareholder	1 represents related shareholder's career experience, Otherwise, give 0
Career experience – General	General	Include CEO/ President, general manager, law career experiences
		1 represents related general career experience; otherwise, give 0
Career experience – Stakeholder	Stakeholder	Include marketing/sales, operations, R&D, HR, public relations, medical/education/govService
		1 represents related stakeholders' career experience. Otherwise, it gives 0
Oversea background	Overseaback	1 represents the related overseas background; otherwise, gives 0
Finance background	Finback	1 represents related finance background; otherwise, it gives 0
CEO's Multiple Identity	CEO's Multiple Identity	CEO's duality ratio through calculating related formula
Return on Assets	ROA	Net profit/average assets
Asset Liability Ratio	Leverage	Total liability/total assets
Tobin's Q	Tobin's Q	Market value divided by total assets
Firm size	Firmsize	The natural log of total sales
Executive Compensation	Compensation	Total executive compensation is divided by the number of executives. Take the natural logarithm of the average executive compensation.

value divided by total asset), executive compensation (the natural logarithm of the total executive compensation divided by the number of the executive). In addition, the firm size is usually measured as the natural log of total sales in CSR studies.

Table 1.4 reports the descriptive statistics for all variables. The number of observations is almost identical, but some variables have fewer observations due

Table 1.4. Descriptive Statistics.

Variable	Obs.	Mean	Std. Dev.	Min	Max
CSRR	32,666	0.383	0.256	0	1
Gender	32,666	0.065	0.247	0	1
Age	32,661	49.629	6.663	24	81
Degree	26,062	3.16	1.241	0	5
MBA	26,062	0.072	0.258	0	1
Shareholder	32,627	0.207	0.405	0	1
General	32,627	0.011	0.102	0	1
Stakeholder	32,627	0.998	0.048	0	1
OveseaBack	32,628	0.085	0.279	0	1
FinBack	32,666	0.072	0.259	0	1
CEO's Multiple Identity	32,666	0.577	0.135	0.333	0.833
ROA	32,666	0.035	0.729	−48.316	108.366
Leverage	32,666	0.441	1.11	−0.195	178.345
Tobin's Q	31,475	0.63	0.248	0.001	1.484
Firmsize	32,652	9.273	0.684	3.928	12.472
Compensation	32,537	5.694	0.313	3.931	7.303

to missing values. CSRR is normalised between zero and one. The average CSRR value is 0.383, and the standard deviation of CSRR is 0.256. The average Gender value is 0.065 and close to zero, indicating that most CEOs are male. The average CEO age is about 49.6 years old.

Table 1.5 shows the correlation matrix among all variables. Many control variables and CEO characteristics correlate highly with the CSR disclosure index. More specifically, a significant correlation exists between CSRR and CEO characteristics, such as the CEO's gender, age, degree, and overseas background. The preliminary correlation analysis supports two hypotheses.

3.2. Methodology

We use pooled panel data to investigate the impact of CEO characteristics and firm performance on CSR activities to run multivariate ordinary lease square (OLS) regressions.

$$\begin{aligned} CSRR_{it} = {} & \beta_0 + \beta_1 Gender_{it} + \beta_2 Age_{it} + \beta_3 Degree_{it} + \beta_4 MBA_{it} + \\ & \beta_5 CareeExp_{it} + \beta_6 OverseaBack_{it} + \beta_7 FinBack_{it} + \\ & \beta_8 CEOMulti_{it} + \beta_9 FirmPerf_{it} + \beta_{10} Firmsize_{it} + \\ & \beta_{11} Compensation_{it} + \varepsilon_{it} \end{aligned} \quad (3)$$

where *i* denotes the sample firm and *t* denotes the year in the sample period.

Table 1.5. Correlations of Variables.

Variables	(1)	(2)	(3)	(4)	(5)	(6)	(7)	(8)	(9)	(10)	(11)	(12)	(13)	(14)	(15)	(16)
(1) *CSRR*	1.000															
(2) *Gender*	−0.018*	1.000														
(3) *Age*	0.101*	−0.042*	1.000													
(4) *Degree*	0.081*	−0.020*	−0.004	1.000												
(5) *MBA*	−0.016*	0.004	−0.051*	−0.709*	1.000											
(6) *Shareholder*	0.062*	0.066*	−0.036*	0.077*	−0.040*	1.000										
(7) *General*	0.013*	0.010	−0.016*	0.025*	−0.019*	0.050*	1.000									
(8) *Stakeholder*	0.006	−0.016*	0.009	0.005	−0.002	−0.004	−0.007	1.000								
(9) *OveseaBack*	0.035*	0.017*	−0.022*	0.142*	−0.016*	0.004	0.017*	−0.024*	1.000							
(10) *FinBack*	0.087*	0.018*	−0.013*	0.077*	−0.033*	0.503*	0.021*	−0.004	0.017*	1.000						
(11) *CEO's Multiple Identity*	−0.011*	−0.021*	0.164*	−0.062*	0.059*	−0.034*	−0.037*	−0.027*	0.050*	0.000	1.000					
(12) *ROA*	0.001	0.000	0.021*	−0.006	0.000	−0.019*	−0.005	0.001	0.001	−0.018*	0.018*	1.000				
(13) *Leverage*	0.009	−0.007	−0.005	0.022*	−0.009	0.042*	0.013*	−0.001	−0.016*	0.047*	−0.032*	−0.358*	1.000			
(14) *Tobin'sQ*	0.154*	−0.027*	0.047*	0.030*	−0.016*	0.047*	0.004	0.027*	−0.046*	0.072*	−0.052*	−0.009	0.040*	1.000		
(15) *Firmsize*	0.397*	−0.053*	0.106*	0.106*	−0.017*	0.058*	0.005	0.025*	−0.011*	0.061*	−0.065*	0.005	0.051*	0.498*	1.000	
(16) *Compensation*	0.227*	−0.017*	0.081*	0.108*	−0.013*	0.054*	−0.001	0.000	0.063*	0.091*	0.009	0.007	0.034*	0.080*	0.307*	1.000

Notes: This table reports pairwise correlations of all variables. * represents statistical significance at the 5% level.

4. RESULTS AND DISCUSSIONS

4.1. Baseline Results

Questions related to measured CEO characteristics are often directly related to CEO selection, creating the possibility that reverse causality leads to positive outcomes (Chatterjee & Hambrick, 2007). Therefore, we use CSR as the dependent variable and introduce various control variables and firm performance measures. Because performance is the most critical measure for the firm, we explore different performance measures as robustness checks. Previous papers often use ROA and Tobin's Q to measure a firm's performance (Jiang et al., 2013; Li et al., 2020; Shah et al., 2019).

We use OLS regression analysis and select explanatory variables such as gender, age, educational degree, overseas background, career experiences, finance experience, and CEO's multiple identities. Additionally, we use the ROA, Tobin's Q, executive compensation, and firm size as control variables to observe the relationship with the dependent variable, CSR activity. The impact of CEO characteristics on CSR is shown in Table 1.6. We find that most CEO characteristics have a significant relationship with CSR activity. The coefficients of *Degree* and *MBA* are significant and positive at 1%, indicating that companies hiring CEOs with higher educational levels or with an MBA degree perform better in CSR. The results suggest that the CEO's educational background is positively related to CSR activity, which is consistent with *H2*.

Table 1.6.   Baseline Regressions.

Variables	CSRR	CSRR
Gender	−0.00218 (0.00584)	−0.00360 (0.00595)
Age	0.00200*** (0.000219)	0.00195*** (0.000223)
Degree	0.00888*** (0.00168)	0.00871*** (0.00171)
MBA	0.0279*** (0.00799)	0.0248*** (0.00813)
Shareholder	0.00514 (000414)	0.00612 (0.00420)
General	0.0729*** (0.0137)	0.0744*** (0.0138)
Stakeholder	−0.0348 (0.0277)	−0.0598** (0.0263)
Overseaback	0.0179*** (0.00486)	0.0174*** (0.00493)
FinBack	0.0504*** (0.00605)	0.0535*** (0.00613)
CEO's Multiple Identity	−0.00683 (0.0108)	−0.00719 (0.0110)
ROA	−0.00172*** (0.000837)	
Tobin's Q		−0. 0505*** (0.00705)
Firmsize	0.137*** (0.00233)	0.146*** (0.00263)
Compensation	0.0864*** (0.00492)	0.0822*** (0.00501)
Constant	−1.470*** (0.0409)	−1.468*** (0.0409)
Observation	25,971	25,103
R-squared	0.188	0.189

Notes: Robust standard errors are in parentheses. *** $p<0.01$, ** $p<0.05$, * $p<0.1$.

For the control variables, we find positive and significant coefficients for *Age*, suggesting that firms with older CEOs perform better in CSR. The result is consistent with the findings by Fabrizi et al. (2014). Both the overseas and finance background has a significant and positive impact on CSR activity, consistent with the findings by Shi and Ye (2019). The positive and significant coefficients of CEO's general-function career experience indicate that CEOs with top executive experience perform better in CSR. The positive and significant coefficients of *Firmsize* show that larger firms are more likely to perform better in CSR. However, the negative coefficients of *ROA* and *Tobin's Q* indicate that more profitable and growing firms are less likely to participate in CSR activities.

4.2. Additional Results

To further test hypotheses, we conduct a more in-depth analysis of the influence of CEO characteristics on CSR activities. Here, we still choose ROA, Tobin's *Q*, executive compensation and firm size as control variables. As discussed in the literature review, one of the possible reasons for the gender gap in compensation is that female CEOs usually manage small companies. Due to such a selection bias, we introduce an additional interaction term between gender and firm size.

$$\begin{aligned} CSRR_{it} = {} & \beta_0 + \beta_1 Gender_{it} + \beta_2 Age_{it} + \beta_3 Degree_{it} + \beta_4 MBA_{it} + \\ & \beta_5 CareeExp_{it} + \beta_6 OverseaBack_{it} + \beta_7 FinBack_{it} + \\ & \beta_8 CEOMulti_{it} + \beta_9 FirmPerf_{it} + \beta_{10} Firmsize_{it} + \\ & \beta_{11} Firmsize_{it} \times Gender_{it} + \beta_{12} Compensation_{it} + \varepsilon_{it} \end{aligned} \tag{4}$$

Table 1.7 shows the robustness check analysis. After adding the interaction term between firm size and gender, we obtain similar results for CEO characteristics and control variables. In addition, the coefficients on *Gender* become significantly positive at 1% level, suggesting that female CEOs engage more in CSR activities. Additionally, the interaction term between *Gender* and *Firmsize* has a significantly negative coefficient, suggesting that the positive relationship between female gender and CSR activities is weakened in large firms. However, the net effect of *Gender* on CSR is positive and significant. Still, we find positive and significant coefficients of *Degree* and *MBA*. The results are consistent with *H1* and *H2*.

H2 indicated that the education level of the CEO has a positive impact on CSR activity. Our results show that CEO's educational and MBA degrees positively impact CSR activity, thus directly supporting this hypothesis. In hypothesis *H1*, we can test whether CEO's female gender has a strong positive relationship with CSR activity. Tables 1.6 and 1.7 show that female CEOs engage more in CSR activities. Such an observation might disappear in large firms, presumably due to the low percentage of female CEOs. Finally, CEO's career experience, finance experience, and oversea background boost the CSR activity.

Table 1.7. Interaction Between Gender and Firm Size.

Variables	CSRR	CSRR
Gender	0.312*** (0.0860)	0.332*** (0.0898)
Age	0.00200*** (0.000219)	0.00195*** (0.000223)
Degree	0.0879*** (0.00168)	0.00861*** (0.00171)
MBA	0.0278*** (0.00799)	0.0245*** (0.00813)
Shareholder	0.00587 (0.00415)	0.00603 (0.00420)
General	0.0713*** (0.0138)	0.0728*** (0.0139)
Stakeholder	−0.0357 (0.0276)	−0.0605** (0.0261)
Overseaback	0.0178*** (0.00486)	0.0173*** (0.00492)
FinBack	0.0496*** (0.00605)	0.0527*** (0.00613)
CEO's Multiple Identity	−0.00512 (0.0108)	−0.00538 (0.011)
ROA	−0.00166** (0.000845)	
Tobin's Q		−0.0511*** (0.00703)
Firmsize	0.139*** (0.00225)	0.148*** (0.00263)
Firmsize × Gender	−0.0344*** (0.00940)	−0.0367*** (0.00980)
Compensation	0.0858*** (0.0492)	0.0825*** (0.00501)
Constant	−1.501*** (0.0416)	−1.493*** (0.0410)
Observation	25,971	25,103
R-squared	0.188	0.189

Robust standard errors are in parentheses. *** $p<0.01$, ** $p<0.05$, * $p<0.1$.

5. CONCLUSIONS

Our research offers several contributions. Firstly, it broadens existing literature by examining executive-level impacts on CSR instead of primarily organisational-level factors. Secondly, we enrich the discourse by investigating the effects of CEO gender and educational background on CSR. Thirdly, we supply CSR-related evidence within an emerging market by scrutinising listed companies in China.

Our findings suggest that firms should prioritise selecting CEOs with higher educational degrees, older ages, and more overseas and finance backgrounds, as these characteristics are associated with a greater propensity for CSR activity. By emphasising these traits, companies can enhance and improve their CSR performance. It also indicates that female CEOs are positively related to CSR activity. Firms should therefore promote gender diversity in leadership positions to capitalise on the benefits of diverse perspectives and enhance CSR performance.

ACKNOWLEDGEMENTS

This research was supported by the Student Partnering with Faculty Research Program of Wenzhou-Kean University [No. WKUSPF2023004] and the Internal Research Support Program of Wenzhou-Kean University [No. IRSPG202205].

REFERENCES

Adams, R. B., & Ferreira, D. (2009). Women in the boardroom and their impact on governance and performance. *Journal of Financial Economics*, *94*(2), 291–309. https://doi.org/10.1016/j.jfineco.2008.10.007

Adams, S. M., Gupta, A., Haughton, D. M., & Leeth, J. D. (2007). Gender differences in CEO compensation: Evidence from the USA. *Women in Management Review*, *22*(3), 208–224. https://doi.org/10.1108/09649420710743662

Barnea, A., & Rubin, A. (2010). Corporate social responsibility as a conflict between shareholders. *Journal of Business Ethics*, *97*(1), 71–86. https://doi.org/10.1007/s10551-010-0496-z

Bertrand, M., & Schoar, A. (2003). Managing with style: The effect of managers of firm policies. *Quarterly Journal of Economics*, *CXVIII*(4), 1169–1208.

Chatterjee, A., & Hambrick, D. C. (2007). It's all about me: Narcissistic chief executive officers and their effects on company strategy and performance. *Administrative Science Quarterly*, *52*(3), 351–386.

Cook, A., & Glass, C. (2018). Women on corporate boards: Do they advance corporate social responsibility? *Human Relations*, *71*(7), 897–924. https://doi.org/10.1177/0018726717729207

Davis, K. (1973). The case for and against business assumption of social responsibilities. *The Academy of Management Journal*, *16*(2), 312–322. https://about.jstor.org/terms

Dean, D. H. (2003). Consumer perception of corporate donations effects of company reputation for social responsibility and type of donation. *Journal of Advertising*, *32*(4), 91–102. https://doi.org/10.1080/00913367.2003.10639149

Fabrizi, M., Mallin, C., & Michelon, G. (2014). The role of CEO's personal incentives in driving corporate social responsibility. *Journal of Business Ethics*, *124*(2), 311–326. https://doi.org/10.1007/s10551-013-1864-2

Flammer, C. (2015). Does product market competition foster corporate social responsibility? Evidence from trade liberalization. *Strategic Management Journal*, *36*(10), 1469–1485. https://doi.org/10.1002/smj.2307

Galbreath, J. (2011). Are there gender-related influences on corporate sustainability? A study of women on boards of directors. *Journal of Management & Organization*, *17*(1), 17–38.

García-Sánchez, I. M., Martínez-Ferrero, J., & Garcia-Benau, M. A. (2019). Integrated reporting: The mediating role of the board of directors and investor protection on managerial discretion in munificent environments. *Corporate Social Responsibility and Environmental Management*, *26*(1), 29–45. https://doi.org/10.1002/csr.1655

Guo, L. (2013). What determines CEO compensation effectively? Taking the case of Henan province as an example. *Journal of Applied Sciences*, *13*(22), 5416–5421.

Hegde, S. P., & Mishra, D. R. (2019). Married CEOs and corporate social responsibility. *Journal of Corporate Finance*, *58*, 226–246. https://doi.org/10.1016/j.jcorpfin.2019.05.003

Hendratama, D. T., & Huang, Y.-C. (2022). Corporate social responsibility of family-controlled firms in Taiwan. *Review of Integrative Business and Economics Research*, *11*(2), 36–60.

Javeed, S. A., & Lefen, L. (2019). An analysis of corporate social responsibility and firm performance with moderating effects of CEO power and ownership structure: A case study of the manufacturing sector of Pakistan. *Sustainability (Switzerland)*, *11*(1). https://doi.org/10.3390/su11010248

Jensen, C., & Meckling, H. (1976). Theory of the firm: Managerial behavior, agency costs and ownership structure. *Journal of Financial Economics*, *3*(4), 305–360.

Jian, M., & Lee, K. W. (2015). CEO compensation and corporate social responsibility. *Journal of Multinational Financial Management*, *29*, 46–65. https://doi.org/10.1016/j.mulfin.2014.11.004

Jiang, F., Huang, J., & Kim, K. A. (2013). Appointments of outsiders as CEOs, state-owned enterprises, and firm performance: Evidence from China. *Pacific Basin Finance Journal*, *23*, 49–64. https://doi.org/10.1016/j.pacfin.2013.01.003

Karagiannidis, I. (2012). The effect of management team characteristics on risk-taking and style extremity of mutual fund portfolios. *Review of Financial Economics*, *21*(3), 153–158. https://doi.org/10.1016/j.rfe.2012.06.009

Kemper, J., Schilke, O., Reimann, M., Wang, X., & Brettel, M. (2013). Competition-motivated corporate social responsibility. *Journal of Business Research*, *66*(10), 1954–1963. https://doi.org/10.1016/j.jbusres.2013.02.018

Kim, M., & Kim, T. (2020). When do CEOs engage in CSR activities? Performance feedback, CEO ownership, and CSR. *Sustainability (Switzerland)*, *12*(19). https://doi.org/10.3390/su12198195

Kuo, Y. C., Wu, Y. M., & Liu, Y. X. (2022). Identifying key factors for sustainable manufacturing and development. *Review of Integrative Business and Economics Research*, *11*(1), 30–50.

Li, H., Hang, Y., Shah, S. G. M., Akram, A., & Ozturk, I. (2020). Demonstrating the impact of cognitive CEO on firms' performance and CSR activity. *Frontiers in Psychology*, *11*. https://doi.org/10.3389/fpsyg.2020.00278

Loury, L. D. (1997). The gender earnings gap among college-educated workers. *ILR Review*, *50*(4), 580–593. https://about.jstor.org/terms

Manner, M. H. (2010). The impact of CEO characteristics on corporate social performance. *Journal of Business Ethics*, *93*(SUPPL. 1), 53–72. https://doi.org/10.1007/s10551-010-0626-7

Rahman, Md. J., & Fang, Y. (2019). The relationship between corporate social responsibility and firm performance in China. *Risk Governance and Control: Financial Markets and Institutions*, *9*(4), 41–48. https://doi.org/10.22495/rgcv9i4p4

Rekker, S. A. C., Benson, K. L., & Faff, R. W. (2014). Corporate social responsibility and CEO compensation revisited: Do disaggregation, market stress, gender matterα. *Journal of Economics and Business*, *72*, 84–103. https://doi.org/10.1016/j.jeconbus.2013.11.001

Shah, S. G. M., Tang, M., Sarfraz, M., & Fareed, Z. (2019). The aftermath of CEO succession via hierarchical jumps on firm performance and agency cost: Evidence from Chinese firms. *Applied Economics Letters*, *26*(21), 1744–1748. https://doi.org/10.1080/13504851.2019.1593932

Shi, B.W., & Ye, X. (2019). Research on the background of executive education and the mechanism of corporate social responsibility. *China Forestry Economics*, *159*(6), 20–40. https://doi.org/10.13691/j. [In Chinese].

Shibuya, K., Hu, E., Kobayashi, N., & Suzuki, H. (2023). Visualizing the project of design for environment to improve the feasibility for corporate social responsibility. *Review of Integrative Business and Economics Research*, *12*(1), 56–70.

Stanley, T. D., & Jarrell, S. B. (1998). Gender wage discrimination bias? A meta-regression analysis. *The Journal of Human Resources*, *33*(4), 947–973. https://about.jstor.org/terms

Tyler, B. B., & Steensma, H. K. (1998). The effects of executives' experiences and perceptions on their assessment of potential technological alliances. *Strategic Management Journal*, *19*(10), 939–965.

Vogel, D. (2005). *The market for virtue: The potential and limits of corporate social responsibility*. Brookings Institution Press.

Wei, J., Ouyang, Z., & Chen, H. A. (2018). CEO characteristics and corporate philanthropic giving in an emerging market: The case of China. *Journal of Business Research*, *87*, 1–11. https://doi.org/10.1016/j.jbusres.2018.02.018

Zou, Z., Wu, Y., Zhu, Q., & Yang, S. (2018). Do female executives prioritize corporate social responsibility? *Emerging Markets Finance and Trade*, *54*(13), 2965–2981. https://doi.org/10.1080/1540496X.2018.1453355

CHAPTER 2

EFFECT OF YEARS OF MARRIAGE ON THE DECISION-MAKING POWER OF WOMEN: A STUDY OF INDIA

Sudatta Banerjee[a], Grahithaa Sarathy[b] and Bincy George[c]

[a]BITS Pilani Hyderabad Campus, Hyderabad, India
[b]University of California, Berkeley, USA
[c]Tata Institute of Social Sciences (TISS) Hyderabad, India

ABSTRACT

In India, women make up 48% of the population, but only around 20% of the labour force. Their empowerment could potentially play a key role in the country's economic growth. At the household level, most of the decisions are taken by males and the attitude of females has been to accept it as a norm. This study measures changing levels of women's empowerment in terms of decision-making capability at the household level at different stages of marriage in the context of India. Data from India's National Family Health Survey is used to create indices based on freedom of movement, personal decisions, and household decisions. Then, these three indices are used to create a women empowerment index. Multiple regression analysis is used to find the relationship between decision-making and the number of years the respondent has been married, controlling for other factors. It is found that the number of years of marriage has a highly significant, positive relationship with the empowerment index, indicating gender differences may indeed be evolving in nature with respect to the number of years married. Additionally, through regressions on the indices

The Finance-Innovation Nexus: Implications for Socio-Economic Development
International Symposia in Economic Theory and Econometrics, Volume 34, 15–26
Copyright © 2025 by Emerald Publishing Limited
All rights of reproduction in any form reserved
ISSN: 1571-0386/doi:10.1108/S1571-038620240000034002

that make up the empowerment index, the above relationship appears to be primarily driven by personal decision-making.

Keywords: Women empowerment; stage of marriage; age of women; decision-making; gender equality

JEL Codes: C3; D1; J12; J16; O1; O12

1. INTRODUCTION

Women empowerment has been described as 'improving the ability of women to access the constituents of development – in particular health, education, earning opportunities, rights, and political participation' (Duflo, 2012). It comprises facets of domestic decision-making, access and control over resources, and freedom of movement. If empowered, women will be able to execute decisions concerning their well-being, family, and finances; put simply, they can have equal rights as males (Banerjee et al., 2020). The positive effect of women empowerment is not only experienced by women themselves; it trickles down to increased labour market participation and more human capital investment, in terms of increased empowerment, education, and health of their children (Banerjee et al., 2019, 2022; Hoddinott & Haddad, 1995). In India, women make up 48% of the population, but only around 20% of the labour force. Their empowerment could potentially play a key role in the country's economic growth and development.

This study intends to measure changing levels of women's empowerment in terms of decision-making capability at different stages of marriage. It tries to find the age at which women, if married, might be more empowered compared to other ages, and how decision-making evolves among spouses with different characteristics. The question addressed is as follows: does women's decision-making capability evolve as the years of marriage increase? The results of this study will help in identifying variables that may boost women's empowerment, and thus help in policy-making.

2. LITERATURE REVIEW

Decision-making is cited frequently by social scientists and individual respondents alike as a dominant basis for assessing equality in marriage (Rosenbluth et al., 1998). Though couples are likely to view their marriages as largely egalitarian, Fox and Murry (2000) note that in actual fact, husbands are likely to have the upper hand in household decision-making. Wanic and Kulik (2011) have addressed the consistent finding that men derive more benefit from marriage than their women counterparts. Gender inequality within a marriage may lead to a status quo that creates a difference in power, and discrimination between men and women (Sattar et al., 2022).

Studies conducted on the effects of empowerment provide a number of variables that can be used to model the empowerment of women. Murugan et al. (2021) find that in the Indian context, women who had completed their secondary education or higher, women who were property owners, and women who had higher levels of intra-household decision-making power were found to be less likely to experience intimate partner violence. A similar study considers the impact of women's financial empowerment on intimate partner violence in Jordan (Akilova & Marti, 2014), and finds that women who take part in financial decision-making are less likely to ever experience any type of intimate partner violence. Women's empowerment measures such as age at first marriage, education, employment, participation in women's groups, and ability to make intra-household decisions were used to determine the role of empowerment in mothers' risk of experiencing neonatal or under-five child death in Nepal, and the first two of these variables were found to play an important role (Pandey et al., 2017). In a study aimed at determining empowerment's effect on female sterilisation in Bihar, education, age, religious affiliation, age at marriage, out-of-home employment and intra-household decision-making were used as indicators of empowerment, though the latter two were not significant correlates of sterilisation status (Murugan & Pandey, 2019).

In the economics literature, multiple approaches have been proposed to model the household decision-making process. A review of the literature conducted by Himmelweit et al. (2013) outlines new home economics, and the unitary, bargaining, and collective model approaches. Gary Becker's (1965) new home economics views household decision-making as a process involving the maximisation of a single unified household utility function, by a single head of household. While the unitary model (Becker, 1965, 1981; Samuelson, 1956) assumes the members of the household to be a single decision-making unit, bargaining models make use of game theory to account for the bargaining involved in decision-making when members of a household have differing preferences. Bargaining literature considers both cooperative and non-cooperative bargaining processes as being capable of affecting the outcome of decision-making (Lundberg & Pollak, 1993; Manser & Brown, 1980; McElroy & Horney, 1981). A generalised version of cooperative bargaining is the more recent collective model (Chiappori, 1988, 1992; Chiappori et al., 2002), which doesn't rely on any one specific bargaining framework in the decision-making process.

Numerous factors have been cited as influencing decision-making in the case of women. Both the bargaining model and the sociology literature stemming from Blood and Wolfe (1960) suggest that a member's influence in household decision-making is dependent upon relative access to resources such as income and education. A woman's degree of involvement in household decision-making may, in such a case, be positively related to their share of household income and relative level of education. In support of this, Bernasek and Bajtelsmit (2002) find that a woman's involvement in household financial decision-making is positively related to her share of the household's total income.

There is also a pressing need to examine the decision-making dynamic in systems where the social norms that prevailed in the past and do so presently are different from those previously considered. Datta Gupta and Stratton (2010) use a two-country analysis to reason that institutions and social norms from different countries can affect bargaining power in a household. Moreover, empirical evidence shows that intra-household relations in developing countries may be more conflictive than equitable (Pearson, 1992). Consequently, we take into consideration studies conducted in developing South Asian countries like India.

Sathar and Kazi (2000) explore elements that impact women's autonomy in decision-making in rural Pakistan, and find that a woman's age and family structure appear to be the strongest determinants. Older women and women in nuclear households have a higher likelihood of involvement in the household decision-making process. Evidence from Nepal shows that a woman's age, employment, and number of living children are positively related to her autonomy in decision-making as captured by four outcome measures: her own health care, making major household purchases, making purchases for daily household needs, and visiting her family and friends (Allendorf, 2007). Furthermore, women living in rural areas are less likely to have autonomy in decision-making as captured by these measures, as are women belonging to higher wealth quintiles (Acharya et al., 2010). Abrar-ul-haq et al. (2017) examine decision-making autonomy as a source of women empowerment in southern Punjab, and conclude that women in rural areas have relatively lower decision-making ability on issues that concern them, their households, and society at large. Education, deprivation level, and ethnicity have also been cited as factors associated with a woman's autonomy in decision-making (Kabeer, 2002).

Findings from studies on women's empowerment can have implications for policy-making. In their attempts to improve income-generating activities, women face constraints that include physical, economic, natural, and sociocultural factors (Abebe & Kasa, 2021). Olaniran and Perumal (2021) argue that in the design and implementation of programmes aimed at improving the livelihood of women, the impact is exponential, and results are achieved expeditiously, when the beneficiaries themselves are actively involved. Membership in such groups has been linked with greater control over income and greater decision-making power (Kumar et al., 2021), making it necessary to understand the nature and the drivers of women empowerment. Empowering women is a goal in itself and also affects various economic indicators positively for example health and education of children, job performance, etc. (Anderson et al., 2017; Basu, 1992; Bautista & Uy, 2023; Dyson & Moore, 1983; Malhotra et al., 2002; Mason, 1995; Pham et al., 2023) and so policy making in this regard becomes necessary.

3. DATA AND VARIABLES

For this study, data were acquired from the NFHS (National Family Health Survey) – four datasets were used. This survey is carried out by the Government of India's Ministry of Health and Family Welfare. The specific dataset chosen for our analysis is the IAIR71FL dataset, obtained from the DHS (Demographic and Health Surveys) website. The IAIR71FL dataset consists of 699,686 observations corresponding to female respondents, and 4,797 variables. From this dataset, we worked on 8,829 observations for which it was possible to compute the number of years married. Of these, 8,828 observations for which the data on occupation categories was available were used for the final regression. Variables of interest were of two categories: potential control variables, and variables that could be used to make indices of empowerment.

The control variables considered were mostly demographic information, based on previous studies in women empowerment literature, including the ages of the respondent and partner (Acharya et al., 2010; Murugan & Pandey, 2019; Sathar & Kazi, 2000), age of the respondent at first marriage (Pandey et al., 2017), education levels of the respondent and partner (Kabeer, 2002, Murugan et al., 2021; Pandey et al., 2017), occupations of the respondent and partner (Murugan & Pandey, 2019; Pandey et al., 2017), number of living children, ownership of property or land (Murugan et al., 2021), type of place of residence (rural or urban) (Abrar-ul-haq et al., 2017; Acharya et al., 2010), wealth index (Blood & Wolfe, 1960), and sex of household head. Based on prior literature, the expectation is that women who are more highly educated, employed, and from urban areas are more likely to be empowered. This would be enhanced by greater access to resources in the form of wealth and fewer children. The control variables used in the regression are briefly described in Table 2.1, listed alphabetically.

The variables that could potentially be part of the indices broadly focused on decision-making ability and independence. These included information on the decision-makers for contraception, the expenditure of income, visits from and to family and friends, large household purchases, movement, medical help, and more.

Table 2.1. List of Variables.

Variable	Description
Age	Age of respondent at the time of filling the survey.
Earns Same as/More than Partner	Categorical variable describing relative income share. The value is 1 if the respondent earns the same as or more than her partner, and 0 otherwise.
Education	Categorical variable that measures the respondent's highest education at four levels: no education (0), primary education (1), secondary education (2), higher education (3).
Employment Status	Categorical variable describing respondent's employment with two categories (binary): unemployed (0), employed (1).
Ownership of Land/ Property	Categorical variable describing the respondent's ownership at three levels: owns neither land nor property (0), owns either land or property (1), owns both land and property.
Partner's Education	Categorical variable that measures the partner's highest education at four levels: no education (0), primary education (1), secondary education (2), higher education (3).
Partner's Employment Status	Categorical variable describing the partner's employment with two categories (binary): unemployed (0), employed (1).
Place of Residence	Binary (categorical) variable, value is set to 1 if the respondent resides in an urban area, and 0 otherwise.
Sex of Household Head	Binary (categorical) variable, value is set to 1 if the household head is female, and 0 otherwise.
Uses Bank/Savings Account	Binary (categorical) variable, value is set to 1 if the respondent owns a bank account that she can use, and 0 otherwise.
Wealth Index	Consists of wealth quintiles, numbered from 0 (poorest) to 4 (richest).
Years Married	Number of years the respondent has been married, at the time of filling the survey.

As described by Osamor and Grady (2016), multiple measures of female autonomy have been used in the literature. Common components were decision-making with regard to household matters, finances, personal healthcare, child healthcare, and freedom of movement. This study considers three components of an overall empowerment index: household decision-making, personal decision-making, and freedom of movement.

4. METHODOLOGY

The variables obtained from the dataset were used to construct three indices relating to a woman's autonomy. These three indices of empowerment are what we use to assess the evolving nature of gender differences in intra-household decision-making. Additionally, we also sum the three indices to generate an overall index of empowerment.

To compute the value of each index, values assigned to the individual variables that comprise the index were summed. Variables such as those that consider who makes decisions, for example, were given positive values if the respondent was the primary decision-maker, since this adds to a woman's choice and thereby, empowerment. On the other hand, some variables, such as those that depict control by the husband, if applicable, take away from a woman's independence and tend to lessen the level of empowerment. These variables were transformed into variables that would have a positive impact (for example, the variable 'husband does not permit respondent to meet female friends' was transformed into 'allowed to meet female friends'), and values were mapped accordingly.

Overall Empowerment Index

$$= Freedom\ of\ Movement\ Index$$

$$+ Personal\ Decisions\ Index + Household\ Decisions\ Index$$

The three indices are described below and listed along with the variables that they comprise.

Freedom of Movement Index: To describe how free a woman is to move by herself. Variables used are categorical variables depicting a woman's choice and permissions to go to the market, go outside the village, visit, or contact family and friends, inform her partner about her location.

Personal Decisions Index: To describe how empowered a woman is when it comes to making decisions that concern her own body and health. Variables used are categorical variables depicting a woman's choice regarding her own body and health, such as decisions on contraception, treatment during pregnancy, visits to a health facility, self-medical help.

Household Decisions Index: To describe to what extent a woman is an active participant of decisions that concern the household at large. Variables used categorical variables depicting the extent of a woman's participation in deciding the expenditure of income.

We estimate the following equation:

$$\begin{aligned}
Indices = \ &\alpha + \beta_1 \text{Years married} + \beta_2 \text{ Age of the respondent} \\
&+ \beta_3 \text{ Number of living children} + \beta_4 \text{Education} \\
&+ \beta_5 \text{ Partners education} \\
&+ \beta_6 \text{ Employment status} + \beta_7 \text{ Partners empolyment status} \\
&+ \beta_8 \text{ Earns same as or more than partner} \\
&+ \beta_9 \text{Ownership of land or property} + \beta_{10} \text{ Place of residence} \\
&+ \beta_{11} \text{ Weath index} + \beta_{12} \text{ Use bank or savings account} \\
&+ \beta_{13} \text{ Sex of the household head} + \varepsilon
\end{aligned}$$

In the above equation, indices represent composite empowerment index, freedom of movement index, personal decisions index and household decisions index.

Multiple regression models may face issues of multicollinearity and heteroskedasticity. These issues lead to unreliable estimators and low precision of least-square estimates of coefficients and standard errors, making the regression analysis uncertain. Accordingly, we have tested the proposed model for multicollinearity and heteroskedasticity. The model's mean value of the variance inflation factor (VIF) commonly used to diagnose multicollinearity was 1.84, and individual VIF values did not exceed 4.64. Both of these values indicate that the model does not significantly suffer from problems caused by multicollinearity. Additionally, heteroskedasticity in the model was corrected for through the use of robust standard errors.

5. RESULTS

5.1. Summary Statistics

The descriptive statistics for the data used in the regression analysis are shown in Table 2.2.

For the binary variables, the summary statistics are as follows (Table 2.3).

5.2. Results

Here regression analysis is carried out with the composite empowerment index, as well as the three decision-making indices as regressands. The results are shown in Table 2.4. It is noted that the main variable of interest, years married, is significantly positively related to the empowerment index. This is also the case when the personal decision index is the dependent variable. The coefficients of the years married variable are insignificant when freedom of movement and household decision indices are regressed against it. This could indicate that the increased decision-making power of women in the later years of their marriage could be attributed to increased autonomy in the governance of their own bodies through personal decision-making.

Table 2.2.   Summary Statistics, A.

Variable	Observations	Mean	Std. Dev.	Min	Max
Age	8,829	38.0079	7.651	15	49
Number of Living Children	8,829	2.7052	1.614	0	10
Years Married	8,829	21.577	8.5697	0	47
Stage of Marriage	8,829	1.7236	0.898	0	4
Education Level	8,829	0.5426	0.8033	0	3
Partner's Education Level	8,829	0.1427	0.501	0	3
Difference in Education	8,829	−1.6049	3.9869	−19	19
Occupation	8,828	0.0893	0.3996	0	3
Partner's Occupation	8,829	0.2634	0.875	0	6
Wealth Index	8,829	1.491	1.2362	0	4
Ownership of Land/Property	8,829	0.1448	0.4986	0	2
Freedom of Movement Index	8,829	3.189	0.6724	0	6
Personal Decisions Index	8,829	2.912	0.9435	1	6
Household Decisions Index	8,829	1.2239	0.7357	0	5
Empowerment Index	8,829	7.325	1.9761	2	17

Table 2.3.   Summary Statistics, B.

Variable	Observations	Frequency (0)	Frequency (1)
Employment Status	8,829	8,304	525
Partner's Employment Status	8,829	7,692	1,137
Residence (Rural/Urban)	8,829	6,870	1,959
Earns Same as/More than Partner	8,829	8,640	189
Uses Bank/Savings Account	8,829	8,233	596

Table 2.4.   Multiple Regression Results.

Variables		Empowerment Index	Freedom of Movement Index	Personal Decision Index	Household Decision Index
Years Married		0.0182***	0.0007	0.0178***	−0.0004
		(0.003)	(0.001)	(0.002)	(0.001)
Age of the		−0.0131***	−0.0001	−0.0125***	−0.0004
Respondent		(0.004)	(0.001)	(0.002)	(0.001)
Number of Living		0.0496***	0.0030	0.0392***	0.0074**
Children		(0.009)	(0.003)	(0.005)	(0.003)
Education	No Education[R]				
	Primary	0.0268	−0.0002	0.0248	0.0022
	Education	(0.038)	(0.014)	(0.024)	(0.013)
	Secondary	−0.1195***	−0.0314**	−0.0649**	−0.0231*
	Education	(0.041)	(0.015)	(0.026)	(0.014)
	Higher	−0.2044	−0.0804	−0.0869	−0.0371
	Education	(0.130)	(0.053)	(0.092)	(0.035)

Table 2.4.   (*Continued*)

Variables		Empowerment Index	Freedom of Movement Index	Personal Decision Index	Household Decision Index
Partner's Education	No Education[R]				
	Primary Education	0.7410*** (0.210)	0.1613* (0.094)	0.2191*** (0.082)	0.3605*** (0.086)
	Secondary Education	1.0216*** (0.181)	0.2630*** (0.080)	0.3928*** (0.069)	0.3658*** (0.073)
	Higher Education	0.0864 (0.453)	−0.0600 (0.216)	−0.1193 (0.177)	0.2658 (0.201)
Employment Status		0.5170*** (0.196)	0.0754 (0.084)	0.1329* (0.072)	0.3087*** (0.085)
Partner's Employment Status		2.3549*** (0.183)	0.7388*** (0.079)	0.7895*** (0.068)	0.8266*** (0.074)
Earns Same as/More than Partner		2.1175*** (0.244)	0.3899*** (0.113)	0.4580*** (0.093)	1.2697*** (0.109)
Ownership of Land/ Property	Owns neither land not property[R]				
	Owns either land or property	0.0946 (0.249)	−0.0011 (0.112)	0.0406 (0.094)	0.0551 (0.099)
	Owns both land and property	−0.5811*** (0.169)	−0.0262 (0.074)	−0.3882*** (0.064)	−0.1666** (0.069)
Place of Residence	Rural[R]				
	Urban	0.0555 (0.039)	0.0380*** (0.014)	0.0044 (0.024)	0.0130 (0.013)
Wealth Index	Poorest[R]				
	Poorer	0.0982*** (0.037)	0.0167 (0.014)	0.0833*** (0.024)	−0.0017 (0.013)
	Middle	0.0928** (0.040)	−0.0069 (0.014)	0.1203*** (0.026)	−0.0206 (0.014)
	Richer	0.2117*** (0.049)	0.0354* (0.018)	0.1659*** (0.031)	0.0103 (0.016)
	Richest	0.2788*** (0.070)	0.0414* (0.024)	0.2292*** (0.043)	0.0081 (0.024)
Uses Bank/Savings Account	No[R]				
	Yes	1.8648*** (0.163)	0.7853*** (0.070)	0.5161*** (0.062)	0.5633*** (0.068)
Sex of Household Head	Male[R]				
	Female	−0.2250*** (0.038)	−0.0003 (0.014)	−0.1747*** (0.022)	−0.0500*** (0.014)
Constant		6.6924*** (0.089)	2.9793*** (0.033)	2.6821*** (0.057)	1.0309*** (0.029)
Observations		8829	8829	8829	8829
Pseudo R-squared		0.565	0.50	0.23	0.63

Note: R-Reference Category; Standard errors in parentheses: *** $p<0.01$, ** $p<0.05$, * $p<0.1$.

Additionally, a woman's empowerment as measured by decision-making power is significantly positively related to the number of living children she has, partner's education, herself and her partner being employed, her income relative to her partner, wealth, and use of a bank account. Notably, partner's employment status, relative income share, and use of a savings account are each associated with an increase of around two points of the empowerment index. The suggestion is that employment and greater income leading to savings accounts have a positive impact on the empowerment of women, and that larger families may help by adding to a woman's support network in making her own decisions. A woman's partner having attained higher education beyond the secondary level does not have a significant impact on her empowerment.

The control variables related to women's own age and education, ownership of land or property, and sex of the household head are negatively and significantly related to the value of the composite empowerment index. The empowerment index is lowered if a woman's highest level of education is secondary, if she owns both land and property, and if she is part of a female-headed household. This suggests that a woman's decision-making freedom could potentially be restricted by responsibilities arising from ownership of land or property and heading a household. The negative relationship with ownership of land or property could also be a result of joint ownership with a partner (Behrman, 2017). Interestingly, in spite of being positively related with the number of years married, the empowerment index is negatively related with a woman's age. This could indicate that younger women are being more outspoken about their rights than older women and the generation gap plays a significant role here.

Largely, women's empowerment as measured by the composite empowerment index appears to be driven by their personal decision-making power. This may be observed by the significance of variable coefficients when the empowerment index and personal decision index are used as regressands, compared to the other two indices that compose the empowerment index. Additionally, though it does not significantly affect the empowerment index, living in an urban area significantly increases a woman's freedom of movement.

6. CONCLUSIONS

This study explored the relationship between decision-making and the number of years the respondent has been married, controlling for other factors in the Indian context with an aim to examine whether the gender differences in household decision-making are evolving with the number of years of marriage. The results are in accordance with various studies which establishes that there existed a relationship between the empowerment of women and decision-making (Abrar-ul-haq et al., 2017; Murugan & Pandey, 2019). Extant socio-economic, political, and household factors play key roles in determining the decision-making power of women.

REFERENCES

Abebe, W., & Kasa, A. (2021). Constraints to women participating in public works for improving income-generating activities in selected districts vis-a-vis productive safety net program of Ethiopia. *Global Social Welfare, 8*(2), 181–185.

Abrar-ul-haq, M., Jali, M. R. M., & Islam, G. M. N. (2017). Decision-making ability as a source of empowerment among rural women of Pakistan. *Global Social Welfare, 4*, 117–125.

Acharya, D. R., Bell, J. S., Simkhada, P., Van Teijlingen, E. R., & Regmi, P. R. (2010). Women's autonomy in household decision-making: A demographic study in Nepal. *Reproductive Health, 7*, 1–12.

Akilova, M., & Marti, Y. M. (2014). What is the effect of women's financial empowerment on intimate partner violence in Jordan? *Global Social Welfare, 1*, 65–74.

Allendorf, K. (2007). Couples' reports of women's autonomy and health-care use in Nepal. *Studies in Family Planning, 38*(1), 35–46.

Anderson, C. L., Reynolds, T. W., & Gugerty, M. K. (2017). Husband and wife perspectives on farm household decision-making authority and evidence on intra-household accord in rural Tanzania. *World Development, 90*, 169–183.

Banerjee, S., Alok, S., & George, B. (2020). Determinants of women empowerment as measured by domestic decision-making: Perspective from a developing economy. In W. A. Barnett & B. S. Sergi (Ed.), *Advanced issues in the economics of emerging markets (International Symposia in Economic Theory and Econometrics* (Vol. 27, pp. 1–12). Emerald Publishing Limited.

Banerjee, S., Alok, S., Kumar, R. & Lakhtakia, S. (2022). Does a woman's life before marriage affect her empowerment level? – Perspective from rural India. *International Journal of Social Economics*, Ahead-of-print. https://doi.org/10.1108/IJSE-05-2022-0329

Banerjee, S., Alok, S., Lakhtakia, S., & Mahapatra, M. S. (2019). Determinants of women empowerment and effect on children's overall health development. *IASSI Quarterly: Contributions to Indian Social Science, 38*(2), 276–291.

Basu, A. M. (1992). *Culture, the status of women, and demographic behaviour: Illustrated with the case of India.* Clarendon Press.

Bautista, M. P. J. T., & Uy, C. (2023). The effects of organizational culture and leadership style on organizational performance in times of covid-19 pandemic. *Review of Integrative Business and Economics Research, 12*(1), 175–194.

Becker, G. S. (1965). A theory of the allocation of time. *The Economic Journal, 75*(299), 493–517.

Becker, G. S. (1981). *A treatise on the family.* Harvard University Press.

Behrman, J. A. (2017). Women's land ownership and participation in decision-making about reproductive health in Malawi. *Population and Environment, 38*, 327–344.

Bernasek, A., & Bajtelsmit, V. L. (2002). Predictors of women's involvement in household financial decision-making. *Journal of Financial Counseling and Planning, 13*(2), 39–47.

Blood, R. O., & Wolfe, D. M. (1960). *Husbands & wives: The dynamics of married living.* Free Press.

Chiappori, P.-A. (1988). Rational household labor supply. *Econometrica, 56*(1), 63–89.

Chiappori, P.-A. (1992). Collective labor supply and welfare. *Journal of Political Economy, 100*(3), 437–467.

Chiappori, P.-A., Fortin, B., & Lacroix, G. (2002). Marriage market, divorce legislation and household labor supply. *Journal of Political Economy, 110*(1), 37–72.

Datta Gupta, N., & Stratton, L. S. (2010). Institutions, social norms, and bargaining power: An analysis of individual leisure time in couple households. *Review of Economics of the Household, 8*(3), 325–343.

Duflo, E. (2012). Women empowerment and economic development. *Journal of Economic Literature, 50*(4), 1051–1079.

Dyson, T., & Moore, M. (1983). On kinship structure, female autonomy, and demographic behavior in India. *Population and Development Review, 9*(1), 35–60.

Fox, G. L., & Murry, V. M. (2000). Gender and families: Feminist perspectives and family research. *Journal of Marriage and Family, 62*(4), 1160–1172.

Himmelweit, S., Santos, C., Sevilla, A., & Sofer, C. (2013). Sharing of resources within the family and the economics of household decision making. *Journal of Marriage and Family, 75*(3), 625–639.

Hoddinott, J. & Haddad, L. (1995). Does female income share influence household expenditures? Evidence from c^ote d'ivoire. *Oxford Bulletin of Economics and Statistics, 57*(1), 77–96.

Kabeer, N. (2002). Resources, agency, achievements: Reflections on the measurement of women's empowerment. *Development and Change, 30*(3), 435–464.

Kumar, N., Raghunathan, K., Arrieta, A., Jilanid, A., & Pandey, S. (2021, October). The power of the collective empowers women: Evidence from self-help groups in India. *World Development, 146.*

Lundberg, S., & Pollak, R. (1993). Separate spheres bargaining and the marriage market. *Journal of Political Economy, 101*(6), 988–1010.

Malhotra, A., Schuler, S. R., & Boender, C. (2002). Measuring women's empowerment as a variable in international development. In *Background paper for the World Bank workshop on poverty and gender: New perspectives* (Vol. 28, pp. 1–58). The World Bank.

Manser, M., & Brown, M. (1980). Marriage and household decision-making: A bargaining analysis. *International Economic Review, 21*(1), 31–44.

Mason, K. O. (1995). *Gender and demographic change: What do we know?* (Vol. 3). International Union for the Scientific Study of Population.

McElroy, M. B., & Horney, M. J. (1981). Nash-bargained household decisions: Toward a generalization of the theory of demand. *International Economic Review, 22*(2), 333–349.

Murugan, V., Khoo, Y.-M., & Termos, M. (2021). Intimate partner violence against women in India: Is empowerment a protective factor? *Global Social Welfare, 8*(2), 199–211.

Murugan, V., & Pandey, S. (2019). Correlates of female sterilization in Bihar: Does women's empowerment matter? *Global Social Welfare, 6*(2), 79–85.

Olaniran, S. O., & Perumal, J. (2021). Enacting community development principles in women empowerment projects: A case study in Ondo state, Nigeria. *Global Social Welfare, 8*(2), 151–158.

Osamor, P. E., & Grady, C. (2016). Women's autonomy in health care decision-making in developing countries: A synthesis of the literature. *International Journal of Women's Health, 8*, 191–202.

Pandey, S., Karki, Y. B., Murugan, V., & Mathur, A. (2017). Mothers' risk for experiencing neonatal and under-five child deaths in Nepal: The role of empowerment. *Global Social Welfare, 4*(3), 105–115.

Pearson, R. (1992). Gender matters in development. In T. Allen & A. Thomas (Eds.), *Poverty and development in the 1990s*. Oxford University Press.

Pham, T. T. P., Truong, G. Q., Nguyen, T. V., & Nguyen, P. V. (2023). The meaning of public service motivation: Human resource management practices in the public sector. *Review of Integrative Business and Economics Research, 12*(2), 1–27.

Rosenbluth, S. C., Steil, J. M., & Whitcomb, J. H. (1998). Marital equality: What does it mean? *Journal of Family Issues, 19*(3), 227–244.

Samuelson, P. A. (1956). Social indifference curves. *The Quarterly Journal of Economics, 70*(1), 1–22.

Sathar, Z. A., & Kazi, S. (2000). Women's autonomy in the context of rural Pakistan. *The Pakistan Development Review, 39*(2), 89–110.

Sattar, T., Ahmad, S., & Asim, M. (2022). Intimate partner violence against women in southern Punjab, Pakistan: A phenomenological study. *BMC Women's Health, 22*(1), 505.

Wanic, R., & Kulik, J. (2011). Toward an understanding of gender differences in the impact of marital conflict on health. *Sex Roles, 65*, 297–312.

CHAPTER 3

POST-PANDEMIC OPERATIONAL PERFORMANCE: REDESIGNING COFFEE SHOPS' INVENTORY MANAGEMENT STRATEGY USING ECONOMIC ORDER QUANTITY, JUST-IN TIME, AND SUPPLIER PARTNERSHIP

Muhammad Ainul Fahmi[a], Wawas Bangun Tegar Sunaryo Putra[c], A'ang Kunaifi[d], Untung Alamsah[b] and Sari Usih Natari[b]

[a]Institut Insan Cendekia Mandiri (ITICM), Sidoarjo 61234, Indonesia
[b]Universitas Padjadjaran, Bandung 45363, Indonesia
[c]Institut Komunikasi dan Bisnis LSPR, Jakarta 10220, Indonesia
[d]Institut Teknologi Sepuluh Nopember, Surabaya 60111, Indonesia

ABSTRACT

COVID-19 has dramatically changed consumer behaviour and has significantly changed all business processes. Business organisations must be able to deal with the pandemic and rapid pace-based changes to enable flexible remote purchases. In this survey, the purpose of the inventory management strategy is to be considered, and the next one is to identify the design change based on the three main factors: economic order quantity, just-in time, and supplier

The Finance-Innovation Nexus: Implications for Socio-Economic Development
International Symposia in Economic Theory and Econometrics, Volume 34, 27–43
Copyright © 2025 by Emerald Publishing Limited
ISSN: 1571-0386/doi:10.1108/S1571-038620240000034003
All rights of reproduction in any form reserved

partnership. The model in this study was built on HCMs or hierarchical component models by placing the 3 main factors as a higher-order construct (HOC) with 11 lower-order constructs (LOCs) that compose each higher construct. The findings in this study show that Inventory Shortages, Just-in Time Delivery by Supplier (JITDS), and Suppliers' Quality (SQ) are the most significant forming components for each construct. The findings can be used to reference the academic and practical reorganisation of inventory management strategies. By empirically investigating the relationship between inventory management strategy components and operational performance, this study contributes to the on-going scholarly discussion on the link between inventory management strategy components and operational performance.

Keywords: Economic order quantity; just-ın time; supplier partnership; operational performance; operations management

JEL Classification Code: C44; M11

INTRODUCTION

The growth of the culinary sector is considered very fast and dynamic, especially in the cafe industry – the growth rate of cafes and restaurants in Bandung is experiencing increasing growth. According to the Central Bureau of Statistics for the City of Bandung through bandungbergerak.id (2020), the growth of cafes and restaurants in the city of Bandung grew by 15.79% from the previous year. This can also be shown by the many publications about various culinary businesses on the internet. With the internet, individuals worldwide can connect, enabling consumers to share their buying experiences via social media. In line with that, various types of culinary and culinary tourism centres exist in various regions of the country. In terms of culinary tourism, one of the most famous in Indonesia is culinary from West Java (Rachmah & Madiawati, 2022).

The city that is the centre of culinary tourism in West Java is Bandung City. The city of Bandung has always been a top destination for culinary delights because of its varied and innovative food. Currently, cafés are considered one of the most popular forms of the culinary business. Generally, visitors who come to the cafe relax while drinking coffee. However, nowadays, cafés have become a must-visit place, especially for young people who are changing their lifestyles. Changes in the lifestyle of young people that are needed to hang out in cafes and the use of social media make them aware of the places they visit (Rachmah & Madiawati, 2022).

On the other hand, the Covid-19 pandemic is a significant event for the supply chain of almost any business. In a different corporate environment, over 18 months after the global pandemic was formally announced, several companies assess the disruptive drag brought on by the severe health catastrophe (Ji & Zhang, 2022). Supply chain disruptions prompt businesses to develop capabilities to lessen the effects of these risk sources and creating new capabilities has been essential to surviving Covid-19. The Covid-19 health issue impacts global supply networks, and Craighead et al. (2020) emphasise how this requires us to 'think in new and foreign ways' as well as other forms of supply chain disruptions.

As a post-pandemic strategy, companies must develop their business plans for sustainability, i.e., build resilient business models post-pandemic (Paula & Bautista, 2023). Making an inventory strategy to enhance the effectiveness of business operations is one way for businesspeople to combat the effects of post-pandemic hazards. Inventory levels are one of the critical factors that Panigrahi (2013) identifies as affecting a firm. According to Yang et al. (2020), a successful supply chain and order fulfilment depend on effectively managed inventory. According to Sitienei and Memba (2015), inventory management balances too little and too much inventory. Wan et al. (2020) confirm that prudent inventory management promotes product diversity while lowering turnover. Based on theoretical assumptions, a company employs the best inventory management strategy to improve operating performance (Gupta & Boyd, 2008; Inman et al., 2009). Therefore, research on inventory management techniques is required to enhance operational performance in the café industry (CR). Because raw materials, semi-finished goods, and completed goods are perishable, the inventory for the CR is the most complicated. However, very little research has specifically addressed the cafe industry. This study will contribute to the long-term viability of the CR in Indonesia, particularly in Bandung for cafe companies to endure the pandemic. In addition, this study is also intended to contribute to ongoing scholarly discussions regarding the relationship between components of inventory management strategies and operational performance.

LITERATURE REVIEW
Economic Order Quantity (EOQ)

The EOQ model is a framework for inventory management that helps firms determine the amount of stock that must be kept reducing expenses associated with using inventory and satisfy consumer requests (Sanni et al., 2020). EOQ, according to Apriyani and Muhsin (2017), is a method for estimating the number of economic orders for each order with a particular order frequency in a corporation. The EOQ requirements are listed as follows by Haekal and Setiawan (2020): (1) The quantity of requests is known and constant; (2) The lead time, or the time between placing an order and receiving it, is also known and constant; (3) The receipt of supplies is immediate and complete; (4) There are no quantity discounts available; (5) Variable costs are simply the cost of ordering and holding inventory for a specific period, and (6) Out of stock can be avoided entirely if orders are placed on time.

The EOQ is the most often developed deterministic inventory model in operations management (Busola & Olaleke, 2020; Eroglu & Ozdemir, 2007; Sanni et al., 2020; Vörös, 2013). Since it predicts the costs associated with ordering and maintaining inventory, EOQ, according to Mwangi and Nyambura (2015), is a preferred strategy for lowering inventory. A 2013 study on inventory management and organisational performance at the Gianchore Tea Processing plant in Kenya's Nyamira District by Mogere et al. found that EOQ considerably enhanced organisational performance. According to Lwiki et al. (2013), most industrial firms rely on EOQ to overcome shortcomings in inventory control and save costs.

Just-in Time (JIT)

According to Haekal and Setiawan (2020), the corporation can lower operating or manufacturing expenses by using just-in-time (JIT), to compete with more competitive rates. JIT's philosophy is to utilise the available time to reduce waste in manufacturing processes. At the Toyota vehicle assembly facility in Japan in the early 1970s, Taiichi Ohno implemented the JIT production method. According to several papers and publications, this approach is a method for reducing or reaching zero inventory. While some perceive it as a new manufacturing technique, others see it as a new way of looking at production. This system conjures up specific thoughts and philosophies in some people while serving as a tactic in others. Some people still think it contains all the above ideas and goes beyond them. Simply-in-time production refers to all components and units of all different sorts of organisations, not just specific elements of one organisation. The transportation of resources and administration of items became just a tiny part of the manufacturing chain. It is a way of thinking and a philosophy that avoids using waste products in any of its endeavours. JIT's primary objectives are to achieve sustainable quality, boost yields, and produce with zero waste through efficient raw resources (Pourasiabi, 2012).

The JIT approach was created for industrial companies to improve operational performance by minimising waste (Abu et al., 2019; Musara, 2012; Narayanapillai, 2014). The JIT technique is seen to be an effective tool for decreasing inventory shortages (IS), waste, and inefficiencies, retaining flexibility while enhancing the speed and performance of the manufacturing process in terms of delivery (Motwani, 2003; Nawanir et al., 2016). According to Stevenson (2005), the JIT strategy aims to remove waste from the production system. This method emphasises maintaining the necessary inventory, ensuring flawless quality, and shortening lead times by reducing lot sizes, queue lengths, and setup times (Abu et al., 2019; Taj & Morosan, 2011; Yang et al., 2020). Thus, JIT emphasises the production of goods only when needed, not earlier or later (Hua et al., 2011).

Strategic Supplier Partnership (SSP)

For manufacturing businesses to increase operating performance by eliminating waste, the JIT technique was developed (Abu et al., 2019; Musara, 2012; Narayanapillai, 2014). The JIT method is seen to be a potent instrument for reducing IS, waste, and inefficiencies, maintaining flexibility while boosting manufacturing process speed and performance in terms of delivery (Motwani, 2003; Nawanir et al., 2016). The goal of the JIT approach is to eliminate all waste from the manufacturing system, according to Stevenson (2005). By lowering lot sizes, queue lengths, and setup times, this technique emphasises retaining the necessary inventory, assuring faultless quality, and cutting lead times (Abu et al., 2019; Taj & Morosan, 2011;

Yang et al., 2020). Companies may purchase high-value products even in periods of supply volatility by proactively collaborating with suppliers and ensuring proper supplier selection (Connor et al., 2020; Hosseini et al., 2019; Qi et al., 2009).

A substantial correlation between SSP and Operation Performance (OP) of industrial organisations has been discovered in earlier research (Agus & Makbhul, 2008; Musau et al., 2017; Qrunfleh & Tarafdar, 2013; Srinivasan et al., 2011). For instance, Agus and Makbhul (2008) investigated how SSP affected the performance of Malaysian manufacturing companies' businesses and the quality of their products. They discovered a beneficial connection between SSP, product quality, and company performance. According to several quantitative research, SSP and business success are positively correlated (Connor et al., 2020; Hussain et al., 2014; Khan & Siddiqui, 2018; Lwiki et al., 2013). As a result, the SSP approach positively impacts inventory management, eventually enhancing the organisation's operational and overall performance.

Hypothesis Development

Based on the assumptions, the EOQ's dimensions are generated. The following assumptions are made that demand will be known and constant, that lead time will be known and constant, that the Cost Components Determination Procedure will be followed precisely, and that the firm will be ready for IS (Lee, 2002; Sanni et al., 2020). Therefore, the hypothesis is obtained as follows:

H1. **The EOQ strategy significantly and positively improves OP in the café business.**

H1a. Demand is Known and Constant (DKC) significantly and positively improves OP.

H1b. Lead Time is Known and Constant (LKC) significantly and positively improves OP.

H1c. Procedure for Determining Cost Components (PDCC) significantly and positively improves OP.

H1d. IS significantly and positively improves OP.

The four objective measures of JIT were adapted from Abdallah and Matsui (2007). This dimension consists of Just-in-Time Delivery by Supplier (JITDS), Information among Actors (IF), Daily Schedule Adherence (DSA), and Customer Requirements (CRs) (see Fig. 3.1). Therefore, the hypothesis is obtained as follows:

H2. **JIT strategy significantly and positively improves OP.**

H2a. JITDS significantly and positively improves OP.

H2b. DSA significantly and positively improves OP.

H2c. IF significantly and positively improves OP.

H2d. CR significantly and positively improves OP.

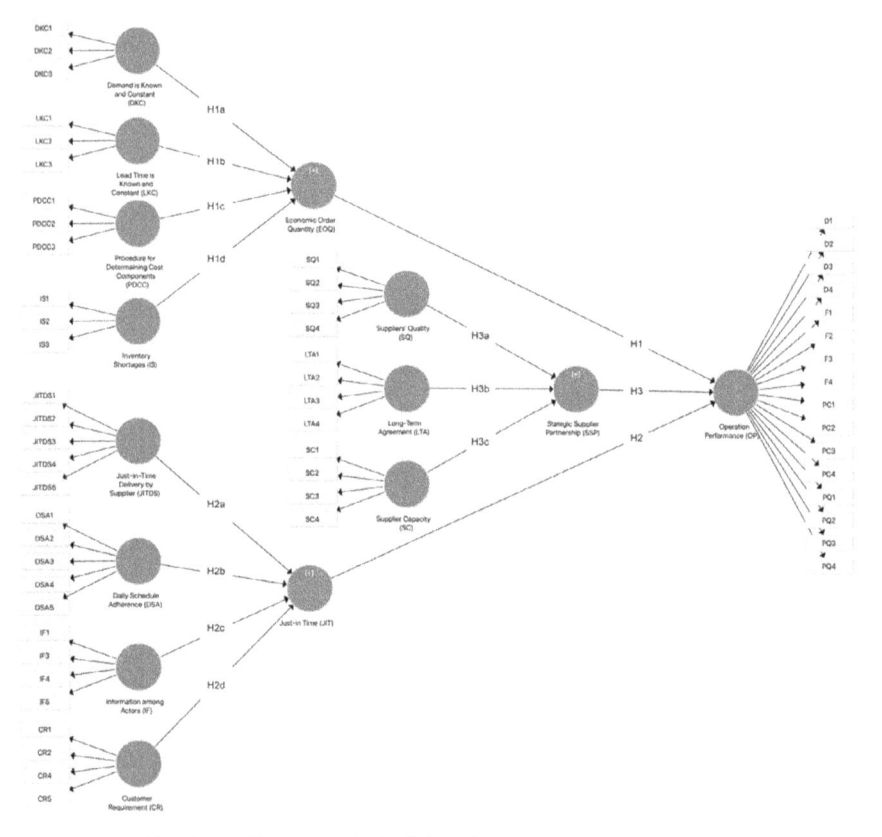

Fig. 3.1. Conceptual Model of the Study. *Source*: Authors.

SSP is measured based on Suppliers' Quality (SQ), Long-Term Agreement (LTA), and Supplier Capacity (SC) (Holweg & Bicheno, 2002; Kosgei & Gitau, 2016; Omoush, 2020). Therefore, the following hypothesis can be obtained:

***H3*. SSP significantly and positively improves OP**.

H3a. SQ significantly and positively improves OP.

H3b. LTA significantly and positively improves OP.

H3c. SC significantly and positively improves OP.

RESEARCH AND METHODOLOGY

This study's respondent population was 76 café businesses in the city of Bandung. This study managed to collect questionnaire data that 74 respondents filled in. All respondents in this study have met the criteria of respondents who are cafe businesses in the city of Bandung, which have sugar supplies. The constructed model in this study was designed using hierarchical component models (HCMs) by placing EOQ, JIT, and Supplier Partnership (SSP) as HOCs. Establishing high-level or HCMs is recommended when testing second-order models containing two-layer construction structures (Putra & Ardianto, 2022). EOQ has three LOCs. Namely, DKC, LKC, and PDCC with measuring items adapted from Lee (2002) and Sanni et al. (2020).

Furthermore, the JIT construct has four LOCs, namely JITDS, DSA, IF and CRs with items adapted from Abdallah and Matsui (2007), Khaireddin et al. (2015), Patnayakuni et al. (2006) and Wong et al. (2011). The SSP construct consists of three LOCs, namely SQ, LTA, and SC, with indicators adapted from Khaireddin et al. (2015) and Nyamah et al. (2022). While the OP construct in this study is the first-order construct with indicators adapted from Wong et al. (2011).

Due to the usage of second-order constructs or HCMs, partial least squares structural equation modelling (PLS-SEM) was employed in this investigation (Andriani & Putra, 2019). Powerful analytical techniques like partial least squares (PLS) may be used with just a few presumptions. The PLS method does not consider dispersion (it does not assume specific data and can be nominal, categorical, ordinal, interval, and ratio). When the assumption of normalcy does not provide a challenge for PLS, it will employ bootstrapping or random doubling. Additionally, PLS does not specify the minimum number of samples employed in a study; PLS can be used for studies with tiny samples. Since PLS is a non-parametric type, data having a normal distribution are not required for PLS modelling (Putra, 2022).

FINDINGS AND DISCUSSIONS

Second-Order Construct Evaluation

The purpose of this factor analysis is to first identify the dimensions of a concept before assessing the degree to which each dimension can account for each variable. The study employed a repeated indicators strategy (Hair et al., 2013). The second-order concept underwent several tests, including convergent validity, variance inflation factor (VIF) collinearity, discriminant validity, and construct reliability (see Fig. 3.2).

Because the measurement model in this study is reflective, an outer loading greater than 0.6 is recommended (Hair et al., 2013; Putra, 2022; Putra & Ardianto, 2022). However, the reflecting indication must be taken out if the outside loading is less than 0.4. Depending on the other item's outer loading (height), it is best to keep or remove the item when the outer loading is between 0.4 and 0.7 (Hair et al., 2013; Henseler et al., 2015). According to this hypothesis, the researchers arrived at a value of 0.6. Additionally, the average variance extracted (AVE) needs to be larger than 0.5; this ratio indicates that the hidden variable has contributed to more than 50% of the variation of the reflective indicator. According to the study's findings (Table 3.1), all measuring items had obtained

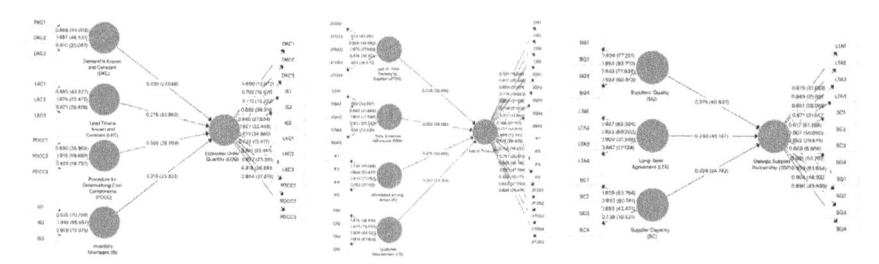

Fig. 3.2. Confirmatory Factor Analysis (CFA) Evaluation of HCMs Constructs.
Source: Authors.

Table 3.1. Loadings Assessment of HCM Constructs.

EOQ's Items	EOQ's LOCs	EOQ's HOC	JIT's Items	JIT's LOCs	JIT's HOC	SSP's Items	SSP's LOCs	SSP's HOC
DKC1	0.866	0.690	CR1	0.875	0.707	LTA1	0.927	0.875
DKC2	0.887	0.702	CR2	0.933	0.807	LTA2	0.933	0.849
DKC3	0.810	0.710	CR4	0.908	0.825	LTA3	0.900	0.851
IS1	0.925	0.850	CR5	0.904	0.774	LTA4	0.847	0.871
IS2	0.945	0.840	DSA1	0.850	0.803	SC1	0.929	0.917
IS3	0.928	0.827	DSA2	0.840	0.759	SC2	0.933	0.907
LKC1	0.885	0.810	DSA3	0.805	0.711	SC3	0.893	0.862
LKC2	0.875	0.732	DSA4	0.831	0.768	SC4	0.738	0.668
LKC3	0.871	0.811	DSA5	0.836	0.727	SQ1	0.939	0.901
PDCC1	0.890	0.827	IF1	0.735	0.668	SQ2	0.953	0.939
PDCC2	0.915	0.818	IF3	0.846	0.779	SQ3	0.942	0.904
PDCC3	0.923	0.844	IF4	0.835	0.756	SQ4	0.934	0.896
			IF5	0.762	0.767			
			JITDS1	0.870	0.837			
			JITDS2	0.886	0.861			
			JITDS3	0.870	0.825			
			JITDS4	0.874	0.834			
			JITDS5	0.823	0.808			

Source: Authors.

outer loading values greater than 0.6 and AVE values greater than 0.50, allowing them to be considered legitimate and capable of measuring each latent variable.

Next, we looked at the VIF data to check for collinearity between the construct elements. In order to investigate the collinearity issue, the researcher employs the inner VIF value. The cut-off number for VIF, according to (Hair et al., 2013), is fewer than 7. Table 3.2 demonstrates that all predictor constructions have a VIF value of less than 7. Consequently, collinearity between construct dimensions is not a concern (Hair et al., 2013; Henseler et al., 2014; Sarstedt et al., 2019). The next phase is to be investigated issues with discriminant validity for each concept with correlation values between components in the model because there are no convergent validity issues.

The heterotrait-monotrait ratio of correlations and the Fornell-Larcker criteria are two testing procedures to assess discriminant validity (Henseler et al., 2014,

2015; Putra, 2022). However, Henseler et al. (2015) recommended prioritising HTML[Inference] over the Fornell-Larcker criteria. This is due to the Fornell-Larcker criteria test's inability to detect discriminant validity, particularly in situations of importance or intricate research models. In order to determine discriminant validity, researchers exclusively employ HTML[Inference] as a test.

By using the bootstrapping method with a resample of 5,000 and aiming for a confidence interval (CI) value of less than or equal to 1.00, it was established that there were no problems with discriminant validity. The year 2015 (Henseler et al., 2015) As seen in the table below (Table 3.3), every supporting indicator used in this study did not have problems with discriminant validity since the CI value for each dimension of the variable was less than or equal to 1.00 between 2.5% and 97.5%. The composite reliability test, which was used to look at all values of the latent variable, produced a composite reliability value of 0.7, indicating that the construct has good reliability. As a result, it can be concluded that the idea has substantial dependability.

Table 3.2. Confidence Interval Assessment of HCM Constructs.

	Original Sample (O)	Sample Mean (M)	2.5%	97.5%
DKC -> EOQ	0.239	0.240	0.222	0.257
IS -> EOQ	0.313	0.314	0.292	0.341
LKC -> EOQ	0.275	0.275	0.259	0.291
PDCC -> EOQ	0.302	0.302	0.284	0.325
CR -> JIT	0.257	0.258	0.236	0.279
DSA -> JIT	0.286	0.287	0.265	0.306
IF -> JIT	0.216	0.215	0.199	0.228
JITDS -> JIT	0.329	0.330	0.311	0.351
LTA -> SSP	0.340	0.340	0.326	0.353
SC -> SSP	0.324	0.324	0.304	0.341
SQ -> SSP	0.375	0.376	0.361	0.396

Source: Authors.

Table 3.3. Significance Level of HCM Constructs.

	Original Sample (O)	t Values	p Values
DKC -> EOQ	0.239	27.658	**0.000**
IS -> EOQ	0.313	23.303	**0.000**
LKC -> EOQ	0.275	32.860	**0.000**
PDCC -> EOQ	0.302	28.509	**0.000**
CR -> JIT	0.257	23.224	**0.000**
DSA -> JIT	0.286	26.080	**0.000**
IF -> JIT	0.216	30.468	**0.000**
JITDS -> JIT	0.329	32.460	**0.000**
LTA -> SSP	0.340	45.147	**0.000**
SC -> SSP	0.324	34.742	**0.000**
SQ -> SSP	0.375	40.937	**0.000**

Source: Authors.

Based on the test results of the second-order CFA (stage), which is used to identify the dimensions of a structure and then determine to what extent each dimension can explain each variable, it was discovered that the entire LOC forming the HOC had a t-statistics value above 1.96. All dimension structures are also members of the HOC because the p-value is less than 0.05.

STRUCTURAL MODEL EVALUATION

The substantive theory of research serves as the foundation for the inner model, sometimes referred to as inner model, which is a model specification of the relationship between latent variables. It explains how latent variables are connected. It is expected that the latent variable, indicator, or manifest variable is on the zero means to scale and that the unit variance is equal to one to eliminate the location parameter (parameter constant) from the model without losing its general nature (Sarstedt et al., 2019; Tenenhaus et al., 2004). To explore the interactions between exogenous and endogenous elements, the inner model test develops a concept- and theory-based model (Putra, 2022). To assess the structural model, the R-square value, which symbolises the model's goodness-of-fit test, is utilised. The R-square value gauges how well the model fits the data. The R-square values for endogenous latent variables of 0.25, 0.50, and 0.75 indicate that the model has minor, medium, and substantial effects on the structural model in the second test (Hair et al., 2013; Putra, 2022). Table 3.4 shows the significant impact of the R-squared value on the structural model used in this investigation.

Calculating the effect size reveals the effect size for each route model (f^2). Effect sizes may be calculated, and according to Henseler et al. (2015), 0.02, 0.15, and 0.35 reflect minor, moderate, and substantial impacts, respectively.

The findings of determining the impact size (f^2) in the study model are shown in Table 3.5, where all routes have value ranges between 0.050 and 4767.937. This study's findings revealed that 12 routes had a substantial impact (0.35) and that two additional linkages had a moderate impact (0.15). Predictive relevance (Q2) for structural models assesses how effectively the observed values are produced. (Hair et al. (2013) claim that the PLS path model has predictive relevance for a construct if the Q^2 value is more significant than zero for certain endogenous latent variables. Based on calculations for predictive relevance (Table 3.4),

Table 3.4.   Model Fit.

	R Square	R Square Adjusted	Q Square	SRMR
OP	0.821	0.818	0.465	0.077
JIT	1.000	1.000	0.602	
EOQ	1.000	1.000	0.617	
SSP	1.000	1.000	0.755	

Source: Authors.

Table 3.5. Effect Size.

	EOQ	JIT	OP	SSP
CR		1032.830		
DSA		1099.769		
DKC	4224.311			
EOQ			0.050	
IF		604.495		
IS	4767.937			
JIT			0.227	
JITDS		1013.715		
LKC	4042.753			
LTA				1117.135
OP				
PDCC	4116.016			
SSP			0.081	
SC				853.815
SQ				1118.995

Source: Authors.

the model has a meaningful predictive value because all values are over 0.000. Additionally, three test models – Chi-square, standardised root means square residual (SRMR), and standard fit index – were used to assess the model's fit in this work (normed fit index). (Bentler & Bonett, 1980) assert that the model is valid if the Chi-square value is more than 0.9 (Chi-square >0.9). The model will be regarded as having a satisfactory fit, according to (Hair et al., 2014), if the SRMR value is less than or equal to 0.1. The repeated indicators technique in this study prevents some values from being computed; hence they are represented as n/a values.

HYPOTHESIS TESTING

Data analysis was done during the model's development and research hypothesis testing. Testing hypotheses enables researchers to address open-ended issues and discover answers to their queries. Hypothesis testing is also conducted to show if each LOC impacts the intended higher-order (Table 3.6).

It is decided at this step whether to accept or reject the research hypothesis put forth in the research model. The route coefficients, *t*-Statistic values obtained from bootstrapping processes, and *p*-values demonstrate the need to evaluate the given hypothesis. Hair et al. (2014) say the path coefficient values fall between -1 and $+1$, with values close to $+1$ signifying a positive link and values of -1 signifying a negative relationship. *t*-Statistics (bootstrapping) is used in tandem to determine the significance of constructs. Ramayah et al. (2017) recommended doing the bootstrapping technique with a re-sample value of 5.000 (Hair et al., 2013). The difference between accepting and rejecting the suggested hypothesis is 1.96. The null hypothesis is accepted if the *t*-statistic result is between -1.96 and 1.96, which means that the hypothesis is rejected (*H0*).

Table 3.6.   Hypothesis Testing.

Path	Original Sample (O)	t Statistics	p Values
EOQ -> OP	**0.232**	**2.834**	**0.005**
DKC -> EOQ -> OP	0.056	2.755	0.006
LKC -> EOQ -> OP	0.063	2.834	0.005
PDCC -> EOQ -> OP	0.070	2.858	0.004
IS -> EOQ -> OP	0.072	2.893	0.004
JIT -> OP	**0.439**	**4.895**	**0.000**
JITDS -> JIT -> OP	0.143	5.023	0.000
DSA -> JIT -> OP	0.132	5.062	0.000
IF -> JIT -> OP	0.099	4.849	0.000
CR -> JIT -> OP	0.104	4.477	0.000
SSP -> OP	**0.277**	**2.744**	**0.006**
SQ -> SSP -> OP	0.102	2.719	0.007
LTA -> SSP -> OP	0.094	2.749	0.006
SC -> SSP -> OP	0.091	2.713	0.007

Source: Authors.

Based on the test results, it was found that the EOQ had a positive ($\beta = 0.232$) and significant ($t = 2.834$, $p = 0.005$) effect on OP. Thus, *H1* was accepted; the higher the EOQ, the level of OP will increase. Furthermore, the findings in this study reveal that all dimensions of the EOQ can influence OP, where DKC is found to have a positive ($\beta = 0.056$) and significant ($t = 2.755$, $p = 0.006$), LKC has a positive ($\beta = 0.063$) and significant ($t = 2.834$, $p = 0.005$), PDCC has a positive ($\beta = 0.070$) effect and significant ($t = 2.858$, $p = 0.004$), and IS has a positive ($\beta = 0.072$) and significant ($t = 2.893$, $p = 0.004$) effect. For this reason, it can be concluded that increasing DKC, LKC, PDCC, and IS can improve OP. An interesting finding in this study is that IS has the most significant influence compared to other components (see Fig. 3.3).

The findings of further research reveal that JIT has a positive ($\beta = 0.439$) and significant ($t = 4.895$, $p = 0.000$) effect on OP. Thus, *H2* is accepted; the higher the JIT, the level of OP will increase. Furthermore, the findings in this study reveal that all dimensions of JIT can influence OP, where JITDS has a positive ($\beta = 0.143$) and significant ($t = 5.023$, $p = 0.000$), DSA has a positive ($\beta = 0.132$) and significant ($t = 5.062$, $p = 0.000$), IF has a positive ($\beta = 0.099$) and significant ($t = 4.849$, $p = 0.000$), and CR has a positive ($\beta = 0.104$) and significant ($t = 4.477$, $p = 0.000$) effect. An interesting finding in this study is that JITDS is the component that has the most significant influence when compared to other components.

The last hypothesis in the study has also been confirmed, where the SSP has a positive ($\beta = 0.277$) and significant ($t = 2.744$, $p = 0.006$) effect on OP. Thus, *H3* is accepted; the higher the SSP, the level of OP will increase. Furthermore, the findings in this study reveal that all dimensions of the SSP can influence OP, where SQ has a positive ($\beta = 0.102$) and significant ($t = 2.719$, $p = 0.007$), LTA has a positive ($\beta = 0.094$) and significant ($t = 2.749$, $p = 0.006$). SC has a positive

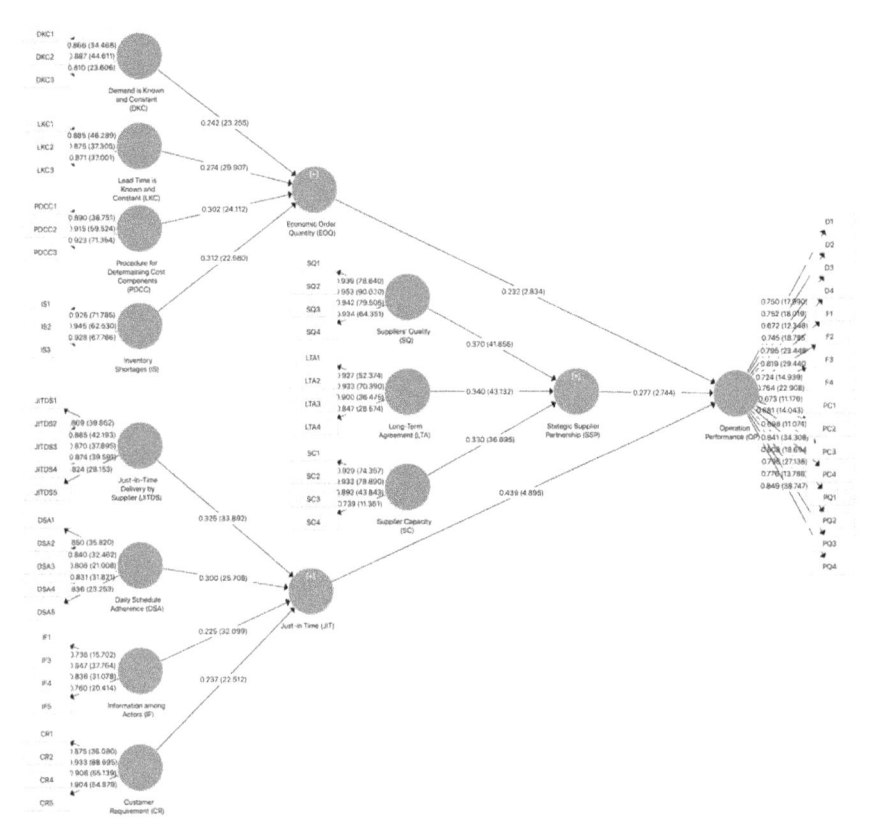

Fig. 3.3. Hypothesis Testing.
Source: Authors.

($\beta = 0.091$) and significant ($t = 2.713$, $p = 0.007$). An interesting finding in this study is that SQ is the most significant influence compared to other components.

CONCLUSIONS

The three first-order hypotheses in this study can be adopted considering the research findings. According to a study by Nyamah et al. (2022), the food and beverage industries utilise the most inventory management methods, including EOQ, JIT, and SSP. The overall findings of the EOQ, JIT, and SSP components in this second-order research impact operational performance (OP) in the CR. This is a study by Mwangi and Nyambura (2015), who discovered that most food and beverage organisations rely on EOQ to address inventory control-related issues. By ensuring that lead time (LKC) and demand (DKC) are predictable and consistent, the EOQ dimension enables the business to guarantee appropriate inventory levels with no shortages at any time (IS). This may assure flexibility, ensure timeliness of delivery, boost product quality, and reduce production costs in corporate operating systems (OP). The JIT approach stresses customisation so that the items produced are utilised to satisfy client criteria in terms of quality, quantity, and price. This study, however, discovered that all JIT dimensions had an impact on parts of operations carried out in the CR. The CR emphasises the JIT strategy because it helps business owners' lower storage, ordering, transportation, and insurance costs. As a result, operational performance (OP) is increased in terms of the dimensions of JITDS, DSA, and information flow among actors (IF). The JIT approach also successfully lowers inventory costs and shortages of basic materials. Because JIT is a practical approach to inventory management, this study is based on the research of Eroglu and Hofer (2011), Koumanakos (2008), and Shin et al. (2015).

All SSP strategy components positively and significantly impact the operational success of the café company. Businesses manage their inventory by creating solid, long-term relationships (LTA) with suppliers and encouraging those suppliers to create significant capacity, according to Hussain et al. (2014), Khan and Siddiqui (2018), Lwiki et al. (2013), and Srinivasan et al. (2011). The SSP technique allows companies to share resources, talents, and experience with their suppliers, making it one of the most popular inventory management systems (SQ).

REFERENCES

Abdallah, A. B., & Matsui, Y. (2007). The relationship between JIT production and Manufacturing strategy and their impact on JIT performance. *Proceedings of the 18th Annual Conference of Production and Operations Management Society*, pp. 1–35.

Abu, F., Gholami, H., Mat Saman, M. Z., Zakuan, N., & Streimikiene, D. (2019). The implementation of lean manufacturing in the furniture industry: A review and analysis on the motives, barriers, challenges, and the applications. *Journal of Cleaner Production, 234*. https://doi.org/10.1016/j.jclepro.2019.06.279

Agus, A., Makhbul, Z. M., & Hassan, Z. (2008). *The importance of strategic supplier partnership in supply chain management in enhancing product quality performance and business performance*, 1–8 [Proceeding of the 13th international conference on ISO 9000 & TQM].

Andriani, R., & Putra, W. B. T. S. (2019). The intersection of marketing and human resource disciplines: Employer brand equity as a mediator in recruitment process. *International Journal of Innovative Science and Research Technology, 4*(12), 465–475.

Apriyani, N., & Muhsin, A. (2017). *Analisis Pengendalian Persediaan Bahan Baku dengan Metode Economic Order Quantity dan Kanban pada PT Adyawinsa Stamping Industries. OPSI, 10*(2). https://doi.org/10.31315/opsi.v10i2.2108

Bentler, P. M., & Bonett, D. G. (1980). Significance tests and goodness of fit in the analysis of covariance structures. *Psychological Bulletin, 88*(3), 588–606. https://doi.org/10.1037/0033-2909.88.3.588

Busola, E. K., & Olaleke, O. O. (2020). Analysis of inventory management practices for optimal economic performance using ABC and EOQ models. *Jurnal of Management (IJM), 11*(7), 835–848.

Connor, N. O., Lowry, P. B., & Treiblmaier, H. (2020). Interorganizational cooperation and supplier performance in high-technology supply chains. *Heliyon, 6*(3). https://doi.org/10.1016/j.heliyon.2020.e03434

Craighead, C. W., Ketchen, D. J., & Darby, J. L. (2020). Pandemics and supply chain management research: Toward a theoretical toolbox. *Decision Sciences, 51*(4). https://doi.org/10.1111/deci.12468

Eroglu, C., & Hofer, C. (2011). Lean, leaner, too lean? the inventory-performance link revisited. *Journal of Operations Management, 29*(4). https://doi.org/10.1016/j.jom.2010.05.002

Eroglu, A., & Ozdemir, G. (2007). An economic order quantity model with defective items and shortages. *International Journal of Production Economics, 106*(2). https://doi.org/10.1016/j.ijpe.2006.06.015

Gupta, M. C., & Boyd, L. H. (2008). Theory of constraints: A theory for operations management. *International Journal of Operations and Production Management, 28*(10). https://doi.org/10.1108/01443570810903122

Haekal, J., & Setiawan, I. (2020). Comparative analysis of raw materials control using JIT and EOQ method for cost efficiency of raw material supply in automotive components company Bekasi, Indonesia. *International Journal of Engineering Research and Advanced Technology, 6*(10), 76–82. https://doi.org/10.31695/ijerat.2020.3661

Hair, J. F. J., Hult, G. T. M., Ringle, C. M., & Sage, M. S. (2013). A primer on partial least squares structural equation modeling. *Long Range Planning, 46*(1–2), 184–185. https://doi.org/10.1016/j.lrp.2013.01.002

Hair, J. F., Sarstedt, M., Hopkins, L., & Kuppelwieser, V. G. (2014). Partial least squares structural equation modeling (PLS-SEM): An emerging tool in business research. *European Business Review, 26*(2), 106–121. https://doi.org/10.1108/EBR-10-2013-0128

Henseler, J., Dijkstra, T. K., Sarstedt, M., Ringle, C. M., Diamantopoulos, A., Straub, D. W., Ketchen, D. J., Hair, J. F., Hult, G. T. M., & Calantone, R. J. (2014). Common beliefs and reality about PLS: Comments on Rönkkö and Evermann (2013). *Organizational Research Methods, 17*(2), 182–209.

Henseler, J., Ringle, C. M., & Sarstedt, M. (2015). A new criterion for assessing discriminant validity in variance-based structural equation modeling. *Journal of the Academy of Marketing Science, 43*(1), 115–135. https://doi.org/10.1007/s11747-014-0403-8

Holweg, M., & Bicheno, J. (2002). Supply chain simulation – A tool for education, enhancement and endeavour. *International Journal of Production Economics, 78*(2), 163–175. https://doi.org/10.1016/S0925-5273(00)00171-7

Hosseini, S., Morshedlou, N., Ivanov, D., Sarder, M. D., Barker, K., & Khaled, A. Al. (2019). Resilient supplier selection and optimal order allocation under disruption risks. *International Journal of Production Economics, 213*, 124–137. https://doi.org/10.1016/j.ijpe.2019.03.018

Hua, G., Cheng, T. C. E., & Wang, S. (2011). Managing carbon footprints in inventory management. *International Journal of Production Economics, 132*(2), 178–185. https://doi.org/10.1016/j.ijpe.2011.03.024

Hussain, W., Hussain, J., Akbar, S., Sulehri, N. A., & Maqbool, Z. (2014). The effects of supply chain management practices (strategic suppliers partnership, information sharing, and postponement) on organizational performance in consumer goods manufacturing industry of Pakistan. *International Journal of Management Sciences, 2*(8), 351–352.

Inman, R. A., Sale, M. L., & Green, K. W. (2009). Analysis of the relationships among TOC use, TOC outcomes, and organizational performance. *International Journal of Operations and Production Management, 29*(4), 341–356. https://doi.org/10.1108/01443570910945819

Ji, W., & Zhang, J. (2022). The impact of COVID-19 on the E-commerce companies in China. *Review of Integrative Business and Economics Research, 11*(1), 155–165.

Khaireddin, M., Abu Assab, M., & Nawafleh, S. (2015). Just-in-time manufacturing practices and strategic performance: An empirical study applied on Jordanian Pharmaceutical Industries. *International Journal of Statistics and Systems, 10*(2), 287–307.

Khan, A., & Siddiqui, D. A. (2018). Information sharing and strategic supplier partnership in supply chain management: A study on pharmaceutical companies of Pakistan. *Asian Business Review, 8*(3), 117–124. https://doi.org/10.18034/abr.v8i3.162

Kosgei, R. C. & Gitau, R. (2016). Effect of supplier relationship management on organizational performance: A case study of Kenya Airways Limited. *International Academic Journal of Procurement and Supply Chain Management, 2*(2), 134–148.

Koumanakos, D. P. (2008). The effect of inventory management on firm performance. *International Journal of Productivity and Performance Management, 57*(5). https://doi.org/10.1108/17410400810881827

Lee, H. L. (2002). Aligning supply chain strategies with product uncertainties. *California Management Review, 44*(3), 105–119. https://doi.org/10.2307/41166135

Lwiki, T., Ojera, P., Box, P., Bagmaseno, P., Nebat, K., Mugenda, G., & Wachira, V. (2013). The impact of inventory management practices on financial performance of sugar manufacturing firms in Kenya. *International Journal of Business, Humanities and Technology, 3*(2), 75–85.

Motwani, J. (2003). A business process change framework for examining lean manufacturing: A case study. *Industrial Management and Data Systems*, *103*(5–6). https://doi.org/10.1108/02635570310477398

Musara, M. (2012). Impact of just-in-time (JIT) inventory system on efficiency, quality and flexibility among manufacturing sector, small and medium enterprise (SMEs) in South Africa. *African Journal of Business Management*, *6*(17). https://doi.org/10.5897/ajbm12.148

Musau, E. G., Namusonge, G., Makokha, E. N., & Ngeno, J. (2017). The effect of inventory management on organizational performance among textile manufacturing firms in Kenya. *International Journal of Academic Research in Business and Social Sciences*, *7*(11), 1032–1046. https://doi.org/10.6007/ijarbss/v7-i11/3543

Mwangi, W., & Nyambura, M. T. (2015). The role of inventory management on performance of food processing companies: A case study of Crown Foods Limited Kenya. *European Journal of Business and Social Sciences*, *4*(04), 64–78.

Narayanapillai, R. (2014). Factors discriminating inventory management performance: An exploratory study of Indian machine tool SMEs. *Journal of Industrial Engineering and Management*, *7*(3), 605–621. https://doi.org/10.3926/jiem.924

Nawanir, G., Lim, K. T., & Othman, S. N. (2016). Lean manufacturing practices in Indonesian manufacturing firms: Are there business performance effects? *International Journal of Lean Six Sigma*, *7*(2), 149–170. https://doi.org/10.1108/IJLSS-06-2014-0013

Nyamah, E. Y., Opoku, R. K., & Kaku, G. (2022). Inventory strategies and performance of food and beverage processing industries. *International Journal of Logistics Systems and Management*, *41*(1–2). https://doi.org/10.1504/IJLSM.2022.120985

Omoush, M. M. (2020). Investigation the relationship between supply chain management activities and operational performance: Testing the mediating role of strategic agility – A practical study on the pharmaceutical companies. *International Business Research*, *13*(2), 74–89. https://doi.org/10.5539/ibr.v13n2p74

Panigrahi, A. (2013). Relationship between inventory management and profitability: An empirical analysis of Indian cement companies. *Asia Pacific Journal of Marketing and Management Research*, *2*(7), 107–120.

Patnayakuni, R., Rai, A., & Seth, N. (2006). Relational antecedents of information flow integration for supply chain coordination. *Journal of Management Information Systems*, *23*(1), 13–49. https://doi.org/10.2753/MIS0742-1222230101

Paula, M., & Bautista, J. T. (2023). The effects of organizational culture and leadership style on organizational performance in times of COVID-19 pandemic. *Review of Integrative Business and Economics Research*, *12*(1), 175–194.

Pourasiabi, H. (2012). Just in Time (JİT) production and supply chain. *International Iron & Steel Symposium, April*, 1221–1227.

Putra, W. B. T. S. (2022). Problems, common beliefs and procedures on the use of partial least squares structural equation modeling in business research. *South Asian Journal of Social Studies and Economics*, *14*(1), 1–20. https://doi.org/10.9734/sajsse/2022/v14i130367

Putra, W. B. T. S., & Ardianto, B. (2022). Why does risk communication matter? Preventive and excessive health behavior among uninfected people. *South Asian Journal of Social Studies and Economics, February*, 56–72. https://doi.org/10.9734/sajsse/2022/v13i230355

Qi, Y., Boyer, K. K., & Zhao, X. (2009). Supply chain strategy, product characteristics, and performance impact: Evidence from Chinese manufacturers. *Decision Sciences*, *40*(4), 667–695. https://doi.org/10.1111/j.1540-5915.2009.00246.x

Qrunfleh, S., & Tarafdar, M. (2013). Lean and agile supply chain strategies and supply chain responsiveness: The role of strategic supplier partnership and postponement. *Supply Chain Management: An International Journal*, *18*(6), 571–582. https://doi.org/10.1108/SCM-01-2013-0015

Rachmah, S. A., & Madiawati, P. N. (2022). Pengaruh storytelling marketing dan electronic word of mouth terhadap Keputusan Pembelian Café Kisah Manis Jalan Sunda di Kota Bandung melalui Content Marketing Creator TikTok. *ATRABIS: Jurnal Administrasi Bisnis (e-Journal)*, *8*(1), 48–60.

Ramayah, T., Yeap, J. A. L., Ahmad, N. H., Halim, H. A., & Rahaman, S. A. (2017). Testing a confirmatory model of Facebook usage in smartPLS using consistent PLS. *International Journal of Business and Innovation*, *3*(2), 1–14.

Riswanto, W., & Prasetyo, S. (2022). Kanban (pull system) development in the cigarette manufacturing production area. *Review of Integrative Business and Economics Research*, *11*(1), 311–318.

Sanni, S., Jovanoski, Z., & Sidhu, H. S. (2020). An economic order quantity model with reverse logistics program. *Operations Research Perspectives*, 7. https://doi.org/10.1016/j.orp.2019.100133

Sarstedt, M., Hair Jr, J. F., Cheah, J. H., Becker, J. M., & Ringle, C. M. (2019). How to specify, estimate, and validate higher-order constructs in PLS-SEM. *Australasian Marketing Journal, 27*(3), 197–211.

Shin, S., Ennis, K. L., & Spurlin, W. P. (2015). Effect of inventory management efficiency on profitability: Current evidence from the US manufacturing industry. *Journal of Economics and Economic Education Research, 16*(1), 98–106.

Sitienei, E., & Memba, F. (2015). The effect of inventory management on profitability of cement manufacturing companies in Kenya: A case study of listed cement manufacturing companies in Kenya. *International Journal of Management and Commerce Innovations, 3*(2), 111–119.

Srinivasan, M., Mukherjee, D., & Gaur, A. S. (2011). Buyer-supplier partnership quality and supply chain performance: Moderating role of risks, and environmental uncertainty. *European Management Journal, 29*(4), 260–271. https://doi.org/10.1016/j.emj.2011.02.004

Stevenson, W. J. (2005). *Operations management* (8th ed.). McGraw-Hill.

Taj, S., & Morosan, C. (2011). The impact of lean operations on the Chinese manufacturing performance. *Journal of Manufacturing Technology Management, 22*(2), 223–240. https://doi.org/10.1108/17410381111102234

Tenenhaus, M., Amato, S., & Vinzi, E. V. (2004). A global goodness-of-fit index for PLS structural equation modelling. *The XLII SIS Scientific Meeting, 1*(2), 739–742.

Vörös, J. (2013). Economic order and production quantity models without constraint on the percentage of defective items. *Central European Journal of Operations Research, 21*(4), 867–885. https://doi.org/10.1007/s10100-012-0277-0

Wan, X., Britto, R., & Zhou, Z. (2020). In search of the negative relationship between product variety and inventory turnover. *International Journal of Production Economics, 222*. https://doi.org/10.1016/j.ijpe.2019.09.024

Wong, C. Y., Boon-Itt, S., & Wong, C. W. (2011). The contingency effects of environmental uncertainty on the relationship between supply chain integration and operational performance. *Journal of Operations Management, 29*(6), 604–615. https://doi.org/10.1016/j.jom.2011.01.003

Yang, L., Li, H., & Campbell, J. F. (2020). Improving order fulfillment performance through integrated inventory management in a multi-item finished goods system. *Journal of Business Logistics, 41*(1), 54–66. https://doi.org/10.1111/jbl.12227

CHAPTER 4

DEVELOPING MANUFACTURING CAPABILITY FOR MICRO, SMALL, AND MEDIUM ENTERPRISES

Lina Anatan

Maranatha Christian University Bandung, Indonesia

ABSTRACT

This study discusses how companies develop their manufacturing capabilities through learning and the mastery of processes and equipment based on the resource-based view. Resources and capabilities are formed through an internal and external learning process, also from processes and equipment owned by the company. Data are collected through surveys and selected based on purposive samples. By involving 61 respondents from micro, small and medium enterprises (MSMEs), the study found that there is no significant influence of internal and external learning on the mastery of production processes and equipment, however, both internal and external learning directly influence manufacturing capability. It is also found that mastery of processes and equipment significantly influences manufacturing capability. It indicates that the achievement of manufacturing capability within the company is strongly influenced by the learning process within the company which is developed based on the resource-based view. This study is expected to contribute to the strategic and operational management literature regarding the implementation of resource-based theory into practices through strategy formulation to develop manufacturing capability, especially in MSMEs.

The Finance-Innovation Nexus: Implications for Socio-Economic Development
International Symposia in Economic Theory and Econometrics, Volume 34, 45–53
Copyright © 2025 by Emerald Publishing Limited
All rights of reproduction in any form reserved
ISSN: 1571-0386/doi:10.1108/S1571-038620240000034004

Keywords: Resource-based view; internal learning; external learning; manufacturing capability; MSME

JEL Classification Code: M19 (Other)

INTRODUCTION

Some of the problems during the Covid-19 pandemic included reduced public demand for micro, small and medium enterprise (MSME) products which had an impact on decreasing MSME income and turnover, scarcity in materials due to mobility restrictions triggered by large-scale social restriction policies to reduce the rate of spread of the virus, difficulties in accessing finance and capital since there are still many MSME are considered to be unbankable, and the low mastery of technology by MSME has resulted in the productivity, performance, and competitiveness of MSMEs are still tending to be low (Catriana, 2021).

To increase the productivity, performance, and competitiveness of MSMEs, especially in the manufacturing sector, the development of manufacturing capabilities needs to receive important attention. The concept of manufacturing capability was first introduced by Hayes and Wheelwright (1984) who defined manufacturing capability as the dimension in which a company chooses to compete. This capability refers to decisions and practices related to the company's operational structure and infrastructure that are developed internally and are difficult to imitate and transfer (Swink & Hegarty, 1998). Peng et al. (2008) define manufacturing capability as process capability and operational outcome. So that it can be concluded that manufacturing capability is the ability to compete, or actual company strength compared to its competitors in the market share where the company operates. In operations management, manufacturing capability is synonymous with quality, delivery, flexibility, and cost (Swink et al., 2007; Ward et al., 1995). For example, cost capability refers to a company's ability to produce at a lower price level than its competitors.

The resource-based view suggests an important strategy in creating competitive advantage through the ownership of unique resources within a company, which are better known as firm-specific resources. The creation of a company's competitive advantage can be done through a cost leadership and differentiation approach (Porter, 1980). Cost leadership can be achieved through low costs which can be achieved through production efficiency. Meanwhile, differentiation can be realised through the creation of brand loyalty and a positive reputation owned by the company. The concept of competitive advantage is closely related to manufacturing capability since competitive advantage can be achieved and maintained when supported by manufacturing capability which can be obtained through the ownership of valuable, rare, non-imitation, and non-substitutable resources.

This research was conducted to examine the effect of internal and external learning on process and equipment ownership and its effect on manufacturing capability and the effect of proprietary process and equipment on manufacturing capability which was analysed using a resource-based view. The model was from Schroeder et al. (2002).

HYPOTHESES DEVELOPMENT

Argyris (1999) defined organisational learning as a learning process that occurs within an organisation or company through a social interaction process within a group or organisational level. Learning is carried out to encourage the company to adapt to the environmental changes through adaptation to company routines. It means when there is a learning process within a company, there will be an increase in knowledge within the company which in turn will be able to increase the company's ability to master the production process and own equipment since with knowledge, companies might improve productivity, performance, and competitiveness become an important factor in determining the profitability that can be achieved by a company.

The resource-based view (RBV) is the basis for company decisions to conduct learning both internally and externally. The concept of external learning was put forward by Gerwin and Kolodny (1992) who identified internal learning as multi-functional training for all human resources in a company. Through this training, human resources are empowered and involved in the production and development process so that the company is more adaptive to change.

Schroeder et al. (2002) suggested external learning as an inter-organisational learning process or in other words, the learning process comes from companies or other organisations, such as suppliers. The supplier's role for the company is to provide input regarding the design of new processes and products which can be in the form of supplier involvement in creating quality and continuous process improvement. Both internal and external learning have an important role in mastering the production process and equipment ownership which will ultimately affect manufacturing capability so that in this study the following hypotheses were developed:

H1. Internal learning affects the proprietary of the production process and equipment.

H2. External learning affects the proprietary of the production process and equipment.

H3. Internal learning affects manufacturing capability.

H4. External learning affects manufacturing capability.

The proprietary of the production process and equipment includes all processes and production equipment owned by the company to support the company's production activities. It is a result of a learning process that is difficult to imitate and of value that needs to be patented and becomes an asset or resource that can be used as a source of company advantage. In addition, the production process and equipment will determine the company's success in developing manufacturing capabilities (Schroeder et al., 2002). Company profitability and sales are something of value and cannot be imitated because each company is unique in terms of the achievements of both which can also be used as indicators of measuring a company's financial performance, so in this study, the following hypothesis was developed:

H5. The proprietary of the production process and equipment affects manufacturing capabilities.

RESEARCH METHOD

The purposive sampling method was used as the sampling method in this study. The judgement used is companies in the manufacturing sector that are included in the criteria for MSMEs based on Law No. 20 of 2008 which classifies MSMEs in class, micro, small, and medium based on assets and turnover. The online survey method is used as a data collection method which is carried out using the Google form. The type of data collected is cross-section data. Cross-section data can be defined as data collected at a certain time and involves many respondents.

The variables in this study were adopted from the research of Schroeder et al. (2002), where the internal learning variable consisted of 11 statements, the internal learning variable consisted of 11 statements, the process ownership, and production equipment variable consisted of 4 statements and the manufacturing capability variable consisted of top 10 statements. All statement items in this study were measured using a 5-point Likert scale, where point 1 represents strongly disagree, point 2 represents disagree, point 3 represents no answer, point 4 represents agree, and point 5 represents strongly agree. Company age and industry type are used as control variables in accordance with studies conducted by Masri and Martani (2014) and Ridho and Suhari (2021). Company age and industry type might be specified as the company's specific characteristics that might influence the process of capability development.

To determine the quality of the research instruments in this study, validity and reliability tests were carried out. According to Hair et al. (2006), an instrument is said to be valid if it is able to measure the data studied accurately, while reliability testing is carried out to determine the consistency of the test results under different conditions for each statement item. Validity testing was carried out using Product Moment Correlation, while reliability testing used Cronbach's Alpha with a Rule of thumb > 0.6 (Sekaran, 2003). To test the hypothesis this study used multiple linear regression analysis. This analytical method is used to predict the effect of several independent variable (X) on the dependent variable (Y). Tests for violations of the classical assumptions include heteroscedasticity tests, multicollinearity tests, and normality tests are also carried out before testing the hypothesis to test the model free from violations of the classical assumptions.

DATA ANALYSIS

Business Profile

Table 4.1 shows the profiles of the 61 MSMEs involved in this research. Based on the age of the MSMEs involved in this study, the majority have been operating for 0–5 years, 23 MSMEs (37.7%), 6–10 years, 19 MSMEs (19%), 11–15 years, 9 MSMEs (14.8%), 16–20 years, 8 MSMEs (13.1%), and more than 20 years, 2 MSMEs (3.3%).

By field of business, 16 MSMEs (26.2%) were engaged in food and beverages, 13 MSMEs (21.3%) were engaged in crafts, 11 MSMEs (18%) were engaged in textiles and garments, 12 MSMEs (19.7%) were engaged in electronics and 9 SMEs (14.8%)

Table 4.1. Business Profile.

Characteristics	Criteria	Frequency	Percentage	Accumulative Percentage
Age	0–5 years	23	37.7	37.7
	6–10 years	19	31.8	68.8
	11–15 years	9	14.8	83.6
	16–20 years	8	13.1	96.7
	>20 years	2	3.3	100
Field of Business	Textile and Garment	11	18	18
	Food and Beverages	16	26.2	44.2
	Crafts	13	21.3	65.5
	Automotives	9	14.8	80.3
	Electronics	12	19.7	100
Number of employees	0–4 employees	15	24.6	24.6
	5–19 employees	21	34.4	59
	20–99 employees	35	41	100
	>100 employees	–	–	–
3 years Performance	Increased > 15%	9	14.8	14.8
	Increased < 15%	20	32.8	47.5
	No changes	12	19.2	67.2
	Decreased > 15%	11	18.0	85.2
	Decreased < 15%	9	14.8	100
Assets	0 – IDR 50 million	10	16.4	16.4
	>IDR 50 – IDR 500 million	23	37.7	93.4
	>IDR 500 m – IDR 10 bil.	28	45.9	100

Source: Data Processed.

in the automotive. Based on the number of workers, the majority of MSMEs have a workforce of between 20 and 99 workers totalling 35 MSMEs (41%), 5–10 workers totalling 21 MSMEs (34.4%), and 15 MSMEs (24.6%) have 0–4 workers.

Based on the performance over the last three years, the majority of MSMEs, 20 MSMEs (32.8%), had an increase in performance of <15%, 12 MSMEs (19.2%) did not experience any change in performance, 11 MSMEs (18.0%) MSMEs stated that their performance in the last 3 years had decreased > 15% and 9 MSMEs (14.8%) stated that they had decreased <15%. Based on the assets owned by the majority of MSMEs in this study, 28 MSMEs (45.9%) confirmed that they had assets > IDR 500 million to IDR 10 billion, 23 MSMEs (37,7%) confirmed they had assets IDR 50 to IDR 500 million, and the remaining 10 MSMEs (16.4%) confirmed they had assets IDR 0-IDR 50 million.

Descriptive Statistic

Table 4.2 summarises the characteristics of the respondents' answers in this study.

Validity and Reliability Analysis

Table 4.3 shows the results of testing the validity using the Product Moment Correlation Coefficient and the results of testing the validity with Cronbach's Alpha.

Table 4.2.   Descriptive Statistic.

Variables	Means	Standard Deviation
IL	3.84–4.39	0.633–1.064
EL	3.66–4.21	0.734–1.015
PPE	2.80–3.90	0.895–1.108
MC	3.67–4.23	0.733–1.054

Source: Data Processed.
Note: IL – internal learning; EL – external learning; PPE – proprietary of the production process and equipment; MC – manufacturing capability.

Table 4.3.   Validity and Reliability Testing.

Variables	Range of *r*-count	Sign	Exclude	Cronbach's Alpha
IL	0.512–0.790	0.000	0	0.855
EL	0.506–0.707	0.000	0	0.824
PPE	0.712–0.834	0.000	0	0.800
MC	0.502–0.820	0.000	0	0.902

Source: Data Processed.
Note: IL – internal learning; EL – external learning; PPE – proprietary of the production process and equipment; MC – manufacturing capability.

Hypothesis Testing

Table 4.4 summarises the results of testing *H1* (internal learning affects the proprietary of the production process and equipment), *H2* (external learning affects the proprietary of the production process and equipment), *H3* (internal learning affects manufacturing capability), *H4* (external learning affects manufacturing capability), and *H5* (the proprietary of the production process and equipment affects manufacturing capability). Prior to testing the hypothesis, the research model has been tested on classical assumptions which include normality tests (using normal probability plots), heteroscedasticity tests (using scatterplots), and multicollinearity tests (using VIF values). The test results show that the research model is free from classic assumption violations.

The results of testing *H1* and *H2* regarding the effect of internal learning and external learning on the proprietary of the production process and equipment show that both internal learning and external learning have no significant effect on the proprietary of the production process and equipment. Based on the results of partial testing with multiple regression analysis, the t value and significance of $t > 0.05$ are good for internal learning ($t = 1.162$, sig-$t = 0.213$), while for external learning ($t = 1.062$, sig.$t = 0.293$), so it can be concluded that both hypotheses are not supported.

The results of the hypothesis testing regarding the influence of internal and external learning on the proprietary production process and equipment are not significant. It can be explained that the internal and external learning processes for MSME actors have not been optimally implemented due to limitations in mastering the resources of MSME actors in Indonesia, the Government is currently very

Table 4.4. Hypotheses Testing.

Dependent and Control Variable	Independent Variables	Standardised β	*t*	Sig. *t*
PPE	Constant	–	1.162	0.250
	IL	0.208	1.250	0.213
	EL	0.175	1.062	0.293
MC	Constant	–	8.543	000
	IL	0.421	3.379	0.002
	EL	0.300	2.343	0.0.23
	PPE	0.331	2.698	0.009
Control Variables	Company age	0.080	0.651	0.517
	Industry type	0.271	2.035	0.047

Source: Data Processed.
Note: IL – internal learning; EL – external learning; PPE – proprietary of the production process and equipment; MC – manufacturing capability.

aggressive to encourage collaboration between universities and the business world and the industrial world, especially MSMEs. One example of a Collaboration Program that is currently being implemented by the Government of Indonesia is the Matching Fund Grant Collaboration.

The results of testing *H3* and *H4* which examine the direct effect of internal and external learning on manufacturing capabilities show that both hypotheses are supported. The partial test results with the multiple linear methods show *t* and significant *t* values as follows: internal learning ($t = 3.379$, sig.$t = 0.002$) and external learning ($t = 2.343$, sig.$t = 0.23$). The results of testing *H5* to test the effect of the proprietary production process and equipment on manufacturing capability show that the hypothesis is supported based on the test results which show the value of $t = 2.698$ and sign.$t = 0.09$.

Discussion

Internal and external learning does not have a significant effect on the proprietary processes and equipment in this study and it can be explained as follows: limited resources such as competence and knowledge of human resources and financial constraints which are the main problems of MSMEs in Indonesia result in the learning process cannot be carried out well. Likewise, financial limitations result MSMEs do not have sufficient capital to invest in technology and equipment, as well as developing process designs to support MSME operational activities (Hamdan, 2021). Nonetheless, MSMEs believe that internal learning, external learning, as well as process and equipment ownership have an important role in developing MSME manufacturing capabilities so that the results of testing the three hypotheses are significant for MSME manufacturing capabilities.

In supporting the development of manufacturing capabilities, both internal and external learning processes need to be implemented by MSMEs. The learning process might focus on causal knowledge, ambiguity, and complex social factors and can be obtained through access to knowledge from external parties if internal MSMEs are difficult to obtain. One of the efforts that can be taken is through the development of external partnerships such as universities as knowledge producers, as well as banks to overcome problems related to financial problems which are one of the internal problems of MSMEs. In the long term, MSMEs are expected to be able to own patents for processes and equipment that provide competitive advantages for MSMEs, and this competitive advantage is largely determined by the achievement of MSME manufacturing capabilities.

CONCLUSION

The results showed that there were two unsupported hypotheses and three supported hypotheses. The unsupported hypothesis is the effect of internal and external learning on the proprietary of the production process and equipment. While the supported hypothesis is the effect of internal learning, external learning, and proprietary production process and equipment on manufacturing capability.

The implications of managerial policies related to this study are that the results of the study are expected to provide benefits to practitioners, especially in managing internal and external learning to improve MSME manufacturing capabilities. Suggestions for future research are to modify the research model by adding other variables such as company performance, and company competitiveness as the dependent variable or to include other variables such as manufacturing strategy or specific manufacturing competence as moderating variables between proprietary of the production process and equipment.

REFERENCES

Argyris, C. (1999). *On organizational learning*. (2nd edn.). Blackwell Business, Oxford.

Catriana, E. (2021) This is the importance of holding ultra micro financing for MSMEs. Kompas.com. https://money.kompas.com/read/2021/02/10/070518926/ini-pentingnya-holdingpembiayaan-ultramikro-untuk-umkm?page=all

Gerwin, D., & Kolodny, H. (1992). *Management of advanced manufacturing technology: Strategy, organization, and innovation*. Wiley/Interscience.

Hair, J. F., Black, W. C., Babin, B. J., Anderson, R. E., & Tatham, R. L. (2006). Multivariate data analysis (6th ed). Pearson Prentice Hall.

Hamdan. (2021). Analysis of the sustainability of MSMEs in the Covid-19 pandemic era. *JEJAK: Journal of Economics and Policy*, 4(1), 183–199.

Hayes, R. H., & Wheelwright, S. C. (1984). *restoring our competitive edge: Competing through manufacturing*. John Wiley.

Masri, I., & Martani, D. (2014). Tax avoidance behaviour towards the cost of debt. *International Journal of Trade and Global Markets*, 7(3), 235–249.

Peng, D. X., Schroeder, R. G., & Shah, R. (2008). Linking routines to operations capabilities: A new perspective. *Journal of Operations Management*, 26, 730–748.

Porter, M. (1980). *Competitive advantage creating and sustaining superior performance*. Free Press.

Ridho, M. R. A., & Suhari, E. (2021). Industry type as control variable between company size, capital structure, and profitability ratio to financial distress. *International Journal of Economics, Business, and Management Research*, 5(12), 173–184.

Schroeder, R. G., Bates, K. A., & dan Junttila, M. A. (2002). A-resource based view of manufacturing strategy and the relationship to manufacturing performance. *Strategic Management Journal, 23*, 105–117.

Swink, M., & Hegarty, W. H. (1998). Core manufacturing capabilities and their links to product differentiation. *International Journal of Operations and Production Management, 18*, 374–396.

Swink, M., Narasimhan, R., & Wang, C. (2007). Managing beyond the factory walls: Effects of four types of strategic integration on manufacturing plant performance. *Journal of Operations Management, 25*(1), 148–64.

Ward, P. T., Bickford, D. J., & Leong, G. K. (1995). Business environment, operation strategy, and performance: An empirical study of Singapore Manufacturers. *Journal of Operation Management, 13*(2), 99–155.

CHAPTER 5

ASSESSING GROWTH OF GREEN FINANCE AND INVESTMENT IN SELECT DEVELOPED AND DEVELOPING COUNTRIES

Sumedha Bhatnagar and Dipti Sharma

Department of Humanities and Social Sciences, Malaviya National Institute of Technology Jaipur, Rajasthan, India

ABSTRACT

This study evaluates the performance of green finance and investment scenarios in 15 carbon emitting countries, among which 7 are developed countries and 8 are developing countries. The principal component analysis is applied to form the global green financing (GF) and investment index, a composite indicator for assessing the multidimensional characteristics of GF and investment. The global green finance and investment index is developed to map the country's overall GF and investing scenario. The indicator is developed on the basis of 30 variables that represent 11 quantitative factors. These factors are aggregated into four parameters: transparency, efficiency, efficacy and resilience. Transparency includes political stability and the development of the countries' capital markets to adapt to the green transition. Efficiency consists of the performance of existing resources and regulatory conditions of the countries. Efficacy refers to the factors related to international engagement and the growth of specific financial instruments. Lastly, resilience includes factors that promote the adaptability of the countries towards a green economy and green financial system. It contains the regulatory structure of the country's growth

The Finance-Innovation Nexus: Implications for Socio-Economic Development
International Symposia in Economic Theory and Econometrics, Volume 34, 55–72
Copyright © 2025 by Emerald Publishing Limited
All rights of reproduction in any form reserved
ISSN: 1571-0386/doi:10.1108/S1571-038620240000034005

of macroeconomic variables. These variables represent social, economic, environmental and governance factors that influence the countries' GF and investment scenario. The countries are ranked on the basis of the composite indicator score. The USA scored the highest rank, and India scored the least. In terms of developed countries, the USA has achieved the highest value, followed by Germany and in developing countries, China has scored the highest performance, followed by Mexico.

Keywords: Green investment; green finance; green finance index; composite indicator; principal component analysis

JEL Classification: O11; Q01; Q5

1. INTRODUCTION

1.1. Green Economy

In the present global scenario, the environment has become an integral part of the country's sustainable economic growth (Boudghene Stambouli et al., 2014; Stern, 2007). UNEP Green Economy Report (Towards a Green Economy Pathways to Sustainable Development and Poverty Eradication, PART II: Investing in energy and resource efficiency, Renewable Energy | UNEP – UN Environment Programme, 2017) defines the green economy as

> the process of reconfiguring businesses and infrastructure to deliver better returns on natural, human and economic capital investments, while at the same time reducing greenhouse gas emission, extracting and using less natural resources, creating less waste and reducing social disparities.

It is a multidimensional concept that pays specific attention to the interface between the economy and the environment (Merino-Saum et al., 2019). The idea has gained attention on a national and international scale. Various countries have developed and reformed their policies to transition their economy towards a green economy. The objective of the green economy is human welfare and reducing environmental risks in the long term (Robins & Zadek, 2016). It is closely related to three prime disciplines ecological economics, industrial ecology and environmental/resource economics.

1.2. Green Finance and Investment

The adoption of the green economic model can be a success when it involves global commitment and a designed framework for a global investment involving both developing and developed countries (Andersen et al., 2020; Green Growth Knowledge Platform, 2013). Green financing (GF) is a ladder to make the transition to a green economy possible. It addresses multiple environmental challenges and converges the economies on a sustainable pathway (Falcone & Sica, 2018). GF is a route to sustainable financial sector development (Berensmann & Lindenberg, 2016). According to the UNEP Enquiry (United Nations Environment Programme, 2019), climate finance is a subset of green finance, which is a further subset of sustainable finance. It states that green finance includes environmental objectives necessary to support sustainability through biodiversity and resource conservation, and it is not limited to climate change mitigation and adaptation.

In contrast, climate finance includes financing limited to climate change mitigation and adaptation activities shown in Fig. 5.1. The operational definition of climate financing adopted by the Organisation for Economic Co-operation and Development (OECD) and other Multilateral Development Banks (MDBs) such as the World Bank states climate financing as 'the capital flows that specifically target low-carbon and climate-resilient development which direct or indirect greenhouse gas mitigation or adaptation objectives or outcomes'. G20 Green Finance Study Group (2016) defined green finance as

> financing of investment that provide environmental benefits in the broader context of environmentally sustainable development. These environmental benefits include, for example, reduction in air, water and land pollution, reduction in greenhouse gas (GHG) emissions, improved energy efficiency while utilizing existing natural resources, as well as mitigation of and adaption to climate change and their co-benefit.

The motive of GF is to encourage the transition towards the green economy. The initiatives include reducing the GHG emissions, promoting the use of renewable energy, controlling pollution, and waste energy management, holistic development of biodiversity and sustainable development of the nation. It is an interaction between the green industry and finance industry for sustainable economic growth.

GF is a channel for directing investment to green projects with the common objective of increasing green growth in the economy. Thus, it includes the concept of green investment. Green investment (GI) refers to the investment that aims to reduce GHG emissions caused by pollution without significantly reducing the production and consumption of non-energy goods. It includes both public and

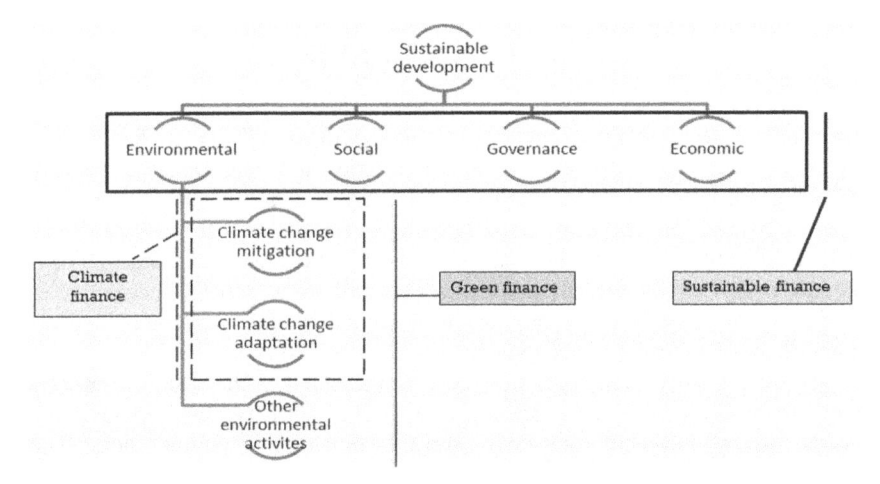

Fig. 5.1.   Demarcation of Sustainable, Green and Climate Finance (*Source*: redrawn from UNEP Inquiry).

private investment. The major components of green investment include investment in low-emission energy supply (renewables, biofuels and nuclear), energy efficiency (in energy supply and energy-consuming sectors) and carbon capture and sequestration. As per the report by UNEP (2015), UNEP (2010) and UNDESA (2011), the global green investment should be at least about 2% of the global gross domestic product (GDP) to shift development towards the low-carbon resource-efficient path (Stern, 2007). The Economics of Climate Change of the United Kingdom has stated that climate change will impose costs of 9% to 13% of the GDP in India by 2100.

Developing countries have always been adversely affected by the systemic biases of the global financial system because they are less resilient and more vulnerable to fluctuations in the world market. They are compelled to follow pro-cyclical macroeconomic policies, leading to greater economic instability and undermining long-term growth (Sundaram, 2013). As per the report by Shakti Sustainable Energy Foundation and Climate Policy Initiative (Damodaran et al., 2019), nearly 40% of capital market activities and bank loans are directly or indirectly at risk due to climate change. The total green investment needed for a successful transition to the green economy is nearly USD 1.8 trillion, with an annual investment of USD 160 billion.

The present chapter attempts to assess the GF and investment scenario of selected 15 countries in terms of factors broadly categorised into four dimensions: transparency, efficiency, efficacy and resilience. The composite indicator is obtained as a combination of several indicators. The chapter has applied principal component analysis (PCA) to calculate a combined score of all the variables categorised into four parameters. The chapter attempts to evaluate the global GF and investment scenario of 15 countries. A composite indicator developed from the factors influencing the scenario reflects the comparative score and rank of the countries.

2. LITERATURE REVIEW

2.1. Green Finance and Green Investment

The financial sector plays an integral role in supporting GF by channelling the resources required for climate mitigation, adaptation and environment protection (Bhatnagar & Sharma, 2022; Taghizadeh-Hesary & Yoshino, 2020). Financial institutions and markets protect the form of insurance, risk controlling mechanisms and other financial instruments such as bonds, loans and equities. GF requires reforms in the present financial system and its measures. Effective implementation of these reforms requires well-defined metrics for comprehensive tracking of the progress of GF (Maheshwari et al., 2016).

The green finance indicators can broadly be measured on the basis of transparency, efficacy, resilience and efficiency. Inderst et al. (2012) extensively reviewed various aspects and definitions of GF and GI provided by previous studies. The study proposed a green investment pyramid that indicates various financial products and ventures with scope for increasing GI. It recommends that GI definition should include governance structure. The study identified that GI can be the standalone definition and can also be the subset of broader definitions such as SRI (social or sustainably responsible investing), long-term investing, thematic investing and double or triple-bottom-line investing (with financial, social and ecological goals).

Zhang et al. (2019) conducted a bibliometric analysis highlighting that green finance is a fast-growing and relevant research area. The study showed that developed countries are more engaged in green finance studies than developing countries. Bhatnagar and Sharma (2022), extended the research and identified ten factors responsible for enabling GF. Wang et al. (2021) conducted a scientometric analysis to explore GF opportunities through energy-related policy reforms. It identified four significant policies for promoting the development of green finance. The four feasible policies for green finance are as follows: carbon tax policy, government subsidy policy, green bond policy and investment policy. The study highlighted that a green bond policy could significantly improve the green financial system.

In their study, Chowdhury et al. (2013) established that GF at the grassroots level can support the global goal of transitioning to a green economy. This requires creating awareness at the grassroots level among the rural population. An increase in micro-financing for green products can be the financial initiative that the countries can adopt. Dikau and Volz (2018) and Volz (2018) discussed the need for the green transformation of the financial system and the role of financial governance. Volz (2018) highlighted that sustainability-themed investment strategies in Asia have increased with the increase in awareness towards climate change, energy and water security. The study concluded that country-specific financial and market instruments should be developed for channelising investments in green projects.

The concept of green financial innovation is in a nascent stage and has enormous growth potential. Bhatnagar et al. (2021) conducted a bibliometric analysis highlighting the industrial revolution's role in adopting GF. Sifa et al. (2021) reviewed the role of Islamic financing for improving the agricultural financing and food sustainability. Wardhana and Universitas Atma Jaya Yogyakarta (2021) investigated the sustainable consumption pattern and environmental awareness among the university students. The study concluded that environmental awareness has positive impact on consumption behaviour of the respondents. Dwijaya Hendratama and Huang (2021) in their study concluded that family owned firm has negative affect on firm's initiatives towards resource use, emission reduction, responsibility towards community, human rights and other CSR strategies.

Dikau and Volz (2018) reviewed various tools and instruments of central banks and financial regulatory agencies for addressing environmental risks and promoting green finance. The study highlighted various tools and instruments to address environmental risk and promote green finance and investment in micro and macro-prudential regulations, green financial market development, credit allocation and various central bank initiatives. It concluded that the government's mandate for promoting green lending and investment could be a very effective initiative in developing countries.

Tran et al. (2020) explored the factors affecting green investments in Vietnam. The study stated that the green financial system comprises green capital and investment. It showed that access to capital for the projects is one of the significant constraints to the investment. The other challenges that significantly impact the investment are lack of legal framework, inadequate and asymmetric availability of information, relatively long-implementation time along with the requirement of large-scale investment and lack of awareness among the investors. Bhatnagar and Sharma (2021) conducted a SWOT analysis to analyse the scope of green finance in India. The barriers and drivers were categorised into strengths, weaknesses, opportunities and threats based on various initiatives undertaken by India. Hafner et al. (2020) identified various investment barriers in green projects. The study developed a theoretical framework and identified solutions to the obstacles. The results highlighted that policy uncertainty and short-termism in the financial system are critical investment obstacles. The study highlighted various other barriers such as lack of long-term climate change policy framework, lack of stability in the prevalent policies, lack of availability of suitable projects and investment possibilities, lack of knowledge and technical expertise, lack of liquidity in the market, lack of financial market instruments and lack of uniformity in climate disclosures.

2.2. Development of Composite Indicator

Samuwai and Hills (2018) analysed the climate readiness of selected Asia-Pacific countries. The study quantified readiness on the basis of three dimensions: policies and institutions, knowledge management and learning and fiscal policy environment. The 48 indicators to measure climate finance were further subjected to PCA. The study concluded that the Asian countries performed better than the Pacific Small Island Developing States (PSIDS) in all three dimensions. There is a significant readiness gap in PSIDS, but they are relatively better-performing countries on policy and institution dimensions.

Edmonds et al. (2020) developed a climate change vulnerability index for 100 nations. The study applied data envelopment analysis for forming the composite indicator. The index calculated endogenous weight within the six sectors selected for analysis. The sectors were identified on the basis of a theoretical framework. Kim et al. (2014) assessed 30 countries on the basis of 12 indicators to evaluate the green growth of the countries. The study's results highlighted that a country's consumption and production patterns significantly impact the country's green growth and transition. The study measured the current status of green growth in the countries. Dabla-Norris et al. (2012) developed a composite index for assessing the public efficiency index of 71 countries using the PCA. The index measured the institutional environment of the countries influencing public investment management. The index was developed on the basis of 17 indicators broadly categorised into four components strategic guidance and project appraisal, project selection, project implementation and management and project evaluation and audit. The index reflected the role of institutions, capacity and investment. The study concluded that most countries had a low capacity to choose public investment projects. According to Schomaker (1997), an ideal indicator should be specific, measurable, achievable or accessible, relevant and aligned with the objective and time bound or sensitive to the timeframe of the policy. According to Serres et al. (2010), an indicator should be relevant, analytically sound and measureable.

Gasser (2020) developed an electricity supply resilience index to measure a nation's electricity resilience. Multi-Criteria Decision Analysis was applied to develop the index. The indicator selection was based on the principles of relevance, credibility, data availability and comparability. Horváth and Vaško (2012) developed the financial stability transparency index for 110 countries from 2000 to 2011. The index was formed on the basis of the financial stability report published by various countries under the framework proposed by the IMF. The index was developed by taking the sum of 12 components of the report. Firmialy and Nainggolan (2019) constructed a sustainability reporting index based on the integrative perception of academic experts, social rating agencies and Indonesian companies. The index was developed on the basis of a theoretical framework and was validated using exploratory factor analysis and the Kinder-Lydenberg-Domini (KLD) method. The index reflects the social performance of the Indonesian public listed companies.

Jha and Bhanu Murthy (2003) proposed a modified methodology for calculating the environmental sustainability index. The authors provided critiques of the Environmental Sustainability Index developed by the World Economic Forum. The composite score of the study is developed using PCA. The justification for applying PCA is that 'it is a statistical technique that linearly transforms a large set of variables into a substantially smaller set of uncorrelated variables. That also represents the larger (original) set of variables'. PCA does not assume the normality assumption of the variables. It also does not consider the status of correlation and covariance among the variables. PCA does not assume hypothetical factors like factor analysis. It reduces the redundant data from the total observations.

Reddy and Nathan (2012) employed the Analytical Hierarchy Process of MCDA to weigh the variables. The study employed What-How-Whom (WHW) framework for categorising the variables. MCDA technique is used for constructing a composite index. Kuo et al. (2021), applied decision-making trial and evaluation laboratory (DEMATEL) for identifying factors influencing enterprise's ability to achieve sustainability practices. The study indicated that eco-design, waste management and laws and regulations are the three most important factors that influences sustainability practices of an enterprise.

Zhou et al. (2020) applied PCA to developing a green finance development index for 30 provinces and municipalities in China. The results showed that green finance has a positive relationship with environmental improvement. It applied global PCA, which combined time series data and PCA. The PCA index was calculated for each year from 2010 to 2017. The study recommended that fiscal policies, transition to a green financial system and policy support for green financial development can significantly and positively impact economic growth and improvement in environmental quality.

3. OBJECTIVES

The study evaluated the GF and investment environment of 15 carbon-emitting countries. It aims to develop a global green finance and investment index for measuring and comparing the growth of green finance in 15 selected countries.

4. METHODOLOGY

4.1. Method

This section includes the methods for selecting countries, indicators and construction of composite indicators. The selected countries are among the top 30 carbon-emitting countries. They are selected based on the comprehensive methodology adopted by (Damodaran et al., 2019). The normalised and aggregate score of carbon emissions, GDP, education index, health index and primary energy consumption for the countries are calculated. The top seven developed and eight developing countries were selected based on the finalised score. A mix of developed and developing countries was selected for conducting a comparative analysis of the countries.

4.1.1. Selection of Indicators

By OECD definition, a composite indicator is formed by compiling individual indicators into a single index on the basis of the underlying model of a multidimensional concept being measured. Ideally, composite indicators should be based on a theoretical framework/definition, which allow individual indicators/variables to be selected, combined and weighted in a manner which reflects the dimension or structure of the phenomenon being measured. OECD handbook guidelines are used for forming the index, as indicated in Fig. 5.2.

A theoretical approach based on a literature review is used for selecting the variables. Bhatnagar and Sharma (2022) categorised factors influencing GF and investment into 10 categories. The study considers quantitative factors gauging the mentioned categories and one additional factor representing environmental performance and the renewable energy sector. Through an extensive literature review, a total of 30 variables measuring 11 broad indicators for GF and investment scenarios are grouped into four broad dimensions: transparency, efficiency, efficacy and resilience. The critical components of the theoretical framework are shown in Fig. 5.3.

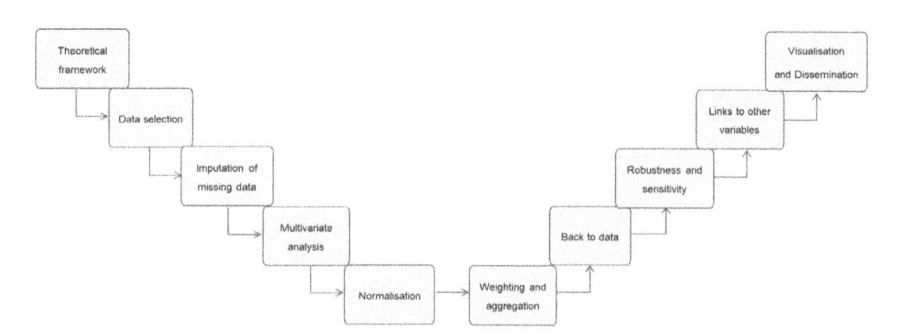

Fig. 5.2. Steps for the Formulation of Composite Indicator (*Source*: Redrawn from OECD Framework).

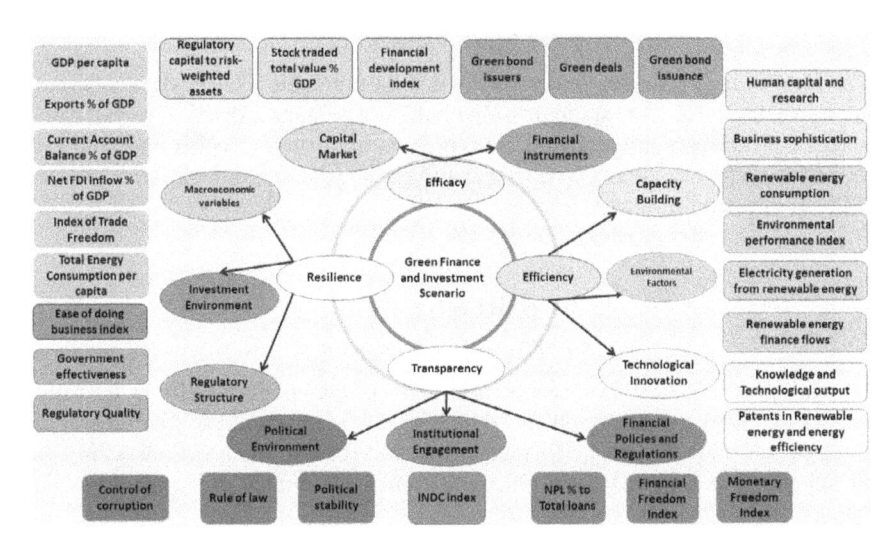

Fig. 5.3. Theoretical Framework of Selected Variables. *Source:* Author's Compilation.

4.1.2. Construction of Composite Indicator

The empirical analysis in this study exploits the potentialities of the PCA method for developing the composite index and calculating combined weights variables in four dimensions. The component score is transformed using the max-min method to make a comparative analysis across countries. The method for transformation is as follows.

$$C_{ij} = \frac{x_{ij} - x_{min}}{x_{max} - x_{min}}$$

C_{ij} is the transformed values of the four dimensions
The component is aggregated using the following formula

$$C_j = \frac{1}{n} \sum_{n=1}^{n=4} w_i \times x_{ij}$$

where $(n = 1, 2, ...n)$ and x_{ij} is a matrix of indicators, showing the ith indicator for country j; w_i is a vector of indicator weights and is given by: $w_i = [w_1, w_2, ..., w_i]$ here weights for the four parameters is 0.25.

The countries are ranked on the basis of individual parameters' factor score and a combined score indicating Global Green Finance and Investment Index. Kaiser-Meyer-Olkin (KMO) and Bartlett test for sphericity is applied to check PCA's appropriateness. The KMO value above 0.5 and the significant *p*-value of the Bartlett test indicate PCA is appropriate for evaluating selected variables. Outliers in data are subjected to the winsorising method in which the 95 percentile values replace the extreme values. This method prevents truncation or trimming of extreme importance.

Reliability is checked by the value of Cronbach's alpha test. The Cronbach's value greater than 0.6 is considered an accepted value. The higher value shows more reliability of the results and appropriate selection of the indicators and data.

4.2. Data Source

The data source for the selected variables is shown in Table 5.1. The data collected are normalised using the standardising method. The standardisation of variables makes the variables unit less, thus making them uniform for further analysis.

The cross-sectional data is collected, and the latest data available from 2005 to 2020 is collected for all the variables.

5. RESULTS

5.1. Theoretical Framework

Horváth and Vaško (2012) measured the impact of the financial sector by the ratio of stock market capitalisation to GDP. The financial instability was measured through the share of non-performing loans and the IMF financial stress index. Przychodzen and Przychodzen (2020) examined the impact of macroeconomic

Table 5.1. Data Source of 30 Variables.

Indicator	Source
1. Regulatory quality	World Bank database, World Governance
2. Control of corruption	Indicators
3. Political stability	
4. Government effectiveness	
5. Rule of Law	
6. Index of Finance freedom	World bank database, World Economic
7. Index of Monetary freedom	Freedom Index
8. Index of Trade freedom	
9. No. of green deals	Climate Bonds Initiative
10. No. of green bond issuers	
11. Green bond issuance by value	
12. Human capital and research	World Intellectual Property Organization
13. Business sophistication	(WIPO), Global Innovation Index
14. Knowledge and technological output	
15. GDP per capita	World Bank database
16. Export % of GDP	
17. Current account balance% of GDP	
18. Net Foreign Direct Investment (FDI) inflow % of GDP	
19. Stock traded % of GDP	
20. Ease of doing business index	
21. Share of bank non-performing loans to total loans	
22. Total energy consumption per capita	
23. Share of renewables in electricity generation	International Renewable Energy Agency
24. Environmental Performance Index	(Wendling et al., 2020)
25. No. of patents in renewable energy and energy efficiency	International Renewable Energy Agency
26. INDC Index	(Tolliver et al., 2020)
27. Financial Development Index	IMF Database
28. Regulatory capital to risk-weighted assets	IMF database
29. Public Renewable energy financial flow	IRENA
30. Renewable energy consumption	BP Statistical Review of World Energy 2021

Source: Author's Compilation.

and institutional variables on the renewable energy production of 27 countries from 1990 to 2014. Macroeconomic variables included in the study are GDP growth, unemployment rate, inflation rate, domestic credit supply, government debt, foreign direct investment, current account balance, GHG emissions, R&D capabilities (R&D expenditure) and integration of countries with the European Union and implementation of Kyoto protocol. According to the study, financial capital is crucial for developing renewable energy projects. A sound financial capital scenario of a country eases access to capital for green projects. The study concluded that government financing and competition policy could play a fundamental role in transitioning towards a low-carbon economy and increasing renewable energy production.

Dutta et al. (2020) empirically explored the relationship between green investment and oil price shocks. The study applied the Markov regime-switching (MRS) model to study the movement in green stock indices with movement in oil prices. The study reveals that oil volatility negatively impacts the stock prices of eco-friendly and green companies. Investment in environmental stock can be risky; thus, proper risk assessment of the stock and assets is crucial for portfolio management. Campiglio et al. (2018) discuss the financial risks arising due to climate change. The perspective article highlights the potential research and policy development areas that the financial institutions and central banks can undertake to address climate-related risks. The research-related interventions include the assessment of climate-related financial risks and macroeconomic modelling of the low-carbon transition. Creel et al. (2015) analysed the link between economic performance and financial stability of 27 countries in the EU from the time period 1960 to 2011. The study measured economic performance with real GDP per capita growth rate, real disposable income per capita growth rate and household consumption per capita growth rate. The private financial investment growth is measured by the growth rate of gross fixed capital formation. Other explanatory variables included are average years of education, government consumption over GDP, trade openness and inflation.

Financial depth was measured through total credit to the private sector by the financial institutions and commercial banks and stock market turnover ratio. Susan et al. (2021) measured profitability of the enterprise through internal and external factors. Internal factors included firm size and debt to equity ratio. The external factor comprised of exchange rate and interest rate. The microeconomic dimension of financial stability is measured through the ratio of non-performing loans to gross loans, banking Z score and stock market volatility. The study developed financial stability index using PCA. The variables included in forming the index were the ratio of capital to total assets, net interest margin, returns on assets, and bank non-performing loans to gross loans, returns on equity and liquid assets and stock market capitalisation growth rate. Tolliver et al. (2020) empirically identified the drivers for the growth of the green bond market. The quantitative analysis of variables included INDC (Intended Nationally Determined Contribution) index, macroeconomic factors, institutional factors and other exogenous factors. Macroeconomic factors measured the size of the economy in terms of GDP, trade openness of the country in terms of total exports as %

of GDP, and growth of the capital market in terms of the total value of stock traded as a percentage of GDP. The institutional factors were measured using the regulatory quality index, the rule of law index and the trade freedom index. The exogenous variable included the INDC index developed in the study. The study concluded that macroeconomic variables substantially impact the issuance of green bonds. Institutional factors and the INDC index positively impact the green bond market and overall green finance. The significant impact of the INDC index reflects the robustness in the adoption of green bonds and transition to a green and low-carbon economy.

In their study, Mohsin et al. (2020) showed that Foreign Direct Investment (FDI) and R&D have a significant role in influencing the financing of green projects. Financing activities promoting energy-efficient technology and developing the renewable energy sector are the most effective pathways for transitioning towards a low-carbon economy. The financial index formulated in the study is the weighted aggregate of R&D, FDI, GDP and financial risk index. The low-carbon index was developed to identify the level of performance of countries. The index reflects the common measure for performance evaluation of the countries in dealing with environmental issues and reducing carbon emissions.

Dafermos et al. (2018) empirically assessed the effect of climate change on the financial stability of a firm and the implication of green quantitative easing on the firm's financial performance. The study highlighted that climate change impacts consumption and production, impacting a company's financial stability. Damages caused due to climate change tends to reduce the consumption and investment demand, reduce the demand for conventional corporate bonds and rise in demand for government securities of risk-aversive investments (due to a rise in investment risks), and reduction in labour-intensive and capital-intensive potential output.

Based on the literature survey, 11 enabling factors were identified. These were categorised into four broad dimensions. To gauge these 11 factors, 30 variables or sub-indicators were identified. Authors' discretion on the basis of discussion with experts, the variables were categorised into four dimensions. Fig. 5.4 shows the theoretical framework that includes the 30 indicators gauging the 11 broad parameters categorised into 4 dimensions.

5.2. Global Green Finance and Investment Index

PCA is applied to the variables categorised into four dimensions: transparency, efficiency, efficacy and resilience. The factor loading of PCA is the weights. The rotated component matrix values are considered as the factor loadings. The factor loading shows the importance of that specific variable in that dimension. The factor loadings are given in Table 5.2. It can be concluded that the rule of law is the most crucial factor in transparency; Environmental Performance Index is in efficiency, green deals in efficacy and GDP per capita in resilience. Similarly, the INDC index, renewable energy finance, regulatory capital to risk-weighted assets and exports as % of GDP contribute least in transparency, efficiency, efficacy and resilience, respectively.

The KMO value represents sampling adequacy. The recommended KMO value in previous literature should be equal to or above 0.6. The study results had

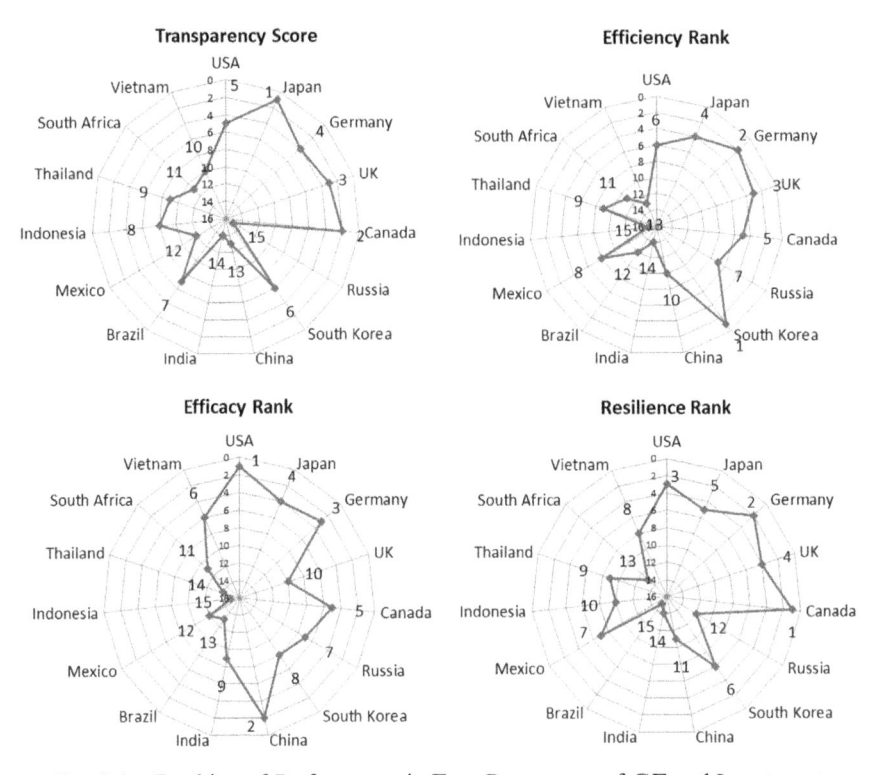

Fig. 5.4. Ranking of Performance in Four Parameters of GF and Investment Scenario of the Selected Countries. *Source:* Authors' Compilation.

Table 5.2. Factor Loadings of Variables.

S.No	Factors	Factor Loadings
	Transparency	
1.	Control of corruption	0.912
2.	Political stability and absence of violence/terrorism	0.879
3.	The rule of law	0.928
4.	INDC index	0.795
5.	Share of bank non-performing loans to total loans	0.802
6.	Index of Financial Freedom	0.823
7.	Index of Monetary Freedom	0.809
	Efficiency	
8.	Human capital and research	0.904
9.	Business sophistication	0.816
10.	Share of renewables in electricity generation	0.173
11.	Environmental performance index	0.943
12.	Renewable energy consumption	0.083
13.	Public Renewable energy financial flow	−0.034
14.	Knowledge and Technological output	0.704
15.	No. of patents in renewable energy and energy efficiency	0.311

(Continued)

Table 5.2.   (*Continued*)

S.No	Factors	Factor Loadings
	Efficacy	
16.	Regulatory capital to risk-weighted assets (2020)	−0.253
17.	Stock traded % of GDP	0.340
18.	Financial development index (2019)	0.458
19.	No. of green bond issuers	0.921
20.	No. of green deals	0.962
21.	Green bond issuance by value	0.896
	Resilience	
22.	GDP per capita	0.928
23.	Export % of GDP	−0.008
24.	Current account balance % of GDP	−0.087
25.	Net FDI inflow % of GDP	−0.107
26.	Index of Trade freedom	0.831
27.	Total energy consumption per capita (2019)	0.724
28.	Ease of doing business index 2019	0.741
29.	Government effectiveness	0.912
30.	Regulatory quality	0.962

Source: Authors' calculation.

a KMO value above 0.6 and the Bartlett's test was significant at 95% significance. Bartlett's test shows the strength of the relationship among variables. The null hypothesis to the difficulty is that the correlation matrix is an identity matrix in which all the diagonal elements are one and all off-diagonal elements are close to zero. The weighted average aggregation method is applied to calculate the composite score of the 15 countries.

The results show that Japan is ranked first in transparency, followed by Canada, the United Kingdom and Germany. In terms of efficacy, the USA has the highest score, followed by China, Germany and Japan. South Korea has the highest score in efficiency, and Canada has the highest score in resilience. The summary of scores of 15 countries is given in Table 5.2. The composite index developed on the basis of these four dimensions is formed by assigning equal weights to all four dimensions. Equal weights are assigned with the assumption that all the dimensions play an equal role in developing the country's green finance and investment environment. The composite score and the ranks of the countries are given in Table 5.3.

The USA has the highest rank, and India has the lowest rank in GF and investment. In terms of developed countries, the USA is the top-ranked country, followed by Germany and Japan. In terms of developing countries, China is ranked first, and Mexico is ranked second. India has the lowest score, which shows that India and Indonesia have the lowest development of GF and enormous potential in developing green finance and investment scenarios.

Fig. 5.4 shows the ranks of 15 countries in the four dimensions of transparency, efficiency, efficacy and resilience. Fig. 5.4 shows that developing countries are ranked lower than developed countries. China is among the top-performing

Table 5.3. Composite Score of Four Dimensions and GGFI Index.

Countries	Transparency Score	Efficiency Score	Efficacy Score	Resilience Score	Composite Score	Rank
USA	0.888	0.719	1.000	0.787	0.212	1
Japan	1.000	0.838	0.472	0.744	0.191	3
Germany	0.943	0.978	0.525	0.866	0.207	2
UK	0.975	0.925	0.117	0.765	0.174	5
Canada	0.992	0.804	0.254	1.000	0.191	4
Russia	0.000	0.485	0.173	0.146	0.050	13
South Korea	0.853	1.000	0.156	0.618	0.164	6
China	0.337	0.237	0.640	0.193	0.088	7
India	0.236	0.035	0.135	0.112	0.032	15
Brazil	0.566	0.220	0.087	0.000	0.055	12
Mexico	0.399	0.317	0.093	0.313	0.070	8
Indonesia	0.521	0.000	0.000	0.230	0.047	14
Thailand	0.463	0.311	0.060	0.243	0.067	9
South Africa	0.460	0.230	0.107	0.138	0.058	11
Vietnam	0.462	0.135	0.186	0.291	0.067	10

Source: Authors' Compilation.

Table 5.4. Reliability (Cronbach's Alpha Values) Values of the Four Dimensions.

S.No	Dimension	Cronbach's Alpha Values
1.	Transparency	0.936
2.	Efficiency	0.863
3.	Efficacy	0.717
4.	Resilience	0.679

Source: Authors' calculation.

countries in all dimensions and the overall GGFI index. The figure also indicates that efficacy is the dimension that reflects extreme fluctuations in developed and developing countries. Russia is a country that has low performance in transparency and resilience.

Table 5.4 shows the Cronbach's alpha values of the dimensions.

6. DISCUSSION

The above analysis shows that the major obstacle to developing green finance and investment in the studied countries is the lack of transparency. The literature strongly supports the results that investment disclosures and reporting can significantly improve transparency and investment decision-making. The accountability of the policies also affects the level of transparency. Dafermos et al. (2018), in their study, highlighted that green quantitative easing gives firms a scope for increasing their profitability and reducing their liquidity problems. The pairing of green quantitative easing with environmental policies can effectively combat climate change damages. The environmental policies include green fiscal policies (such as carbon taxes and green public investment), green finance policies (such as green loans, subsidies and differentiated capital requirements) and regulatory interventions. Inderst et al. (2012) gave importance to the governance structure. The structure includes integration of environmental standards, clarification of fiduciary duties in the related context, increased transparency through appropriate reporting and disclosure guidelines, capacity building and development of its expertise, creation of a database for monitoring performances of investments and removal of regulatory barriers to investment in the form of high-interest rates and low-liquidity of assets.

7. CONCLUSION

The study results show the countries' scores on the basis of PCA. It reveals that among the selected countries, the USA is ranked first with a score of 0.212, followed by Germany with a score of 0.207, respectively. Among the developing countries, China is ranked 7th with a score of 0.088 and Mexico is ranked 8th with a score of 0.070.

The study unveils that developing countries are struggling in the transparency dimension, whereas developed countries have a relatively lower score in the efficacy dimension. To the author's best knowledge, this study is one of its kind in terms of methodology and the variables selected for forming the composite indicator. The study results have important policy implications for policymakers, investors and other stakeholders.

ACKNOWLEDGEMENTS

The authors would like to express gratitude towards the reviewers and the editor's comments. Their reviews have helped in improving the manuscript.

REFERENCES

Andersen, T. M., Bhattacharya, J., & Liu, P. (2020). Resolving intergenerational conflict over the environment under the pareto criterion. *Journal of Environmental Economics and Management, 100*. https://doi.org/10.1016/j.jeem.2019.102290

Berensmann, K., & Lindenberg, N. (2016). Green finance: Actors, challenges and policy recommendations.

Bhatnagar, S., Sharma, D., & Agrawal, S. (2021). *Can Industry 4.0 revolutionize the wave of green finance adoption: A bibliometric analysis* (pp. 515–525). https://doi.org/10.1007/978-981-16-3033-0_49

Bhatnagar, S., & Sharma, D. (2021). Green financing in India: Identifying future scope for innovation in financial system. *International Journal of Green Economics, 15*(3), 185–212. https://doi.org/10.1504/IJGE.2021.120875

Bhatnagar, S., & Sharma, D. (2022). Evolution of green finance and its enablers: A bibliometric analysis. *Renewable and Sustainable Energy Reviews, 162*, 112405. https://doi.org/10.1016/J.RSER.2022.112405

Boudghene Stambouli, A., Khiat, Z., Flazi, S., Tanemoto, H., Nakajima, M., Isoda, H., Yokoyama, F., Hannachi, S., Kurokawa, K., Shimizu, M., Koinuma, H., & Yassaa, N. (2014). Trends and challenges of sustainable energy and water research in North Africa: Sahara solar breeder concerns at the intersection of energy/water. *Renewable and Sustainable Energy Reviews, 30*, 912–922.

Campiglio, E. et al. (2018). Climate change challenges for central banks and financial regulators. *Nature Climate Change, 8*(6), 462–468. https://doi.org/10.1038/s41558-018-0175-0

Creel, J., Hubert, P., & Labondance, F. (2015). Financial stability and economic performance. *Economic Modelling, 48*, 25–40. https://doi.org/10.1016/J.ECONMOD.2014.10.025

Dabla-Norris, E. et al. (2012). Investing in public investment: An index of public investment efficiency. *Journal of Economic Growth, 17*(3), 235–266. https://doi.org/10.1007/s10887-012-9078-5

Dafermos, Y., Nikolaidi, M., & Galanis, G. (2018). Climate change, financial stability and monetary policy. *Ecological Economics, 152*(May), 219–234. https://doi.org/10.1016/j.ecolecon.2018.05.011

Damodaran, A. et al. (2019). *Building a consensus on the definition of green finance*. https://shaktifoundation.in/wp-content/uploads/2019/08/Building-a-Consensus-on-the-Definition-of-Green-Finance-1.pdf

Dikau, S., & Volz, U. (2018). *ADBI Working Paper Series Central Banking, Climate Change and Green Finance* (p. 867). https://www.adb.org/publications/central-banking-climate-change-and-green-

Dutta, A., Jana, R. K., & Das, D. (2020). Do green investments react to oil price shocks? Implications for sustainable development. *Journal of Cleaner Production, 266*, 121956. https://doi.org/10.1016/J.JCLEPRO.2020.121956

Dwijaya Hendratama, T., & Huang, Y.-C. (2021). Corporate social responsibility of family-controlled firms in Taiwan. *Review of Integrative Business and Economics Research, 11*(2), 36–60.

Edmonds, H. K., Lovell, J. E., & Lovell, C. A. K. (2020). A new composite climate change vulnerability index. *Ecological Indicators, 117*(November 2019), 106529. https://doi.org/10.1016/j.ecolind.2020.106529

Falcone, P. M., & Sica, E. (2018). Policy pathways for green finance in biomass production: The case of Italy. *Economics and Policy of Energy and the Environment, 2018*(2), 135–149. https://doi.org/10.3280/EFE2018-002007

Firmialy, S. d., & Nainggolan, Y. A. (2019). Constructing the ideal SRI (sustainability reporting index) framework for Indonesian market: Combined perspectives from rating agencies, academics, and practitioners. *Social Responsibility Journal, 15*(5), 573–596. https://doi.org/10.1108/SRJ-07-2016-0128

G20 Green Finance Study Group. (2016). G20 Green Finance Synthesis Report 2016. *G20 Green Finance Synthesis Report* (August), 1–11. http://g20.org/English/Documents/Current/201608/P020160815359441639994.pdf

Gasser, P., Cinelli, M., Labijak, A., Spada, M., Burgherr, P., Kadziński, M., & Stojadinović, B. (2020). Quantifying electricity supply resilience of countries with robust efficiency analysis. *Energies, 13*(7), 1535.

Green Growth Knowledge Platform. (2013). *Moving towards a common approach on green growth indicators, green growth knowledge platform scoping paper*. https://www.greengrowthknowledge.org/node/4620/

Hafner, S. et al. (2020). Closing the green finance gap – A systems perspective. *Environmental Innovation and Societal Transitions, 34*(November 2019), 26–60. https://doi.org/10.1016/j.eist.2019.11.007

Horváth, R., & Vaško, D. W. (2012). *Central bank transparency and financial stability: Measurement, determinants and effects*. http://ies.fsv.cuni.cz.

Inderst, G., Stewart, F., & Kaminker, C. (2012). *Defining and measuring green investments: Implications for institutional investors' asset allocations* (p. 24). OECD Publishing. https://doi.org/10.1787/5k9312twnn44-en

Jha, R., & Bhanu Murthy, K. V. (2003). A critique of the environmental sustainability index. *papers.ssrn.com*. Retrieved March 10, 2022, from https://papers.ssrn.com/sol3/papers.cfm?abstract_id=380160

Kim, S. E., Kim, H., & Chae, Y. (2014). A new approach to measuring green growth: Application to the OECD and Korea. *Futures, 63*, 37–48. https://doi.org/10.1016/j.futures.2014.08.002.

Kuo, Y.-C., Wu, Y.-M., & Liu, Y.-X. (2021). Identifying key factors for sustainable manufacturing and development. *Review of Integrative Business and Economics Research, 11*, 60.

Maheshwari, A., Avendano, F., & Stein, P. (2016). *Measuring progress on green finance – Findings from a survey*. http://unepinquiry.org/wp-content/uploads/2016/09/5_Outline_Framework_for_Measuring_Progress_on_Green_Finance.pdf

Merino-Saum, A. et al. (2019). Unpacking the Green Economy concept: A quantitative analysis of 140 definitions. *Journal of Cleaner Production, 242*. https://doi.org/10.1016/j.jclepro.2019.118339

Mohsin, M. (2020). Developing low carbon finance index: Evidence from developed and developing economies. *Finance Research Letters, 43*, 101520.

Przychodzen, W., & Przychodzen, J. (2020). Determinants of renewable energy production in transition economies: A panel data approach. *Energy, 191.* https://doi.org/10.1016/j.energy.2019.116583

Reddy, B., & Nathan, H. (2012). *Selection criteria for sustainable development indicators.* Retrieved March 10, 2022, from http://oii.igidr.ac.in:8080/xmlui/handle/2275/117

Renewable Energy | UNEP - UN Environment Programme. (2017). *Towards a green economy pathways to sustainable development and poverty eradication, PART II: Investing in energy and resource efficiency.* Retrieved April 12, 2022, form https://wedocs.unep.org/bitstream/handle/20.500.11822/22010/6.0_renewableenergy.pdf?sequence=1&amp%3BisAllowed=

Robins, N., & Zadek, S. (2016). The financial system we need – From momentum to transformation. *The Financial System We Need,* (October), 1–87. https://doi.org/10.18356/f6dfe210-en

Samuwai, J., & Hills, J. M. (2018). Assessing climate finance readiness in the Asia-Pacific region. *Sustainability (Switzerland), 10*(4). https://doi.org/10.3390/su10041192

Schomaker, M. (1997). Development of environmental indicators in UNEP. *FAO Land and Bulletin (FAO).* Retrieved June 1, 2022, from https://agris.fao.org/agris-search/search.do?recordID=XF1998077665

Serres, A. De, Murtin, F., & Nicoletti, G. (2010). *A framework for assessing green growth policies* (p. 774). https://www.oecd-ilibrary.org/docserver/5kmfj2xvcmkf-en.pdf?expires=1600810515&id=id&accname=guest&checksum=A3F6A4D6539CCC67EC1130D061661DBA

Sifa, E. N. et al. (2021). Islamic financing to improve farmers' welfare and food sustainability: A literature review. *Review of Integrative Business and Economics Research, 11*, 234.

Stern, N. (2007). The economics of climate change: The stern review. *The Economics of Climate Change: The Stern Review, 9780521877,* 1–692. https://doi.org/10.1017/CBO9780511817434

Sundaram, J. (2013). A Global Green New Deal for Sustainable Development. *JSTOR.* Retrieved April 12, 2022, from https://www.jstor.org/stable/23528052

Susan, M., Winarto, J., & Gunawan, I. (2021). The determinants of corporate profitability in Indonesia Manufacturing Industry. *Review of Integrative Business and Economics Research, 11*, 184.

Taghizadeh-Hesary, F., & Yoshino, N. (2020). Sustainable solutions for green financing and investment in renewable energy projects. *Energies, 13*(4). https://doi.org/10.3390/en13040788

Tolliver, C., Keeley, A. R., & Managi, S. (2020). Drivers of green bond market growth: The importance of Nationally Determined Contributions to the Paris Agreement and implications for sustainability. *Journal of Cleaner Production, 244.* https://doi.org/10.1016/j.jclepro.2019.118643

Tran, T. T. T. et al. (2020). The factors affecting green investment for sustainable development. *Decision Science Letters, 9*(3), 365–386. https://doi.org/10.5267/j.dsl.2020.4.002

UNEP. (2015). The Financial System We Need: Aligning the Financial System With Sustainable Development Policy Summary. *The UNEP Inquiry Report,* (October), p. 112. www.unep.org/inquiry

United Nations Environment Programme. (2019, March). *Sustainable Finance Progress Report,* p. 26. https://unepinquiry.org/publication/sustainable-finance-progress-report/

Volz, U. (2018). *Fostering green finance for Asian Development Bank Institute* (p. 814). https://www.adb.org/sites/default/files/publication/403926/adbi-wp814.pdf

Wang, M., Li, X., & Wang, S. (2021). Discovering research trends and opportunities of green finance and energy policy: A data-driven scientometric analysis. *Energy Policy, 154*, 112295. https://doi.org/10.1016/J.ENPOL.2021.112295

Wendling, Z. A. et al. (2020). *2020 Environmental Performance Index.* New Haven. epi.yale.edu

Wardhana, D. Y., & Universitas Atma Jaya Yogyakarta. (2021). Environmental awareness, sustainable consumption and green behavior amongst university students. *Review of Integrative Business and Economics Research, 11*, 242.

Zhang, D., Zhang, Z., & Managi, S. (2019). A bibliometric analysis on green finance: Current status, development, and future directions. *Finance Research Letters, 29*(February), 425–430. https://doi.org/10.1016/j.frl.2019.02.003

Zhou, X., Tang, X., & Zhang, R. (2020). Impact of green finance on economic development and environmental quality: A study based on provincial panel data from China. *Environmental Science and Pollution Research, 27*(16), 19915–19932. https://doi.org/10.1007/s11356-020-08383-2

CHAPTER 6

INVESTIGATING FACTORS AFFECTING INVESTOR DECISION TO SELL INDONESIA GOVERNMENT RETAIL BONDS PORTFOLIO

Ahmad Danu Prasetyo[a], Taffy Ukhtia Panduputri[a], Prawira Fajarindra Belgiawan[a], Yunieta Anny Nainggolan[a], Subhan Noor[b], Riky Candra[b], Sri Putri Siregar[b] and Yuddy Hendranata[b]

[a]*School of Business and Management, Institut Teknologi Bandung, Jl Ganesa No. 10, Lb. Siliwangi, Bandung, 40132, Indonesia*
[b]*Directorate General of Budget Financing and Risk Management, Indonesia Ministry of Finance, Indonesia, Jl Dr. Wahidin Raya No.1, Central Jakarta, 10710, Indonesia*

ABSTRACT

Government bonds are debt securities issued by the central government, where investors are to receive returns in the form of an annual coupon rate periodically. This leads investors tend to hold their portfolio after purchasing due to the guaranteed returns of the government bonds. However, another strategy for gaining returns is to sell the eligible portfolios in the secondary market. This research aims to investigate the factors behind investors' decisions whether to sell their government retail bonds portfolio and the length of their portfolio hold days. Towards a secondary dataset of existing government retail bonds

The Finance-Innovation Nexus: Implications for Socio-Economic Development
International Symposia in Economic Theory and Econometrics, Volume 34, 73–89
Copyright © 2025 by Emerald Publishing Limited
All rights of reproduction in any form reserved
ISSN: 1571-0386/doi:10.1108/S1571-038620240000034006

investors in Indonesia and secondary market rate, logistic regression analysis was employed to inspect their selling decisions, while the decision tree classification method investigated their hold days. Results show that both the decision to sell bonds portfolio in the secondary market and the period of hold days are highly affected by its comparative return performance towards other investment alternatives, represented by excess returns. This study contributes to the behavioural finance field by answering the lack of investigation for investors' selling decisions, particularly for government retail bonds, which will enhance the understanding of portfolio rebalancing in portfolio management studies.

Keywords: Decision tree; excess return; logistic regression; government bonds; SBN retail

JEL Codes: E62; G41; H63

1. INTRODUCTION

In Indonesia, government retail bonds are called *Surat Berharga Negara* (SBN), which are issued as an attempt to support the funding of national economic development, especially in lieu of the COVID-19 pandemic (Indonesia's Ministry of Finance, 2022). As the government took mitigation steps to minimise the effect of the virus, economic activity was greatly affected by the lockdown measures. The impact of the spread of this virus was also experienced by the financial market (Paramitha & Faturohman, 2022).

Indonesia Stock Exchange (IDX) stated that there are two types of Indonesian Government Securities, which are Sovereign Debt Instruments and State Sharia Securities. Under the classification by the Directorate General of Budget Financing and Risk Management (DJPPR) of the Ministry of Finance, the division can be classified further into Indonesian Retail Bonds (ORI), Retail Saving Bonds (SBR), Retail Sukuk (SR) and Savings Sukuk (ST).

Generally, research has been abundant in touching on the topic of factors behind investors' decision to invest in government bonds products. Investors will consider negotiating between expected returns and faced risk, where investment is carried out if the perceived risk can be compensated by a large amount of return (Rosdiana, 2020). Other risk-return relation studies are also conducted by Nguyen et al. (2019), Formánková et al. (2019) and Fitria et al. (2019). In government bonds, investors will receive the returns in the form of a fixed annual coupon rate periodically. This leads to the tendency of investors to employ the 'buy-and-hold' strategy, a principle behaviour of most investors whereupon the purchase of an asset, they keep it until the maturity date (Ahroum et al., 2018).

However, some types of investment bonds, in this particular context namely ORI and SR, are eligible for trade in the secondary market and investors may decide to sell their bond portfolio based on their considerations. Profits can be obtained by selling the bonds at a higher price than the purchase price (Hendrocahyo, 2021). Based on the statistics of sold Retail Government Bonds

(SBN Retail), tradable types of bonds make up most of the sales (DJPPR, 2021), where Sukuk Retail securities are sold in total over 54.5 trillion rupiahs and ORI are sold over 65.5 trillion rupiahs, more than the sum of their non-tradable counterparts. This indicates a huge appeal of tradable bonds among investors, yet few have examined the aspect of tradability in the intention of purchasing Government Bonds. Moreover, there has also been scant study on the factors behind investors' decision to sell back their tradable Indonesian Government Bonds (SBN) in the secondary market.

Investors' decision to trade in the secondary market can be traced back to the volatility of a price (Al Aziz et al., 2019). As the main problem of the Indonesian secondary market is the demand for securities (Nasution, 2019), it is imperative to understand the factors behind the transaction of securities in the secondary market. This current research aims to fill the gap in the literature by examining the determinants of investors' choice to trade their Government Bonds (SBN) portfolio on the secondary market. Hartono (2019) compared the potential return from investing in SBN retail and from investing in blue chip stocks (Hartono, 2019). This study contributes to expanding on it by also incorporating comparisons towards mutual funds and gold investment, in addition to using more comprehensive historical data. Moreover, the factors affecting the range of hold days of investment products are also investigated. This expansion will help scholars, portfolio managers, and investors in general to enhance the understanding of portfolio rebalancing in portfolio management studies.

2. GOVERNMENT RETAIL BONDS (SBN RETAIL)

2.1. Government Retail Bonds in Indonesia

SBN Retail or Indonesia Retail Government Bonds is an investment instrument issued by the government and sold to individual Indonesian citizens through regulated selling agents. The issuance in particular realises the government policy to broaden the local investor base to increase demand and market liquidity, to support national development activities. Upon investment in SBN Retail, investors will receive income in the form of coupon rate on a regular basis, or each coupon payment period.

The SBN Retail can further be classified into four types: ORI, SBR, SR, and ST (DJPPR Website). Principally, ORI and SBR are conventional type investments, while SR and ST are Sukuks, which are instruments based on the sharia principle. Structurally, ORI and SR are SBN Retail in the form of bonds, different from SBR and ST which are forms of savings (Hendrocahyo, 2021). Table 6.1 shows the overlapping characteristics of the four SBN retail types.

Coupon rates are the interest rates paid by bond issuers as a percentage of the face value. Based on information in the Ministry of Finance website page, ORI and SR have a fixed rate coupon, while Retail Saving Bonds (SBR) and ST offer a 'floating with floor' coupon rate with minimum limit of 5.1% and 4.8%, respectively (DJPPR). SBN Retail are issued in series for every issuing date, with possibly differing coupon rates for each series of the same bond type. For example, SR

Table 6.1. Characteristics of SBN Retail Investment Types.

	Bond-Type (ORI, SR)	Savings-Type (SBR, ST)
Coupon	Fixed	Floating with floor
Tenor	± 3 years	± 2 years
Tradable	Yes	No

series SR014 issued in February 2021 offered a fixed coupon rate of 5.47% while series SR013 issued in August 2020 offered 6.05%.

Sukuks are issued in accordance with Islamic principles, thus having sharia attributes, while SBR and ORI are classified as conventional investment types. Hamzah (2008) stated sharia investment is a type of investment directed to have halal and good returns and is sustainable. Different from debt-based conventional instruments, sukuks are certificate of rights towards a tangible asset or project on a large scale. Sukuk transactions are based on underlying assets (Fitriyah & Ryandono, 2019), serve as funding for infrastructure development or economic sectors with intense labour (Al Aziz et al., 2019). Investment towards sukuks is gaining tractions as demands from investors in Indonesia, where the majority of the population are Muslims. In the last seven years alone, domestic sharia bond issuance has exhibited a significant increase from 6 issuance with a total of 740 billion rupiahs to 47 issuance with a total of 7.715 trillion rupiahs (Azis et al., 2021).

Investing in SBN Retail is technically free from default risk, or the condition where the issuer is unable to pay the coupon and principal. In this case, it is guaranteed by the Law on Government Securities (SUN) and funds are provided in the state budget (APBN) annually. There is still market risk involved, should the investors decide to conduct their transaction in the secondary market, with capital loss possibility due to a lower selling price than the buying price (BI.go.id). Among the SBN Retail products, ORI and SR are the two types eligible for trade on the secondary market, meaning investors of these SBN Retail products can choose to resell them for capital gain.

Selling agents, also commonly referred to as Distribution Partners, are officially appointed entities responsible for assisting in marketing, offering and/or selling SBN Retail to retail investors (Yenny & Umanto, 2023). There are 24 banks currently registered as SBN retail selling agents, with 5 fintech companies and seven securities companies. Financial technology is an emerging field that includes payment-related innovations and technologies to promote personal and corporate payments and online alternative lending (Wu et al., 2021, 2022). Investree, Modalku, and CoinWorks are three Indonesian fintech businesses in charge of delivering SBN retail products.

2.2. Other Investment Alternatives in Indonesia

SBN Retail is one among many investment alternatives available for individual investors in Indonesia. Outside the government-issued bond instrument, investors may choose to invest in other alternatives such as deposits, mutual funds, gold, or stocks, based on how they estimate the risks and benefits of each instrument.

2.3. Excess Return and Bond Yield

A bond's yield can be considered the expected earnings gained from fixed-income investment over a particular period of time, expressed as a percentage or interest rate. Yield calculations are apparent in the secondary market, and fluctuate based on market conditions. In this case, it is also called current yield, where it represents the bond's future earning power, estimated by dividing the bond's total income by its market price.

Investors' decision to resell their **SBN** portfolio is related to the expectation of gained return from the secondary market transaction. In this case, the **SBN** Retail portfolio's return performance expressed in yield is compared to the return gained from other investment alternatives: gold, deposits, stocks, equity funds, fixed-income funds and discretionary funds. This comparison is expressed as an excess return.

3. METHOD

This study utilises the quantitative method of big data analysis towards secondary data of investor transactions, obtained from the DJPPR of the Ministry of Finance database, and supporting external data from the secondary market.

3.1. Secondary Dataset

The secondary data in observation is an assemblage of a dataset consisting of: (1) data of SBN Retail investors registered in the internal database of DJPPR; (2) data of stock returns (year-on-year) from the IHSG index database (Yahoo! Finance); (3) data of time deposits, fixed-income mutual funds, equity funds, and discretionary funds return (year-on-year) data obtained from Indonesian Economic and Financial Statistics Bank Indonesia (BI.go.id); (4) data of the year-on-year return of gold asset; and (5) yield data of each SBN products of corresponding time period from internal DJPPR database.

The five datasets are compiled into one large database, where the merging adapts according to transaction date and type of SBN series. The time range of observed data is from November 2019 to August 2021, with only tradable SBN series to be analysed, namely ORI from ORI016 to ORI019, and SR from SR012 to SR014 (see Table 6.2).

Considering the objective of the study and the characteristics of the collected dataset, secondary data analysis is carried out using a classification approach. In machine learning, classification analysis is a form of supervised learning intended to group data into a target attribute or dependent variable as accurately as possible. Classification modelling is generally predictive, where models are constructed through constant learning based on a number of training datasets, and the model is intended to predict the membership of an observation in a testing dataset according to the target attribute.

In this study, the objective of predicting SBN investors' range of hold days is accomplished using the decision tree classification method using **IBM SPSS** software, while the prediction of the probability of whether investors will sell their owned SBN portfolio or not is done using logistic regression.

Table 6.2.   Constituent Variables of the Dataset.

Variables	Description	Variable Type
ID_GUID	Unique code identification for each investor	Categorical
Order date	Transaction date for SBN product purchase by an investor	Timestamp
Buy juta	SBN product purchase amount	Continuous
Series name	Series of the SBN product in transaction	Categorical
Sell date	Transaction date for SBN product sold by the investor	Timestamp
MIDIS	Selling agent for the SBN product purchased	Categorical
CHANNEL	Transaction channel for the SBN product	Categorical
Wait days	Range (in days) between the availability date of the SBN product to the purchase date by the investor	Continuous
Coupon	The coupon amount for the corresponding SBN product	Continuous
Syariah	Sharia type of related SBN product (sharia or conventional)	Categorical
Tenor	Range of days between the settlement date and maturity date	Continuous
Sell_YN	Binary variable stating whether investor sells their SBN product or not	Categorical
Hold	Range of days investor holds their SBN product before selling	Continuous
Excess return **deposito**	The excess return of deposits; the difference between deposits return (yoy) and yield of corresponding SBN product	Continuous
Excess return **saham**	Excess return from stocks; the difference between stock return (yoy) and yield of the corresponding SBN product	Continuous
Excess return **reksadana saham**	Excess return from equity funds; the difference between equity funds return (yoy) and yield of the corresponding SBN product	Continuous
Excess return **reksadana pendapatan tetap**	Excess return from fixed-income funds; the difference between fixed-income funds return (yoy) and yield of the corresponding SBN product	Continuous
Excess return **reksadana campuran**	Excess return from discretionary funds; the difference between discretionary funds return (yoy) and yield of the corresponding SBN product	Continuous
Excess return **emas**	Excess return from gold investment; the difference between gold return (yoy) and yield of the corresponding SBN product	Continuous
Inflasi	Inflation rate on the corresponding date	Continuous

3.2. Logistic Regression

Binary logistic regression is a statistical method almost similar to a linear regression regarding its objective to predict a dependent variable based on existing independent variables (Hair et al., 2010). Logistic regression analysis is applied to the secondary dataset to determine the probability of investor reselling their owned SBN Retail portfolio or not. Thus, in this case, the dependent variable is a binary variable of sell (Y) or not sell (N), while the independent variables are the excess return of other investment alternatives, the categorical variable of selling agents (bank, fintech companies, or securities company), the continuous variable of purchased SBN products amount (in millions of rupiahs), wait days, tenor and the length of hold days.

3.3. Decision Tree

As a classification method, decision trees have several advantages: they are easy to interpret and visualize, can handle categorical, continuous, and missing data, are non-parametric (Alpaydin, 2020), robust to noise, and computationally efficient for large datasets. The algorithm used for the decision tree in this case is the CRT algorithm. For this algorithm, maximising object homogeneity under the same node is the main purpose (IBM SPSS, 2012), by basing the splitting criterion calculation on Gini Index and using the *postpruning* technique. Splitting criterion is a calculation criterion to determine which variable is used to test the observed, and then do the classification based on the calculation. The Gini Index criterion consistently splits internal nodes into two branches, whether the variable type is continuous or categorical. Seeing the number of independent variables observed, the *postpruning* method may result in a more accurate model by considering the interaction effect of existing variables and preventing overfitting.

Decision tree modelling is carried out towards the secondary dataset to determine the hold days range, which states for how long investors would hold their SBN Retail products before reselling to the secondary market if they chose to do so. The targeted attribute of this classification is named **hold range**, a range of days divided into seven classes: less than 100 days, between 100 and 200 days, 200 and 300 days, 300 and 400 days, 400 and 500 days, 500 and 600 days, and above 600 days. Meanwhile, the independent variables are the excess return of other investment alternatives (deposits, stocks, equity funds, fixed-income funds, discretionary funds, gold), purchase amount, selling agents, purchase channel, wait days, sharia type, and binary variable of their decision to sell or not.

4. RESULTS AND DISCUSSION

4.1. Classification of Investors' Decision to Sell (Logistic Regression)

Binary logistic regression analysis is done using IBM SPSS software, resulting in the output of the model summary table as attached below (Table 6.3).

The above model summary table shows the variance of independent variables, or how much the observed independent variables can explain or affect the targeted dependent variable. Referring to the Nagelkerke R^2 or pseudo R2 of the model, it is obtained that the resulting logistic regression model shows that the independent variables such as excess returns, purchase amount, wait days, tenor and hold days, and selling agents can explain 99.2% of the dependent variable of investors' decision to resell or not. Furthermore, the Hosmer–Lemeshow test result illustrates that the significance value of the logit model is 0.619, indicating that the fit of the produced logistic regression model is fairly good.

In this case, binary logistic regression estimates the probability of investor reselling their SBN portfolio to the secondary market. If the probability of the estimated dependent variable has a value above 0.5, it will be categorised into the 'sell' class, otherwise, it is included in the 'not sell' classification. The classification table above displays a comparison between the classification predicted by the logit model and the actual observed cases (Table 6.4).

The resulting logit model shows a very high percentage of correct prediction towards investors' decision to resell their SBN portfolio. The model predicts with 100% accuracy of all the investors who decide not to sell their portfolio (N), where the prediction is compared to observation. On the other hand, 99.6% accuracy is shown for the model predicting investors who decide to sell their portfolio (Y). Moreover, there are 312 cases of false negatives, where investors are predicted to

Table 6.3.   Model Summary for Logistic Regression.

Model Summary			
Step	−2 Log likelihood	Cox & Snell R^2	Nagelkerke R^2
1	4531.049	0.673	0.992
Hosmer–Lemeshow Test			
Step	Chi-square	df	Sig.
1	5.334	7	0.619

Table 6.4.   Classification Table of Logistic Regression.

Observed		Predicted		
		SELL_YN		Percentage Correct
		N	Y	
SELL_YN	N	215138	0	100.0
	Y	312	72907	99.6
Overall Percentage				99.9

not sell their portfolios, when actually it is observed that they did. Overall, the accuracy of this model's prediction based on the available data is 99.9%.

Table 6.5 shows the statistics of each variable included in the logistic regression model. Wald test illustrates the statistical significance of each independent variable, whose value is listed in the Sig. column. All independent variables show the value $p < 0.05$, indicating significance towards the model's dependent variable, which in this case is the decision to resell the SBN portfolio.

The column labelled B in the table indicates the coefficient for independent variables in the logistic regression equation expressing probability of investor decision to resell their SBN portfolio. The significance of each independent variable is shown by the value of Exp(B) or generally called odds ratio. An odd ratio higher than 1 indicates a positive correlation with the observed dependent variable. However, the interpretation of the odds ratio for continuous and categorical variables are different. For categorical variables, a positive relation by odds ratio means the inclusion of the case in that category increases the probability of the target variable. In a continuous variable, the same correlation applies, only the value is affecting unit value of the corresponding variable (Table 6.5).

In this case, the categorical variable bank selling agent has an odd ratio of 11.29, while the fintech selling agent is 12.49. This implies that investor transaction through banks holds a 11.29 higher possibility of reselling in comparison of transactions through securities companies (as a reference point). Meanwhile, transaction through a fintech company holds 12.49 times more probability of reselling than transactions through a securities company. It is also observed that three particular continuous variables, which are stock excess return, fixed-income funds excess return, and gold investment excess return, have an exceedingly high value of odds ratio, indicating their significant effect towards the classification of investors' reselling decision. In summary, based on the obtained logistic regression model, small increments in the value of stock excess return or fixed-income

Table 6.5.　Variables in the Logistic Regression Equation.

	B	S.E.	Wald	df	Sig.	Exp(B)	95% C.I.for EXP(B)	
							Lower	Upper
ExcessReturn_Deposito	−15.350	5.676	7.313	1	0.007	0.000	0.000	0.015
ExcessReturn_Saham	141.041	20.920	45.455	1	0.000	1.792E+61	2.796E+43	1.149E+79
ExcessReturn_RD_Saham	−126.966	24.059	27.850	1	0.000	0.000	0.000	0.000
ExcessReturn_RD_PendapatanTetap	41.405	7.196	33.108	1	0.000	9.590E+17	7.189E+11	1.279E+24
ExcessReturn_RD_Campuran	−49.183	24.951	3.885	1	0.049	0.000	0.000	0.756
ExcessReturn_Emas	10.540	1.766	35.602	1	0.000	37785.271	1185.124	1204706.484
MIDIS_Sekuritas (ref.)			13.793	2	0.001			
MIDIS_Bank	2.424	0.655	13.695	1	0.000	11.291	3.127	40.762
MIDIS_Fintech	2.525	0.769	10.784	1	0.001	12.491	2.768	56.374
SYARIAH	−0.885	0.173	26.089	1	0.000	0.413	0.294	0.579
BUY_JUTA	0.000	0.000	19.404	1	0.000	1.000	1.000	1.000
WAIT_DAYS	0.022	0.009	6.668	1	0.010	1.022	1.005	1.040
TENOR	−0.041	0.018	5.317	1	0.021	0.960	0.927	0.994
HOLD	−0.007	0.001	23.234	1	0.000	0.993	0.990	0.996
Constant	−681.588	126.967	28.818	1	0.000	0.000		

funds excess return or gold excess return will significantly increase the probability of investors to resell their SBN portfolio.

In contrast, excess return for deposits, equity funds, discretionary funds, alongside sharia type, tenor and hold days have a negative correlation with the prediction of reselling the SBN portfolio. The high value of the excess return for deposits, equity funds, or discretionary funds indicates a decrease in the probability that investors resell their SBN portfolio. Negative correlations are also displayed by sharia variable, tenor and hold days. If the SBN portfolio has sharia type, a longer period of tenor and longer days of holding the portfolio, the probability of reselling is lower. Meanwhile, purchase amount has an odds ratio of 1, indicating that this variable has no effect on the probability of investor reselling or not reselling their portfolio.

This result indicated that investors of sharia-type SBN retail products with longer periods of tenor have the tendency to implement a buy-and-hold strategy instead of reselling. This finding supported Alqahtani's (2017) study where *sukuk* with short or medium maturity periods is traded more on the secondary market (Al Aziz et al., 2019).

4.2. Classification of Investors Hold Days (Decision Tree)

In order to determine the classification of days investors spend in holding their SBN retail portfolio, the decision tree method was utilised. Decision tree analysis using **IBM SPSS** software produced an output of a model summary table as attached below, including the parameters employed (see Table 6.6).

Table 6.6. Model Summary Output of SPSS Decision Tree.

Specifications	Growing Method	CRT
	Dependent Variable	HOLD_RANGE
	Independent Variables	ExcessReturn_Deposito, ExcessReturn_Saham, ExcessReturn_ReksadanaSaham, ExcessReturn_ReksadanaPendapatanTetap, ExcessReturn_ReksadanaCampuran, ExcessReturn_Emas, BUY_JUTA, MIDIS, CHANNEL, WAIT_DAYS, SYARIAH, SELL_YN
	Validation	Cross Validation
	Maximum Tree Depth	5
	Minimum Cases in Parent Node	100
	Minimum Cases in Child Node	50
Results	Independent Variables Included	ExcessReturn_Emas, ExcessReturn_ReksadanaPendapatanTetap, ExcessReturn_Deposito, ExcessReturn_ReksadanaCampuran, ExcessReturn_ReksadanaSaham, ExcessReturn_Saham, SYARIAH, WAIT_DAYS, BUY_JUTA, CHANNEL, MIDIS, SELL_YN
	Number of Nodes	39
	Number of Terminal Nodes	20
	Depth	5

Classification of hold range attributes based on the 12 independent variables using the CRT algorithm produced a decision tree of a total of 39 nodes, with 20 terminal nodes and a tree depth of 5 layers. The terminal node or leaf node represents the outermost part of the tree, which determines the object's classification. In this case, each terminal node shows how the observed cases are included in one of the predetermined seven hold range classifications (see Figs. 6.1 and 6.2).

Decision tree formation begins at the root node of the dependent variable (hold range), which shows that from the 288,357 total transactions, it is predicted that as many as 33% of investors hold their SBN portfolio for less than 100 days, 18.4% hold their portfolios between 100 and 200 days, 22% of total hold portfolios between 200 and 300 days, 13.7% investors hold between 300 and 400 days, while 6.5% hold the portfolios between 400 and 500 days, 0.1% hold for 500 to 600 days, and 6.3% hold for more than 600 days. This root node is split into two branches based on the value of the gold excess return variable, namely branch for an excess return of gold ≤ -11.585 and branch for an excess return of gold > -11.585, which in turn results in other nodes branching out to produce final classification represented in 20 terminal nodes in the diagram.

The final classification is based on the combination of independent variables of nodes passed over the object cases in the branching from the root node until the terminal node. Classification detail of the range of the days investor hold their portfolio based on the optimum independent variables' combination can be seen in Table 6.7.

Referring to the table above, it is predicted that in the case of a gold excess return with a value less than -11.585, combined with the value of deposits excess return less than 0.0805 and the corresponding SBN portfolio is of sharia type, then the investor will hold the portfolio for less than 100 days before reselling it to the secondary market. On the other hand, for a similar combination of excess return value, if the SBN portfolio is of conventional type (non-sharia), the model predicts investors to hold the portfolio between 100 and 200 days. Prediction of the range of days for portfolio holding for SBN investors can be done by looking at the combination of independent variables in the resulting table, especially by looking at the value of excess return from other investment types and sharia type of the SBN portfolio of the holder.

The next output is regarding the classification of the target attribute. Referring to Table 6.8, the decision tree model produced a rather high accuracy on average, as much as 90.9%. This model succeeds in predicting correctly 91.9% of investors with 100 to 200 hold days, 96.3% of investors with hold days between 200 and 300 days, 98.5% of investors with hold days between 300 and 400 days, 97.9% of investors with hold days between 400 and 500 days, and 99.6% investors with hold days less than 100 days. However, the model fails to correctly predict any of the investors who hold their portfolio between 500 and 600 days, and is only able to predict a fraction of investors with hold days of over 600 days (0.3%).

Aside from the output of the overall decision tree model evaluation, the model also illustrates the significance of each independent variable towards the resulting tree model through an output of independent variable importance. The independent variable importance table estimates how much the model's prediction value might

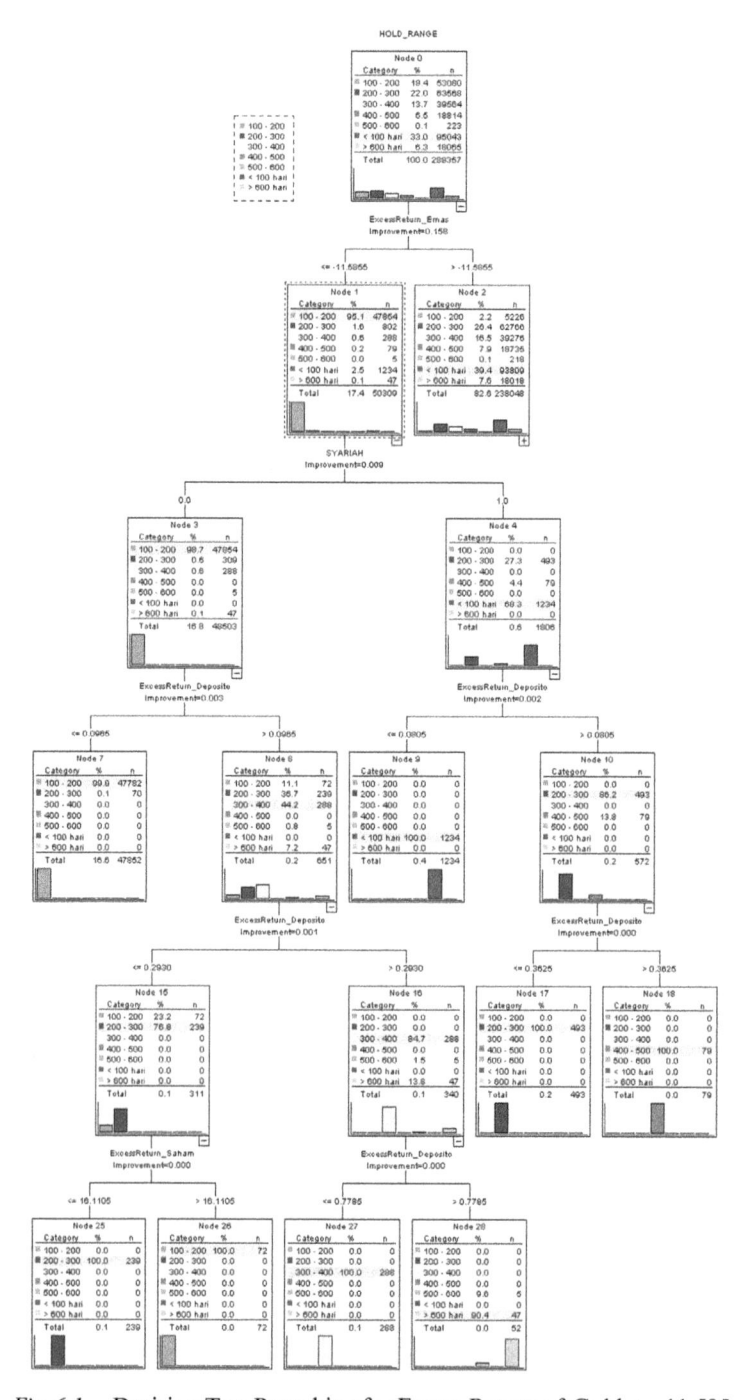

Fig. 6.1. Decision Tree Branching for Excess Return of Gold ≤ −11.585.

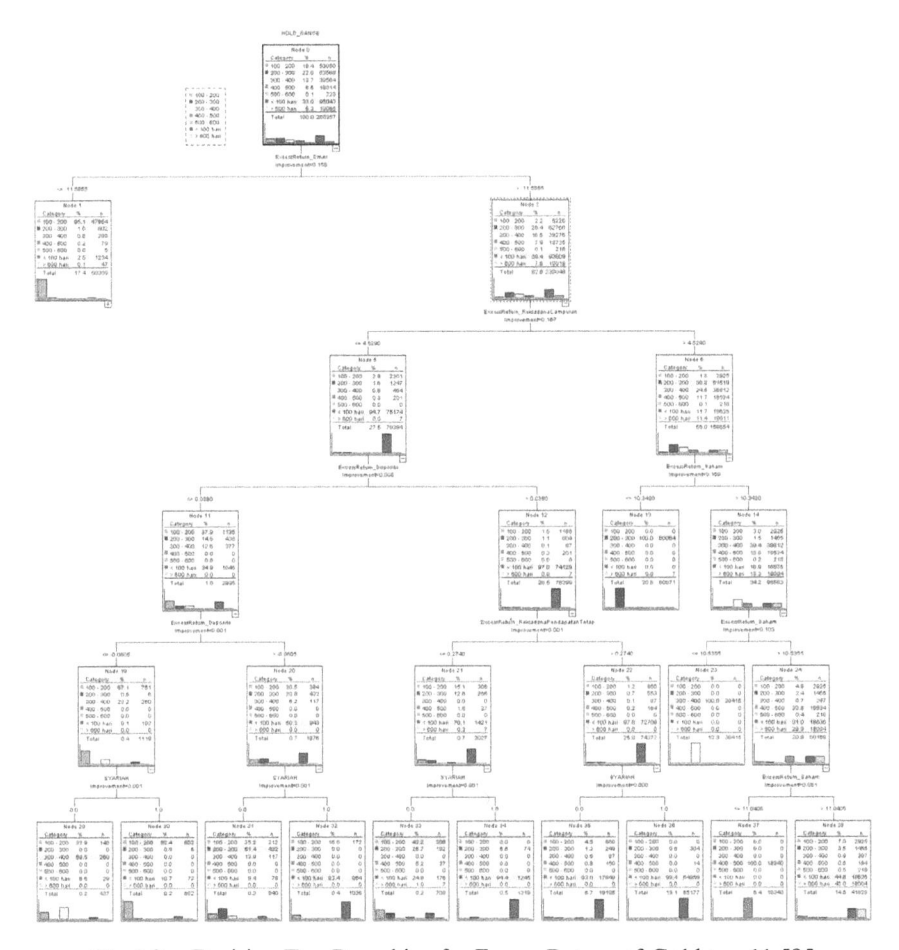

Fig. 6.2. Decision Tree Branching for Excess Return of Gold > -11.585.

change should each of the independent variable change (Alabi et al., 2013). Based on the importance value in Table 6.9, the model will undergo the most significant change when the value of stock excess return and discretionary funds excess return are changed. The value of normalised importance is calculated as the difference between the importance value and the highest independent variable importance value.

Based on the output above, it can be concluded that the factor most affecting how long investors may hold their SBN portfolio is the excess return of stocks and discretionary funds with a normalised importance percentage of 100%. This effect is followed by other high-significance factors: the excess return of equity funds (99.6%), the excess return of gold investment (93.8%), the excess return of fixed-income funds (86.9%), and the excess return of deposits (76.4%). Under the 50% significance are the binary variable of selling decision (37.5%), sharia type of the portfolio (27%), wait days (5%), purchase amount (0.9%) and selling agents and transaction channel (0.3% each).

Table 6.7. Classification of Hold Days' Range Based on Independent Variables Path.

Classification	Independent Variable Combinations
< 100 days	Emas ≤ −11,585; Syariah; Deposito ≤ 0,0805
	Emas > −11,585; Reksadana Campuran ≤ 4,529; −0,0605 < Deposito ≤ 0,038; Syariah
	Emas > −11,585; Reksadana Campuran ≤ 4,529; Deposito > 0,038; Reksadana Pendapatan Tetap ≤ −0,274; Syariah
	Emas > −11,585; Reksadana Campuran ≤ 4,529; Deposito > 0,038; Reksadana Pendapatan Tetap > −0,274; Non-Syariah
	Emas > −11,585; Reksadana Campuran ≤ 4,529; Deposito > 0,038; Reksadana Pendapatan Tetap > −0,274; Syariah
	Emas > −11,585; Reksadana Campuran > 4,529; Saham > 11,0405
100–200 days	Emas ≤ −11,585; Non-syariah; Deposito ≤ 0,0965
	Emas ≤ −11,585; Non-syariah; 0,0965 < Deposito ≤ 0,293; Saham > 16,11
	Emas > −11,585; Reksadana Campuran ≤ 4,529; Deposito ≤ −0,0605; Syariah
	Emas > −11,585; Reksadana Campuran ≤ 4,529; Deposito > 0,038; Reksadana Pendapatan Tetap ≤ −0,274; Non-syariah
200–300 days	Emas ≤ −11,585; Non-syariah; 0,0965 < Deposito ≤ 0,293; Saham ≤ 16,11
	Emas ≤ −11,585; Syariah; 0,0805 < Deposito ≤ 0,3625
	Emas > −11,585; Reksadana Campuran ≤ 4,529; −0,0605 < Deposito ≤ 0,038; Non-syariah
	Emas > −11,585; Reksadana Campuran > 4,529; Saham ≤ 10,342
300–400 days	Emas ≤ −11,585; Non-syariah; 0,293 < Deposito ≤ 0,778
	Emas > −11,585; Reksadana Campuran ≤ 4,529; Deposito ≤ −0,0605; Non-syariah
	Emas > −11,585; Reksadana Campuran > 4,529; 10,342 < Saham ≤ 10,535
400–500 days	Emas ≤ −11,585; Syariah; Deposito > 0,3625
	Emas > −11,585; Reksadana Campuran > 4,529; 10,535 < Saham ≤ 11,0405
500–600 days	-
>600 days	Emas ≤ −11,585; Non-syariah; Deposito > 0,778

Note: Metrics for gold, stocks, deposits, and mutual funds are represented by excess return value.

Table 6.8. Classification Matrix for Decision Tree Result.

Observed	Predicted							
	100–200	200–300	300–400	400–500	500–600	< 100 days	> 600 days	Percent Correct
100– 200	48763	212	148	0	0	3957	0	91.9%
200– 300	258	61228	0	0	0	2082	0	96.3%
300– 400	0	117	38963	0	0	484	0	98.5%
400– 500	37	0	0	18419	0	358	0	97.9%
500– 600	0	0	0	0	0	218	5	0.0%
< 100 days	249	79	29	0	0	94686	0	99.6%
> 600 days	7	7	0	0	0	18004	47	0.3%
Overall Percentage	17.1%	21.4%	13.6%	6.4%	0.0%	41.5%	0.0%	90.9%

Notes: Growing Method: CRT.
Dependent Variable: HOLD_RANGE.

Table 6.9. Independent Variables Importance.

Independent Variable	Importance	Normalised Importance
ExcessReturn_Saham	0.589	100.0%
ExcessReturn_ReksadanaCampuran	0.588	100.0%
ExcessReturn_ReksadanaSaham	0.586	99.6%
ExcessReturn_Emas	0.552	93.8%
ExcessReturn_ReksadanaPendapatanTetap	0.512	86.9%
ExcessReturn_Deposito	0.449	76.4%
SELL_YN	0.221	37.5%
SYARIAH	0.159	27.0%
WAIT_DAYS	0.030	5.0%
BUY_JUTA	0.005	0.9%
MIDIS	0.002	0.3%
CHANNEL	0.002	0.3%

Notes: Growing Method: CRT.
Dependent Variable: HOLD_RANGE.

5. CONCLUSION

This research aims to investigate the factors affecting Indonesian individual investors in the decision to resell their retail government bonds to the secondary market. Through a statistical analysis of logistic regression and decision tree method towards an existing investor database, it is found that reselling behaviour is related to the expected return from a capital gain in the secondary market. In this case, the return performance of the government retail bonds yield is compared to the expected return of other types of investment, mainly: gold, deposit, equity funds, discretionary funds, fixed-income funds and stocks, where the comparison is expressed in excess return.

Specifically, the logistic regression analysis to determine factors behind the probability of investor reselling behaviour results in a high-accuracy model where the most significant determinants are the excess return of stocks, fixed-income funds, and excess return of gold, next to a categorical variable of transaction through fintech and bank selling agents. Meanwhile, the decision tree analysis to classify the time length of hold days using the CRT algorithm shows an overall prediction accuracy of 90.9%. Based on the decision tree model established, it is found that the length of time investors spend before reselling their SBN portfolios is mostly influenced by the excess return value of stocks, discretionary funds, equity funds, gold, fixed-income funds, deposits, and whether the product is sharia or not.

Policy-wise, since this study revealed a relationship between SBN retail and other types of investment, the findings can be used by the government or selling agents to highlight the prospect of investors reselling their SBN retail products to potential and existing investors on the secondary market. The increased trading volume of SBN retail products on the market can help the price of the SBN product itself and enhance economic development in general.

ACKNOWLEDGEMENTS

The authors acknowledge financial support from the School of Business and Management, Institut Teknologi Bandung through Penelitian, Pengabdian Masyarakat dan Inovasi (PPMI) research program 2022. The authors also thank to all the parties who have participated in data collection and Indonesia's Ministry of Finance for supported the data. This paper was *presented at: the SIBR 2022 (Osaka) Conference on Interdisciplinary Business and Economics Research, 30*[th] *June – 1*[st] *July 2022, Osaka, Japan.*

REFERENCES

Ahroum, R., Touri, O., Sabiq, F. Z., & Achchab, B. et al. (2018). Investment strategies with rebalancing: How could they serve Sukuk secondary market?. *Borsa Istanbul Review*, *18*(2), 91–100. https://doi.org/10.1016/J.BIR.2017.08.004

Al Aziz, M. F., Beik, I. S., & Firdaus, A. (2019). Factors influencing the price of Indonesia Sovereign Sukuk in Secondary Market. *Share: Jurnal Ekonomi dan Keuangan Islam*, *8*(1). https://doi.org/10.22373/share.v8i1.4162

Alabi, M. A., Issa, S., & Afolayan, R. B. (2013). An application of artificial intelligent neural network and discriminant analyses on credit scoring. *Math Theory Model*, *11*, 20–28.

Alpaydin, E. (2020). *Introduction to machine learning*. MIT press.

Azis, M. A., Wardhani, A. M., Pradivta, I. W. N. B., & Prahasto, S. (2021). Analysis of factors affecting the demand of retail sukuk. *Indonesian Interdisciplinary Journal of Sharia Economics*, *3*(2), 149–164.

Direktorat Jenderal Pengelolaan Pembiayaan dan Risiko. (2021). Dataset of existing SBN ritel investor [Unpublished raw data]. Kementerian Keuangan Republik Indonesia.

Fitria, Y., Rahadi, R. A., Afgani, K. F., Putranto, N. A. R., Murtaqi, I., & Faturohman, T. (2019). The influence of demographic, financial literacy and information factors on investment decision among millenial generations in Bandung. *European Journal of Business and Management Research*, *4*(6).

Fitriyah, N. L., & Ryandono, M. N. H. (2019). Determinan Terhadap Yield Sukuk Ritel Negara (Studi Tahun 2009 – 2017). *Jurnal Ekonomi Syariah Teori dan Terapan*, *6*(9), 1741–1755. https://doi.org/10.20473/VOL6ISS20199PP1741-1755

Formánková, S., Trenz, O., Faldík, O., Kolomazník, J., & Sládková, J. (2019). Millennials' awareness and approach to social responsibility and investment – Case study of the Czech Republic. *Sustainability*, *11*(2), 504.

Hair, J. F., Black, W. C., Babin, B. J., Anderson, R. E., & Tatham, R. et al. (2013). *Multivariate data analysis*. Pearson Education.

Hartono. (2019). Perbandingan Potensi Return Investasi Surat Berharga Negara (SBN) Ritel dan Return Saham Blue Chip. *Jurnal Ekonomi*, *21*(1), 32–45. http://ejournal.borobudur.ac.id/index.php/1/article/view/528

Hendrocahyo, H. (2021). Pengaruh Tingkat Kupon, Jenis SBN Ritel, Implementasi E-SBN, & Penurunan Nominal Pemesanan Terhadap Tingkat Partisipasi Investor Milenial SBN Ritel. *Jurnal Pasar Modal dan Bisnis*, *3*(2), 1–20. https://doi.org/10.37194/JPMB.V3I2.80

Kementerian Keuangan Republik Indonesia. (2022). Penerbitan ORI022 Memperoleh Tingkat Keritelan Terbaik. Retrieved August 4, 2024, from https://www.djppr.kemenkeu.go.id/penerbitanori022memperolehtingkatkeritelanterbaik

Nasution, D. (2019). *Masih Dangkal, Pendalaman Pasar Keuangan Belum Cukup Berhasil*. https://www.cnbcindonesia.com/market/20190102101206-17-48683/masih-dangkal-pendalaman-pasar-keuangan-belum-cukup-berhasil

Nguyen, L., Gallery, G., & Newton, C. (2019). The joint influence of financial risk perception and risk tolerance on individual investment decision-making. *Accounting & Finance*. John Wiley & Sons, Ltd, *59*(S1), 747–771. https://doi.org/10.1111/ACFI.12295

Paramitha, S., & Faturohman, T. (2022). analysis of optimal portfolio allocation using sharpe ratio before and during Covid-19 pandemic: A case study of PT Jasa Raharja. *Review of Integrative Business and Economics Research*, *11*(1), 201.

Rosdiana, R. (2020). Investment Behavior in Generation Z and Millennial Generation. *Dinasti International Journal of Economics, Finance & Accounting*, *1*(5), 766–780. https://doi.org/10.38035/DIJEFA.V1I5.595

Wu, P. C., Liu, S. Y., & Huang, C. W. (2022). The impact of FinTech Index on P2P lending rate. *Review of Integrative Business and Economics Research*, *11*(2), 79–94.

Wu, P. C., Liu, S. Y., & Yang, M. F. (2021). Estimation of P2P lending rates and lending strategies. *Review of Integrative Business and Economics Research*, *11*(2), 61–78.

Yenny, I., & Umanto, U. (2023). The effectiveness of retail government bond issuance policy through the electronic system as an instrument of state budget financing. *Return: Study of Management, Economic and Business*, *2*(11), 1173–1189.

CHAPTER 7

AN EMPIRICAL EXAMINATION OF INTRINSIC MOTIVATION, PERFORMANCE APPRAISAL SATISFACTION, AND PERFORMANCE OUTCOMES AMONG EMPLOYEES IN SELECT SERVICE SECTOR ORGANIZATIONS

A. Suryanarayana

Osmania University, India

ABSTRACT

The empirical research examined the effect of intrinsic motivation (IM) and employees' performance appraisal satisfaction (PAS) on performance outcomes (POs) viz., organisational commitment (OC) and turnover intention (TI). The existence of significant differences among variables under study due to different demographic factors was also tested. A questionnaire survey approach was used as a method of heterogeneous data collection involving 302 employees from 3 select service sector organisations (SSOs). To test the hypothesised relationships, results were interpreted based on mean values, standard deviation (SD), percentage, correlation analysis, regression analysis, and one-way ANOVA tests which are the accepted tools and are appropriate to interpret the data in a study of this kind. Empirical evidence supported the direct relationships of IM and

The Finance-Innovation Nexus: Implications for Socio-Economic Development
International Symposia in Economic Theory and Econometrics, Volume 34, 91–120
Copyright © 2025 by Emerald Publishing Limited
All rights of reproduction in any form reserved
ISSN: 1571-0386/doi:10.1108/S1571-038620240000034008

PAS with OC and TI. The findings also indicated that IM and PAS are more than the normal in most of the cases across the demographic groups. Significant differences were observed on perceptions of PAS and OC due to gender, years of service, and level or current position of employees. Further research studies are needed to establish the predictors of IM, PAS, and POs in different organisational contexts. Several important practical and research implications of the research results are discussed in this chapter.

Keywords: Intrinsic motivation; performance appraisal satisfaction; organisational commitment; turnover intention; performance outcomes

JEL Classification Code: M12

1. INTRODUCTION

Human capital has always been regarded as one of the critical resources of organisations, and the quality of these resources has a direct effect on the organisational profitability (Fakhimi & Raisy, 2013). Efficient and motivated employees are regarded to be committed towards their jobs while simultaneously enhancing the organisational performance (Ahmed & Shaheen, 2011). But in real organisations, employees are frequently switching their workplaces due to various reasons and it has been a painful issue for the organisations (Saeed et al., 2014). In developing countries too, employees' TI is leading to actual turnover and their low commitment has become a critical issue in workplaces in recent years (Bhattarai, 2014). Managers are trying to minimise their turnover ratio while also saving recruitment and selection costs. These problems of low commitment and turnover are mostly due to a lack of stability and job security for employees (Lee & Chen, 2013). The same problems are also existent among employees working in service organisations. Adhikari and Gautam (2011) mentioned about the challenges to motivate employees and make them feel safe and secure in their jobs in organisations. When the employees' motivation level is low, it is a challenge for human resource (HR professionals) to maintain a stable, motivated, and committed workforce. The employees' tendency to switch jobs and employees' low commitment level and productivity have led to a situation of stress for both the employees and management in service organisations creating disharmony between the two parties (Bhattarai, 2014). Research conducted in different manufacturing and service sectors reveals that HR practices have a key role to play in the success of organisations (Adhikari & Gautam, 2011).

Therefore, the role of HR professionals becomes critical to integrate HR and business strategies and to maintain a healthy employment relationship, making people engaged at work and motivating them for commitment. Personnel related areas like job design, HR planning, performance appraisal (PA) system, recruitment, selection, compensations, motivation strategies, and employee relations come under human resource management (HRM). One of the important functions of HRM is to develop motivation strategies to motivate employees at work and ultimately retain them. Motivation is the factor that stimulates desire and energy in people to be continually interested and committed to a job or to make an effort to attain a goal. Ryan and Deci (2000) highlighted that IM has a large effect on employees' attitudes and performance. When employees enjoy their work and find jobs interesting, they will put a considerable effort to perform their tasks efficiently and also have an influence on other aspects of employee behaviour (Choong et al., 2011). The authors also indicated a finding that IM is more significantly related to OC as compared to extrinsic motivation. And, when employees are intrinsically motivated, they are less likely to quit their jobs. Kuvaas (2006) highlighted that negative and a significant correlation between employees' IM and TI have been reported in previous studies due to the fact that employees with interesting, enjoyable, and exciting jobs are more committed and they are less likely to be attracted by extrinsic rewards offered by other organisations. Previous studies also provide empirical evidence on the relationship of IM with OC and TI (e.g. Sajjad et al., 2013; Yundong, 2015; Zadeh et al., 2016). Another critical function of HRM that makes organisation a success is PA (Marquardt, 2004). As mentioned by Abbas (2014), employee PA is an effective tool or vehicle for the assessment of employee performance and the implementation of strategic initiatives for the improvement of employee efficacy.

Many organisations primarily use the PA appraisal to evaluate and motivate employees. So, it is crucial for organisations to know about employees' PAS and their reactions that might affect OC and the productivity level of employees and the organisation as a whole. Employee perception of fairness of PA is a significant factor in employee acceptance and PAS decisions. Many scholars have studied PA systems and their impacts on employees' POs especially on the job performance, EC, and TI in different contexts (Fakhimi & Raisy, 2013; Kuvaas, 2006; Vignaswaran, 2005). For example, a Malaysian study showed the relationship between PAS and POS in the form of the job performance, affective OC, and employee turnover (Vignaswaran, 2005). Specifically, the perceptions of procedural unfairness in PA can adversely affect employee's OC, job satisfaction, trust in management, performance, work-related stress, organisation citizenship behaviour, theft, and inclination to litigate against their employer (Bekele et al., 2014). The present study, therefore, aims to examine the effect of IM and PAS on employees' POs (TI and OC). The service sector is an important component of any country's economy and skilled HR are considered assets especially to these industries. And therefore, it is important to motivate and retain them to achieve the desired organisational goals. There have been only limited studies on the effect of IM and PAS on employee performance outcomes (EPOs) in the service sector. Moreover, no such study has been found in existence in banking, information technology (IT), and international non-government organisation (INGO) sectors. So, this study aims to look into service providers from these three sectors.

1.1. Objectives of the Study

The general objective of this study is to investigate the effect of IM and PAS on EPOs. The other objective of this research is to find out whether there are any differences in the perceptions of IM, PAS, and POs on the basis of demographic variables. In order to achieve these research objectives, the specific objectives are formulated as:

(i)   To assess employees' levels of IM and PAS in select SSOs.
(ii) To examine the effect of IM and PAS on EPOs among employees in the SSOs.
(iii) To examine whether there are any differences in the perceptions of IM, PAS, and employee outcomes on the basis of different demographic variables.

2. REVIEW OF LITERATURE

This section presents an overview of both theoretical and research-based literature on IM, PAS, and their relationships with EPOs viz., OC and TI. Emphasis is given to the study-related constructs of IM, PAS, OC, and TI. Direct relationships between the variables under study have been proposed on the basis of reviewed literature. A theoretical framework has been formulated to present the proposed relationships. The majority of the research studies reviewed belongs to the Western context and Asia due to the unavailability of relevant studies in the local context.

2.1. Intrinsic Motivation

IM can be defined as the inner drive of an individual providing him/her energy or force to work for better outcomes (Farwa & Niazi, 2013). Over the decades, IM has been an important construct reflecting the natural human propensity to learn and assimilate. The quality of experience and performance of an individual can vary due to the motivational reasons either intrinsic or extrinsic (Ryan & Deci, 2000).

Other research evidence is available from the studies carried out by Vroom (1964) and Porter and Lawler (1968) and as cited in Jeswani (2016), Farwa and Niazi (2013), Jeswani (2016), Kuvaas (2006), Malik and Aslam (2013), Mohamed Aly and El-Shanawany (2016), Farwa and Niazi (2013), and Ganesan and Weitz (1996). Over the decades, IM has been an important construct reflecting the natural human propensity to learn and assimilate; the quality of experience and performance of an individual can vary due to the motivational reasons may be intrinsic or extrinsic (Ryan & Deci, 2000). Previous research evidence proves that holding the ability constant for most jobs, highly motivated employees perform at significantly higher rates than unmotivated employees (Porter & Lawler, 1968; Vroom, 1964; as cited in Jeswani, 2016).

The employee having IM is more autonomous and works for better outcomes like creativity, performance, and involvement (Farwa & Niazi, 2013). Employees sometimes refuse to do a particular task when their IM is low even though higher pay and benefits are available (Farwa & Niazi, 2013). It has been established that certain activities can enhance work effectiveness by raising the level of employees' IM (Jeswani, 2016). It focuses on enriching employees' attitudes, experiences, and skills (Kuvaas, 2006). As empirically stated in previous researches, IM has both positive and negative impacts on employee work-outcomes like OC and TI (e.g. Farwa & Niazi, 2013; Ganesan & Weitz, 1996; Jeswani, 2016; Mohamed Aly & El-Shanawany, 2016).

2.2. Performance Appraisal Satisfaction

PA is among the most important practices of management which include all the systematic procedures used in organisations to assess the employees' performance (Singh & Rana, 2015). The existence of the PA principles has been observed since the early 1900s (Vance et al., 1992). As per to Vignaswaran (2005), it was designed to support a top-down and control-oriented style of management at that point of time. Studies by Fletcher (2001), Keeping and Levy (2000), Saleem and Shah (2015), Kuvaas (2006), Saxena and Rai (2015), Hepner (1930), Katavich (2013), Ali et al. (2012), Keeping and Levy (2000), Saxena and Rai (2015), and Fakhimi and Raisy (2013) are of relevance in the context of PAS. PA has increasingly become part of a more strategic approach to integrating HR activities and business policies. It is now being seen as a generic term covering activities through which organisations develop employees' competence, enhance performance, and distribute rewards (Fletcher, 2001).

There are several research works that have been done in many countries like Turkey, the Netherlands, the USA, the UK, Australia, Malaysia, Bangladesh, and Singapore to represent the importance of PA in different sectors like banking, telecommunication, educational, non-profit organisation, and health (Saleem & Shah, 2015). During the last 10 years, the number of studies which examined the effects of PA systems on employees has increased and the foundation of these researches is that employees' opinions regarding the PA process are highly critical to the long-term effectiveness and the success of the system as well (Vignaswaran, 2005). Kuvaas (2006) indicated that even though PAS is the most frequently measured appraisal reaction and there is extensive research on factors that contribute to PAS or other reactions, there is a lack of empirical evidence on why and how satisfaction with PA matters. Hepner (1930) found that when the aims of the PA system were openly and honestly communicated, employees' trust in the PA systems increased. There is evidence that employee dissatisfaction with the PA system is commonly reported when employee reactions to PA were assessed (Katavich, 2013). The lack of satisfaction with the PA process in organisations is considered one of the symptoms of the organisational diseases as mentioned by Ali et al. (2012). There are four main constructs which have been used to investigate employee reactions to PA systems: satisfaction, fairness, utility, and accuracy with PA systems (Keeping & Levy, 2000) as diagrammatised later in Fig. 7.1. Of these four, it has been suggested that PAS is the preferred construct as it has the ability to capture other constructs, such as fairness and utility (Katavich, 2013).

2.3. Organisational Commitment

OC is the degree to which an employee links with a specific organisation and its objective and willing to retain membership in the organisation (Danish et al.,

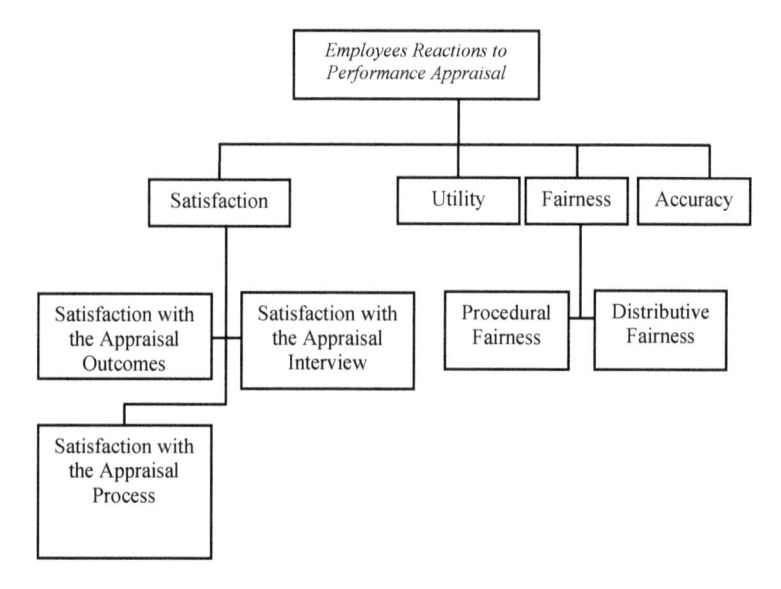

Fig. 7.1.   Employee Reactions to PA System. *Source*: As modified and adapted to the diagram provided by Keeping and Levy (2000).

2015). It has attracted considerable attention over recent years and has become a central objective of HRM (Armstrong, 2006). It is largely studied by researchers such as Mowday et al. (1979), Ahmad et al. (2014), Mowdray (1992), Allen and Meyer (1990), and Bhattarai (2014).

2.4. Turnover Intention

TI is defined as individuals' own estimated probability that they are permanently leaving the organisation at some point in the near future (Wu, 2012). It is an important factor which influences employee productivity and organisational effectiveness (Barak et al., 2001). In the world of tough competition, turnover is a painful issue for the organisations (Saeed et al., 2014). Many scholars highlighted that TI is the single best predictor of turnover and a key element in the study of employee behaviour (Wu, 2012). Research studies by Wright and Bonett (2007), Wu (2012), and Staw (1980) throw much light on TI.

2.5. Intrinsic Motivation and Performance Outcomes

Past researches showed that IM is significantly related to employee work outcomes such as performance, satisfaction, commitment, and morale (Asiedu, 2017). Employees who have IM are more autonomous and work for better outcomes like creativity, performance, and involvement (Farwa & Niazi, 2013). It has been established by earlier researchers that work effectiveness can be enhanced by raising the level of employees' IM (Jeswani, 2016).

2.6. Intrinsic Motivation and Organisational Commitment

IM is associated with the employees' responsibilities towards the organisation and commitment is one of the responsibilities among them (Zadeh et al., 2016). Choong et al. (2011) indicated that IM is more significantly compared with OC than extrinsic motivation. As internal motivation emphasises on action process, people will be satisfied and get pleasure by doing their work. Many researches in the past empirically stated the direct positive relationship between IM and OC. Other studies of relevance are those by Farwa and Niazi (2013), Zadeh et al. (2016), and Choong et al. (2011).

2.7. Intrinsic Motivation and Turnover Intention

Various researches on the relationship between IM and TI established that IM is negatively correlated with TI (Jeswani, 2016). Zadeh et al. (2016) emphasised that the effect of self-determination theory is seen on employees' enhanced behaviour and performance, reducing the perception of TI. Similarly, Khan et al. (2009) highlighted the importance of IM for employees' OC and reducing intention to leave their jobs. Few researches empirically stated the relationship between IM and TI in different contexts and domains such as the subsequent studies by Khan et al. (2009) and Jeswani (2016).

2.8. Performance Appraisal Satisfaction and Performance Outcomes

PAS has been associated with a variety of individual-level outcomes like job satisfaction, OC, job involvement, employee motivation, TI, job stress, and employee performance which are important in OB studies (Vignaswaran, 2005).

Thomas (1990) identified five outcomes of PAS, that is improved performance, reduced employee turnover, increased motivation, existence of feelings of equity among employees, linkage between performance, and rewards (Bekele et al., 2014). Katavich (2013) also studied PAS.

2.9. Performance Appraisal Satisfaction and Organisational Commitment

Roberts and Reed (1996) indicated that PAS is positively related to OC due to the enhancement of employee participation and perceived clarity of goals within the PA process. Studies by Meyer et al. (2002), Bekele et al. (2014), Katavich (2013), Singh and Mohanty (2011), and Singh and Rana (2015) also investigated the impact of PAS on OC.

2.10. Performance Appraisal Satisfaction and Turnover Intention

Employees who perceive the PA process as being fair will also perceive the organisation as being trustworthy and build feelings of trust towards the organisation (Ismail & Gali, 2016). Boxall et al. (2003), Vigoda (2000), and Katavich (2013) focused on the same. In empirical studies carried out by Bekele et al. (2014), Ahmed et al. (2010), Katavich (2013), Vignaswaran (2005), and Rajendran (2005), PAS was

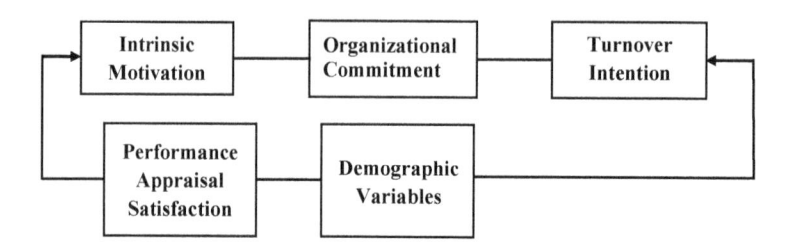

Fig. 7.2.   Conceptual Framework of the Study*.
*As developed the researcher.

negatively related to employee TI. As shown in Fig. 7.1 (Keeping & Levy, 2000), this research which has intended to predict employees' PAS is to focus on one of the three main components of the appraisal system.

They are about satisfaction having three sub-components viz., the appraisal process, the appraisal interview, and the appraisal outcomes (Keeping & Levy, 2000). The employees' reactions to PA system are further explained under the three sub-components viz., utility, fairness, and accuracy. The present study defines PAS as a positive reaction to the appraisal process, interview, and the outcomes and will measure employees' PAS on the basis of these criteria.

2.11. Theoretical Framework

A pictorial representation of the proposed interrelationships between different study variables is presented in this theoretical framework. Based on the above literature review, the following theoretical framework has been proposed for the study. The direct relationships between IM and PAS with POs (OC and TI) are shown clearly in Fig. 7.2.

3. RESEARCH METHODOLOGY

The main aim of this section is to describe the research design including research variables, validity and reliability, unit of analysis, population, and sample and to make the variables under study operational. Likewise, instruments used for measurement, pre-testing the questionnaire, research hypotheses, and research procedure of the study are discussed in detail. This study takes the form of a quantitative design. A descriptive research design was employed for the study as it permits the researcher to gather information from a large sample of people relatively quickly and inexpensively (Asiedu, 2017). This research discovers the cause and effect relationship of IM and PAS with employee POs viz., OC and TI. Therefore, it can also be known as a correlation research (Farwa & Niazi, 2013). This is a cross-sectional study as data are collected from organisations relating to different sectors at the same point of time. Primary data were generated through a survey method using self-administered questionnaires under non-experimental research design.

3.1. Research Design

- *Research variables*: The present study has established IM and PAS as independent variables and POs viz., TI and OC as dependent variables.
- *Validity and reliability*: In the present study, validated instruments are used to measure the variables under study and they were again made operational and tested in the context of the study to comply with content validity.
- The research questions and hypotheses were formulated on the basis of comprehensive literature review of available empirical studies and established empirical relationships to measure construct validity.
- Likewise, to establish criterion-related validity, SPSS statistical software that is widely used is used for data analysis and interpretation of the results. After obtaining the real data, instruments were again examined using confirmatory factor analysis (CFA) and Cronbach alpha to ensure the reliability of the findings.
- *Unit of analysis*: For the present study, the units of analysis are individuals and the sample constituted individuals from three service sectors viz., banking, IT, and INGOs. The respondents are *appraisees* whose performance is evaluated internally.
- *Population and sample*: Among the various service sectors, Banking, IT, and INGOs are some of the industries conducting PA regularly either on a half yearly or yearly basis. Hence, this study has taken these sectors as the overall population.

Due to the non-availability of total population, the non-probability sampling method, especially quota sampling, is used to select the sample for the study. In the first stage, the quotas or control categories of the population are developed. The quota from banking sector consists of those banks categorised under 'A class' by the Central Bank of the nation. There are altogether 28 such banks currently operating in the country. The study included bankers from all the hierarchical levels to ensure the validity of data. And, the quota from the IT sector included both large- and medium-sized software development companies operating in the nation's capital to ensure the validity of the results. Medium-sized organisations included companies with at least 15 software engineers, whereas large-sized IT companies have at least 50 software engineers.

Participants included the core software development team like web designer, iOS developer, android developer, PHP developer, and quality analyst. The sample excluded members from the management team. Likewise, the quota from non-profit sector is INGOs that are members of the Association of International NGOs (AIN) in the country. According to its website, AIN has altogether 140 members (AIN, 2017). And, in the second stage, after the development of quotas of the population, some of the companies from these quotas are selected for data collection purpose as samples on convenience or judgement basis as per availability.

The most important criterion for selecting an organisation as a sample for the study is the presence of regular PA process in that organisation. The total sample size is estimated to be 450 respondents from the select SSOs.

However, while selecting the individual respondents, the control variables like gender, age, and years of service, as well as current level, marital status, educational level, and earning of the respondents are considered to the extent data is available. The basic sampling plan is presented in Table 7.1.

Table 7.1. Sampling Plan.

Domain: Service Industry		
Population	Selected Quotas	Estimated Sample Size
Banks	'A' class banks	150
IT companies	Large and medium sized*	150
INGOs	Listed by AIN	150
Total sample size		450

*Medium- and large-sized organisations include companies with at least 15 and 50 software engineers, respectively.

3.2. Making the Research Variables Operational

The variables under study, namely, IM, PAS, OC, and TI are made operational as stated below.

(a) *IM*: It is the behaviour that is driven by internal rewards, that is an employee is motivated towards achieving organisational goals by self-motivation (Ryan & Deci, 2000).
(b) *PAS*: It is the positive reaction of the employees to PA process, interview, and the outcomes (Keeping & Levy, 2000). The study used these criteria to measure PAS of the sample *ratees* or appraisees.
(c) *OC*: It is an employee's feeling of organisations' ownership, being motivated towards work, and willingness to continue with the organisation for a considerable time is known (Danish et al., 2015).
(d) *TI*: It is an individuals' own estimated probability that they are permanently leaving the organisation at some point in the near future (Wu, 2012).

3.3. Measures

A questionnaire consisting of four instruments that were previously developed and validated viz., (IM, PAS, OC, and TI) including some general information was provided to the participants. General information consisted of questions that include participants' personal details like gender, age, years of service, current level of the job, marital status, educational level, and salary. All these instruments were based on 5-point Likert scale (where 1, strongly disagree; 2, disagree; 3, neutral; 4, agree; 5, strongly agree) for the purpose of uniformity of participants' responses.

a. *PAS*: The measure of employees' satisfaction with PA developed by Meyer and Smith (2000) was used to measure PAS level.

The scale consists of seven items concerning the overall satisfaction with PA activities within an organisation and employees' perceptions of their organisation's commitment to conducting developmental PA.

b. *IM*: A commonly used questionnaire developed by Cameron and Pierce (1994) is used to measure employees' intrinsic work motivation. The scale consists of six items.

c. *OC*: A six-item scale derived from Lincoln and Kalleberg's (1990) study was used to measure OC (Marsden et al., 1993 as cited in Dail, 2002). One item is reverse scored item in the scale.
d. *TI*: A commonly used questionnaire by Meyer and Smith (2000) was used to measure employees' TIs. The scale consists of five items.

Summary of measures: The instruments have been used by several researchers in previous studies and were able to establish the validity and reliability to capture the perceptions of variables under study. The Cronbach's alpha value for each of the FOUR variables viz., PAS, IM, OC, and TI and as reported by previous researchers is shown in Table 7.2.

3.4. Demographic Variables

Demographic variables to record the characteristics of respondents like gender, age, years of service, current level, marital status, educational level, and earning are included in the study and are used as control variables during analysis of direct relationships between variables of the study are subsequently coded to ease the statistical analysis.

3.5. Pre-testing Questionnaires and Pilot Study

The pilot survey was conducted with 30 respondents working in 2 organisations (a software development company and a bank branch) based on convenience and was explained about the significance of the study and the importance of the respondents' cooperation. These participants are those employees whose performances on their jobs were appraised recently. A separate sheet was attached to record if there were any confusion in the questionnaire. The time taken to complete the whole questionnaire was recorded.

3.6. Research Hypothesis

Based on the review of literature, four hypotheses are developed to investigate the relationships between IM, PAS, and POs viz., OC and TI.

Table 7.2. Summary of Measures.

Instrument	Variable	Cronbach's Alpha
I. Meyer and Smith (2000)		0.86
7-Items Likert scale	PAS	Rajendran (2005)
II. Cameron and Pierce (1994)	IM	0.91
6-Items Likert scale		Rajendran (2005)
III. Lincoln and Kalleberg's (1990)	OC	0.78
6-Iitems Likert scale		Marsden et al. (1993)
IV. Meyer and Smith (2000)	TI	0.91
5-Items Likert scale		Rajendran (2005)

H1. IM will positively influence OC.

H2. IM will negatively influence TI.

H3. PAS will positively influence OC.

H4. PAS will negatively influence TI.

- *Research procedure*: Under research procedure, administration of the questionnaire, collection of data, data processing, and data analysis are provided.

3.7. Administration of the Questionnaire

Before the distribution of the questionnaires, the purpose of the study was explained to the respondents and it was also ensured that the collected data to be used at aggregate level for the purpose of academic research only. Fifteen organisations were selected on convenience basis from different sectors, that is eight 'A' class banks, four (two small and two large) software development companies, and three INGOs. The data collection was done as per sampling plan described earlier. Two methods viz., online survey and distribution of questionnaires manually to the respondents were used for the collection of data based on the choice of the respondents. From an online survey, 68 responses were collected. Likewise, 325 questionnaires are distributed to employees working in different INGOs, banks, and software development companies operating out of the nation's capital city.

Out of the 325 distributed questionnaires, 249 questionnaires were returned with the response rate of 76.62%. Therefore, the total responses received are 317.

3.8. Data Processing

The collected responses were then screened for missing data and those which had similar responses throughout the questionnaires. Fifteen responses were found unusable for the study purpose and the research data for the present study was then reduced to 302. The information about required sample size, sample organisations, and collected and useful responses has been presented in Table 7.3. The usable responses were then entered into SPSS windows statistical package after appropriate coding of the items and study variables for further analysis of data.

Table 7.3.   Number of Samples Required and Collected.

Population	Required Sample Size	No. of Organisations	Collected Responses	Useful Responses
Banks	150	8	138	128
IT companies	150	4	105	103
INGOs	150	3	74	71
Total	450	15	317	302

3.9. Characteristics of the Respondents

The personal information of the respondents according to different demographic variables viz., gender, age, years of service, current level, marital status, educational level, and earning is summarised in Table 7.4.

3.10. Data Analysis

All statistical analyses as shown below were carried out using the SPSS software, version 21.

(a) *Descriptive analysis* – To analyse data on the basis of distribution and frequency across the demographic, independent, and dependent variables.
(b) *CFA* – To test whether measures of a construct are consistent with the nature of the same construct used in the study.

Table 7.4. Summary of the Profiles of the Respondents.

Variables	Frequency (%)
Gender	
Male	189(62.58)
Female	113(37.42)
Age	
15–24	46(15.23)
25–34	214(70.86)
35–44	33(10.92)
45 and above	9(2.98)
Years of service	
Less than 1 year	33(10.92)
Between 1 and 3 years	116(38.41)
Between 3 and 5 years	64(21.19)
Above 5 years	89(29.47)
Current level	
Senior	60(19.86)
Middle	160(52.98)
Junior	82(27.15)
Marital status	
Single	163(53.97)
Married	137(45.36)
Divorced	2(0.66)
Widowed	0
Educational level	
Up to higher secondary	4(1.32)
Bachelor's degree	150(49.67)
Master's degree	140(46.36)
Above Masters'	8(2.65)
Earning (NRs.)	
Up to 25,000	38(12.58)
25,001–50,000	155(51.32)
50,001–75,000	63(20.86)
Above 75,000	46(15.23)

(c) *Reliability analysis* – To check the internal consistency of the scales used to measure study variables in the context under study.
(d) *Correlation analysis* – To measure the relationship between IM, PAS, and OC and TI.
(e) *Regression analysis* – To infer causal relationships between the independent and dependent variables.
(f) *One-way ANOVA* – To find whether there is any statistically significant differences in the perception of study variables across different demographic variables.

3.11. Validation of Research Instruments

The present research used duly validated instruments developed by different scholars for the purpose of data collection. Though the questionnaire was pre-tested, further validation was still necessary before administering them among the respondents. As they were mostly developed and contextualised in Westernised world, it is very much necessary to establish contextual validation in the country's service sector. CFA technique was used to confirm if all the items explaining a particular construct (e.g. PAS) could be clubbed together to represent the construct itself. Later, internal consistency and reliability of instruments were tested using Cronbach's alpha values. Both the techniques are explained in detail.

3.12. Confirmatory Factor Analysis

CFA techniques were used to test whether the models in the present study fitted the collected data. There are four models in the present study viz., PAS (seven items), IM (six items), OC (six items), and TI (five items) as the latent variables.

The CFA for these models was performed using AMOS 21 (analysis of moment structure) for Windows and maximum likelihood estimation was used for analysis. The four CFA models included all the remaining items after item deletion linked to their corresponding latent variables. Standardised factor loadings of the latent variables on their respective items were checked to test models that fitted the sample data. On a conventional liberal-to-conservative continuum, setting a cut-off factor loading at 0.4 would be the lowest acceptable threshold and setting a cut-off at 0.6 or 0.7 would be the most conservative as suggested by Matsunaga (2010). However, the present study used the lowest acceptable threshold and those items with standardised factor loadings of 0.4 or less were removed before continuing with the analysis. Two items, item PA6 from PAS scale and one reversed item OC2_R from OC scale that failed to meet the cut-off value 0.4,

Table 7.5. CFA-Model Fit Statistics.

Model	χ^2	df	Probability Level	GFI	AGFI	RMSEA	NFI	CFI	TLI
PAS	4.74	4	0.32	1.00	1.00	0.03	1.00	1.00	1.00
IM	9.36	6	0.16	1.00	0.96	0.04	0.99	1.00	0.99
OC	4.10	5	0.54	1.00	0.98	0.00	0.98	1.00	1.00
TI	3.40	2	0.18	1.00	0.97	0.05	1.00	1.00	0.99

were removed. Table 7.5 presents the several fit indices cut-off criteria values for the four CFA models. It shows the factor structures after the items were dropped below 0.4 and when the good fit for models was established. The CFA model fit statistics for PAS and OC models were improved after the deletion of those two items. Likewise, the CFA fit statistics for the other two IM and TI models are also satisfactory. Therefore, all the models were accepted for further analysis.

3.13. Reliability Analysis

Reliability analysis was conducted after models were finalised by CFA. Cronbach values of the validated instruments are above 0.7 and are found to be reliable enough to capture the intended study variables. The variables could then be used for further analyses. The Cronbach values for the instruments are tabulated in Table 7.6.

3.14. Level of IM

The mean and SD values representing the level of IM with respect to different demographic variables are presented in Table 7.7.

Table 7.6. Reliability Test Results.

Instruments	No. of Items	Cronbach's Alpha Value
PAS	6	0.82
IM	6	0.83
OC	5	0.70
TI	5	0.82

Table 7.7. Mean and SD of IM as per the Demographic Groups.

Groups	N	IM	
		Mean	SD
Gender			
Male	189	3.67	0.61
Female	113	3.61	0.59
Age			
15–24	46	3.71	0.51
25–34	214	3.63	0.60
35–44	33	3.58	0.72
45 and above	9	3.93	0.55
Years of service			
Less than 1 year	33	3.77	0.50
Between 1 and 3 years	116	3.58	0.60
Between 3 and 5 years	64	3.60	0.63
Above 5 years	89	3.72	0.62
Current level			
Senior	60	3.71	0.65
Middle level	160	3.63	0.60
Junior	82	3.63	0.58

(Continued)

Table 7.7. *(Continued)*

Groups	N	IM	
		Mean	SD
Marital status			
Single	163	3.67	0.55
Married	137	3.63	0.65
Divorced	2	3.00	0.24
Widowed			
Educational level			
Up to higher secondary	4	3.83	0.91
Bachelor's degree	150	3.72	0.56
Master's degree	140	3.59	0.59
Above Masters'	8	3.15	1.11
Earning (Rs.)			
Up to 25,000	38	3.63	0.51
25,001–50,000	155	3.68	0.57
50,001–75,000	63	3.56	0.57
Above 75,000	46	3.68	0.79

3.15. Level of PAS

The mean and SD values representing the level of PAS with respect to different demographic variables are presented in Table 7.8

3.16. Relationships Between IM, PAS, and Work Outcomes

The results from the Pearson correlation coefficient are used to assess the nature and strength of the relationship between the variables under the study.

The mean and SD values of each of the study variables are tabulated in Table 7.9. The mean score 3.49 (SD = 0.60) suggests that employees have a high level of satisfaction about their PA system at their work. The IM level of the employees working in nation's service sector is above average with mean score 3.65 (SD = 0.60). Likewise, they perceive their OC level at work above average, mean score 3.39 (SD = 0.59). It can be observed that the employees are committed with their present jobs, but they have the intention to switch their jobs (mean 2.93, SD = 0.78). Table 7.9 also illustrates the Pearson's correlation coefficients of the variables under study. It can be observed that there exists a positive and significant relationship between PAS and OC that has a significant correlation value of 0.42 at level 10% level of significance. But, TI has a negative relationship with PAS at 0.01 significance levels with a correlation value of 0.27. Likewise, IM has a positive relationship with OC and a negative relationship with TI with correlation values 0.42 and 0.27, respectively, at 0.01 significance level.

The regression results as depicted in Tables 7.10 and 7.11 show the same results from correlation analysis. R square values in the model summary data explain that 25% of variability in OC and 11% variability in TI are accounted by IM and PAS, meaning that IM and PAS both are important predictors of OC and TI.

The standardised beta coefficients are statistically significant at 5% level of significance. Also, the positive beta values show the positive relationships of OC

Table 7.8. Mean and SD of PAS According to the Demographic Groups.

Groups	N	PAS	
		Mean	SD
Gender			
Male	189	3.50	0.58
Female	113	3.46	0.65
Age			
15–24	46	3.49	0.53
25–34	214	3.48	0.61
35–44	33	3.46	0.72
45 and above	9	3.76	0.35
Years of service			
Less than 1 year	33	3.66	0.51
Between 1 and 3 years	116	3.43	0.53
Between 3 and 5 years	64	3.27	0.70
Above 5 years	89	3.66	0.60
Current level			
Senior	60	3.53	0.56
Middle	160	3.47	0.59
Junior	82	3.50	0.65
Marital status			
Single	163	3.47	0.54
Married	137	3.52	0.66
Divorced	2	2.75	0.59
Widowed	0	0	0
Educational level			
Up to higher secondary	4	3.67	0.30
Bachelor's degree	150	3.47	0.53
Master's degree	140	3.52	0.63
Above Masters'	8	3.23	1.21
Earning (Rs.)			
Up to 25,000	38	3.53	0.58
25,001–50,000	155	3.45	0.58
50,001–75,000	63	3.39	0.64
Above 75,000	46	3.70	0.59

Table 7.9. Correlations Between Variables Under Study.

	Mean	SD	PAS	IM	OC	TI
PAS	3.49	0.60	1			
IM	3.65	0.60	0.51**	1		
OC	3.39	0.59	0.42**	0.44**	1	
TI	2.93	0.78	−0.27**	−0.29**	−0.28**	1

**Correlation is significant at the 0.01 level (2-tailed).
*$p < 0.05$; **$p < 0.01$

Table 7.10. Regression Results of OC as Dependent Variable and IM & PA as Independent Variables.

Model Summary				
Model	R	R Square	Adjusted R Square	Std. Error of the Estimate
1	0.50[a]	0.25	0.24	0.51

[a]Predictors: (constant), IM, PAS

Coefficients[a]					
Model	Un-standardised Coefficients		Standardised Coefficients	t	Sig.
	B	Std. Error	Beta		
1 (Constant)	1.39	0.20		6.83	0.00
PAS	0.26	0.06	0.27	4.60	0.00
IM	0.30	0.06	0.30	5.16	0.00

[a]Dependent variable: OC

Table 7.11. Regression Results of TI as Dependent Variable and IM and PA as Independent Variables.

Model Summary				
Model	R	R Square	Adjusted R Square	Std. Error of the Estimate
1	0.33[a]	0.11	0.10	0.74

[a]Predictors: (constant), IM, PAS

Coefficients[a]					
Model	Un-standardised Coefficients		Standardised Coefficients	t	Sig.
	B	Std. Error	Beta		
1 (Constant)	4.66	0.29		15.96	0.00
PAS	−00.22	0.08	−0.17	−2.63	0.01
IM	−0.27	0.08	−0.21	−3.26	0.00

[a]Dependent variable: TI

with IM and PAS. Likewise, the negative values show the negative relationships of TI with IM and PAS.

3.17. Effect of Demographic Variables

The mean differences about IM, PAS, OC, and TI with respect to different demographic variables have been presented. The statistical significance of mean differences of the study variables according to different demographic factors is measured with the help of one-way ANOVA.

To examine the effect of gender among employees working in service sectors on their perception of IM, PAS, OC, and TI, the subjects were divided into two groups, male and female employees. In Table 7.12, the results indicate that gender does not have any statistically significant difference among them in their perceptions about PAS, IM, and TI but do have statistically significant difference among them about perceptions on OC. The *p*-value of PAS, IM, and TI was greater than 0.05 ($p < 0.05$) and that of OC was less than 0.05 ($p < 0.05$) which indicates that only mean differences of OC were statistically significant. The mean differences in the variables under study due to gender are presented in Table 7.12.

The descriptive statistics presented in Table 7.13 shows that the highest difference between males and females exist in OC (0.17 points) as compared to PAS, IM, and TI.

To examine the effect of age among employees working in service sectors on their perception of IM, PAS, OC, and TI, the subjects were divided into four age groups – between 15 and 24 years of age, between 25 and 34 years of age, between 35 and 44 years of age, and above 45 years of age. In Table 7.14, the results indicate that age does not have any statistically significant difference among them in their perceptions about PAS, IM, OC, and TI. The *p*-value of PAS, IM, OC, and TI was greater than 0.05 ($p < 0.05$) which indicates that none of the study variables have statistically significant difference due to varying age groups.

To examine the effect of years of service or tenure among employees working in service sectors on their perception of IM, PAS, OC, and TI, the subjects were divided into four groups – less than 1 year, between 1 and 3 years, between 3 and 5 years, and above 5 years.

In Table 7.15, the results indicate that years of service do not have any statistically significant difference among them in their perceptions about IM, OC, and TI but do have statistically significant difference among them about perceptions on PAS. The

Table 7.12.   ANOVA Outputs of Gender for Study Variables.

Variables	*F*	Sig.
PAS	0.29	0.59
IM	0.85	0.36
OC	5.42	0.02*
TI	3.76	0.05

*The mean difference is significant at 0.05 significance levels.

Table 7.13.   Mean Differences of Gender for Variables Under Study.

		N	Mean	SD
PAS	Male	189	3.50	0.58
	Female	113	3.46	0.65
IM	Male	189	3.67	0.61
	Female	113	3.61	0.59
OC	Male	189	3.32	0.62
	Female	113	3.49	0.52
TI	Male	189	3.00	0.77
	Female	113	2.82	0.77

Table 7.14. ANOVA Outputs of Age for Variables Under Study.

Variables	F	Sig.
PAS	0.64	0.59
IM	1.06	0.37
OC	0.88	0.45
TI	1.82	0.14

*The mean difference is significant at 0.05 significance levels.

Table 7.15. ANOVA Outputs of Years of Service for Study Variables.

Variables	F	Sig.
PAS	6.67	0.00*
IM	1.47	0.22
OC	2.26	0.08
TI	1.59	0.19

*The mean difference is significant at 0.05 significance levels.

p-value of IM, OC, and TI was greater than 0.05 ($p > 0.05$) and that of PAS was less than 0.05 ($p < 0.05$) which indicates that only mean differences of PAS were statistically significant. To find out between which groups the difference is significant, post-hoc test analysis results are presented in Table 7.15. The results presented in Table 7.16 about post-hoc analysis show that PAS differs significantly among employees with tenure less than 1 year, between 1 and 3 years, and above 5 years, but no significant difference is found among employees with tenure between 3 and 5 years. Also, it can be referred that employees with tenure between 3 and 5 years have the highest level of satisfaction with PA as compared to others with the mean difference value of 0.39.

To examine the effect of current level among employees working in service sectors on their perception of IM, PAS, OC, and TI, the subjects were divided into three groups – senior level, middle level, and junior level. In Table 7.17, the results indicate that the current level does not have any statistically significant difference among them in their perceptions about IM, PAS, and TI but do have statistically significant difference among them about perceptions on OC.

The p-value of IM, PAS, and TI was greater than 0.05 ($p > 0.05$) and that of OC was less than 0.05 ($p < 0.05$) which indicates that only mean differences of OC were statistically significant. To find out as to between which groups the difference is significant, post-hoc test analysis results are presented in Table 7.17.

In Table 7.18, results from post-hoc analysis show that OC differs significantly among employees working in senior- and junior-level positions but no significant difference is found among employees working in middle-level positions. Also, it can be referred that employees working in senior-level positions have the highest level of commitment as compared to others with the mean difference value of 0.27.

To examine the effect of marital status among employees working in service sectors on their perception of IM, PAS, OC, and TI, the subjects were divided

Table 7.16. Post-hoc Test Results According to Years of Service.

Dependent Variable Between Years		Mean Difference	Std. Error	Sig.
PAS　Less than 1 year	1–3	0.23	0.12	0.25
	3–5	0.39*	0.13	0.02
	Above 5 years	0.01	0.12	1.00
Between 1 and 3 years	Less than 1 year	−0.23	0.12	0.25
	3–5	0.15	0.09	0.42
	Above 5	−0.23	0.08	0.06
Between 3 and 5 years	Less than 1 year	−0.39*	0.13	0.02
	1–3 years	−0.15	0.09	0.42
	Above 5 years	−0.38*	0.10	0.00
Above 5 years	Less than 1 year	−0.01	0.12	1.00
	1–3	0.23	0.08	0.06
	3–5	0.38*	0.10	0.00

Table 7.17. ANOVA Outputs of Current Level for Variables Under Study.

Variables	F	Sig.
PAS	0.24	0.78
IM	0.38	0.68
OC	3.78	0.02*
TI	2.06	0.13

*The mean difference is significant at 0.05 significance levels.

Table 7.18. Post-hoc Test Results According to Current Level.

		Mean Difference	Std. Error	Sig.
OC　Senior	Middle	−0.15	0.09	0.22
	Junior	−0.27*	0.10	0.02
Middle	Senior	0.15	0.09	0.22
	Junior	−0.12	0.08	0.38
Junior	Senior	0.27*	0.10	0.02
	Middle	0.12	0.08	0.33

*The mean difference is significant at 0.05 significance levels.

into four age groups – single, married, divorced, and widowed. In Table 7.19, the results indicate that marital status does not have any statistically significant difference among them in their perceptions about PAS, IM, OC, and TI. The p-value of PAS, IM, OC, and TI was greater than 0.05 ($p < 0.05$) which indicates that none of the study variables have statistically significant difference due to marital status.

To examine the effect of educational level among employees working in service sectors on their perception of IM, PAS, OC, and TI, the subjects were divided into four age groups – up to higher secondary, Bachelor's degree, Master's degree, and above Master's degree. In Table 7.20, the results indicate that educational level does not have any statistically significant difference among them in their perceptions about PAS, IM, OC, and TI. The p-value of PAS, IM, OC, and TI is

Table 7.19. ANOVA Outputs of Marital Status for Variables Under Study.

Variables	F	Sig.
PAS	1.88	0.15
IM	1.39	0.25
OC	0.90	0.41
TI	2.28	0.10

*The mean difference is significant at 0.05 significance levels.

Table 7.20. ANOVA Outputs of Educational Level for Study Variables.

Variables	F	Sig.
PAS	0.78	0.51
IM	3.16	0.06
OC	2.88	0.07
TI	0.57	0.64

*The mean difference is significant at 0.05 significance levels.

Table 7.21. ANOVA Outputs of Earning per Month for Study Variables.

Variables	F	Sig.
PAS	2.60	0.52
IM	0.65	0.59
OC	1.74	0.16
TI	0.50	0.68

*The mean difference is significant at 0.05 significance levels.

greater than 0.05 ($p < 0.05$) which indicates that none of the study variables have any statistically significant difference due to educational level.

To examine the effect of earning per month among employees working in service sectors on their perception of IM, PAS, OC, and TI, the subjects were divided into four earning groups – up to Rs. 25,000, between Rs. 25,001 and 50,000, between Rs. 50,001 and 75,000, and above Rs. 75,000. In Table 7.21, the results indicate that earning per month do not have any statistically significant difference among them in their perceptions about PAS, IM, OC, and TI. The p-value of PAS, IM, OC, and TI was greater than 0.05 ($p < 0.05$) which indicates that none of the study variables have statistically significant differences due to earning level of employees.

4. RESULTS

This section aims to present the employees' perceptions of different variables proposed under study and the relationships that are established. It analyses and interprets the results of the empirical research undertaken from the data obtained using various techniques. The hypotheses formulated are tested to address the research issues.

Table 7.22. Summary of Hypotheses Testing.

Hypothesis	Independent Variables	Dependent Variables	Hypothesised Relationships	Findings
H1	IM	OC	Positive	Supported
H2	IM	TI	Negative	Supported
H3	PAS	OC	Positive	Supported
H4	PAS	TI	Negative	Supported

4.1. Hypothesis Testing

Based on the results of correlation and regression analysis made, the hypothesis regarding the positive relationship between IM and OC and the hypothesis regarding negative relationship between IM and TI are supported. Therefore, *H1* and *H2* are fully supported.

Likewise, *H3* regarding positive relationship between PAS and OC and *H4* regarding the negative relationship between PAS and TI are also fully supported. The summary of hypothesis testing has been presented Table 7.22.

5. SUMMARY, DISCUSSION, IMPLICATIONS, AND CRITIQUING

This section presents the major findings of the study, and a discussion on the same that is relevant in the context under study is presented along with their practical and research implications. A critique of the study highlighting the limitations and possibility of further improvements is also made at the end.

5.1. Summary

The major focus of the present empirical study is to examine the effect of IM and PAS on OC and TI among 302 employees working in three different service sectors (Banking, INGOs, and IT companies) located in the capital city of the nation. It also aimed to test the significant differences in the employees' perceptions about the variables under study due to different demographic factors. Four hypotheses are examined to test the direct effects of IM and PAS on POs. The findings of the study proved that there is a direct positive relationship between IM and OC and a negative direct relationship between IM and TI. Evidence is also found to establish positive direct relationship between PAS and OC and a negative relationship between PAS and TI. The results also indicated that none of the demographic variables have any statistically significant difference in the employees' perceptions about IM and TI. But gender, years of service, and current work positions *do* have statistically significant difference in the employees' perception about PAS and OC. There is a higher level of OC in females than in males and also in senior-level employees as compared to middle and lower levels. Employees with tenure between 3 and 5 years have the highest level of satisfaction with PA.

5.2. Discussions

Most of the findings of the study are in the hypothesised direction. *H1* and *H2* stated the influence of IM on OC positively and TI negatively. The results are similar to the previous findings in both the cases. A study conducted in Malaysian Private Universities among 247 academicians found that IM is significantly correlated with the three components of commitment, namely, affective, continuance, and normative commitment (Choong et al., 2011). Similarly, same are the results in the study of Zadeh et al. (2016) conducted among 250 physical education teachers. Likewise, Ganesan and Weitz (1996) in their study found the strong effect of IM on TI. Significant and empirical correlation between IM and TI was also found in a study by Khan et al. (2009).

These findings also have relevance in the local context as a research conducted in the nation's insurance industry by Bhattarai (2014) also empirically confirmed these relationships. The results of the correlation and regression analysis showed that PAS had a positive impact on OC accepting *H3* that when an *appraisee* is satisfied with the PA system in her or his organisation, the OC level is high. This finding is consistent with the findings of other previous studies like that of Katavich (2013) and a number of studies (e.g. Kuvaas, 2006; Singh & Mohanty, 2011; Singh & Rana, 2015). The existence of the above relationship in select SSOs can be explained by a certain cultural context of our society. For example, PA outcomes in our society are driven by an increase in pay in most of the organisations. The reason behind it can be that in a developing country, a large chunk of people is still struggling to fulfil their basic needs, and in such scenarios, monetary benefits become most important. Therefore, it can be concluded when PA is linked to monetary benefits employees are likely to be satisfied and exhibit higher levels of OC. A study by Shrestha (2015) found that OC of the employees affected significantly by the role of supervisor and training programmes. It can be inferred that PAS plays an important role in enhancing employees OC level in SSOS, specifically in banking, INGOs, and IT companies.

The results also provide empirical evidence supporting *H4* about the negative relationship between PAS and TI. It shows that when an appraisee is unsatisfied with the PA system, employees plan to quit the job in the near future or start seeking and searching for new opportunities. This finding provides additional empirical evidence to various previous researches (e.g. Ahmed & Akbar, 2010; Bekele et al., 2014; Katavich, 2013; Rajendran, 2005; Vignaswaran, 2005) about the negative influence on employees' TI due to PA process at their organisations. The relevance of this finding is also commented by Biswakarma (2016) in his study conducted in select commercial banks. He wrote that two factors viz., promotion speed and remuneration growth of the employees are vital to retain and encourage them towards their contribution in the effectiveness and productivity of the organisations. These two factors are the outcomes of PA system. It can also be inferred that when the outcomes of PA are not satisfactory or as per their expectation, they are likely to have a future plan to quit their jobs. Also, different studies have found negative correlations between PAS and TI as mentioned by Kuvaas (2006) in his study. He further wrote that employees working on exciting and interesting roles are less interested in quitting their jobs.

The one-way ANOVA results indicated that gender does have statistically significant difference among them in their perceptions about OC among employees, but there is no statistically significant difference among them about IM, PAS, and TI. It means that males and females working in different service sectors, that is banking, INGOs, and IT companies, have varying levels of OC. The results found that females are more committed towards their jobs than males. This finding is supported by similar results of those studies in the past which indicated the existence of some differences in the level of OC due to gender (Kokubun, 2017). The OC level of females might be high due to various reasons like pay, working environment, and facilities offered in the local context. For example, banks provide provident fund, insurance facilities, loan facilities, and safe as well as good working environment rather than high salaries. This factor is a motivating factor for females than males. As per societal and cultural values in the nation, males are more responsible to earn for living than the females. In the same way, the relationship between gender and TI has also been examined in numerous earlier studies. The results depicted that the TI in females was high as compared to males due to lower pays, tenure, and weak attachments to their jobs (Jusoff et al., 2009).

Cotton and Tuttle (1986) in their study found that females are more likely to quit their current jobs than their male counter-parts. But in the present study, there is no statistically difference found in the perception of TI due to gender in SSOS. One of the reasons behind this finding might be job insecurity. The trend about people management in these sectors shows that there is no fear of job insecurity for employees. For example, INGOs provide high-salaried jobs, but they hire employees mostly on contract basis or on project basis for a short period of time. This could be a de-motivating factor for both males and females resulting in TI. In the like manner, previous studies also established differences in PAS and IM due to the impact of gender (e.g. Arnania-Kepuladze, 2010; Gautam & Adhikari, 2016; Sturman, 2003; Tiraieyari & Uli, 2011; Ufuophu-Biri & Iwu, 2014). The previous results contradict the findings of the present study in this context. The results found no statistically significant differences in the perceptions of PAS and IM levels. The reasons behind this finding could be equal treatment of both the gender in these organisations in terms of pay, promotion, benefits, facilities, and working environment. Hence, there is no question of difference in their perceptions about PAS. The study found statistically significant differences in the perception of PAS due to years of service or tenure.

The respondents in the present study were divided into four groups according to years of service as (i) less than 1 year, (ii) between 1 and 3 years, (iii) between 3 and 5 years, and (iv) above 5 years. Employees with long and short tenure in an organisation have different factors of IM and organisations are required to provide promotion packages and other facilities keeping such factors in mind. But in real scenarios, these practices are very limited and this might be a reason for differences in the perceptions of PAS. The results also indicated significant differences in the perception of OC due to current level or position of employees. The respondents in the present study were divided into three groups – senior level, middle level, and junior level. Specifically, it is found that employees working in senior-level positions have the highest level of commitment as compared to others. This finding is contradictory to those from the study by Shrestha (2015) that was conducted in local financial institutions. She found that job position does not have any significant difference on OC of employees in financial institutions. The contradiction in results may be due to the choice of sample in both the studies. The present study collected data from three select SSOs operating inside the valley unlike that of Shrestha (2015) who used the sample from only financial institutions operating out of valley. Therefore, it might be the case that OC of employees working in INGOs and IT companies may differ due to their current work position. One reason for the high OC level of senior-level employees in these organisations may be that INGOs and IT companies pay handsome salaries and a number of benefits to senior-level staffs. However, the present finding is similar to the results obtained from a study conducted by Hung and Wu (2016). Finally, this study empirically establishes the effect of IM and PAS on POs viz., OC and TI.

5.3. Practical and Research Implications

The findings of this empirical work have both practical and research implications. The result can be a guideline for HR managers in preparing policies related to motivating employees and for designing PA systems in their organisations. The knowledge about the effect of employees' PA and their IM level on POs is gained. The study can be insightful about the importance to motivate employees and improve their PA systems in SSOS to address critical issues like turnover. It is found that IM has a direct impact on employees' OC and TI. So, it will be wise to hire employees who are self-motivated than those who need to be motivated.

The recruitment team at these companies can include some questions indicating self-motivation in the interviews or written tests during the hiring process. Therefore, this finding can have significant practical implications in developing efficient and committed work teams at these companies. The hiring and motivation strategies for service industries can have valuable input from the current research findings. The direct relationship of PAS with OC and TI is also established. Therefore, HR managers can further investigate about the ways to improve PA systems and motivation strategies in their organisations that will enhance employee motivation and OC level of employees as well as to reduce employees' TI in SSOS. The results indicated that level of IM and PAS is above average in most of the cases across various demographic groups. Therefore, it is a positive sign that the service industries, that is banking, INGOs, and IT companies in the nation are giving importance to motivation strategies and PA practices in their organisations. However, they need to improve these processes to make them more outcome-oriented and transparent. Another finding depicted that there is statistically significant difference in perceptions of OC due to gender and current level has practical implication. The HR personnel in these organisations should first understand motivating factors for each gender (males and females) and each position/level (junior, middle, and senior) and provide appropriate motivating factors like pay packages, promotion criteria, job security, and other facilities.

Likewise, it was found significant difference in the perception of PAS due to years of service. On the basis of this finding, it would be wise to develop motivation strategies for employees according to their tenure. For example, special recognition of employees who have served the company for five years on its annual day may be considered. The implications of this study are not only limited to practice but do have a few research implications. It helps reveal the importance of IM and PAS and its relationships with POs like OC and TI in the context of three select SSOs. Further research can be suggested to measure the predictors of IM and PAS attempt to investigate the effect of PAS on other types of employee outcomes such as job satisfaction, job involvement, and employee absenteeism. PA may lead to better compensation and promotion. Therefore, future research may use both intrinsic and extrinsic motivation (promotion, rewards) as the mediating variables and/or as moderating variables. Likewise, IM itself can be examined as a moderating variable in the same study. Additional factors like organisational structure, working environment, and culture may mediate/moderate the relationship between IM/PAS and POs. The service industries need to further explore these relationships with different samples and contexts to enhance the validity and generalisability of the results. Therefore, HR department and managers from service sector industries are recommended to develop motivation strategies and enhance PA process and systems based on the above results to align with targets like high employees' OC level and minimum turnover.

REFERENCES

Abbas, M. Z. (2014). Effectiveness of performance appraisal on performance of employees. *IOSR Journal of Business and Management, 16*(6), 173–178.

Adhikari, D. R., & Gautam, D. K. (2011). Employees' commitment and organizational performance: A typological framework. *SEBON Journal, 5*(1), 1–17.

Ahmad, N., Iqbal, N., Javed, K., & Hamad, N. (2014). Impact of organizational commitment and employee performance on the employee satisfaction. *International Journal of Learning, Teaching and Educational Research, 1*(1), 84–92.

Ahmed, A., Hussain, I., Ahmed, S., & Akbar, M. F. (2010). Performance appraisal's impact on attitudinal outcomes and organisational performance. *International Journal of Business and Management, 5*(10), 62–68.

Ahmed, I., & Ahmar, N. (2010). Relationship among rewards, recognition and performance: Mediating role of intrinsic motivation. *Journal of American Science, 6*(8).

AIN. (2017). 2017 *Salary guide. Accounting and finance.* https://www.ainjobs.com/pdfs/AIN_2017_Salary_Guide.pdf

Ahmed, Z., & Shaheen, W. A. (2011). Impact of employee commitment on organizational performance. *Arabian Journal of Business and Management Review, 1*(3), 87–98.

Ali, S. B., Mahdi, A., & Malihe, J. (2012). The effect of employees' performance appraisal procedure on their intrinsic motivation. *International Journal of Academic Research in Business and Social Sciences, 2*(12), 161–168.

Allen, N. J., & Meyer, J. P. (1990). The measurement and antecedents of affective, continuance and normative commitment to the organization. *Journal of Occupational Psychology, 63*, 1–18.

Aly, M., & El-Shanawany, S. (2016). The impact of performance appraisal on employee motivation in the public sector. *International Journal of Scientific and Research Publications, 6*(5), 661–665.

Armstrong, M. (2006). *A handbook of human resource management practice* (10th ed.). Kogan Page Limited.

Arnania-Kepuladze, T. (2010). Gender stereotypes and gender feature of job motivation: Differences or similarity? *Problems and Perspectives in Management, 8*(2), 84–93.

Asiedu, R. (2017). *Impact of intrinsic motivation on health workers: A case study of Suntreso Government Hospital* (pp. 245–253) [1st international conference on competency-based training and research]. Kumasi.

Barak, M. E. M., Nissly, J. A., & Levin, A. (2001). Antecedents to retention and turnover among child welfare, social work, and other human service employees: What can we learn from past research? A review and metanalysis. *Social Service Review*, *75*(4), 625–661.

Bekele, A. Z., Shigutu, A. D., & Tensay, A. T. (2014). The effect of employees' perception of performance appraisal on their work outcomes. *International Journal of Management and Commerce Innovations*, *2*(1), 136–173.

Bhattarai, G. (2014). Role of intrinsic motivation in the relationship between performance appraisal satisfaction and employee outcomes [Unpublished report].

Biswakarma, G. (2016). Organizational career growth and employees turnover intentions: An empirical evidence from private commercial banks. *International Academic Journal of Organizational Behavior and Human Resource Management*, *3*(2), 10–26.

Boxall, P., Macky, K., & Rasmussen, E. (2003). Labour turnover and retention in New Zealand: The causes and consequences of leaving and staying with employers. *Asia Pacific Journal of Human Resources*, *41*(2), 195–214.

Choong, Y.-O., Wong, K. L., & Lau, T.-C. (2011). Intrinsic motivation and organizational commitment in the Malaysian private higher education institutions: An empirical study. *Journal of Arts, Science & Commerce*, *2*(4), 91–100 & 40–50.

Comerion, P., & Pierce, J. L. (1994). The moderating effect of supervisory involvement on appraisal reactions. *Journal of Occupational and Organizational Psychology*, *67*(3), 223–234.

Cotton, J. L., & Tuttle, J. M. (1986). Employee turnover: A meta-analysis and review with implications for research. *Academy of Management Review*, *11*(1), 55–70.

Dail, L. F. (2002). *Taking the measure of work*. Sage Publications India Pvt. Ltd.

Danish, R. Q., Ramzan, S., & Ahmad, F. (2015). Effect of formalization on organizational commitment; interactional role of self-monitoring in the service sector. *American Journal of Economics, Finance and Management*, *1*(4), 229–235.

Fakhimi, F., & Raisy, A. (2013). Satisfaction with performance appraisal from the employees' perspective and its behavioral outcomes (case study of headquarters offices of Bank Refah). *European Online Journal of Natural and Social Sciences*, *2*(3), 296–305.

Farwa, U.-e., & Niazi, G. (2013). Impact of intrinsic motivation on organizational commitment: An Islamic banking perspective. *Journal of Asian Development Studies*, *2*(2), 85–94.

Fletcher, C. (2001). Performance appraisal and management: The developing research agenda. *Journal of Occupational and Organizational Psychology*, *74*(4), 473–487.

Ganesan, S., & Weitz, B. (1996). The impact of staffing policies on retail buyer job attitudes and behavior. *Journal of Retailing*, *72*, 31–56.

Gautam, P. K., & Adhikari, N. (2016). Gender differences on employee motivation and job involvement with job rotation practices. *Journal of Interdisciplinary Studies*, *2*(1), 46–59.

Hepner, H. W. (1930). Factors affecting employee morale. *The Personnel Journal*, *8*(6), 435–446.

Hung, C., & Wu, J. (2016). The impact of position difference on employees organizational commitment after the merger of life insurance companies. *Merging Markets Finance and Trade*, *52*(4), 843–852. https://doi.org/10.1080/1540496X.2015.1117870

Ismail, H. N., & Gali, N. (2016). Relationships among performance appraisal satisfaction, work–family conflict and job stress. *Journal of Management and Organization*, *22*(6), 1–17. https://doi.org/10.1017/jmo.2016.15

Jeswani, S. (2016). Do intrinsic motivations influence turnover intention? Structural equation modeling approach among technical faculty members. *International Journal of Business and General Management*, *7*(4), 1–20.

Jusoff, K., Jiri, M., Khan, A., & Samah, B. A. (2009). Factors influencing performance appraisal system: A case study of the Malaysian armed forces. *Journal of Politics and Law*, *2*(1), 45.

Katavich, K. M. (2013). *The importance of employee satisfaction with performance appraisal systems*. At Massey University.

Keeping, L. M., & Levy, P. E. (2000). Performance appraisal reactions: Measurement, modeling, and method bias. *Journal of Applied Psychology*, *85*(5), 708.

Khan, A., Khan, I., Ahmed, S., & Zakirullah, Z. (2009). Relationship between employee's motivation and turnover intention: Empirical study of traffic police of district Charsadda. *Sarhad Journal of Management Sciences*, *2*(2), 113–127.

Kokubun, K. (2017). The moderating effect of gender on the organizational commitment-rewards relationship. *International Journal of Business and Management, 12*(7), 1–16.

Kuvaas, B. (2006). Performance appraisal satisfaction and employee outcomes: Mediating and moderating roles of work motivation. *The International Journal of Human Resource Management, 17*(3), 504–522.

Lee, C. H., & Chen, C. J. (2013). The relationship between employee commitment and job performance: A review and research agenda. *Social Behavior and Personality: An International Journal, 41*(3), 443–458.

Lincoln, J. R., & Kalleberg, A. L. (1990). *Culture, control, and commitment: A study of work organization and work attitudes in the United States and Japan.* Cambridge University Press.

Malik, M. S., & Aslam, S. (2013). Performance appraisal and employee's motivation: A comparative analysis of telecom industry of Pakistan. *Pakistan Journal of Social Sciences (PJSS), 33*(1), 179–189.

Marquardt, M. J. (2004). *Optimizing the power of action learning.* Soundview Executive Book Summaries.

Marsden, P. V., Kalleberg, A. L., & Cook, C. R. (1993). Gender differences in organizational commitment: Influences of work positions and family roles. *Work and Occupations, 20*(3), 368–390.

Matsunaga, M. (2010). How to factor-analyze your data right: Do's, don'ts, and how-to's. *International Journal of Psychological Research, 3*(1), 97–110.

Meyer, J. P., Allen, N. J., & Topolnytsky, L. (2002). Affective, continuance, and normative commitment to the organization: A meta-analysis of antecedents, correlates, and consequences. *Journal of Vocational Behavior, 61*(1), 20–52. https://doi.org/10.1006/jvbe.2001.1842

Meyer, J. P., & Smith, C. A. (2000). HRM practices and organizational commitment: Test of a mediation model. *Canadian Journal of Administrative Sciences, 17*(4), 319–331. https://doi.org/10.1111/j.1936-4490.2000.tb00231.x

Mowday, R. T., Steers, R. M., & Porter, L. W. (1979). The measurement of organizational commitment. *Journal of Vocational Behavior, 14*, 224–247.

Mowdray, R. W. (1992). *Human resource management.* Dryden Press.

Porter, L. W., & Lawler, E. E. (1968). *Managerial attitudes and performance.* R. D. Irwin.

Rajendran, V. (2005). *The relationship between performance appraisal satisfaction and employee outcomes: A study conducted in Peninsular Malaysia.* University of Malaya.

Roberts, G., & Reed, T. (1996). Performance appraisal participation, goal setting and feedback. *Review of Public Personnel Administration, 16*, 29–60.

Ryan, R. M., & Deci, E. L. (2000). Intrinsic and extrinsic motivations: Classic definitions and new directions. *Contemporary Educational Psychology, 25*, 54–67. https://doi.org/10.1006/ceps.1999.1020

Saeed, R., Mussawar, S., Lodhi, R. N., Iqbal, A., Nayab, H. H., & Yaseen, S. (2014). Factors affecting the performance of employees at work place in the banking sector of Pakistan. *International Journal of Human Resource Studies, 4*(2), 192–202.

Sajjad, A., Ghazanfar, H., & Ramzan, M. (2013). Impact of motivation on employee turnover in telecom sector of Pakistan. *Journal of Business Studies Quarterly, 5*(1), 76–92.

Saleem, H., & Shah, F. M. (2015). Impact of performance appraisal on job satisfaction in banking sector of Pakistan. *International Journal of Management Sciences and Business Research, 4*(10), 74–82.

Saxena, N., & Rai, H. (2015). Impact of performance appraisal on organizational commitment & job satisfaction. *International Journal of Engineering and Management Sciences, 6*(2), 95–104.

Shrestha, I. (2015). Organizational commitment of female employees of financial institutions. *The Journal of Business Studies, IX*(1), 126–136.

Singh, R., & Mohanty, R. (2011). Performance appraisal satisfaction and OC: Moderating roles of employees' cultural values. *International Journal of Indian Culture and Business Management, 4*(3), 272–297.

Singh, S. P., & Rana, S. (2015). The impact of performance appraisal on organizational commitment of bank employees. *International Journal of Science and Research (IJSR), 4*(4), 2964–2967.

Staw, B. M. (1980). The consequences of turnover. *Journal of Occupational Behavior, 1*, 253–273.

Sturman, M. C. (2003). *Searching for the inverted U-shaped relationship between time and performance: Meta-analyses of the experience/performance, tenure/performance, and age/performance relationships.* School of Hotel Administration Collection.

Thomas, K. W. (1990). Intrinsic motivation and how it works. *Training & Development Journal, 44*(8)

Tiraieyari, N., & Uli, J. (2011). Moderating effects of employee gender and organizational tenure in competency-performance relationships. *African Journal of Business Management, 5*(33), 12898–12903. https://doi.org/10.5897/AJBM11.2399

Ufuophu-Biri, E., & Iwu, C. G. (2014). Job motivation, job performance and gender relations in the broadcast sector in Nigeria. *Mediterranean Journal of Social Sciences, 5*(16), 191–196. https://doi.org/10.5901/mjss.2014.v5n16p191

Vance, C. M., McClaine, S. R., Boje, D. M., & Stage, H. D. (1992). An examination of the transferability of traditional performance appraisal principles across cultural boundaries. *Management International Review, 32*(4), 313–326.

Vignaswaran, R. (2005). *Performance appraisal satisfaction: A study among employees in automobile component manufacturing units in India.* Sudha Publications.

Vigoda, E. (2000). Organizational politics, job attitudes, and work outcomes: Exploration and implications for the public sector. *Journal of Vocational Behavior, 57*, 326–347. https://doi.org/10.1006/jvbe.1999.1742

Vroom, V. H. (1964). *Work and motivation.* John Wiley & Sons.

Wright, T. A., & Bonett, D. G. (2007). Job satisfaction and psychological well-being as nonadditive predictors of workplace turnover. *Journal of Management, 33*(2), 141–160. https://doi.org/10.1177/0149206306297582

Wu, X. (2012). *Factors influencing employee turnover intention: The case of retail industry in Bangkok, Thailand* [Unpublished MBA Thesis]. University of the Thai Chamber of Commerce.

Yundong, H. (2015). Impact of intrinsic motivation on OC: Empirical evidences from China. *International Business and Management, 11*(3), 31–44. https://doi.org/10.3968/7723

Zadeh, A. A., Moradi, J., & Veisi, K. (2016). The relationship between intrinsic motivation and organizational commitment among physical education teachers of Sanandaj City. *International Journal of Life Science and Pharma Research, 2*, 49–55.

CHAPTER 8

ANALYSIS OF INTELLECTUAL CAPITAL AND FINANCIAL PERFORMANCE OF TEXTILE AND GARMENT INDUSTRIES IN INDONESIA

Ratu Shavira[a], Niki Lukviarman[a] and Erna Setiany[b]

[a]Faculty of Economics and Business, Andalas University, Padang, Indonesia
[b]Faculty of Economics and Business, Universitas Mercu Buana, Jakarta, Indonesia

ABSTRACT

This study investigates the influence of intellectual capital on the financial performance of textile and garment companies in Indonesia. In this study, three proxied of value-added intellectual capital are used to represent intellectual capital: value-added human capital (VAHU), value-added structural capital, and value-added capital employed (VACA). The sample consists of 72 firm years of textile and garment companies publicly traded on the Indonesian Stock Exchange between 2016 and 2019 and was chosen using a purposive sampling method that fit the study's requirements utilising panel data analysis. In this study, multiple regression analysis was used to test the hypothesis. According to the study, not all proxies of intellectual capital have an impact on a company's financial performance. Return on assets (ROA) is influenced by VAHU, while asset turnover and ROA are only affected by VACA. Structural capital value-added has no impact on any financial performance measurements. In this analysis, physical capital was the most important element impacting financial performance.

The Finance-Innovation Nexus: Implications for Socio-Economic Development
International Symposia in Economic Theory and Econometrics, Volume 34, 121–131
Copyright © 2025 by Emerald Publishing Limited
All rights of reproduction in any form reserved
ISSN: 1571-0386/doi:10.1108/S1571-038620240000034009

Since intellectual capital has a significant impact on financial success as measured by profitability ROA, it has a considerable relationship with ROA.

Keywords: Intellectual capital; financial performance; value-added human capital; structural capital value-added; value-added capital employed

JEL Codes: O11; Q01; Q5

INTRODUCTION

The development of technological innovation and increasing business competition made companies aware that they needed innovation capabilities, information, and knowledge of human resources to compete. So the company is forced to change its business strategies (Komnenic & Pokrajčić, 2012). Many organisations that are reviewing their organisational structures and internal processes under the banner of agile transformation are confused because they lack experience in this area and do not know how to proceed or which aspects of their existing governance and operations need to be reviewed (Nakano & Oura, 2022). Organisational agility is the capacity to adapt to unanticipated environmental changes, it enables businesses to achieve and maintain competitive advantage in a dynamic and demanding business environment (Tibon, 2022).

A labour-intensive industry was forced to survive in market competition (Bontis et al., 1999), so the executives must develop strategies for managing physical and financial assets and pay more attention to the intangible assets contained in the company. Barney (1991) explains that intangible assets have valuable properties, are difficult to imitate, rare, and difficult to substitute, and can be used as strategic assets that provide a competitive advantage. One example of asset intangibility is the knowledge and competencies possessed by employees. One approach in this knowledge asset is intellectual capital. In practice, if a company refers to business based on knowledge, companies in Indonesia can compete by using the competitive advantage obtained through creative innovation generated by the intellectual capital owned by the company.

In general, intellectual capital is defined as an intangible asset that significantly impacts a company's overall performance and success even though it is not explicitly presented in the balance sheet (Ghosh & Mondal, 2009; Joshi et al., 2013), however. There is no mutual agreement regarding the definition of intellectual capital because each study has a different definition (Ghosh & Mondal, 2009). The company's awareness of the importance of intellectual capital is the company's foundation to be superior and competitive, providing added value for the company (Solikhah et al., 2010). With the existence of intellectuals as an added value in the company, intellectuals influence the company's financial performance. In the forecasting process involving multiple future possibilities, many computations rely on assumptions to indicate items associated with the probability of the future (Nursaadah & Faturohman, 2022). One of them is profitability and efficiency. Profitability relates to the company's efforts to maintain the company in the future. High profitability reflects a good company's financial performance.

Companies use intellectual capital to maintain and increase profitability by utilising the company's resources efficiently and adequately. Efficiency concerning the company's efforts to maintain its performance is reflected in its efficiency in managing its assets, which is still related to intellectual capital.

A previous study has revealed that intellectual capital has an inconsistent impact on a company's financial performance (Chowdhury et al., 2018). Chu et al. (2011), Firer and Williams (2003), Wahyuni and Utami (2018), and Setiany et al. (2020) discovered that intellectual capital has a beneficial effect on the financial performance of a corporation. According to studies, only human capital indicators on intellectual capital have an impact on return on assets (ROA), return on equity (ROE), and asset turnover (ATO) (Komnenic & Pokrajčić, 2012). Meanwhile, intellectual capital has an impact on corporate productivity as measured by ATO, has an impact on firm profitability as measured by ROE, but has no impact on ROA, according to Chowdhury et al. (2018). This research contradicts Solikhah et al. (2010), who found no evidence of intellectual capital having a positive impact on corporate value. Chu et al. (2011) studied at how intellectual capital affected MBV (market to book value), ROA (return on asset), ROE (return on equity), and ATO (asset turnover). It shows that all financial performance measures have a negative relationship with human capital indices. Human capital has a negative influence on financial performance as measured by ROA and Tobin's Q, according to Solechan (2017), while structural capital has a negative impact on EPS, ROA, and Tobin's Q.

LITERATURE REVIEW AND HYPOTHESIS FORMULATION

Resource-Based Theory

Penrose initiated the argument in 1955 that a company is a collection of productive resources whose development varies according to the decisions of the managerial party in the company. RBT is a theory which states that company resources are heterogeneous and provide a unique character for each company (Kor & Mahoney, 2000). Resources must have value-adding properties, are scarce, difficult to imitate, and cannot replace other resources to obtain and survive competitive advantages. The resource-based theory considers that companies' economic value and advantages in competing for lie in the ownership of these resources and how effective is the use of these resources (Barney, 1991).

Stakeholders Theory

Stakeholders are groups or individuals identified as influencing or influencing the achievement of organisational goals (Freeman & Reed, 1983). According to stakeholder theory, maintaining relationships with stakeholders encompasses all types of business partnerships. Stakeholder theory states that all components of the stakeholder have the right to be appropriately treated in the context of value-added intellectual capital (VAIC), a technique for measuring intellectual capital. The organisation must be managed for the advantage of these stakeholders. To create value, this management makes full use of the company's potential in the form of personnel (human capital), physical assets, and structural capital. An increase in assets, followed by an increase in operating outcomes, increases the trust of outsiders, such as creditors and investors, in a company (Sanil et al., 2018; Suhendra, 2014). The company's financial performance will improve as its value-added increases. The company's growth will be improved, resulting in an increase in the company's worth in the eyes of stakeholders.

Financial Performance

According to Ulum et al. (2008), performance can be defined as a company's achievement over a period of time that represents the company's health. Meanwhile, financial performance refers to a company's financial position as assessed and examined through financial ratios. Financial performance is one of the company's methods for meeting its obligations to investors and achieving its objectives. Financial ratios, according to Brealey et al. (2008), are a company's financial analysis tool for analysing financial data contained in the company's financial statements to measure a company's performance. There are four categories of financial ratios, according to Brealey et al. (2008): leverage ratios, liquidity ratios, efficiency ratios, and profitability ratios.

The financial performance of the organisation is measured using profitability and efficiency ratios in this study. The profitability ratio is a metric used to evaluate a company's capacity to profit from its operations (Kasmir, 2011). The efficiency ratio, on the other hand, is a financial ratio study that determines how well organisations use their assets to generate profits (Brealey et al., 2008).

Intellectual Capital

Various groups have interpreted intellectual capital in different ways. There is no formal definition of intellectual capital because there is no standard assessment method. Still, according to Stewart (1997) (in Marr et al., 2004), intellectual capital is a resource owned in the form of knowledge supported by an information process to develop relationships with outsiders to produce high-value economic benefits for the organisation in the future. Intellectual capital is a notion that refers to non-physical capital or intangible assets that are linked to human knowledge and experience, as well as the technology used. According to Bontis et al. (1999), intellectual capital is divided into three indicators: human capital, structural capital, and customer capital, all of which contribute value to the organisation and provide it with a competitive edge.

Value-Added Intellectual Capital

The VAIC method was created by Pulic (2000) to offer information on the value generation efficiency of assets possessed by businesses, both tangible and intangible assets. The ability of the company to develop value-added products is the starting point for this strategy (VA). The most objective indication of corporate performance is value-added, which demonstrates a company's ability to produce value (Pulic, 2000; Puntilo, 2009). The difference between output (revenue, which includes all items and services sold to the market) and input is used to calculate the VA (all expenses used to get revenue-exempt employee expenses). Pulic (2000) invented VAIC, which consists of three basic indicators:

a. *Human capital efficiency (HCE) or value-added human capital (VAHU)*. HCE is a measure of how much value is added to human capital. This relationship demonstrates human capital's ability to add value to the firm. HCE is defined as a company's ability to generate additional value for every dollar spent on human capital, or how much additional value is added by labour (Ulum et al., 2008). HCE is a critical metric for organisations that can add value. Human capital is a resource that is responsible for a company's success in attaining its goals by employing a workforce with the necessary knowledge, expertise, and abilities so that the company can profit from it. As a result of the evidence indicating that HCE has an impact on the company's financial success, the hypothesis can be stated as follows:

H1. There is a positive influence between HCE on financial performance.

b. *Structural capital value-added (STVA) or structural capital efficiency (SCE)*. SCE is an indicator of the ratio of structural capital to value-added. This ratio measures the amount of structural capital needed to make money from value-added and indicates how successful structural capital is in value creation (Tan et al., 2007). Companies with a good and robust structural capital can support the work sauna, encourage employees to work better, and increase company profitability and productivity (Zeghal & Maaloul, 2010). Human resources and infrastructure suitable for high efficiency and technology transfer are the most crucial aspects. As long as there are sufficient human resources, it is possible to create structural cutting-edge technology (Nguyen et al., 2022). Based on this, the following hypothesis can be drawn:

H2. There is a positive influence between SCE on financial performance.

c. *Value-added capital employed (VACA) or capital employed efficiency (CEE)*. It is the indicator ratio of value-added to capital employed. CEE describes how much value the company adds is generated from the capital used and is an indicator of the company's better utilise physical capital (Kuryanto & Syafaruddin, 2008). Pulic (2000) assumes that companies that use capital employed well and efficiently will produce a greater return from the capital employed unit than other companies. So it can be concluded that using good and efficient capital employed will improve a company's financial performance. Based on this, the hypothesis can be taken as follows:

H3. There is a positive influence between CEE on financial performance.

METHODS

The population used in this study were companies operating in the textile and garment industries listed on the Indonesia Stock Exchange for 2016–2019 consisting of 21 companies. Based on the sample criteria, the total number of companies that match the criteria is 18 out of 21 companies with a total of 72 observations. The dependent variable in this research is financial performance as measured by ROA, ROE, and ATO. Meanwhile, the independent variable consists of three VAIC indicators based on Pulic (2000), Puntilo (2009), and Ulum et al. (2008) as follows:

$$VAIC = HCE + SCE + CEE \tag{1}$$

The calculation phase of each VAIC indicator is as follows:

$$HCE = VA/HC \tag{2}$$

$$VA = OUT - IN \tag{3}$$

where
HCE = human capital efficiency (ratio of VA to HC)
VA = value-added
HC = human capital (measured by total employee salaries)
OUT = output (measured by total revenue)
IN = input (measured by total operating costs excluding salaries and employee benefits)

$$SCE = SC/VA \tag{4}$$

$$SC = VA - HC \tag{5}$$

where
SCE = structural capital efficiency
SC = structural capital
VA = value-added
HC = human capital (measured by total employee salaries)

$$CEE = VA/CE \tag{6}$$

$$CE = TA - CL \tag{7}$$

where
CEE = capital employed efficiency
VA = value-added
CE = capital employed
TA = total asset
CL = current liabilities.

Hypothesis testing is done by using multiple linear regression analysis with the following equations:

$$ATO_{it} = \alpha_0 + \beta_1 HCE_t + \beta_2 SCE_{it} + \beta_3 CEE_{it} + \beta_4 LEV_{it} + \beta_5 SIZE_{it} + \varepsilon_{it} \tag{8}$$

$$ROA_{it} = \alpha_0 + \beta_1 HCE_{it} + \beta_2 SCE_{it} + \beta_{55} SIZE + {}_{2\beta4e} LEV_{it} \tag{9}$$

$$ROE_{it} = \alpha_0 + \beta_1 HCE_{it} + \beta_2 SCE_{it} + \beta_3 CEE_{it} + \beta_4 LEV_{it} + \beta_5 SIZE_{it} + \varepsilon_{it} \tag{10}$$

where

α = constant

β = coefficient

ATO = assets turnover, measured by proportion of net sales divided to the total assets

ROA = return on assets, measured by the proportion of total assets

ROE = return on equities, measured by the proportion of earnings before income and tax to equity

CEE = capital employed efficiency

HCE = human capital efficiency

SCE = structural capital efficiency

LEV = leverage, measured by debt-equity-ratio

SIZE = company size, measured by the natural log of the total asset

ε = error

RESULTS AND DISCUSSION

Analysis of Variable Descriptions

Table 8.1 shows the descriptive statistics.

Regression Results

Table 8.2 shows the calculated F value obtained by all three equations. p-values are significantly below 0.05. This result means that all equations are fit, and the independent variable fits to predict the dependent variable. Table 8.3 shows the multiple linear regression results of all three equations.

Table 8.1. Descriptive Statistics.

Variables	Minimum	Maximum	Mean	Std. Deviation
HCE	−13.606	20.917	2.60397	6.287578
SCE	−4.834	135.784	2.57902	15.965269
CEE	−.681	0.944	0.10919	0.231859
LEV	−166.749	31.224	−2.56249	26.082144
SIZE	26.684	30.726	28.19922	1.66686
ATO	0.017	0.809	0.94874	0.790494
ROA	−0.223	0.207	−0.00887	0.074075
ROE	−3.189	1.621	−0.02710	0.527566
SALE	20.184	23.231	22.12322	1.71686

Table 8.2. Goodness of Fit Results.

Regression	R Equation	R Square	Adjusted R Square	Std. Error of the Estimate	F	Sig
1	0.594 [a]	0.373	0.299	0.665521	6.831	0.000 [b]
2	0.761 [a]	0.582	0.542	0.050559	17.324	0.000 [b]
3	0.522 [a]	0.182	0.112	0.498505	2.800	0.029 [b]

Table 8.3. Regression Results.

Regression Equation	Unstandardised Coefficients		Standardised Coefficient	t	Sig.
	B	Std. Error	Beta		
Regression coefficient 1 (constant)	−6.120	1.719		−2.145	0.002
HCE	0.017	0.015	0.132	1.086	0.282
SCE	0.001	0.005	0.021	0.209	0.835
CEE	1.062	0.412	0.311	2.577	0.012
LEV	−0.001	0.003	−0.032	−0.312	0.756
SIZE	0.228	0.070	0.366	3.538	0.001
SALE	0.148	0.034	0.321	3.132	0.001
2 (constant)	−0.368	0.210		−1.1422	0.061
HCE	0.005	0.001	0.433	4.399	0.000
SCE	0.000	0.000	0.073	0.890	0.377
CEE	0.121	0.031	0.379	3.868	0.000
LEV	−3.045E-5	0.000	−0.011	−0.131	0.896
SIZE	0.008	0.005	0.132	1.287	0.082
SALE	0.007	0.005	0.114	1.913	0.094
3 (constant)	−0.141	1.423		−1.062	0.548
HCE	0.007	0.011	0.086	0.633	0.529
SCE	0.000	0.004	0.011	0.101	0.920
CEE	0.309	0.309	0.136	1.001	0.321
LEV	0.007	0.002	0.360	3.176	0.002
SIZE	0.002	0.052	0.006	0.056	0.956
SALE	0.001	0.011	0.001	0.016	0.556

where:

Equation 1: $ATO_{it} = \alpha_0 + \beta_1 HCE_t + \beta_2 SCE_{it} + \beta_3 CEE_{it} + \beta_4 LEV_{it} + \beta_5 SIZE_{it} + \beta_5 SALE_{it} + \varepsilon_{it}$

Equation 2: $ROA_{it} = \alpha_0 + \beta_1 HCE_{it} + \beta_2 SCE_{it} + \beta_3 SIZE + \beta_{4c} LEV_{it} + \beta_5 SALE_{it}$

Equation 3: $ROE_{it} = \alpha_0 + \beta_1 HCE_{it} + \beta_2 SCE_{it} + \beta_3 CEE_{it} + \beta_4 LEV_{it} + \beta_5 SIZE_{it} + \beta_6 SALE_{it} + \varepsilon_{it}$

Note: Significant levels at *10%, **5%, and ***1%, respectively.

THE INFLUENCE BETWEEN HCE ON FINANCIAL PERFORMANCE

Human capital refers to a company's ability to develop solutions based on the knowledge held by its employees. The regression results indicate that HCE has no significant impact on ATO, according to the regression results in Table 8.3 in hypothesis testing with the t-statistical test, with a p-value of 0.282, which is higher than 0.05. The findings of this study are consistent with Chowdhury et al. (2018) research. The study showed significant findings on the impact of HCE on ROA, as indicated by a p-value of 0.000, which is below the threshold of 0.05. This suggests that HCE had a positive effect on ROA. This finding corroborates the findings of Chen et al. (2005) and Komnenic and Pokrajčić (2012). However, the p-value of 0.529 for the HCE effect on ROE is greater than 0.05, suggesting that HCE does not have a significant impact on ROE. These results align with the findings of Chowdhury et al. (2018).

THE INFLUENCE BETWEEN SCE ON FINANCIAL PERFORMANCE

A high SCE number implies that the organisation can complete all routine corporate processes and that the company structure supports employees' efforts to get the best possible results. SCE does not affect the overall financial performance measures of ATO, ROA, and ROE, according to the p-value of SCE on financial performance. The results reveal that the p-value for all three SCE effects on ATO, ROA, and ROE equations is higher than the 0.05 error limit. Celenza and Rossi (2014), Chen et al. (2005), Chowdhury et al. (2018), and Firer and Williams (2003) all found similar results (Komnenic & Pokrajčić 2012). As a result, it can be inferred that the company has not fully utilised its structural capital and, hence, has not benefited from competitive advantages.

THE INFLUENCE BETWEEN CEE ON FINANCIAL PERFORMANCE

CEE is a term that explains how businesses manage their physical and financial capital. The higher the CEE value, the better managed intellectual capital is, and the more likely it is to influence financial performance. According to the results, CEE has a beneficial influence on ATO and ROA, with a p-value less than 0.05. Chen et al. (2005), Chowdhury et al. (2018), Chu et al. (2011), Komnenic and Pokrajčić (2012), and Ulum et al. (2008) have all undertaken research in this area. On the other hand, the CEE does not affect ROE when the p-value is greater than 0.05 (i.e., p-value 0.321). The findings are linked to the resource-based theory, which states that a company's resources are made up of physical, human, and organisational resources that contribute value to the company's productivity and profitability.

DISCUSSION, CONCLUSIONS, AND LIMITATIONS

This research aims to find out how intellectual capital affects a company's bottom line. The findings reveal that the HCE results have no apparent impact on firm productivity as assessed by ATO. There is no influence on ROE, but it does have a considerable impact on ROA. In SCE, no effect on all financial performance measures was discovered. In the meantime, the CEE has a significant impact on ATO and ROA but no impact on ROE.

The findings of this study back up those of Firer and Williams (2003), who discovered that not all aspects of intellectual capital are related to financial success metrics. While other financial performance does affect by intellectual capital, intellectual capital has a substantial impact on financial performance as measured by profitability ROA. This finding suggests that only capital- employed efficiency has an impact on financial KPIs like ROA and ATO. Physical capital is also found to be the most crucial factor influencing financial performance, and intellectual capital has a strong link to ROA. According to Chowdhury et al. (2018), Dzenopoljac et al. (2017), and Firer and Williams (2003), intellectual capital has only a financial impact on a company's performance.

ACKNOWLEDGEMENT

The authors acknowledge the full financial support from GRP Strategic in this research.

REFERENCES

Barney, J. (1991). Firm resources and sustained competitive advantage. *Journal of Management, 17*(1), 99–120. https://doi.org/10.1177/014920639101700108

Bontis, N., Dragonneti, N. C., Jacobson, K., & Roos, G. (1999). The knowledge toolbox: A review of the tools to measure and manage intangible resources. *European Management Journal, 17*(4), 391–402. https://doi.org/10.1016/S0263-2373(99)00019-5

Brealey, R. A., Myers, S. C., & Marcus, A. J. (2008). *Fundamentals of corporate finance* (3rd ed.). McGraw-Hill. https://doi.org/10.1017/CBO9781107415324.004

Celenza, D., & Rossi, F. (2014). Intellectual capital and performance of listed companies: Empirical evidence from Italy. *Measuring Business Excellence, 18*(1), 22–35. https://doi.org/10.1108/MBE-10-2013-0054

Chen, M. C., Cheng, S. J., & Hwang, Y. (2005). An empirical investigation of the relationship between intellectual capital and firms' market value and financial performance. *Journal of Intellectual Capital, 6*(2), 159–176. https://doi.org/10.1108/14691930510592771

Chowdhury, L. A. M., Rana, T., Akter, M., & Hoque, M. (2018). Impact of intellectual capital on financial performance: Evidence from the Bangladeshi textile sector. *Journal of Accounting and Organizational Change, 14*(4), 429–454. https://doi.org/10.1108/JAOC-11-2017-0109

Chu, S. K. W., Chan, K. H., Yu, K. Y., Ng, H. T., & Wong, W. K. (2011). An empirical study of the impact of intellectual capital on business performance. *Journal of Information and Knowledge Management, 10*(1), 11–21. https://doi.org/10.1142/S0219649211002791

Dzenopoljac, V., Yaacoub, C., Elkanj, N., & Bontis, N. (2017). Impact of intellectual capital on corporate performance: Evidence from the Arab region. *Journal of Intellectual Capital, 18*(4), 884–903. https://doi.org/10.1108/JIC-01-2017-0014

Firer, S., & Williams, S. M. (2003). Intellectual capital and traditional measures of corporate performance. *Journal of Intellectual Capital, 4*(3), 348–360. https://doi.org/10.1108/14691930310487806

Freeman, R. E., & Reed, D. L. (1983). Stockholders and stakeholders: A new perspective on corporate governance. *California Management Review, 25*(3), 88–106. https://doi.org/10.5897/ajmr2014.7057

Ghosh, S., & Mondal, A. (2009). Indian software and pharmaceutical sector IC and financial performance. *Journal of Intellectual Capital, 10*(3), 369–388. https://doi.org/10.1108/14691930910977798

Joshi, M., Cahill, D., Sidhu, J., & Kansal, M. (2013). Intellectual capital and financial performance: An evaluation of the Australian financial sector. *Journal of Intellectual Capital, 14*(2), 264–285. https://doi.org/10.1108/14691931311323887

Kasmir. (2011). *Analisis Laporan Keuangan*. PT Raja Grafindo Persada.

Komnenic, B., & Pokrajčić, D. (2012). Intellectual capital and corporate performance of MNCs in Serbia. *Journal of Intellectual Capital, 13*(1), 106–119. https://doi.org/10.1108/14691931211196231

Kor, Y. Y., & Mahoney, J. T. (2000). Penrose's resource-based approach: The process and product of research creativity. *Journal of Management Studies, 37*(1), 109–139. https://doi.org/10.1111/1467-6486.00174

Kuryanto, B., & Syafaruddin, M. (2008). The effect of intellectual capital on company performance. *Simposium Nasional Akuntansi, 11* (SNA 11). https://doi.org/10.1136/jmg.6.3.347

Marr, B., Schiuma, G., & Neely, A. (2004). Intellectual capital – Defining key performance indicators for organizational knowledge assets. *Business Process Management Journal, 10*(5), 551–569. https://doi.org/10.1108/14637150410559225

Nakano, Y., & Oura, F. (2022). A proposal of efficient agile implementation process model to enterprise organization by involving indirect departments. *Review of Integrative Business and Economics Research, 11*, 111–124.

Nguyen, P., Pham, T., Trieu, H., Lam, L., & Tran, K. (2022). Opportunities and challenges for developing a sustainable software city: Lessons from Quang Trung Software City in Vietnam. *Review of Integrative Business and Economics Research, 11*(3), 38-60.

Nursaadah, M., & Faturohman, T. (2022). The application of risk-based new venture technique for startup valuation (Case Study: Vee Naturals). *Review of Integrative Business and Economics Research, 11*, 166–183.

Pulic, A. (2000). VAICTM – An accounting tool for intellectual capital management. *International Journal Technology Management, 20*(5/6/7/8), 702–714.

Puntilo, P. (2009). Intellectual capital and business performance: Evidence from Italian banking industry. *Journal of Corporate Finance, 12*(4), 97–115.

Sanil, H. S., Noraidi, A. A. A. bin, & Ramakrishnan, S. (2018). The impact of different firm sizes on capital structure determinants among listed consumer product firms in Malaysia. *Journal of Economic Info, 5*(2), 1–6. https://doi.org/10.31580/jei.v5i2.104

Setiany, E., Syamsudin, S., Sundawini, A., & Putra, Y. M. (2020). Ownership structure and firm value: The mediating effect of intellectual capital. *International Journal of Innovation, Creativity, and Change, 13*(10), 1697–1711.

Solechan, A. (2017). The effect of intellectual capital efficiency on the financial performance of companies in Indonesia. *Jurnal Kajian Akuntansi, 1*, 87–100.

Solikhah, B., Abdul Rohman, H., & Meiranto, W. (2010). Implications of intellectual capital on financial performance, growth, and market value; empirical studies with a simplistic specification approach. *Makalah Simposium Nasional Akuntansi XIII Purwokerto*, pp. 1–29. https://doi.org/10.1017/CBO9781107415324.004

Stewart, T. A. (1997). *Intellectual capital: The new wealth of organizations*. Doubleday.

Suhendra, E. S. (2014). Factors impacting capital structure in Indonesian food and beverage companies. *International Conference on Eurasian Economies*, 75–82. https://doi.org/10.36880/c05.00896

Tan, H. P., Plowman, D., & Hancock, P. (2007). Intellectual capital and financial returns of companies. *Journal of Intellectual Capital, 8*(1), 76–95. https://doi.org/10.1108/14691930710715079

Tibon, M. V. P. (2022). Organizational agility among selected SMEs in the Philippines during the Covid-19 Pandemic: Genesis and implications. *Review of Integrative Business and Economics Research, 11*, 253–259.

Ulum, I., Ghozali, I., & Chariri, A. (2008). Intellectual capital and financial performance of the company; an analysis with partial least squares approach. *Simposium Nasional Akuntansi XI, 19*(19), 23–24.

Wahyuni, P. D., & Utami, W. (2018). Pengaruh good corporate governance dan intellectual capital disclosure terhadap cost of equity capital. *Profita: Komunikasi Ilmiah dan Perpajakan, 11*(3), 359–383.

Zeghal, D., & Maaloul, A. (2010). Analyzing value-added as an indicator of intellectual capital and its consequences on company performance. *Journal of Intellectual Capital, 11*(1), 39–60. https://doi.org/10.1108/14691931011013325

CHAPTER 9

DOES THE COVID-19 PANDEMIC AFFECT THE CAPITAL STRUCTURE OF STEEL COMPANIES IN INDONESIA?

Ayudya Puti Ramadhanty and Taufik Faturohman

School of Business and Management, Bandung Institute of Technology, Indonesia

ABSTRACT

The COVID-19 pandemic hit the demand for steel products and their derivatives by 40–50%. As a result, productivity and factory operations will inevitably suffer. Therefore, when fulfilling funding demands that will arise if the company has an appropriate capital structure, the corporation must choose between rising debt (on the liability side) or issuing shares for external funding as viable financial alternatives. This empirical study examines the effects of the COVID-19 pandemic on capital structure before and during the pandemic. This study implemented a descriptive quantitative approach, measured using a method based on panel regression and system Generalised Method of Moments (GMM) using the secondary data quarterly from 2018 to 2021 with the samples of eight steel companies listed on the IDX. The study findings show that COVID-19 influences the capital structure; firm-specific variables like COVID-19 profitability positively affect the capital structure, whereas liquidity, earning volatility, and non-debt tax shield negatively affect the capital structure. Meanwhile, the result of system GMM shows that only COVID-19 and liquidity significantly affect the debt ratio.

The Finance-Innovation Nexus: Implications for Socio-Economic Development
International Symposia in Economic Theory and Econometrics, Volume 34, 133–145
Copyright © 2025 by Emerald Publishing Limited
All rights of reproduction in any form reserved
ISSN: 1571-0386/doi:10.1108/S1571-038620240000034011

Keywords: Capital structure; COVID-19; steel industry; debt ratio; trade-off theory; pecking order theory

JEL Codes: O11; Q01; Q5

1. INTRODUCTION

The COVID-19 pandemic has severely impacted global and national economies. The country's economy will be boosted if COVID outbreaks are contained, but there is a significant chance of ongoing financial difficulties until 2020 (World Bank, 2020). The building, processing, and manufacturing sectors significantly impact the iron and steel business. Steel demand is driven mostly by the building and infrastructure sectors and the processing and manufacturing industries. According to Indonesian Iron and Steel Industry Association's (IISIA's) forecasts, finished steel consumption in 2020 will shrink by 5.3% due to the expanding COVID-19 pandemic and a loss in GDP in these industries (Indonesian Iron and Steel Industry Association, 2021).

Imported steel from China and Vietnam is the most common source. A total of 0.6 million tons of steel bars and sections are imported from outside, while local production is just 0.6 million tons. A total of 380,000 tons come from China, whereas just 20,000 come from Vietnam. Domestic steels often cost 15–35% more than imported steel. A dumping operation is considered to have occurred, and the quality did not meet the SNI criteria (Sandi, 2020).

Steel imports in Indonesia steadily rose from 2015, when they totalled 5.2 million tons, to 6.9 million tons in 2019. The low level of installed production capacity (utilisation) in the country's steel plants and the influence on facility closures are all impacted by the country's high steel imports. Hundreds of thousands of tons of Chinese steel are also suspected of smuggling into Indonesia. Predatory pricing at the outset, followed by evasive tactics towards the conclusion. The decline in the steel sector may be attributed to China's attack on imported steel (Sandi, 2020).

Demand for steel products and derivatives has fallen by 40–50% due to several challenges facing the steel sector in Indonesia, including the COVID-19 pandemic, according to the head of the IISIA. As a result, productivity and industrial operations will diminish. It is a necessary consequence. It affects Indonesian steel firms' capital structure choices. Financial decisions made by the firm, such as those regarding capital structure, can impact the company's financial performance, namely profitability. Different findings from empirical studies indicated that debt could either have a good or negative impact on performance (Susan, Winarto, & Gunawan, 2022).

Thus, in this research, we evaluate the influence of the COVID-19 crisis and other factors on the capital structure of Indonesian steel businesses. Different pandemic effects on capital structure and how these pandemics impact enterprises' performance have been shown in previous research. For this study, Sheikh's (2015) research on the drivers of capital structure in Pakistani manufacturing enterprises might serve as a guide.

2. LITERATURE REVIEW

2.1. Capital Structure

According to Gitman and Zutter (2015, pp. 560–560), there are two types of capital structures: long-term debt and equity. When it comes to maximising the value of a company, it is essential to consider debt and equity to help a firm lower its cost of capital. The Trade-off and Pecking Order Theory of capital structure is the most relevant for this research. Debt financing has certain advantages, but it also has some drawbacks, according to the trade-off principle. Following the Trade-Off Theory, firms must consider both the benefits and downsides of borrowing money to make an informed decision. The company will have to put aside money to pay off the debt in the future. If a company's costs and advantages of leverage are balanced at the margin, it can optimise its value via its capital structure (Acaravci, 2015).

There is also a connection between the 'Pecking Order Theory' and the 'information imbalance'. This idea suggests that internal financing is superior to external money (Demirguc-Kunt, Martinez-Peria, & Tressel, 2016). The company's operating operations provide the cash for this internal project. If the firm's operating operations are unable to cover the company's financial demands, the company will choose external funding. According to this hypothesis, retained profits, debt, and equities are the three most effective. A tax shield is an advantage of using debt to support alternative investments. This study uses the debt-to-assets ratio as a proxy for capital structure (Drobetz & Fix, 2005).

2.2. Determinants of Capital Structure

2.2.1. COVID-19 pandemic

The COVID-19 epidemic affects the company's financial status due to decreased economic activity and uncertainty about the expiry date, which raises the risk of bankruptcy. Armadani et al. (2021) state that firms impacted by the pandemic need to analyse leverage since it can be used to mitigate and forecast the company's future so that it may be taken into account in making corporate decisions. According to Schneiderman (2020) on Yang and Zhang (2022), government revenue has declined sharply due to the pandemic, and costs have risen, which has caused considerable losses to our economy and tax base. With less government support, those manufacturing companies need to bear more costs. When assessing a company's capacity to satisfy immediate and long-term obligations, leverage ratios are often used. The leverage ratio measures how much of a company's net worth is derived from borrowing. Because of this, the company's revenue must exceed its debt to avoid financial trouble (Arohmawati & Pertiwi, 2021). Furthermore, Gropp and Heider (2010) use an interaction dummy to examine the influence of capital limitations on bank leverage.

H1a. There is a significant relationship between COVID-19 and capital structure.

2.2.2. Liquidity

The capacity of a business to satisfy its short-term financial commitments is referred to as 'liquidity.' For each share a corporation has, its current ratio tells us how much money it stands to gain. The greater the agency's capacity to pay its expenses is, the higher this current ratio proportion rises (Arumbarkah & Pelu, 2019). The capacity of infrastructure companies to pay their current obligations is reflected in their high liquidity. When it comes to making loans, borrowers need much liquidity. For steel companies, a large supply of funds is needed to keep their projects operating; therefore, capital structure financing is the appropriate mix.

H1b. There is a significant relationship between liquidity and capital structure.

2.2.3. Earning Volatility

Several empirical studies have shown that a company's ideal debt level decreases as the volatility of its profits increases. Because of this, if a company's profits are more volatile, it is more likely to be late on its payments. Profit volatility may reduce a company's ability to service its debt, creating a negative correlation between earning volatility and leverage. Many empirical studies have shown a strong negative correlation between leverage and earnings volatility (Bradley et al., 1984; Booth et al., 2001; Fama & French, 2002; Jong et al., 2008; Viviani, 2015). According to the trade-off theory and the pecking order theory, firms with greater earnings volatility should employ more cautious leverage in their capital structures to avoid financial difficulty. Using the trade-off theory, companies attempt to maximise shareholder value by weighing the advantages of borrowing against the possible costs of borrowing. Following the pecking order theory, organisations with more unpredictable revenues would keep greater loan capacity on hand to avoid the need to issue more costly loans in the future (Shivdasani & Zenner, 2005).

H1c. There is a significant relationship between earning volatility and capital structure.

2.2.4. Non-Debt Tax Shield

The non-debt tax shield (NDTS), according to Nadeem Wang (2015), is a tax advantage that encourages enterprises with high taxable income to take on debt. When a tax deduction like depreciation increases, the tax advantage of debt reduces. Non-debt tax advantages like depreciation and amortisation result in the NDTS. Companies with high NDTS rates will utilise low debt levels to conduct their operations since cash flow becomes the company's capital. According to Acaravci (2015), the higher a company's tax rate, the more significant the advantages of debt.

H1d. There is a significant relationship between NDTSs and capital structure.

2.2.5. Profitability

In order to determine whether or not a business can generate a profit, the return on assets (ROA) is used. A company's ability to generate profits increases in direct proportion to its level of debt. As a proportion of total assets, the ratio shows how much the firm owes in overall debt and how much money creditors have supplied to the company. A company's profitability and leverage should thus be as high as possible. Higher leverage percentages indicate that those with high overall debt values are more likely to reduce the profitability of a company's debt load that exceeds its assets, placing the latter at risk and impairing its day-to-day business operations. On the other hand, the company's profitability is negatively impacted by the increased fulfilment of debt obligations. It is less risky for a corporation to employ minimal debt since it will not have to pay huge interest.

H1e. There is a significant relationship between profitability and capital structure.

3. RESEARCH METHOD

3.1. Data

The IDX is a secondary data source in this research using quantitative methods. IDX-IC companies comprise most of the study's samples, notably those producing steel. Steel firms in this industry were selected because of the COVID-19 pandemic. It was found in this research that Saranacentral Bajatama Tbk, Citra Tubindo Tbk, Gunawan Dianjaya Steel Tbk, HK Metals Utama Tbk, and PT Steel Pipe Industry Indonesia were the eight firms analysed. Analysis and hypothesis testing are conducted using panel regression tests to examine the influence of liquidity, earnings volatility, NDTS, and profitability on a company's capital structure. The crisis 0–1 dummy is used in the model to indicate the COVID crisis. It also affects the economy between the third quarter of 2020 and the fourth quarter of 2021. The IDX official website (www.idx.co.id), as well as individual bank financial statements, are utilised.

3.2. Variables

This research uses the Debt Ratio (DR) as a proxy for capital structure. COVID-19, liquidity (CR), earnings volatility, NDTS, profitability (ROA), and firm size are all independent factors in this research. Table 9.1 has a definition of each variable.

3.3. Model

An independent *t*-test is performed to determine whether the pre-crisis and crisis means vary significantly. Steel businesses' leverage in Indonesia is assessed using fixed-effect models to examine the effects of the crisis and other independent variables on their financial position.

$$DR_{it} = \alpha_i + \beta_1 COVID_{it} + \beta_2 CR_{it} + \beta_3 EVOL_{it} + \beta_4 NDTS_{it} + \beta_5 ROA_{it} + \beta_6 SIZE_{it} + \varepsilon$$

Table 9.1.   Definition of Variables.

Variables	Definition
Dependent Variable	
Debt Ratio (DR_{it})	Ratio of total debt to total assets.
Independent Variables	
COVID-19 ($COVID_{it}$)	Crisis 0 dummy before pandemic, and 1 dummy during the pandemic.
Liquidity (CR_{it})	Ratio of current assets to current liabilities.
Earning Volatility ($EVOL_{it}$)	Ratio of standard deviation of the first difference of profit before depreciation, interest, and taxes to average total assets.
Non-debt Tax Shield ($NDTS_{it}$)	Ratio of depreciation expense to total assets.
Profitability (ROA_{it})	Ratio of net profit before taxes to total assets.
Control Variable	
Firm Size ($SIZE_{it}$)	Natural logarithm of sales.

where

DR_{it} = debt ratio of firm i at time t.
$COVID_{it}$ = COVID-19 i at time t.
CR_{it} = current ratio i at time t.
$EVOL_{it}$ = earning volatility i at time t.
$NDTS_{it}$ = non-debt tax shield i at time t.
ROA_{it} = profitability i at time t.
$SIZE_{it}$ = size of firm i at time t.
ε = standard error.

For a particular period, panel data regression may be used to simulate the impact of one or more predictor variables on the response variable. In order to estimate a panel data regression model, three approaches are available: the Common Effect Model (CEM), the Fixed Effects Model (FEM), and the Random Effects Model (REM). Correlation matrices are used to look for data that may be multicollinear. Using the Generalised Moment of Method, we looked at whether or not this model was endogenous. According to the GMM (generalised technique of moments), an economic model's parameters may be estimated by integrating observed data with population moment criteria (Zsohar, 2018). A lag term is included in the model as an endogeneity check for accounting for unobservable endogeneity. The first difference between GMM and the system GMM are two typical GMM estimations used to estimate linear auto-regressive models. Stata 16's XTABOND2 modules with the system-GMM are used in this investigation.

4. RESULT

4.1. Descriptive Statistic

Table 9.2 presents summary statistics for the dependent and explanatory variables.

Table 9.2.   The Descriptive Result of Observations.

	DR	COV	CR	EVOL	NDTS	ROA	SIZE
Mean	0.481273	0.510417	2.167245	0.002430	0.011588	0.001218	26.44038
Maximum	0.915088	1.000000	6.027566	0.185329	0.039620	0.139449	29.21737
Minimum	0.157376	0.000000	0.276971	−0.288435	0.000504	−0.238352	22.50968
Std. Dev.	0.241441	0.502516	1.587510	0.059664	0.008572	0.051150	1.700952
Observations	96	96	96	96	96	96	96

Source: Faturohman and Noviandy, 2022.

4.2. Classical Assumption Test

Table 9.3 demonstrates that most of the explanatory variables' cross-correlation terms are moderate. It suggests that multicollinearity among the explanatory factors is not an issue.

Hypothesis zero (*H0*) is accepted based on Wooldridge's autocorrelation test, which yields an *F*-count of 0.0568, significantly higher than the 0.05 test significance threshold. There is no first-order autocorrelation in the model utilised; hence the premise of non-autocorrelation is not violated by it.

4.3. Model Selection Test

Chow and Hausman's tests are used to identify which regression model is most appropriate for model selection. This study's regression model will be determined by the best model that can be found. This test is used to find the optimal regression model between the Pooled Least Squares or CEM and the Fixed Effect Model (FEM). The Hausman Test (also known as the Hausman specification test) can be used to find the endogenous regressions (predictor variables) in a regression model. If equations 1 and 2 have *p*-values less than $= 5\%$, the Chow test has rejected the null hypothesis. A FEM is preferable since the null hypothesis has been ruled out (FEM). Thus, the Hausman test must be used to continue model testing. This table has two *p*-values that are lower than $= 5\%$. Hence, the null hypothesis is ruled out based on these data. The FEM offers a better fit for these equations since the null hypothesis has been rejected.

Table 9.3.   Pearson Correlation Coefficient Matrix.

	COV	CR	EVOL	NDTS	ROA	SIZE
COV	1.000000					
CR	0.029208	1.000000				
EVOL	0.061943	0.195945	1.000000			
NDTS	0.077458	−0.103576	−0.097163	1.000000		
ROA	0.061575	0.171338	0.979768	−0.102591	1.000000	
SIZE	−0.060650	−0.270144	0.089388	0.301091	0.065570	1.00000

4.4. Panel Data Regression Result

The COVID-19 pandemic is shown to influence the capital structure in Table 9.4 favourably, but the CEM and REM have the opposite effect. It is agreed that the time before and during COVID-19 has the significance of the model is less than 0.05. Capital structure is less important to investors because of their thoughts and other opinions that do not change before or throughout the epidemic as a consequence. Even if COVID-19 is considered, investors will continue to invest their money before and throughout the pandemic since the infrastructure will continue to operate. Suppose a pandemic or other large-scale disaster occurs. In that case, the firm must be able to execute or maintain its objectives or strategy and look for methods to increase operational efficiency so that the debt ratio does not grow substantially.

FEM, CEM, and REM results show that the Current Ratio is significant and have a negative relationship with the debt ratio, with a significance level of less than 0.05. Debt finance is often used by companies with a large amount of cash. The amount of a firm's capital structure supported by debt will be inversely or weakly correlated with the current ratio of that company, according to Demirguc-Kunt et al. (2016). Management may take steps to guarantee that steel businesses have a high current ratio, which lowers the company's debt and reduces the risk of bankruptcy due to a high current ratio. In order to contribute to the growth of a company's value in the pandemic era, companies must reduce their outstanding debt and better manage the value of their current assets. However, despite the country's limited and undeveloped bond market and high-cost long-term bank loans, Indonesian manufacturing businesses depend heavily on short-term financing. It is possible that the company holds too much cash, which encourages managers to overspend on excessive extra income. In order to control their managers' additional consumption, firms with fewer collateralised assets may choose a higher level of debt (Qasim, Rizov, & Zhang, 2021).

Table 9.4.   Panel Data Regression Results.

Variable	Model CEM	Model FEM	Model REM
	Coef. $(P > t)$	Coef. $(P > t)$	Coef. $(P > t)$
C	1,7597 (0,000)	−0,0122 (0,108)	−0,48829 (0,333)
COV	−0,0237 (0,373)	0,0165 (0,0285)	0,01655 (0,285)
CR	−0,1315 (0,000)	−0,0393 (0,007)	−0,03932 (0,007)
EVOL	−1,4182 (0,211)	−1,3302 (0,037)	−1,33024 (0,037)
NDTS	6,3399 (0,000)	−3,9953 (0,008)	−3,99539 (0,008)
ROA	2,5043 (0,57)	1,5065 (0,044)	1,50659 (0,044)
SIZE	−0,0398 (0,000)	0,0122 (0,006)	0,05363 (0,006)
R-squared	0,7390	0,9320	0,4472
Adj. R-squared	0,7215	0,9212	0,4792
Prob $> F$	0,0000	0,0010	0,000
No. of obs	96	96	96
No. of groups	8	8	8

Source: Faturohman and Noviandy, 2022.
Note: $^*\rho < 0.1$, $^{**}\rho < 0.05$, $^{***}\rho < 0.001$.

A debt-to-earnings ratio of less than 0.05 negatively correlates with earnings volatility. The correlation between earnings volatility and its predicted negative correlation is statistically significant. These findings support the trade-off theory, which states that organisations with less unpredictable revenues should have higher debt levels since they are better at meeting contract deadlines. With a lack of bonds in Indonesia, businesses depend significantly on bank loans to support their operations. Because many of these banks have been privatised, it is difficult for them to provide loans in advantageous conditions, particularly to businesses with erratic revenue patterns. Consequently, enterprises with fluctuating profit margins have to take on less debt. Businesses face business risk when their operational strategy and industry dynamics, as well as their vulnerability to economic fluctuations (such as changes in interest rates and commodity prices), are impacted by these factors (Bhagat, 2017).

With the fixed-effect model, a NDTS has a negative impact on the capital structure, which indicates that lower debt is needed to fulfil the capital structure demands if there is a greater NDTS (Hoffmann, Martin, & Pablo, 2017). The average NDTS for manufacturing businesses in Indonesia is 0.033, which indicates that the degree of NDTS is relatively low. On the other hand, manufacturing businesses have a high level of fixed assets owing to their large number of assets (Atmajaya, 2008). Depreciation costs for industrial companies are highly substantial. Depreciation charges may be deductible to help firms save money on their taxes (Khémiri & Noubbigh, 2018). Companies with many fixed assets and depreciation expenses will have a more modest capital structure or utilise their capital more often since they can deduct it. Tax deductions and depreciation expenses are reduced when fewer fixed assets are owned. In order to take advantage of the tax credit for interest paid on debt, firms are encouraged to use more debt than equity in their capital structure. This study's results support the trade-off hypothesis, which claims that companies would choose debt financing since it gives tax advantages (Spitsin, Vukovic, Anokhin, & Spitsina, 2020). In conclusion, it can be inferred that Indonesian manufacturing enterprises take NDTSs into account when making capital structure choices (Suryani & Sari, 2020).

The *t*-test findings suggest that profitability positively impacts capital structure in the FEM. In light of the ROA coefficient of 0.15605 and the probability value of 0.044, *H1* has been approved. It is said that profitability and leverage have a positive connection because good profitability increases debt usage and gives firms an incentive to take advantage of tax benefits for interest payments. It is important that profitability is influenced by the company's capital structure, which includes the composition of the capital structure and the quantity of debt in the capital structure. According to a corporation's capital structure, long-term debt may indirectly affect profitability by comparing the company's total equity to its long-term debt. Since the firm would seek financing from outside to finance its operations at a low cost of capital, raising its debt will boost profitability in this situation. It is accepted in the Trade-off Theory. Based on the theory of Modigliani and Miller (Bauer, 2014), a firm with a high-profit margin should use debt to fund its operations first. This theory argues that utilising debt is more profitable than using the equity. Because they think they have a stable financial foundation, companies with considerable capital prefer to take on debt. More significant profits mean more opportunities to borrow money from outside the company as a debt.

Larger banks have been proven to have a favourable impact on leverage. Larger companies might attract higher deposits since they have lower capital positions. The variable size has a positive and significant effect on the debt ratio, as shown in the opposite outcome. The trade-off concept suggests that more prominent companies should take on more debt to deploy risk and benefit from lower interest-payment taxes. Based on the statistical study, the regression coefficient for business size is positive at 0.058. For the company size variable, the t-test statistical findings yielded a significant value of 0.000, which is less than the tolerance for error of 0.05. The size of the firm strongly impacts capital structure. According to the results, a corporation's capital structure rises in proportion to its growth. The smaller a firm is, the smaller its capital structure will be. Large firms will have an easier time getting investors and securing financing than small ones. With easy access to information, large firms can be more flexible. A creditor or lender, in reality, likes to lend to more significant enterprises since they have more options. Indrajaya et al. (2011), Salehi & Manesh (2012), and Cekrezi (2013) all found that firm size had a considerably significant relationship with capital structure.

4.5. GMM Result

GMM is performed on the data to address endogeneity issues and ensure the findings' robustness. When one equation's explanatory variable becomes an independent variable in another, this is known as endogeneity. Even if the number of observations is reduced due to equipment usage, the outcome is consistent with what we have already discovered. Unlike previous results, earnings volatility, non-debt tax shelter, profitability, and size had little influence on capital structure. The idea that a pandemic would impact the essential elements of a company's financial structure is widely acknowledged. Model system-GMM, on the other hand, demonstrates that the leverage ratio rises before and during the crisis, in line with the results of the FEM.

It is possible to test the GMM system by looking at the outcomes of AR (1) and AR (2), which are the first and second-order autocorrelated disturbances, respectively. The null hypothesis is frequently rejected in tests for (1), but the value of AR serves as an essential indication (2). When looking at Table 9.4, it can be seen that the p-value of AR (1) shows a negligible value. However, when looking at the model's AR (2), the p-value is above the alpha value of 5%, which means there is no serial autocorrelation in errors for this GMM system model. For the GMM system model, the Sargan test produced a p-value of 0.441.

Due to these findings, the GMM model's instruments may be considered valid. The best model is the one that can be understood, as there is no serial autocorrelation in error and a valid instrument in the model's feasibility test. Endogeneity is no longer an issue thanks to the GMM test. COVID-19 and liquidity are variables with consistent study outcomes. As a consequence of these findings, it may be deduced that the total debt-to-assets ratio favoured the COVID-19 period.

Another component affecting Indonesian steel businesses' capital structure is liquidity, which was tested in both studies. In other words, the capital structure suffers because of the constancy of liquidity. The debt ratio is negatively related to business size in the GMM test findings, as seen in the graphs. The findings of the FEM test are inversely compatible with this.

Leveraged financing will become increasingly challenging if large firms' liquidity decreases. Due to a decreased degree of liquidity, large firms need to acquire more funds from outside investors. As a result of their greater market access, transparency, reduced credit risk, increased resilience in times of crisis, and cheaper agency costs, large firms have more leverage. Due to a lack of money in the company's coffers, significant corporations are forced to use external cash as debt to finance investments or other needs.

5. CONCLUSION

Across all empirical research, the current ratio and COVID-19 are related to the debt ratio. According to empirical research, the debt-to-equity ratio has a negative impact on liquidity. According to the pecking order hypothesis, this is more in line with the predictions of the trade-off theory. Smaller companies have lower debt ratios than larger ones. This data supports the hypothesis that the likelihood of bankruptcy is inversely proportional to the size of the business. According to the theoretical trade-off hypothesis, the debt-to-equity ratio is inversely related to profit volatility. Because of this, the fact that liquidity substantially negatively impacts the debt ratio shows that firms have excess cash, which may encourage managers to spend more than the appropriate amount of perquisites. Companies with fewer assets that may be collateralised end up borrowing a more significant amount in order for their management to be reined. Because of the NDTS, businesses with a large number of fixed assets and high depreciation charges will have a smaller capital structure or utilise their capital more often because of the tax deduction. Finally, research on varying profitability has shown some interesting results. The debt-to-profitability ratio positively correlates with profitability, supporting the trade-off theory. There is no significant correlation between debt ratio and profitability, earnings volatility, non-debt tax ratio, or firm size, according to the GMM test.

REFERENCES

Acaravci, S. K. (2015). The determinants of capital structure: Evidence from the Turkish Manufacturing Sector. *International Journal of Economics and Financial Issues*, 5(1), 158–171.

Ahmad, Z., Abdullah, N. M., & Roslan, S. (2012). Capital structure effect on firms performance: Focusing on consumers and industrials sectors on Malaysian Firms. *International Review of Business Research Papers*, 8(5), 137–155.

Armadani, A., Fisabil, A. I., & Salsabila, D. T. (2021). Analysis of company bankruptcy ratio during the Covid-19 Pandemic. *Journal of Accounting*, 13(1), 99–108.

Arohmawati, P. P., & Pertiwi, T. K. (2021). Predicting of Financial Distress with the Altman Z- Score model of retail companies listed on IDX. *Balance: Economic Journal*, 17(2), 273–280.

Arumbarkah, & Pelu. (2019). Effect of liquidity, profitability, leverage and growth on dividend policy with firm size as moderating variable. *CESJ: Center of Economic Students Journal, 2*(2), 23–36.

Atmajaya, L. S. (2008). *Financial management theory and practice.* Andi.

Faturohman, T. & Noviandy, R. (2022). *An Empirical Analysis of Firm-specific Determinants of Capital Structure Before and During COVID-19 Pandemic: Evidence from Listed Hotels, Restaurants, and Tourism Entities on the Indonesia Stock Exchange.* 10.1108/S1571-038620220000030008.

Baihaqi, N., Geraldina, I., & Wijaya, S. (2021). The effect of capital structure on firm value on COVID-19 pandemic emergency conditions. *Journal of AKUNIDA, 7*(1), 72–84.

Bauer, P. (2014). Determinants of capital structure: Empirical evidence from the Czech Republic. *Czech Journal of Economics and Finance (Finance a uver)*, 2–21.

Bhagat, S. (2017). *Financial crisis, corporate governance, and bank capital.* Cambridge University Press.

Booth, L., Aivazian, V., Demirguc-Kunt, A., & Maksimovic, V. (2001). Capital structures in developing countries. *The Journal of Finance, 56*(1), 87–130.

Bradley, M., Jarrell, G. A., & Kim, E. H. (1984). On the existence of an optimal capital structure: Theory and evidence. *The Journal of Finance, 39*(3), 857–878.

Cekrezi, A. (2013). Impact of firm specific factors on capital structure decision: An empirical study of Albanian Firms. *European Journal of Sustainable Development, 2*(4), 135.

Chinaemerem, & Anthony, O. (2018). Impact of Capital Structure on the Financial Performance of Nigerian Firms. *Oman Chapter of Arabian Journal of Business and Management Review.*

Cortez, M., & Susanto, S. (2012). The determinants of corporate capital structure: Evidence from Japanese manufacturing companies. *Journal of International Business Research.*

Demirguc-Kunt, A., Martinez-Peria, M. S., & Tressel, T. (2016). *The impact of the global financial crisis on firms capital structure.* Policy Research Working Paper.

Drobetz, W., & Fix, R. (2005). What are the determinants of the capital structure? Evidence from Switzerland. *Swiss Journal of Economics and Statistics (SJES), 141*(1), 71–113.

Fama, E. F., & French, K. R. (2002). Testing trade-off and pecking order predictions about dividends and debt. *Review of financial studies*, 1–33.

Ghosh, R., & Chatterjee, S. (2018). Capital structure, ownership and crisis: How different are banks? *Journal of Financial Regulation and Compliance, 26*(2), 300–330.

Gitman, L. J., & Zutter, C. J. (2015). *Principles of managerial finance* (14th ed.). Essex Pearson Education Limited.

Gottardo, P., & Moisello, A. M. (2014). The capital structure choices of family firms: Evidence from Italian medium-large unlisted firms. *Journal of Managerial Finance, 40*(3), 254–275.

Gropp, R., & Heider, F. (2010). The determinants of bank capital structure. *Review of Finance, 14*(4), 587–622.

Hoffmann, S., Martin, P. R., & Pablo. (2017). Capital structure in the Chilean Corporate Sector: Revisiting the stylized facts. *Research in International Business and Finance.*

Indonesian Iron and Steel Industry Association. (2021, March 27). *Produksi Baja Nasional Tahun 2020 Meningkat |Update Konsumsi Baja Tahun 2020 dan Outlook 2021.* https://www.iisia.or.id/post/view/id/produksi-baja-nasional-tahun-2020-meningkat-di-tengah-penurunan-konsumsi-baja-selama-pandemi-covid19

Indrajaya, G., Herlina, H., & Setiadi, R. (2011). The Effect of Asset Structure, Company Size, Growth Rate, Profitability and Business Risk on Capital Structure: Empirical Study on Mining Sector Companies Listed on the Indonesia Stock Exchange Period 2004-2007. *Accurate Scientific Journal of Accounting, 06*, 523–539.

De Jong, A., Kabir, R., & Nguyen, T. T. (2008). Capital structure around the world: The roles of firm- and country-specific determinants. *Journal of banking & Finance, 32*(9), 1954–1969.

Khémiri, W., & Noubbigh, H. (2018). Determinants of capital structure: Evidence from Sub-Saharan African firms. *The Quarterly Review of Economics and Finance, 70*, 150–159.

Koech, S. K. (2013). *The effect on capital structure on profitability of financial firms listed at Nairobi Stock Exchange.* Department of Business Administration, Kenyatta University.

Lim, T. C. (2012). Determinants of capital structure empirical evidence from financial services listed firms in China. *International Journal of Economics and Finance, 4*(3), 191–203.

Mohammad, K. U. (2021). How bank capital structure decision-making change in recessions: Covid-19 Evidence from Pakistan. *Asian Journal of Economics and Banking*, 2615–9821.

Nurcaya, I. A. (2020, Mei 21). *Pelaku Usaha Sebut Implementasi SNI Baja Jadi Kado di Masa Pandemi Covid-19.* https://ekonomi.bisnis.com/read/20200521/257/1243411/pelaku-usaha-sebut-implementasi-sni-baja-jadi-kado-di-masa-pandemi-covid-19

Qasim, S., Rizov, M., & Zhang, X. (2021). Financial constraints and the export decision of Pakistani firms. *International Journal of Finance and Economics, 26*(3), 4557–4573.

Salehi, M., & Manesh, N. B. (2012). A study of the roles of firm and country on specific determinates in capital structure: Iranian evidence. *International Management Review, 8*(2), 51–62.

Sandi, F. (2020, January 28). *Bukan Cuma China, Baja Impor Vietnam Obrak-Abrik Pasar RI.* https://www.cnbcindonesia.com/news/20200128062844-4-133218/bukan-cuma-china-baja-impor-vietnam-obrak-abrik-pasar-ri

Sethi, P., & Tiwari, R. (2016). New evidence on determinants of capital structure from the Indian Manufacturing Industry. *Corporate Ownership and Control Journal, 13*(3), 82–88.

Sheikh, N. A. (2015). Capital structure determinants of non financial listed firms in service sector: Evidence from Pakistan. *Pakistan Journal of Social Sciences, 35*, 1051–1059.

Shivdasani, A., & Zenner, M. (2005). How to choose a capital structure: Navigating the debt-equity decision. *Journal of Applied Corporate Finance, 17*(1), 26–35.

Spitsin, V., Vukovic, D., Anokhin, S., & Spitsina, L. (2020). Company performance and optimal capital structure: Evidence of transition economy (Russia). *Journal of Economic Studies.* https://www.emerald.com/insight/0144-3585.htm

Strebulaev, I. A. (2007). Do tests of capital structure theory mean what they say? *The Journal of Finance, American Finance Association, 62*(4), 1747–1787.

Susan, M., Winarto, J., & Gunawan, I. (2022). The determinants of corporate profitability in indonesia Manufacturing Industry. *Review of Integrative Business and Economics Research, 11*(1), 184–190.

United Nations Conference on Trade and Development. (2020). *The Covid-19 Shock to Developing Countries: Towards a "whatever it takes" programme for the two-thirds of the world's population being left behind.* United Nations.

Viviani, J.-L. (2015). Capital structure determinants: An empirical study of French Companies in the Wine Industry. *International Journal of Wine Business Research, 20*(2), 171–194.

Wang, N. (2015). Determinants of capital structure: An empirical study of firms in manufacturing industry of Pakistan. *Managerial Finance, 37*(2), 117–133.

World Bank. (2020). *World development report 2020: Trading for development in the age of global value chains.* World Bank. Available at: https://www.worldbank.org/en/publication/wdr2020.

Yang, Y., & Zhang, J. (2022). The impact of Covid-19 on the performance of Chinese Online-Educational Industry. *Review of Integrative Business and Economics Research, 11*(4), 91–100.

Zsohar, P. (2018). *Short introduction to the generalized method of moments.* Central European University.

CHAPTER 10

DOES THE SEARCH VOLUME INDEX ASSOCIATE WITH STOCK RETURN IN THE INDONESIAN CAPITAL MARKET?

Nadia Shakira Nasr and Taufik Faturohman

School of Business and Management, Institut Teknologi Bandung, Indonesia

ABSTRACT

This study examines the relationship between the Search Volume Index (SVI) and stock return during the COVID-19 pandemic. SVI shows how many people search for a particular query over a specified period or region. This study is based on secondary financial data collected from 25 companies from the LQ45 index listed on the Indonesia Stock Exchange. Data collection uses a weekly period use financial data from March 2019 to March 2020. To examine the relationship between the SVI and stock return, this study uses the Fama-French three-factor model with the SVI as the independent variable using the regression methodology.

Keywords: Search volume index; behavioural finance; Fama-French three factors model; stock return; abnormal returns

JEL Codes: G12; G14

The Finance-Innovation Nexus: Implications for Socio-Economic Development
International Symposia in Economic Theory and Econometrics, Volume 34, 147–159
Copyright © 2025 by Emerald Publishing Limited
All rights of reproduction in any form reserved
ISSN: 1571-0386/doi:10.1108/S1571-038620240000034012

1. INTRODUCTION

The efficient market hypothesis is one of the traditional finance theories which became the pillar that formed the body of knowledge of traditional finance. Capital asset pricing models (CAPMs) by Sharpe (1964) and the three-factor models by Fama and French (1993) are theories that use the efficient market hypothesis as their core foundation. The CAPM assumes that all investors have access to all available public information and reach the same expectations about the future (Bratton & McCahery, 2015). If only a few investors have access to certain information that is not readily available to all, then the market is not considered an efficient market. This assumption is in line with the efficient market hypothesis.

Kahneman (1973), popularly known as the 'Fathers of Behavioural Finance', argues that psychological evidence discovers that investors can only handle a certain amount of information at any time. Kahneman states that attention is a deficient cognitive activity; given the reality, investors do not always have access to all available information, the only limited information that attracts their attention. This may undermine the efficient market hypothesis and raise questions about whether and to what extent market prices reflect investor interest.

University Paul Krugman (2012) describes a financial scenario in which asset prices appear to be based on unrealistic or contradictory future expectations, which should never have happened if traditional asset pricing models' premise of an efficient market holds true. Traditional asset pricing models are giving false assurance that the financial bubble moment will never bust.

Barber and Odean (2008) developed the 'investor recognition hypothesis', which states given the large number of stocks that investors can choose from. Still, with their limited attention, they cannot make decisions based on a deep understanding of each stock. This causes increased investor attention to a company causing a temporary increase in stock prices.

Merton (1987) introduced the investor recognition hypothesis, which states that highly new information would improve the visibility of a company's stock among investors who do not own it and may persuade some of them to buy it. Increased stock visibility will result in a rise in the stock's investor base since there is a shortage of visibility among investors.

It is considered challenging to ascertain the level of investor attention because there is a shortage of information and a reliable proxy. Various researchers try to explain investor attention with various proxies such as advertisements (Fehle et al., 2005; Grullon et al., 2004; Lou, 2014), TV program appearances (Takeda & Yamazaki, 2006), and media coverage (Fang & Peress, 2009). However, the above studies are limited in that there is no guarantee that investors actually pay attention to such advertisements and news media.

Joseph Stiglitz, George Akerlof, and Michael Spence are the three economists who issued the Asymmetric Information Theory in 2001. This theory explains that information differences arise because there are parties who know more about internal information and company prospects in the future than other parties.

The development of increasingly advanced information technology has become a new opportunity for investors to get a better understanding of the condition of the efficient market hypothesis. A high level of understanding of information becomes a consideration for investors to place their funds in the capital market. The internet is able to encourage the economic growth of a country, where the activity of searching for information through the Internet has become one of the preferred methods by potential investors (Bank et al., 2011).

McKinsey defines big data as datasets that are too large for traditional database software tools to acquire, store, manage, and analyse. Big data enables us to do computer analysis and uncover patterns, trends, and relationships, particularly in human behaviour and interactions. Da et al. (2011) and Bank et al. (2011) propose the idea of solving and explore what is the best proxy to measure investor attention by using the Search Volume Index (SVI) as their proxy.

SVI as a proxy of investor attention. Da et al. (2011) and Bank et al. (2011) propose an idea to measure investor attention using one of the big data measurements provided by Google, Google SVI, using tools called Google Trends.

This research will contribute to pioneering emerging markets such as the Indonesian capital market. This research will quantify the market behaviour by using the SVI as a proxy and understand their relationship with stock returns and abnormal stock returns.

2. HYPOTHESIS DEVELOPMENT

Assuming that investor attention is captured by the SVI, some studies provide evidence supporting this hypothesis (Bank et al., 2011; Da et al., 2011; Takeda & Wakao, 2014).

H1a. SVI is positively associated with stock return.

The prior studies report a positive relationship between SVI and abnormal return (Da et al., 2011; Ekinci & Bulut, 2021; Joseph et al., 2011). Following prior studies, we pose the following hypothesis.

H1b. SVI is positively associated with abnormal stock return.

3. METHODOLOGY

3.1. Data and Data Collection

These research samples are listed companies on the LQ45 index, an index that is calculated every six months or semi-annually by the research division of the Indonesia Stock Exchange. LQ45 index consists of 45 companies that have been included in the top 60 companies with the highest market capitalisation (MK) in the last 12 months, have been included in the top 60 companies with the highest transaction value in a regular market in the last 12 months, have been listed in the Indonesia Stock Exchange for at least three months and have good financial conditions, the prospect of growth, high transaction value and frequency.

In conducting this research, the researcher uses a weekly period of two periods, from March 2019 to March 2020, considered before the COVID-19 pandemic, and March 2020 – March 2021, considered during the COVID-19 pandemic. The data used are 25 companies that meet the LQ45 criteria and have always existed on the LQ45 index for two years.

To collect SVI data, we did the following steps based on Takeda and Wakao (2014):

1. Exclude the term 'Tbk' from the company name
2. Exclude 'Holdings' and 'Group' from the company name unless the terms make the company name too general
3. Add abbreviated versions of the company name
   a. Use the stock ticker
   b. Check SVIs for the abbreviations and delete from the list if their SVIs are below 1/10 of the highest SVI
   c. Excluding abbreviations that considered too general
4. Check the 'related keywords' section and if there is anything irrelevant is included and found, exclude it from the results
5. Exclude the firms whose SVIs are 0 more than five weeks.

The data used in this research is panel data. Panel data is a combination of cross-section and time-series data. Time series data is specific data collected across different time periods. Cross-section data is a specific set of data collected in a single period (Gujarati & Porter, 2009). All the data required for our research is gathered using Bloomberg and Google Trends.

3.2. Research Models

In this research, we conduct two regressions with the dependent variable abnormal stock return $(R_{i,t} - R_{f,t})$ and stock return (R_i) and the independent variable SVI. We are trying to explain the relationship between these variables. In the model that was used by Ekinci and Bulut (2021), We replicate the model that Ekinci used based on the French-Fama three-factor model on a Turkey market setting in an Indonesia market setting.

$$R_{i,t} - R_{f,t} = \alpha + \beta \, SVI + \beta \, (R_{m,t} - R_{f,t}) + \beta_1 SMB_{i,t} + \beta_2 HML_{i,t} + \varepsilon_{i,t} \quad (3.1)$$

$R_{f,t}$ is the risk-free rate at time t, $R_{m,t}$ is the market return at time t, and $R_{m,t} - R_{f,t}$ is the risk premium at time t. $SMB_{i,t}$ is the difference between the simple average returns of small and large stocks based on MK. $HML_{i,t}$ is the difference between the simple average returns of high and low book-to-market stocks.

Brennan et al. (2002) examine how non-risk characteristics such as MK and price-to-book ratio have explanatory power relative to the risk-based asset pricing model. They show that the size and book-to-market effects are more significant in the characteristic model than in the Fama-French factor model. However, we should note that the pooled-data model assumes all stocks have the same factor betas in the Fama-French model. To mitigate the possible problem arising from these uniform betas, we replace SMB with a firm-specific log of MK and HML with a firm-specific price-to-book value ratio (PBR). We also add the COVID-19 pandemic variable to see the impact of the COVID-19 pandemic on the relationship between SVI and stock return.

The first model is model (3.2), which explains the relationship between SVI and stock return. The second model is model (3.3), which explains the relationship between SVI and abnormal stock returns. We suspect that the SVI has a positive association with the stock return and the abnormal stock return to previous studies conducted by Bank et al. (2011), Joseph et al. (2011), Da et al. (2011), Takeda and Wakao (2014), and Ekinci and Bulut (2021).

$$R_{i,t} = \alpha + \beta\, \text{SVI} + \beta\, (R_{m,t} - R_{f,t}) + \beta_1 \text{MK}_{i,t} + \beta_2 \text{PBR}_{i,t} + \beta_3 \text{COVID} + \varepsilon_{i,t} \quad (3.2)$$

$$R_{i,t} - R_{f,t} = \alpha + \delta \text{SVI} + \beta\, (R_{m,t} - R_{f,t}) + \beta_1 \text{MK}_{i,t} + \beta_2 \text{PBR}_{i,t} + \beta_3 \text{COVID} + \varepsilon_{i,t} \quad (3.3)$$

3.3. Data Analysis

Gujarati and Porter (2009) explain several methods to perform regression with data in the form of panel data. Among them are the common effect model (CEM), fixed effect model (FEM), and random effect model (REM). In selecting the right regression model, we tested several tests Chow, Hausman, and Lagrange multiplier (LM). Chow test is a pre-test to determine the model's common effect or random effect, the Hausman test is a pre-test to determine the random effect or FEM, and the LM test is a pre-test to determine the Common Effect or REM as the most appropriate model used in estimating panel data.

Classical assumption testing needs to be done so that the regression analysis meets the BLUE criteria (Best, Linear, Unbiased Estimator) (Gujarati & Porter, 2017). The classical assumption test conducted in this study consisted of a normality test, autocorrelation test, heteroscedasticity test, and multicollinearity test.

Gujarati and Porter (2017), the normality test in linear regression aims to test whether in the regression the residual variable has a normal distribution or not. In testing for normality, we used the Shapiro-Wilk method. Gujarati (2007) autocorrelation is a condition in which there is a correlation between members of the observation that is ordered by time or space. Autocorrelation testing can use the run test method, whether the observations of varname are serially independent – that is, whether they occur in random order – by counting how many runs there are above and below a threshold. Gujarati and Porter (2009) multicollinearity is a condition with a perfect or precise linear relationship between some or all the explanatory variables in a regression model. In multicollinearity testing, we use the variance inflation factor (VIF). Gujarati and Porter (2009) heteroscedasticity is a condition where the variance varies from observation to observation, or the models' residual does not have a constant variance. Heteroscedasticity can occur if the model has some data loner (outliers). In autocorrelation testing, we use the Wald test method.

We did several tests for our hypothesis, joint test (*F*-stat), coefficient determination (R2), and individual test (*t*-Stat). Gujarati and Porter (2013) joint test or *F*-stat can be used to determine whether all the independent variables have a significant or insignificant effect on the dependent variable. *t*-stat can be used to test the truth of the hypothesised results from the sample. This *t*-stat is used to determine the effect of each independent variable on the dependent variable, whether it has an effect or not. The coefficient determination or R2 can be used to measure the goodness of fit of a regression; the higher value of R2, the model can explain the high portion of the dependent variables (Gujarati & Porter, 2017).

4. RESULT

4.1. Descriptive Statistics

4.2. Model 1 Analysis

In conducting the model selection test, the researcher performs the Hausman and Chow tests. The results of the Hausman test showed that the null hypothesis was accepted so that the random effects method was chosen, and then the Chow test showed that the null hypothesis was accepted so that the fixed effect method was chosen (Tables 10.1 and 10.2).

We performed a multicollinearity test using the VIF method on the regression model. Our result shows that each variable has a VIF value ($<$) of 10 and a tolerance value greater than 0.01. Therefore, we can confidently say that our

Table 10.1. Descriptive Statistic.

	Obs	Mean	Std. Dev.	Min	Max
Search Volume Index	2,600	18.8153800	17.8372500	0	115
Return	2,600	−0.0014276	0.0681710	−0.4194906	0.3485237
Abnormal Return	2,600	0.0114186	0.2001505	−1.1006750	0.5402076
Risk Premium	2,600	0.0179519	3.0201140	−15.2650000	8.5530000
Market Capitalisation Log	2,600	17.9932200	1.3348350	14.8701700	20.5872000
Market Capitalisation	2,600	1.43+08	1.80e+08	2,871,000	8.73e+08
Price-to-Book Ratio	2,600	3.9625070	9.5086120	0.2931000	73.4404000

Table 10.2. Model Selection Test for Model 1.

	p-value			Model Selection
	Hausman Test	Chow Test	LM Test	
Model 1	0.0000	0.0002	−	Fixed Effects

model is free from multicollinearity problems. We conducted an auto-correlation test using the run test method on the regression model. Looking at the result of auto-correlation for our model, the value of the run test is greater (>) than the significance value (0.05). Therefore, we can confidently say that our model is free from auto-correlation. We tested using the Wald test method on the regression model to see if there was a problem with the heteroscedasticity of the model. Our results show that the value of the heteroscedasticity test of 0.000 is smaller (<) than the significance value of 0.05, which means that the model has a heteroscedasticity problem. This research will use the robust variance estimates method to overcome the problem of heteroscedasticity in the model (Freedman, 2006). Since the number of observations from panel data has reached 100 (this study uses 2,600 observation data), this study assumes that the data are normally distributed (Altman & Bland, 1995) (Table 10.3).

Our results show that the independent variable simultaneously affects the dependent variable with a prob F-stat value of 0.000 which is lower (<) than the significance value of 0.05. Our model has a within R-square of 0.4234, which means that the dependent variable, namely returns, can be explained by the independent variable SVI of 42.43%. Variables outside the model explain the remaining 57.57% (Table 10.4).

Our model also shows that the SVI has a p-value $> |t|$ of 0.558 which means we should accept the null hypothesis that there is no significant correlation between SVI and return. The coefficient of 0.0000547 shows that the effects of the SVI are

Table 10.3. Classical Assumption Test for Model 1.

Multicollinearity Test	VIF	Tolerance	Decision
Search Volume Index	1.19	0.8403361	Free Multicollinearity Problem
Risk Premium	1.01	0.9900990	Free Multicollinearity Problem
Market Capitalisation Log	1.20	0.8333333	Free Multicollinearity Problem
Price-to-Book Ratio	1.13	0.8849558	Free Multicollinearity Problem
	z	**Prob $> |z|$**	**Decision**
Auto-correlation Test	0.35	0.72	Free Auto-correlation Problem
Heteroscedasticity Test	727.63	0.0000	Heteroscedasticity Problem

Table 10.4. Search Volume Index and Stock Return Regression Summary.

Return	Coefficient	t-stat	$p > |t|$
Search Volume Index	0.0000547	0.59	0.558
Risk Premium	0.141599	12.89	0.0000*
Market Capitalisation Log	0.029581	7.35	0.0000*
Price-to-Book Ratio	0.0003061	1.55	0.134
COVID	0.0069284	3.35	0.003*
Intercept	−0.53958	−7.47	0.0000*
Within R-Square	0.4232		
F-Stat	0.0000		

Note: *, **, *** denote statistical significance levels at 0.01, 0.05 and 0.10, respectively.

lower compared to the coefficient of risk premium of 0.1411599, the coefficient of the MK of 0.029581, and the coefficient of price-to-book ratio of 0.0003061.

Our model shows the result from our control variable, MK has a p-value $< |t|$ of 0.000 and risk premium has a p-value $< |t|$ of 0.000, which means we should reject the null hypothesis that there is a significant correlation between MK and return also risk premium and return. Besides that, price-to-book ratio has a p-value $> |t|$ of 0.134 means we should accept the null hypothesis that there is no significant correlation between price-to-book ratio and return.

When viewed from the perspective of the COVID-19 period, our model shows that COVID-19 has a significant positive influence on return at a 90% significance level, indicating that the presence of the COVID-19 pandemic increases the return. The coefficient of COVID-19 0.0069284 shows the positive relationship between returns and COVID-19, meaning that when entering the COVID-19 period, stock returns will increase. As we can see, Fig. 10.1 shows an increase in stock returns during COVID-19 compared to before COVID-19.

4.3. Model 2 Analysis

We perform the Hausman and Chow tests in the model selection test. the results of the Hausman test show that the null hypothesis is accepted so that the random effects method is chosen, then the results of the LM test show that the null hypothesis is accepted so that the common effects method is chosen, and finally the Chow test shows that the null hypothesis is accepted so that the common effects method is chosen (Table 10.5).

We performed a multicollinearity test using the VIF method on the regression model. Our result shows that each variable has a VIF value ($<$) of 10 and a tolerance value greater than 0.01. Therefore, we can confidently say that our model is free from multicollinearity problems. We conducted an auto-correlation test using the run test method on the regression model. Looking at the result of

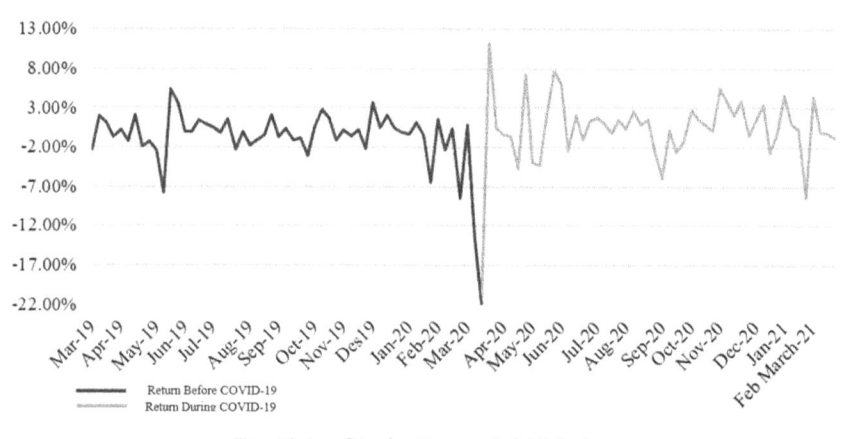

Fig. 10.1. Stocks Return LQ45 Index.

Table 10.5.   Model Selection Test for Model 2.

	p-value			Model Selection
	Hausman Test	Chow Test	LM Test	
Model 2	0.9793	1.0000	1.0000	Common Effects

auto-correlation for our model, the value of the run test is greater ($>$) than the significance value (0.05). Therefore, we can confidently say that our model is free from auto-correlation. We tested using the Wald test method on the regression model to see if there was a problem with the heteroscedasticity of the model. Our results show that the value of the heteroscedasticity test of 0.000 is greater ($>$) than the significance value of 0.05, which means that the model is free from heteroscedasticity problem (Table 10.6).

After conducting regression from our model, our results show that the independent variable simultaneously affects the dependent variable with a prob *F*-stat value of 0.000 which is lower ($<$) than the significance value of 0.05. Our model is within *R*-square of 0.5102 means that the independent variable, abnormal returns, can be explained by the independent variable SVI of 51.02%. In contrast, the remaining 48.98% is explained by variables outside the model (Table 10.7).

Table 10.6.   Classical Assumption Test for Model 2.

Multicollinearity Test	VIF	Tolerance	Decision
Search Volume Index	1.19	0.8403361	Free Multicollinearity Problem
Risk Premium	1.01	0.9900990	Free Multicollinearity Problem
Market Capitalisation Log	1.20	0.8333333	Free Multicollinearity Problem
Price-to-Book Ratio	1.13	0.8849558	Free Multicollinearity Problem
	z	**Prob $> \mid z \mid$**	**Decision**
Auto-correlation Test	-0.04	0.97	Free Auto-correlation Problem
Heteroscedasticity Test	7.47	0.9998	Free Heteroscedasticity Problem

Table 10.7.   Search Volume Index and Abnormal Stock Return Regression Summary.

Abnormal Return	Coefficient	*t*-stat	$p > \mid t \mid$
Search Volume Index	-0.0001020	-0.61	0.545
Risk Premium	0.4754800	51.94	0.0000*
Market Capitalisation Log	-0.0001600	-0.07	0.943
Price-to-Book Ratio	-0.0000470	-0.15	0.879
COVID	-0.0375571	-6.36	0.0000*
Intercept	0.0339658	0.85	0.398
Adjusted *R*-Square	0.5102		
***F*-Stat**	0.0000		

Note: *, **, *** denote statistical significance levels at 0.01, 0.05 and 0.10, respectively.

Our model also shows that the SVI has a p-value $> |t|$ of 0.545 which means we should accept the null hypothesis that there is no significant correlation between SVI and abnormal return. The coefficient of -0.0001200 shows that the effects of the SVI are lower compared to the coefficient of risk premium of 0.47548 and the coefficient of price-to-book ratio of -0.000047.

Our model shows the result from our control variable, MK has a p-value $> |t|$ of 0.943 and price-to-book ratio has a p-value $> |t|$ of 0.879, which means we should accept the null hypothesis that there is no significant correlation between MK and abnormal return also price-to-book ratio and abnormal return. Besides that, risk premium has a p-value $< |t|$ of 0.0000, which means we should reject the null hypothesis that there is a significant correlation between risk premium and abnormal return.

When viewed from the perspective of the COVID-19 period, our model shows that COVID-19 has a significant positive influence on return at a 90% significance level, indicating that the presence of the COVID-19 pandemic increases the return. The coefficient of COVID-19 -0.000047 shows that the relationship between abnormal returns and COVID-19 is negative, meaning that abnormal returns will decrease when entering the COVID-19 period. As we can see, Fig. 10.2 shows that there is an increase in stock returns during COVID-19 when compared to before COVID-19.

5. CONCLUSION AND RECOMMENDATION

This research finds that the SVI does not positively correlate with return and abnormal return. Both models in this study show the effect of COVID-19 has a significant influence on return and abnormal return, indicating the presence of the COVID-19 pandemic increases the stock return and decreases the abnormal return. This finding is in line with the conditions of return and abnormal return during March 2019–March 2021 on Tables 10.1 and 10.2.

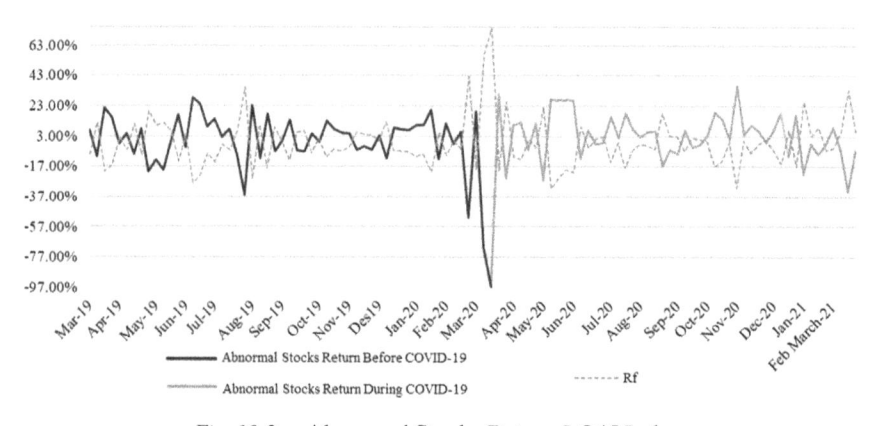

Fig. 10.2.   Abnormal Stocks Return LQ45 Index.

In this study, the regression results of the independent variable SVI do not positively correlate with the dependent variable return and abnormal return. It contradicts with Ekinci and Bulut's (2021) finding that the SVI positively correlates with stock return in the Turkey market and Takeda and Wakao (2014) show that the SVI positively correlates with stock returns in the Japanese market. This may happen where the SVI is not significant with stock returns and abnormal returns because the value of the SVI in this study is lower compared to the benchmark paper conducted by Ekinci and Bulut (2021) in turkey BIST100 (This study has a mean SVI of 18.81 compared to Ekinci and Bulut (2021) has a mean SVI of 28.81).

ACKNOWLEDGEMENT

We express our deep thanks to the supervisors for their kindness and helpful comments and suggestions on this research.

REFERENCES

Adachi, Y., Masuda, M., & Takeda, F. (2017). Google search intensity and its relationship to the returns and liquidity of Japanese startup stocks. *Pacific-Basin Finance Journal, 46*, 243–257. https://doi.org/10.1016/j.pacfin.2017.09.009

Ahmad Zaluki, N. A., & Ramdi, Z. (Eds.) (2013). *The effect of market excess return, size, market-to-book ratio and earnings yield on stock returns.* International Business Management.

Altman, D. G., & Bland, J. M. (1995). Statistics notes: The normal distribution. *BMJ (Clinical Research ed.), 310*(6975), 298. https://doi.org/10.1136/bmj.310.6975.298

Aouadi, A., Arouri, M., & Teulon, F. (2013). Investor attention and stock market activity: Evidence from France. *Economic Modelling, 35*, 674–681. https://doi.org/10.1016/j.econmod.2013.08.034

Apuke, O. D. (2017). Quantitative research methods: A synopsis approach. *Kuwait Chapter of Arabian Journal of Business and Management Review, 6*(11), 40–47. https://doi.org/10.12816/004336

Bank, M., Larch, M., & Peter, G. (2011). Google search volume and its influence on liquidity and returns of German stocks. *Financial Markets and Portfolio Management, 25*(3), 239–264. https://doi.org/10.1007/s11408-011-0165-y

Barber, B. M., & Odean, T. (2008). All that glitters: The effect of attention and news on the buying behavior of individual and institutional investors. *The Review of Financial Studies, 21*(2), 785–818. https://doi.org/10.1093/rfs/hhm079

Blitz, D., Falkenstein, E. G., & van Vliet, P. (2013). Explanations for the volatility effect: An overview based on the CAPM assumptions. *SSRN Electronic Journal.* https://doi.org/10.2139/ssrn.2270973

Bodie. (2017). *Investments* (11th ed.). McGraw-Hill Education.

Bratton, W., & McCahery, J. A. (Eds.) (2015). *Institutional investor activism: Hedge funds and private equity, economics and regulation.* Oxford University Press.

Brennan, M. J., Wang, A. W., & Yihong, X. (Eds.) (2002). *A simple model of intertemporal capital asset pricing and its implication for Gama-French Three-Factor Model.* https://conference.nber.org/confer/2002/aps02/xia.pdf

Chai, D. et al. (2019). Internet search intensity and its relation with trading activity and stock Returns. *International Review of Finance*, (irfi.12268). https://doi.org/10.1111/irfi.12268

Chemmanur, T. J., & Yan, A. (2019). Advertising, attention, and stock returns. *The Quarterly Journal of Finance, 09*(03), 1950009. https://doi.org/10.1142/s2010139219500095

Chen, Y., & Liang, B. (2004). Timing ability in the focus market of Asian country. *Journal of Finance, 59*(6), 2871–2901.

Cramer, D., & Howitt, D. L. (2004). *The SAGE dictionary of statistics: A practical resource for students in the social sciences*. SAGE Publications.

Da, Z., Engelberg, J., & Gao, P. (2011). In search of attention. *The Journal of Finance*, 66(5), 1461–1499. https://doi.org/10.1111/j.1540-6261.2011.01679.x

Ekinci, C., & Bulut, A. E. (2021). Google search and stock returns: A study on BIST 100 stocks. *Global Finance Journal*, 47(100518), 100518. https://doi.org/10.1016/j.gfj.2020.100518

Fama, E. F. (1970). Efficient capital markets: A review of theory and empirical work. *The Journal of Finance*, 25(2), 383. https://doi.org/10.2307/2325486

Fama, E. F., & French, K. R. (1993). Common risk factors in the returns on stocks and bonds. *Journal of Financial Economics*, 33(1), 3–56. https://doi.org/10.1016/0304-405x(93)90023-5

Fang, L., & Peress, J. (2009). Media coverage and the cross-section of stock returns. *The Journal of Finance*, 64(5), 2023–2052. https://doi.org/10.1111/j.1540-6261.2009.01493.x

Fehle, F., Tsyplakov, S., & Zdorovtsov, V. (2005). Can companies influence investor behaviour through advertising? Super bowl commercials and stock returns. *European Financial Management*, 11(5), 625–647. https://doi.org/10.1111/j.1354-7798.2005.00301.x

Foerster, S. R., & Karolyi, G. A. (1999). The effects of market segmentation and investor recognition on asset prices: Evidence from foreign stocks listing in the United States. *The Journal of Finance*, 54(3), 981–1013. https://doi.org/10.1111/0022-1082.00134

Freedman, D. A. (2006). *On the So-called 'Huber Sandwich Estimator' and 'Robust Standard Errors.'* http://www.stat.berkeley.edu/~census/mlesan.pdf

Gervais, S., Kaniel, R., & Mingelgrin, D. H. (2001). The high-volume return premium. *The Journal of Finance*, 56(3), 877–919. https://doi.org/10.1111/0022-1082.00349

Grullon, G., Kanatas, G., & Weston, J. P. (2004). Advertising, breadth of ownership, and liquidity. *The Review of Financial Studies*, 17(2), 439–461. https://doi.org/10.1093/rfs/hhg039

Guidi, F., Gupta, R., & Maheshwari, S. (2011). Weak-form market efficiency and calendar anomalies for Eastern Europe equity markets. *Journal of Emerging Market Finance*, 10(3), 337–389. https://doi.org/10.1177/097265271101000304

Gujarati, D. (2007). *Econometria*. McGraw-Hill Interamericana.

Gujarati. (2014). *Econometrics by example* (2nd ed.). Palgrave MacMillan. https://doi.org/10.1007/978-1-137-37502-5

Gujarati, D., & Porter, D. (2009). *Essentials of econometrics* (4th ed.). McGraw-Hill Professional.

Gujarati, D. N., & Porter, D. C. (2017). *Basic econometrics* (6th ed.). McGraw-Hill Education.

Gujarati, D., Porter, D., & Gunasekar, S. (2013). *Basic Econometrics*. McGraw-Hill.

Hartono, J. (2013). *Teori Portofolio dan Analisis Investasi*. BPFE.

Hartono, J. (2017). *Teori portofolio dan analisis investasi ed. 11*. BPFE.

Hassett, K. (2002). *Bubbleology*. Crown Publishing Group.

Joseph, K., Babajide Wintoki, M., & Zhang, Z. (2011). Forecasting abnormal stock returns and trading volume using investor sentiment: Evidence from online search. *International Journal of Forecasting*, 27(4), 1116–1127. https://doi.org/10.1016/j.ijforecast.2010.11.001.

Kahneman, D. (1973). *Attention and effort*. Prentice Hall.

Kim, N. et al. (2019). Google searches and stock market activity: Evidence from Norway. *Finance Research Letters*, 28, 208–220. https://doi.org/10.1016/j.frl.2018.05.003

Lehavy, R., & Sloan, R. G. (2008). Investor recognition and stock returns. *Review of Accounting Studies*, 13(2–3), 327–361. https://doi.org/10.1007/s11142-007-9063-y

Li, Z., Shi, Y., Chen, W., & Kargbo, M. (2014). Do attention-grabbing stocks attract all investors? Evidence from China. *Emerging Markets Finance and Trade*, 50(sup6), 158–183. https://doi.org/10.1080/1540496x.2014.1013856

Lou, D. (2014). Attracting investor attention through advertising. *The Review of Financial Studies*, 27(6), 1797–1829. https://doi.org/10.1093/rfs/hhu019

Markowitz, H. (1952). Portfolio selection. *The Journal of Finance*, 7(1), 77. https://doi.org/10.2307/2975974

Merton, R. C. (1987). A simple model of capital market equilibrium with incomplete information. *The Journal of Finance*, 42(3), 483. https://doi.org/10.2307/2328367

Mubarok, F., & Fadhli, M. M. (2020). Efficient Market Hypothesis and forecasting in the industrial sector on the Indonesia Stock Exchange. *Journal of Economics Business and Accountancy Ventura, 23*(2). https://doi.org/10.14414/jebav.v23i2.2240

Odean, T. (1998). Volume, volatility, price, and profit when all traders are above average. *The Journal of Finance, 53*(6), 1887–1934. https://doi.org/10.1111/0022-1082.00078

Search Engine Market Share Indonesia. (n.d.). StatCounter Global Stats. Retrieved June 12, 2022, from https://gs.statcounter.com/search-engine-market-share/all/indonesia

Seasholes, M. S., & Wu, G. (2005). Predictable behavior, profits, and attention. *SSRN Electronic Journal.* https://doi.org/10.2139/ssrn.686193.

Sharpe, W. F. (1964). Capital asset prices: A theory of market equilibrium under conditions of risk. *The Journal of Finance, 19*(3), 425–442. https://doi.org/10.1111/j.1540-6261.1964.tb02865.x

Sharpe, W. F. E. (n.d.). *all. 2005. Investasi. Edisi Keenam, Jilid 1. Indeks (terjemahan).* Jakarta.

Shefrin, H., & Statman, M. (1985). The disposition to sell winners too early and ride losers too long: Theory and evidence. *The Journal of Finance, 40*(3), 777–790. https://doi.org/10.1111/j.1540-6261.1985.tb05002.x

Shefrin, H., & Statman, M. (2000). Behavioral portfolio theory. *Journal of Financial and Quantitative Analysis, 35*(2), 127. https://doi.org/10.2307/2676187

Shleifer, A. (2000). *Inefficient markets: An introduction to behavioural finance. Clarendon lectures in economics.* Oxford University Press.

Singh, J. E., Babshetti, V., & Shivaprasad, H. N. (2021). Efficient market hypothesis to behavioral finance: A review of rationality to irrationality. *Materials Today: Proceedings.* https://doi.org/10.1016/j.matpr.2021.03.318

Statman, M. (1999). Behaviorial finance: Past battles and future engagements. *Financial Analysts Journal, 55*(6), 18–27. https://doi.org/10.2469/faj.v55.n6.2311

Takeda, F., & Wakao, T. (2014). Google search intensity and its relationship with returns and trading volume of Japanese stocks. *Pacific-Basin Finance Journal, 27,* 1–18. https://doi.org/10.1016/j.pacfin.2014.01.003

Takeda, F., & Yamazaki, H. (2006). Stock price reactions to public TV programs on listed Japanese Companies. *Economics Bulletin, 13*(7). http://www.accessecon.com/pubs/EB/2006/Volume13/EB-06M20002A.pdf

Tversky, A., & Kahneman, D. (2013). Judgment under uncertainty: Heuristics and biases. In *Handbook of the fundamentals of financial decision making* (pp. 261–268). World Scientific.

University Paul Krugman. (2012). *End this depression now!* W. W. Norton & Company.

Vlastakis, N., & Markellos, R. N. (2012). Information demand and stock market volatility. *SSRN Electronic Journal.* https://doi.org/10.2139/ssrn.1558434

CHAPTER 11

THE IMPACT OF WORKING CAPITAL MANAGEMENT ON FIRM VALUE AND PROFITABILITY OF LISTED PROPERTY AND REAL ESTATE FIRMS IN INDONESIA DURING THE COVID-19 PANDEMIC

Rifaldi Yunus Mahendra and Taufik Faturohman

School of Business and Management, Institut Teknologi Bandung, Indonesia

ABSTRACT

Since the first COVID-19 outbreak in Indonesia, the demand for property and real estate has plunged. The point to consider during an economic crisis and one of the appropriate solutions to withstand the impacts of the economic crisis is to carry out efficient working capital management (WCM). Furthermore, the efficient WCM also contributes positively to the value creation and profitability of the firm. This study aims to empirically analyse and examine the impact of WCM on firms' market valuation and profitability of listed property and real estate firms in Indonesia over the period 2018Q3–2021Q3. This study employs panel data regression and the two-step system generalised method of moment (GMM) to deal with unobservable heterogeneity and endogeneity issues. The results show that WCM components significantly affect firms' value and profitability. In addition, the

The Finance-Innovation Nexus: Implications for Socio-Economic Development
International Symposia in Economic Theory and Econometrics, Volume 34, 161–176
Copyright © 2025 by Emerald Publishing Limited
All rights of reproduction in any form reserved
ISSN: 1571-0386/doi:10.1108/S1571-038620240000034013

COVID-19 pandemic has also proven to have a significant negative impact on firms' value and profitability.

Keywords: Working capital management; property and real estate industry; firm value; profitability; Indonesia; credit policy

JEL Classification: C33; C58; G01; G31; L85

1. INTRODUCTION

The pandemic of the coronavirus disease 2019 (COVID-19) has disrupted every aspect of human life worldwide. Furthermore, it has affected domestic and international economic activities (Fordian and Raharja, in press). It also has pushed the Indonesian economy into a disaster.

According to the Commercial Property Survey carried out by Bank Indonesia, shown in Fig. 11.1, the Commercial Property Demand Index (CPDI) from the third quarter of 2019 to the fourth quarter of 2021 experienced slowing growth on an annual basis. However, the CPDI from the first quarter to the second quarter of 2021 experienced a slight increase in growth compared to the fourth quarter of 2020 (Bank Indonesia, 2020a).

The impact of the COVID-19 pandemic on the property and real estate industry is disrupting firms' operations, marketing activities, and the completion of planned property projects. Furthermore, not only are sales expected to stagnate, but also the risk of bad credit from debtors. These issues will lead to the firm's liquidity problems. This is in line with research (Simon et al., 2017), which stated that the global economic crisis affected firms' liquidity and working capital management (WCM), which consequently led to their low performance. The economic

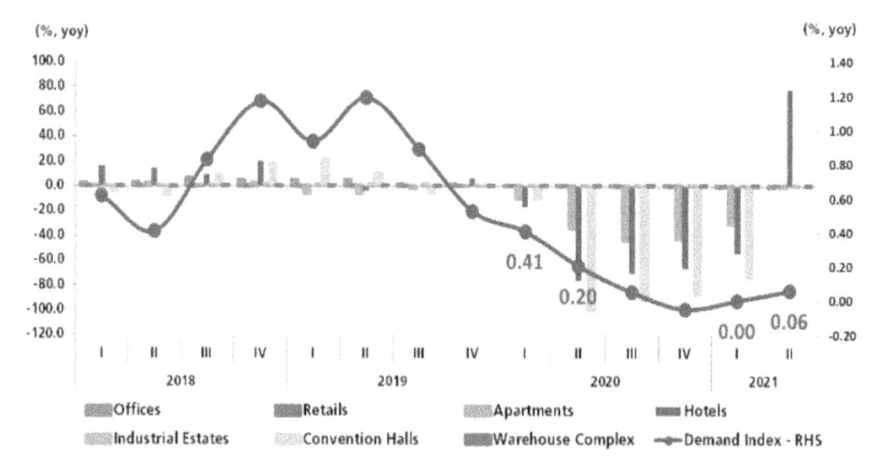

Fig. 11.1. Commercial Property Development Index Growth (% YoY). *Source*: Bank Indonesia.

crisis affects business performance and working capital as a measure of liquidity and business profitability of all sizes, which will eventually affect the firm's market valuation (Akgün & Memiş Karataş, 2020).

As far as we know, a study was conducted to analyse whether WCM affects the profitability of property and real estate firms in Indonesia over the 2013–2017 period. This study used panel data regression, and the result implies that CCC had a significant negative effect on the profitability of property and real estate firms in Indonesia (Firmansyah et al., 2018). However, the study is based on historical financial data from 2013 to 2017, which does not consider the economic crisis caused by the COVID-19 pandemic.

The ability of the firms to withstand and cope with the effects of economic turbulence triggered by the COVID-19 pandemic depends on how well firms could keep up with the changes in how firms manage their working capital activities such as debtors, inventories, and creditors efficiently (Nandy & Sussan, 2021). Thus, this study aims to empirically analyse and examine the impact of WCM on firms' market valuation and profitability of listed property and real estate firms in Indonesia during the COVID-19 pandemic.

2. LITERATURE REVIEW AND HYPOTHESES DEVELOPMENT

Working capital is an essential component of every firm's value creation and profitability (Michel et al., 2020). However, in early 2020, the world faced an unprecedented global phenomenon, the COVID-19 pandemic, which triggered the global health and economic crisis. The global economic crisis impacted firms' liquidity and WCM, which resulted in poor performance (Simon et al., 2017). As a strategy for firms' resiliency in facing the economic crisis due to the COVID-19 pandemic, one of the appropriate solutions for firms' managers is to carry out efficient WCM since firms' managers have access to more firms' information such as firms' future performance, strategy, changes in firms' characteristics, and market conditions (Yovi et al., 2022).

This strategy also contributes positively to the value creation and profitability of the firm (Javid & Zita, 2014). The decisions that must be taken by firms' managers are vital for every firm related to the need to maximise firms' profits and value, as well as the impact of the decision on firms' ability to deal with the economic crisis caused by the COVID-19 pandemic (Susan et al., 2022). The following sections of this research provide a detailed review of the literature on the relationship of each working capital component to firm market valuation and profitability.

2.1. Days Sales Outstanding (DSO)

DSO measures the number of days a firm needs to collect payment after a sale has been made (Gitman & Zutter, 2015). Some previous studies conducted by Farhan et al. (2021) and Vural et al. (2012) found a positive relationship between DSO and firm value, indicating that loosening credit policy by granting customers more time to make payments will lead to an increase in firm market valuation. On the other hand, most previous studies found a negative relationship between the two variables (Abuzayed, 2011; Bhatia & Srivastava, 2016; Essel & Brobbey, 2021). It implies that shortening the collection period will lead to an increase in firm market valuation. Thus, the following is the hypothesis proposed:

H1a. The relationship between DSO and firm market valuation is estimated to be negative.

In terms of firms' profitability, extending trade credit to customers has the potential to lock in the resources viable to debtors, which will increase the firm's opportunity costs and eventually hurt profits (Braimah et al., 2021). Furthermore, most previous studies also found a negative relationship between both variables (Bhatia & Srivastava, 2016; Deloof, 2003; Vural et al., 2012). Thus, the following is the hypothesis proposed:

H1b. The relationship between DSO and firm profitability is estimated to be negative.

2.2. Days Inventory Outstanding (DIO)

DIO measures the number of days a firm needs to hold inventory before turning it into cash (Gitman & Zutter, 2015). Some previous studies conducted by Afrifa et al. (2014) and Vural et al. (2012) found a positive relationship between DIO and firm value, indicating that increasing the delay for inventories to be converted into cash leads to an increase in firm market valuation (Baños-Caballero et al., 2014; Braimah et al., 2021). On the contrary, most previous studies found a negative relationship between both variables (Abuzayed, 2011; Bhatia & Srivastava, 2016; Essel & Brobbey, 2021; Farhan et al., 2021). It implies reducing the delay for inventories to be converted into cash leads to an increase in firm market valuation. Thus, the following is the hypothesis proposed:

H2a. The relationship between DIO and firm market valuation is estimated to be negative.

As regards the firm's profitability, maintaining high inventory levels means the firm's capital is locked up in working capital and also increases holding costs which will deteriorate the firm's profits (Braimah et al., 2021; Deloof, 2003). Furthermore, most previous studies (Bhatia & Srivastava, 2016; Braimah et al., 2021; Vural et al., 2012) show a negative relationship between DIO and firm profitability. Therefore, the following is the hypothesis proposed:

H2b. The relationship between DIO and firm profitability is estimated to be negative.

2.3. Days Payable Outstanding (DPO)

DPO measures the number of days a firm needs to pay back its accounts payable (Gitman & Zutter, 2015). Most previous studies (Abuzayed, 2011; Essel &

Brobbey, 2021; Vural et al., 2012) show a positive relationship between DPO and firm value. It implies that delaying payments to creditors could increase firm profitability and market valuation (Braimah et al., 2021). On the other hand, some previous studies conducted by Bhatia and Srivastava (2016) and Farhan et al. (2021) found a negative relationship between DPO and firm value, indicating that excessive payment delays may put doubt on the firm's creditworthiness. In addition, it might result in the firm losing advantageous credit terms from existing and potential creditors. Therefore, the following is the hypothesis proposed:

H3a. The relationship between DPO and firm market valuation is estimated to be positive.

Regarding the firm's profitability, some previous studies (Bhatia & Srivastava, 2016; Braimah et al., 2021; Vural et al., 2012) show a positive relationship between DPO and firm profitability. Therefore, it makes financial sense since if a firm takes longer to pay its accounts payable to creditors, its working capital volume will decrease, increasing its profitability (Hussain et al., 2021). Thus, the following is the hypothesis proposed:

H3b. The relationship between DPO and firm profitability is estimated to be positive.

2.4. Cash Conversion Cycle (CCC)

CCC measures the number of days a firm needs to convert cash invested in its operations into cash (Gitman & Zutter, 2015). Some previous studies conducted by (Afrifa et al., 2014; Vural et al., 2012) found a positive relationship between CCC and firm value, indicating that a more prolonged CCC reduces breakage and supply costs while attracting more customers, resulting in increased firm market valuation (Baños-Caballero et al., 2014). On the contrary, most previous studies (Abuzayed, 2011; Bhatia & Srivastava, 2016; Essel & Brobbey, 2021) show a negative relationship between CCC and firm value. It implies that accelerating the conversion of its investments in working capital into cash flows leads to an increase in firm value. Thus, the following is the hypothesis proposed:

H4a. The relationship between CCC and firm market valuation is estimated to be negative.

The longer the CCC means, the more inefficient the firm manages liquidity. Thus, shortening the CCC allows a firm to increase its liquidity, gain financial flexibility, and avoid the potential risk of cash out and financial distress, which tends to increase firm profitability (Baños-Caballero et al., 2014). Therefore, the following is the hypothesis proposed:

H4b. The relationship between CCC and firm profitability is estimated to be negative.

3. METHODOLOGY

3.1. Data Collection

The data collected is in the form of panel data, which is based on secondary historical financial data collected from 39 property and real estate firms listed on the Indonesia Stock Exchange (IDX). The data collected is quarterly over the period 2018Q3–2021Q3. It is divided into two periods, namely financial data from 2018Q3 to 2019Q4, considered the period before the COVID-19 pandemic, and 2020Q2 to 2021Q3, considered the period during the COVID-19 pandemic. The historical financial data are also retrieved from Stockbit. Stockbit is a simple stock investing app that provides complete information about firms listed on the IDX.

3.2. Research Variables

The dependent variables used in this study are Tobin's Q and Gross Operating Profit (GOP). Tobin's Q is used as a proxy of firm market valuation, and GOP is used as a proxy of firm profitability. Tobin's Q is used because it has been employed as the primary measure of firm market valuation since it has better distributional properties (Afrifa et al., 2014). Meanwhile, GOP is used since it provides an actual measure of firms' operating activities of which the WCM component is a critical component (Ban˜os-Caballero et al., 2012). As regards the independent variable, this study adopts four components of WCM as independent variables consisting of DSO, DIO, DPO, and CCC.

In line with previous studies, this study employs some variables that are known to impact firm market valuation and profitability as control variables. Furthermore, this study utilises a dummy variable as a control variable, which is COVID_CRISIS, to understand firms' overall situation. The value of this dummy variable is equal to 0, which indicates the period before the COVID-19 pandemic, and 1 implies the period during the COVID-19 pandemic. The abbreviation, calculation, and related literature for all the variables are shown in Table 11.1.

3.3. Empirical Model Specification

In order to analyse and examine the relationship between the WCM components and firms' value as well as profitability, this study employs panel data regression and the two-step system GMM. These two estimation techniques are utilised to deal with unobservable heterogeneity and endogeneity issues. All WCM components and various control variables described previously are introduced in the estimation models. The models used to test the hypotheses developed previously are as follows:

$$
\begin{aligned}
\text{TOBINSQ} = \alpha &+ \beta_1\text{DSO}_{it} + \beta_2\text{LEV}_{it} + \beta_3\text{TA\_TURN}_{it} + \beta_4\text{LEV}_{it} \\
&+ \beta_5\text{FIRM\_SIZE}_{it} + \beta_6\text{CURR\_RAT}_{it} + \beta_7\text{NWC}_{it} + \quad \textbf{(Model 1A)} \\
&\beta_8\text{CATAR}_{it} + \beta_9\text{CTR}_{it} + \beta_{10}\text{COVID\_CRISIS}_{it} + \varepsilon_{it}
\end{aligned}
$$

$$
\begin{aligned}
\text{GOP} = \alpha &+ \beta_1\text{DSO}_{it} + \beta_2\text{LEV}_{it} + \beta_3\text{TA\_TURN}_{it} + \beta_4\text{LEV}_{it} \\
&+ \beta_5\text{FIRM\_SIZE}_{it} + \beta_6\text{CURR\_RAT}_{it} + \beta_7\text{NWC}_{it} + \quad \textbf{(Model 1B)} \\
&\beta_8\text{CATAR}_{it} + \beta_9\text{CTR}_{it} + \beta_{10}\text{COVID\_CRISIS}_{it} + \varepsilon_{it}
\end{aligned}
$$

Table 11.1. Research Variables.

Variables	Abbreviation	Calculation
Dependent Variables		
Tobin's Q	TOBINSQ	(Total market value + Book value of liabilities) /
Gross Operating Profit	GOP	Total assets
		(Sales–COGS) / (Total assets–Financial assets)
Independent Variables		
Days Sales Outstanding	DSO	(Accounts receivable / Sales) * Days in a quarter
Days Inventory Outstanding	DIO	(Inventories / COGS) * Days in a quarter
Days Payable Outstanding	DPO	(Accounts Payable / Purchases) * Days in a quarter
Cash Conversion Cycle	CCC	DSO + DIO - DPO
Control Variables		
Financial Leverage	LEV	Total debts / Total assets
Total Asset Turnover Ratio	TA_TURN	Sales / Total assets
Firm Size	FIRM_SIZE	Natural logarithm of total assets
Current Ratio	CURR_RAT	Current asset / Current liabilities
Net Working Capital	NWC	Current asset - Current liabilities
Current Assets to Total Assets Ratio	CATAR	Current asset / Total assets
Cash Turnover Ratio	CTR	Cash / Sales
The COVID-19 Pandemic	COVID_CRISIS	(0, 1)

$$TOBINSQ = \alpha + \beta_1 DIO_{it} + \beta_2 LEV_{it} + \beta_3 TA\_TURN_{it} + \beta_4 LEV_{it}$$
$$+ \beta_5 FIRM\_SIZE_{it} + \beta_6 CURR\_RAT_{it} + \beta_7 NWC_{it} + \quad \textbf{(Model 2A)}$$
$$\beta_8 CATAR_{it} + \beta_9 CTR_{it} + \beta_{10} COVID\_CRISIS_{it} + \varepsilon_{it}$$

$$GOP = \alpha + \beta_1 DIO_{it} + \beta_2 LEV_{it} + \beta_3 TA\_TURN_{it} + \beta_4 LEV_{it}$$
$$+ \beta_5 FIRM\_SIZE_{it} + \beta_6 CURR\_RAT_{it} + \beta_7 NWC_{it} + \quad \textbf{(Model 2B)}$$
$$\beta_8 CATAR_{it} + \beta_9 CTR_{it} + \beta_{10} COVID\_CRISIS_{it} + \varepsilon_{it}$$

$$TOBINSQ = \alpha + \beta_1 DPO_{it} + \beta_2 LEV_{it} + \beta_3 TA\_TURN_{it} + \beta_4 LEV_{it}$$
$$+ \beta_5 FIRM\_SIZE_{it} + \beta_6 CURR\_RAT_{it} + \beta_7 NWC_{it} \quad \textbf{(Model 3A)}$$
$$+ \beta_8 CATAR_{it} + \beta_9 CTR_{it} + \beta_{10} COVID\_CRISIS_{it} + \varepsilon_{it}$$

$$GOP = \alpha + \beta_1 DPO_{it} + \beta_2 LEV_{it} + \beta_3 TA\_TURN_{it} + \beta_4 LEV_{it}$$
$$+ \beta_5 FIRM\_SIZE_{it} + \beta_6 CURR\_RAT_{it} + \beta_7 NWC_{it} \quad \textbf{(Model 3B)}$$
$$+ \beta_8 CATAR_{it} + \beta_9 CTR_{it} + \beta_{10} COVID\_CRISIS_{it} + \varepsilon_{it}$$

$$TOBINSQ = \alpha + \beta_1 CCC_{it} + \beta_2 LEV_{it} + \beta_3 TA\_TURN_{it} + \beta_4 LEV_{it}$$
$$+ \beta_5 FIRM\_SIZE_{it} + \beta_6 CURR\_RAT_{it} + \beta_7 NWC_{it} \quad \textbf{(Model 4A)}$$
$$+ \beta_8 CATAR_{it} + \beta_9 CTR_{it} + \beta_{10} COVID\_CRISIS_{it} + \varepsilon_{it}$$

$$GOP = \alpha + \beta_1 CCC_{it} + \beta_2 LEV_{it} + \beta_3 TA\_TURN_{it} + \beta_4 LEV_{it}$$
$$+ \beta_5 FIRM\_SIZE_{it} + \beta_6 CURR\_RAT_{it} + \beta_7 NWC_{it} \quad \textbf{(Model 4B)}$$
$$+ \beta_8 CATAR_{it} + \beta_9 CTR_{it} + \beta_{10} COVID\_CRISIS_{it} + \varepsilon_{it}$$

4. RESULT AND DISCUSSION

4.1. Descriptive Statistics

The descriptive statistical analysis is shown in Table 11.2.

4.2. Panel Data Regression Analysis

Panel data regression is employed in this study since it is possible to control for unobservable heterogeneity, which allows for the elimination of biases resulting from the presence of individual effects (Caballero et al., 2010). The most common panel data models for analysing and examining relationships between dependent and independent variables are the Fixed Effects (FE) and Random Effects (RE) models (Altaf & Shah, 2018). In this study, the Hausman test is employed for choosing the preferred panel data model, FE or RE model. Furthermore, since this study uses panel data models, it is able to relax the classical assumption tests (Biørn, 2017). Hence, it is not necessary to perform some of the classical assumption tests.

In addition, this study also uses cluster-robust Huber/white standard errors on FE models and Generalised Least Square (RE models) to take care of heteroscedasticity and serial correlation (Gujarati & Porter, 2009; Schmidheiny, 2012). The multicollinearity test is still being carried out using the variance inflation factor (VIF) as a measure of multicollinearity. The VIF test results are lower than 10 in any cases. In other words, the results imply that no multicollinearity issue is found in the estimation models (Jr et al., 2018). Therefore, it can be concluded that all models satisfied the classical assumption tests.

4.2.1. Panel Data Regression Result of WCM Impact on Firm Value

Table 11.3 shows the result of panel data regressions between independent and control variables with firm value (Tobin's Q) as a dependent variable. The

Table 11.2.   Descriptive Analysis.

Variables	Obs.	Mean	Std. Dev.	Min	Max
TOBINSQ	468	0.9686	0.7146	0.0000	0.8304
GOP	468	0.0486	0.0442	−0.0311	0.3026
DSO	468	118.6155	219.0462	−92.9500	1441.3100
DIO	468	2476.7652	6470.4701	2.3200	104990.7800
DPO	468	138.1808	241.8902	0.0172	2030.2400
CCC	468	2457.1999	6437.3475	−111.5800	104956.0700
LEV	468	0.3835	0.1897	0.0415	1.1080
TA_TURN	468	0.0390	0.0313	−0.0100	0.2900
FIRM_SIZE	468	29.1383	1.4240	24.9338	31.7962
CURR_RAT	468	3.1461	2.6749	0.1800	24.4500
NWC	468	2.1730	4.7500	−7.4670	33.949
CATAR	468	0.3840	0.2092	0.0274	0.8996
CTR	468	2.4972	2.8903	0.0045	25.4385
COVID_CRISIS	468	0.5000	0.5005	0.0000	1.0000

Note: Obs. stands for the number of observations; Std. Dev. for standard deviation; Min. for minimum; and Max. for maximum.

Table 11.3. Panel Data Regression Result of WCM Impact on Firm Value.

	(1A)	(2A)	(3A)	(4A)
	TOBINSQ	TOBINSQ	TOBINSQ	TOBINSQ
DSO	0.0105			
	(0.517)			
DIO		−0.0264**		
		(0.012)		
DPO			−0.0041	
			(0.721)	
CCC				−0.0240**
				(0.048)
LEV	0.1604	0.2645	0.1702	0.2317
	(0.490)	(0.260)	(0.465)	(0.322)
TA_TURN	0.6280*	0.0642	0.4877	0.1728
	(0.074)	(0.868)	(0.216)	(0.656)
FIRM_SIZE	−1.0328	−1.1158	−1.0244	−1.1050
	(0.234)	(0.199)	(0.234)	(0.201)
CURR_RAT	−0.0180	−0.0075	−0.0182	−0.0106
	(0.609)	(0.831)	(0.605)	(0.763)
NWC	−0.0027	−0.0030	−0.0024	−0.0026
	(0.583)	(0.543)	(0.631)	(0.598)
CATAR	0.0594	0.1459	0.0626	0.1036
	(0.724)	(0.393)	(0.711)	(0.540)
CTR	−0.0091	−0.0147	−0.0104	−0.0137
	(0.577)	(0.361)	(0.518)	(0.397)
COVID_CRISIS	−0.0898***	−0.0845***	−0.0914***	−0.0841***
	(0.000)	(0.000)	(0.000)	(0.000)
Constant	1.7451	1.9510	1.7610	1.9367
	(0.167)	(0.123)	(0.160)	(0.124)
No of observation	468	468	468	468
No of companies	39	39	39	39
R-squared	0.064	0.079	0.063	0.073
Hausman	0.885	0.861	0.836	0.820
Estimation	RE	RE	RE	RE

Note: ***, **, and * denote a *p*-value in parentheses of 0.01, 0.05, and 0.1, respectively.

Hausman test results show that the model fails to reject the null hypothesis, so the estimation model preferred is the RE model. The panel data regression results show that DSO has a non-significant positive influence on firm value. Thus, *H1a* is not accepted due to a lack of statistical significance, as in the research of (Sawarni et al., 2021; Vural et al., 2012). Meanwhile, DIO appears to have a statistically significant negative impact on firm value. Therefore, *H2a* is accepted, as in the research of (Essel & Brobbey, 2021; Sawarni et al., 2021). It implies that reducing the delay for inventories to be converted into cash leads to an increase in firm market valuation (Baños-Caballero et al., 2014; Braimah et al., 2021).

DPO is proven to have a statistically non-significant impact on firm value. Thus, *H3a* is not accepted due to a lack of statistical significance, as in the research of Bhatia and Srivastava (2016). On the contrary, CCC seems to have a significant negative effect on firm value. Hence, *H4a* is accepted, as in the research of Bhatia and Srivastava (2016) and Essel and Brobbey (2021). It implies that accelerating the conversion of its investments in working capital into cash flows leads to an increase in firm value. Furthermore, the total asset turnover ratio, leverage, and current assets to total assets ratio fail to have a significant positive impact on firms' value. Meanwhile, the firm size, current ratio, net working capital, and cash turnover ratio have a negative effect on firms' value but fail to be statistically significant in this study. However, the dummy variable COVID_CRISIS seems to have a strong negative significant influence on firm value. It indicates that the more severe the economic crisis triggered by the COVID-19 pandemic, the lower the Indonesian property and real estate firms value (Zimon & Tarighi, 2021).

4.2.2. Panel Data Regression Result of WCM Impact on Firm Profitability
Table 11.4 shows the result of panel data regressions between independent and control variables with firm profitability (GOP) as a dependent variable. The

Table 11.4. Panel Data Regression Result of WCM Impact on firm Profitability.

	(1B)	(2B)	(3B)	(4B)
	GOP	GOP	GOP	GOP
DSO	0.0118			
	(0.120)			
DIO		−0.0063**		
		(0.043)		
DPO			−0.0059	
			(0.458)	
CCC				0.0016
				(0.749)
LEV	0.0943	−0.1158*	0.1032	0.0901
	(0.356)	(0.063)	(0.296)	(0.374)
TA_TURN	1.8733***	1.7210***	1.6948***	1.8238***
	(0.000)	(0.000)	(0.000)	(0.000)
FIRM_SIZE	−1.7076	0.3963***	−1.8656*	−1.7245
	(0.141)	(0.008)	(0.100)	(0.138)
CURR_RAT	0.0106	0.0048	0.0099	0.0111
	(0.341)	(0.685)	(0.405)	(0.325)
NWC	−0.0001	−0.0006	0.0003	0.0003
	(0.734)	(0.743)	(0.377)	(0.365)
CATAR	0.3134***	0.2093***	0.3157***	0.3030***
	(0.000)	(0.000)	(0.000)	(0.000)
CTR	0.0802***	0.0664***	0.0787***	0.0787***
	(0.000)	(0.000)	(0.000)	(0.000)
COVID_CRISIS	−0.0284**	−0.0266***	−0.0296**	−0.0303**
	(0.044)	(0.001)	(0.026)	(0.026)
Constant	2.3966	−0.5820***	2.6626	2.4409
	(0.156)	(0.007)	(0.107)	(0.149)
No of observations	468	468	468	468
No of companies	39	39	39	39
R-squared	0.630	0.613	0.629	0.627
Hausman	0.000	0.147	0.000	0.000
Estimation	FE	RE	FE	FE

Note: ***, **, and * denote a *p*-value in parentheses of 0.01, 0.05, and 0.1, respectively.

Hausman test results show that models 1B, 3B, and 4B reject the null hypothesis, so the estimation model preferred is the FE model. However, model 2B fails to reject the null hypothesis, so the RE model is the appropriate estimation model. The panel data regression results show that DSO seems to have a non-significant positive impact on firm profitability. Therefore, *H1b* is not accepted due to a lack of statistical significance, as in the research of (Khan & Ghazi, 2013). Meanwhile, DIO is proven to have a statistically significant negative influence on firm profitability. Thus, *H2b* is accepted, as in the research of Braimah et al. (2021) and Deloof (2003). It indicates that reducing the delay for inventories to be converted into cash will boost firm profitability. On the other hand, DPO failed to have a statistically significant impact on firm profitability. Hence, *H3b* is not accepted, as in the research of Hussain et al. (2021) and Khan and Ghazi 82013).

Similarly, the relationship between GOP and CCC, proposed in *H4b*, is not accepted since CCC is proven to have a statistically non-significant impact on firm profitability. However, some control variables seem to have a statistically significant influence on firm profitability. For example, total asset turnover ratio, firm size, current assets to total assets ratio, and cash turnover ratio. In addition, the dummy variable COVID_CRISIS is proven to have a highly significant negative influence on firm profitability. It implies that the economic crisis triggered by the COVID-19 pandemic will hurt the Indonesian property and real estate firms' profitability (Zimon & Tarighi, 2021).

4.3. Generalised Method of Moment (GMM) Analysis

In addition to the panel data regression, the two-step system GMM is also employed to analyse the dynamic panel data. This robust estimation method is employed to deal with unobservable endogeneity and heterogeneity issues in regression models, as well as to produce consistent and unbiased results. The dynamic panel data model consists of the lagged dependent variable as an independent variable to assist in solving autocorrelation and endogeneity issues along with help control inverse causality and bias results triggered by omitted variables (Essel & Brobbey, 2021; Vural et al., 2012).

In addition, this study includes the squared values of WCM components (DSO^2, DIO^2, DPO^2, CCC^2) to take care of the possibility of any nonlinear relationship between WCM and firm value also profitability (Ban˜os-Caballero et al., 2012; Essel & Brobbey, 2021). This study utilises the Hansen J statistic (overidentification test) to detect invalidity of the system GMM instruments and AR(2) statistic to test the absence of second-order serial correlation in the residues (Rey-Ares et al., 2021). Based on the two-step system GMM results, AR(2) test results show the models do not suffer from second-order serial correlation since the values are not significant, and Hansen test results reveal that the instruments used in the two-step system GMM are also valid and not overidentified.

4.3.1. Two-Step System GMM Results of WCM Impact on Firm Value

The empirical evidence shown in Table 11.5 reflects that the significant and positive coefficients of the lagged dependent variable ($TOBINSQ_{(t-1)}$) indicate that

Table 11.5. Two-Step System GMM Result of WCM Impact on Firm Value.

	(1A)	(2A)	(3A)	(4A)
	TOBINSQ	TOBINSQ	TOBINSQ	TOBINSQ
TOBINSQ$_{(t-1)}$	1.0051**	1.0105**	1.0034*	1.0147**
	(0.037)	(0.045)	(0.054)	(0.038)
DSO	−0.0044			
	(0.801)			
DSO^2	0.0018			
	(0.734)			
DIO		−0.0070		
		(0.804)		
DIO^2		0.0011		
		(0.806)		
DPO			−0.0422	
			(0.280)	
DPO^2			0.0117**	
			(0.030)	
CCC				−0.0246
				(0.370)
CCC^2				0.0037
				(0.420)
LEV	0.0014	0.0189	−0.0024	0.0156
	(0.990)	(0.820)	(0.974)	(0.894)
TA_TURN	0.3050	0.2635	0.2200	0.2595
	(0.549)	(0.635)	(0.376)	(0.613)
FIRM_SIZE	0.1455	0.1423	0.1834	0.1427
	(0.495)	(0.526)	(0.346)	(0.472)
CURR_RAT	−0.0012	0.0007	−0.0054	0.0014
	(0.989)	(0.994)	(0.956)	(0.988)
NWC	0.0001	0.0002	0.0005	0.0001
	(0.967)	(0.900)	(0.768)	(0.967)
CATAR	−0.0055	−0.0086	−0.0068	−0.0011
	(0.977)	(0.967)	(0.974)	(0.995)
CTR	−0.0025	−0.0013	−0.0027	−0.0009
	(0.880)	(0.935)	(0.871)	(0.956)
COVID_CRISIS	0.0327	0.0319	0.0304	0.0336
	(0.283)	(0.315)	(0.374)	(0.277)
Constant	−0.2243	−0.2156	−0.2458	−0.1880
	(0.593)	(0.646)	(0.574)	(0.606)
No of observation	390	390	390	390
No of companies	39	39	39	39
Number of instruments	14	14	14	14
AR(2)	0.395	0.399	0.379	0.399
Hansen test	0.133	0.126	0.098	0.123

Note: ***, **, and * denote a *p*-value in parentheses of 0.01, 0.05, and 0.1, respectively.

the firm value in the previous quarter positively influences the current firm value. Furthermore, the majority of WCM components and their quadratic forms do not seem to significantly affect the firm value, i.e., the statistical evidence on the effect of the DSO, DIO, CCC, and their quadratic forms (DSO^2, DIO^2, CCC^2) fails to have a significant impact on firm value. Thus, *H1a*, *H2a*, and *H4a* are not accepted due to a lack of statistical significance, as in the research of Abuzayed (2011) and Vural et al. (2012).

However, the quadratic form of **DPO** seems to have a significant positive effect on firm value. Therefore, *H3a* is accepted, as in the research of Abuzayed (2011) and Essel and Brobbey (2021). In addition, it indicates that delaying payments to creditors could lead to increased firm market valuation (Braimah et al., 2021). Furthermore, all control variables, including the dummy variable COVID-19 pandemic, are empirically proven to have not a significant influence on firm value.

4.3.2. Two-Step System GMM Results of WCM Impact on Firm Profitability
The result of the two-step system GMM shown in Table 11.6 reflects that the significant and positive coefficients of the lagged dependent variable (GOP$_{(t-1)}$)

Table 11.6. Two-Step System GMM Result of WCM Impact on Firm Profitability.

	(1B)	(2B)	(3B)	(4B)
	GOP	GOP	GOP	GOP
GOP$_{(t-1)}$	0.1337***	0.1326***	0.1276***	0.1313***
	(0.006)	(0.008)	(0.009)	(0.009)
DSO	0.0486***			
	(0.000)			
DSO^2	−0.0123***			
	(0.000)			
DIO		−0.0127		
		(0.205)		
DIO^2		0.0014		
		(0.474)		
DPO			−0.0098	
			(0.668)	
DPO^2			−0.0001	
			(0.990)	
CCC				−0.0025
				(0.763)
CCC^2				−0.0007
				(0.623)
LEV	−0.1408*	−0.1108	−0.1209	−0.1412*
	(0.070)	(0.162)	(0.102)	(0.076)
TA_TURN	1.6606***	1.6539***	1.5062***	1.6266***
	(0.001)	(0.001)	(0.003)	(0.001)
FIRM_SIZE	0.4433**	0.4189**	0.4507***	0.4297**
	(0.012)	(0.025)	(0.008)	(0.021)
CURR_RAT	0.0092	0.0141	0.0078	0.0115
	(0.528)	(0.333)	(0.601)	(0.432)
NWC	−0.0010	−0.0015*	−0.0013*	−0.0015*
	(0.120)	(0.054)	(0.056)	(0.060)
CATAR	0.1050*	0.1305*	0.1132**	0.1286**
	(0.070)	(0.051)	(0.050)	(0.049)
CTR	0.0619***	0.0601***	0.0603***	0.0600***
	(0.000)	(0.000)	(0.000)	(0.000)
COVID_CRISIS	−0.0188**	−0.0163*	−0.0190**	−0.0141*

(Continued)

Table 11.6. (*Continued*)

	(1B)	(2B)	(3B)	(4B)
	GOP	GOP	GOP	GOP
	(0.044)	(0.066)	(0.036)	(0.093)
Constant	−0.6995***	−0.5969**	−0.6417**	−0.6163**
	(0.007)	(0.031)	(0.012)	(0.026)
No of observations	468	468	468	468
No of companies	39	39	39	39
Number of instruments	13	13	13	13
AR(2)	0.244	0.275	0.487	0.465
Hansen test	0.483	0.455	0.749	0.572

Note: ***, **, and * denote a *p*-value in parentheses of 0.01, 0.05, and 0.1, respectively.

indicate that the current firm's profitability is positively influenced by its profitability in the previous quarter. Furthermore, DSO seems to have a significant positive. In contrast, the quadratic form of DSO (DSO²) has a significant negative impact on firm profitability. Previous studies found a positive relationship (Abuzayed, 2011; Braimah et al., 2021) but also a negative correlation between these variables (Bhatia & Srivastava, 2016; Vural et al., 2012).

In this regard, the empirical evidence for the Indonesian property and real estate firms partially agrees with the previous studies. Thus, *H1b* is accepted. Furthermore, the relationship between DSO, DSO², and GOP implies that firms could increase their profitability by loosening credit policy, but this positive effect does not last indefinitely. If the credit policy is too loose, it will reduce the company's profits (Braimah et al., 2021; Rey-Ares et al., 2021). However, the rest of the WCM components (DIO, DPO, CCC) and their quadratic forms (DIO², DPO², CCC²) fail to influence firm profitability significantly. Hence, *H2b*, *H3b*, and *H4b* are not accepted due to a lack of statistical significance, as in the research of Abuzayed (2011) and Vural et al. (2012).

The dummy variable COVID_CRISIS is proven to have a significant negative impact on firms' profitability, implying that the economic crisis triggered by the COVID-19 pandemic will decrease the Indonesian property and real estate firms' profitability (Zimon & Tarighi, 2021).

5. CONCLUSION

After applying panel data regression and two-step system GMM on 39 firms listed on the IDX covering 2018Q3–2021Q3, the firms' value is proved to have a negative relationship with DIO and CCC. However, the two-step system GMM result shows that DPO positively affects firms' value. It indicates that pursuing shorter DIO and CCC while relying on shorter-term financing through longer DPO leads to an increase in firms' value. Furthermore, the dummy variable COVID_CRISIS is proven to have a strong negative significant influence on firms' value. The findings also reveal a positive relationship between DSO and firms' profitability, but DIO seems to have a negative association with firms' profitability. It implies that loosening credit policy to some extent while reducing the delay for inventories to be converted into cash will boost firms' profitability.

ACKNOWLEDGEMENTS

Gratefulness to the Almighty God who has given his blessings, so this study has finished. This study was also supported by our colleagues, who provided insight and expertise that assisted this study.

REFERENCES

Abuzayed, B. (2011). Working capital management and firms' performance in emerging markets: The case of Jordan. *International Journal of Managerial Finance, 8*(2), 155–179. https://doi.org/10.1108/17439131211216620

Afrifa, G. A., Tauringana, V., & Tingbani, I. (2014). Working capital management and performance of listed SMEs. *Journal of Small Business and Entrepreneurship, 27*(6), 557–578. https://doi.org/10.1080/08276331.2015.1114351

Akgün, A. İ., & Memiş Karataş, A. (2020). Investigating the relationship between working capital management and business performance: Evidence from the 2008 financial crisis of EU-28. *International Journal of Managerial Finance, 17*(4), 545–567. https://doi.org/10.1108/IJMF-08-2019-0294

Altaf, N., & Shah, F. A. (2018). How does working capital management affect the profitability of Indian companies? *Journal of Advances in Management Research, 15*(3), 347–366. https://doi.org/10.1108/JAMR-06-2017-0076

Baños-Caballero, S., García-Teruel, P. J., & Martínez-Solano, P. (2012). How does working capital management affect the profitability of Spanish SMEs? *Small Business Economics*, 517–529. https://doi.org/10.1007/s11187-011-9317-8

Bank Indonesia. (2020a). *Perkembangan Properti Komersial (PPKOM) Triwulan II - 2020.*

Baños-Caballero, S., García-Teruel, P. J., & Martínez-Solano, P. (2014). Working capital management, corporate performance, and financial constraints. *Journal of Business Research, 67*(3), 332–338. https://doi.org/10.1016/j.jbusres.2013.01.016.

Bhatia, S., & Srivastava, A. (2016). Working capital management and firm performance in emerging economies: Evidence from India. *Management and Labour Studies, 41*(2), 71–87. https://doi.org/10.1177/0258042X16658733.

Biørn, E. (2017). *Econometrics of panel data methods and applications* (1st ed.). Oxford University Press.

Braimah, A., Mu, Y., Quaye, I., & Ibrahim, A. A. (2021). Working capital management and SMEs profitability in emerging economies: The Ghanaian Case. *SAGE Open, 11*(1). https://doi.org/10.1177/2158244021989317.

Caballero, B.-S., Martínez, S. P., & García, T. P. (2010). Working capital management in SMEs. *Accounting and Finance, 50*(457), 511–527.

Deloof, M. (2003). Does working capital management affect profitability of Belgian firms?. *Journal of Business Finance and Accounting, 30*(3–4), 573–588. https://doi.org/10.1111/1468-5957.00008

Essel, R., & Brobbey, J. (2021). The impact of working capital management on the performance of listed firms: Evidence of an emerging economy. *International Journal of Industrial Management, 12*(1), 389–407. https://doi.org/10.15282/ijim.12.1.2021.6994

Farhan, N. H. S. et al. (2021). An analysis of working capital management in India: An urgent need to refocus. *Cogent Business and Management, 8*(1). https://doi.org/10.1080/23311975.2021.1924930

Firmansyah, J., Siregar, H., & Syarifuddin, F. (2018). Does working capital management affect the profitability of property and real estate firms in Indonesia? *Jurnal Keuangan dan Perbankan, 22*(4), 695–707. https://doi.org/10.26905/jkdp.v22i4.2438

Fordian, D., & Raharja, S. J. (in press). Share return volatility during the COVID-19 pandemic in the Indonesia Stock Exchange. *International Journal of Trade and Global Markets* [Preprint].

Gitman, L. J., & Zutter, C. J. (2015). *Principles of managerial finance* (14th ed.). Pearson Education Limited.

Gujarati, D. N., & Porter, D. C. (2009). *Basic econometrics* (5th ed.). McGraw-Hill/Irwin.

Hussain, S. et al. (2021). Macroeconomic factors, working capital management, and firm performance– A static and dynamic panel analysis. *Humanities and Social Sciences Communications, 8*(1). https://doi.org/10.1057/s41599-021-00778-x

Javid, S., & Zita, V. P. M. (2014). Impact of working capital policy on firm's profitability: A case of Pakistan Cement Industry. *Research Journal of Finance and Accounting, 5*(5), 182–191.

Jr, J. F. H. et al. (2018). *Multivariate Data Analysis.* https://doi.org/10.1002/9781119409137.ch4

Khan, G. A., & Ghazi, I. U. (2013). Working capital management and firm performance in Karachi Stock Exchange (KSE). *Management and Administrative Sciences Review, 1*(1), 1–13.

Michel, L. et al. (2020). Working capital management and profitability of wine firms in France: An empirical analysis. *International Journal of Entrepreneurship and Small Business, 41*(3), 368. https://doi.org/10.1504/ijesb.2020.10032621

Nandy, S., & Sussan, F. (2021). Did the market indices of G7 countries recover evenly from the start of COVID-19 (January 2020) through December 2021? *Review of Integrative Business and Economics Research, 11*, 39–49.

Rey-Ares, L., Fernández-López, S., & Rodeiro-Pazos, D. (2021). Impact of working capital management on profitability for Spanish fish canning companies. *Marine Policy, 130.* https://doi.org/10.1016/j.marpol.2021.104583

Sawarni, K. S., Narayanasamy, S., & Ayyalusamy, K. (2021). Working capital management, firm performance and nature of business: An empirical evidence from India. *International Journal of Productivity and Performance Management, 70*(1), 179–200. https://doi.org/10.1108/IJPPM-10-2019-0468

Schmidheiny, K. (2012). *Panel data: Fixed and random effects* (pp. 1–15). Unversitat Basel.

Simon, S., Sawandi, N., & Abdul-Hamid, M. A. (2017). The quadratic relationship between working capital management and firm performance: Evidence from the Nigerian economy. *Journal of Business and Retail Management Research, 12*(1), 94–108. https://doi.org/10.24052/jbrmr/v12is01/tqrbwcmafpeftne

Susan, M., Winarto, J., & Gunawan, I. (2022). The determinants of corporate profitability in Indonesia Manufacturing Industry. *Review of Integrative Business and Economics Research, 11*(1), 184–185.

Vural, G., Sökmen, A. G., & Çetenak, E. H. (2012). Affects of working capital management on firm's performance: Evidence from Turkey. *International Journal of Economics and Financial Issues, 2*(4), 488–495.

Yovi, A. et al. (2022). Real earnings management practices in Indonesia: Opportunist or efficient earnings management practices? *Review of Integrative Business and Economics Research.*

Zimon, G., & Tarighi, H. (2021). Effects of the COVID-19 global crisis on the working capital management policy: Evidence from Poland. *Journal of Risk and Financial Management, 14*(4), 169. https://doi.org/10.3390/jrfm14040169

CHAPTER 12

EMPIRICAL ANALYSIS OF THE EFFECTS OF MICROECONOMICS AND MACROECONOMICS FACTORS ON BANK-RISK TAKING BEHAVIOUR BEFORE AND AFTER COVID-19: EVIDENCE FROM REGIONAL DEVELOPMENT BANK (BPD) IN INDONESIA

Vinka Amalia Hasta Barata and Taufik Faturohman

School of Business and Management, Institut Teknologi Bandung, Jl. Ganesha no 10 Bandung, West Java 40132, Indonesia

ABSTRACT

Regarding the crisis caused by the COVID-19 pandemic, regional development banks or Bank Pembangunan Daerah *(BPD) are affected by the problem of non-performing loan (NPL) that plagues national banks. This study aims to find which microeconomic and macroeconomic factors significantly influence the regional development banks' risk-taking behaviour and the effect COVID-19 pandemic on NPL. Microeconomic factors to be examined include credit growth, profitability, capitalisation, capital adequacy, bank size, credit volume, bank liquidity, and operational inefficiency. Macroeconomic factors to be*

The Finance-Innovation Nexus: Implications for Socio-Economic Development
International Symposia in Economic Theory and Econometrics, Volume 34, 177–194
Copyright © 2025 by Emerald Publishing Limited
All rights of reproduction in any form reserved
ISSN: 1571-0386/doi:10.1108/S1571-038620240000034014

examined include regional economic growth, deposit density (DD), deposits per branch (DB), and specialisation index (SI). This study employs a fixed effect panel data model with robust standard errors. The findings show evidence that credit volume is the only microeconomic factor that significantly influences regional development banks' risk-taking behaviour. Meanwhile, DD, DB, and SI are the macroeconomic factors that significantly influence regional development banks' risk-taking behaviour. The effects of the COVID-19 pandemic significantly influence regional development banks' risk-taking behaviour.

Keywords: Non-performing loan; regional development bank; bank risk-taking behaviour; COVID-19; Indonesia

JEL Classifications: G21; G28; C33

1. INTRODUCTION

The economic development of a country depends on the stability of the financial system. Theoretical and empirical studies show that the development of the financial sector has a positive impact on economic growth and the financial system instability will negatively affect the economic growth (Akdogu & Umutlu, 2014; Creel et al., 2015). Akdogu and Umutlu (2014) stated that the financial system is highly vulnerable and prone to crises that can trigger financial instability.

In the context of Indonesia, the banking sector dominates Indonesia's financial system. As of the second quarter of 2020, the total assets of Indonesia's financial system accounted for IDR 12,017 trillion of which 73.37% or IDR 8,817 trillion represent banks (Otoritas Jasa Keuangan, 2020). As a result, the stability of Indonesia's banking sector is critical to the country's financial system.

To fund their operations, the majority of Indonesian banks still rely on loans (Alexandri & Santoso, 2015). Considering this fact and the important role of the banking sector in financial stability, it is important to examine bank credit risk as a measurement of bank performance. The ratio of non-performing loans (NPLs) is used as a major indicator to measure bank credit risk that affects the banking system of the country.

Different industries across many countries experienced abnormal changes in economic and financial indicators as a result of the COVID-19 epidemic (Nandy & Sussan, 2022), including the NPL of regional development banks in Indonesia. Data from the Central Bank of Indonesia has shown that the gross NPL of the national banking sector had increased to 3.24% in the second quarter of 2021 from 2.53% in December 2019 before the COVID-19 pandemic occurred (Katadata, 2021). Regional development banks or *Bank Pembangunan Daerah* (BPD), as one of the commercial banks that play an important role in the regional economy (Sintha, 2018), are also affected by the problem of NPL that plagues national banks. However, regional development banks were more resilient when facing the crisis caused by the COVID-19 pandemic as can be seen from its NPL of 2.9% in the second quarter of 2021, lower than the NPL of the national banking sector.

2. LITERATURE REVIEW

2.1. Regional Development Banks in Indonesia

Regional Development Bank or BPD operate like any other commercial bank to provide financial services; however, it was established and partially or wholly owned by the regional government (Agustin et al., 2013). The existence of regional development banks cannot be separated from the regional economy. The establishment of regional development banks is to encourage development in the regions. Regional development banks are directed to support infrastructure development, MSMEs, agriculture, and other economic activities in the context of regional development. The role of regional development banks has tremendous potential in the era of regional autonomy, namely as an accelerator and at the same time dynamising the economy which aims to drive development in the region (Herdhayinta & Supriyono, 2019; Sintha, 2018).

2.2. Determinants of NPL in Regional Development Banks

Given that the main function of banks is to collect and distribute funds, the main risk faced by all types of banks, including regional development banks, is credit risk. Credit risk can be indicated by a high ratio of NPL. The increase in NPL can be caused by microeconomic factors, measured by internal bank management, and macroeconomic factors (Georgiou, 2012).

2.2.1. Microeconomic Factors

The microeconomic factors used in this study are bank-specific variables that reflect the performance of banks and their management. Bank management behaviour through balance sheet metrics is typically related to moral hazard as changes in all of these factors are tied to actions made by management (Kingu et al., 2017) and the positive behaviour of management can contribute to banks' performance and effectiveness (Suryanarayana, 2022). In the banking industry, moral hazard is a notion that encompasses a wide range of principal-agent issues (Berger & DeYoung, 1997).

The first microeconomic factor to be investigated is credit growth which reflects the credit policy and loan growth of banks. Some studies were carried out at the cross-country level (Abid et al., 2014; Ciukaj & Kil, 2020; Riyazahmed & Baranwal, 2021), showed that rapid growth of loans will increase NPL. Those findings are in line with studies conducted in Indonesia which showed that credit growth, in both conventional banks (Shonhadji, 2020) and regional development banks in particular (Rokhim & Yanti, 2014), has a positive relationship with NPL. Banks with more expansive credit policies tend to have worse credit risk.

However, Vithessonthi (2016) found that this situation applies only before the crisis period occurs. After a crisis or recession, credit growth actually improves the credit risk. This result is due to the banks' expectations of future credit quality. Similar to what Barra and Ruggiero (2021) found in Italy, credit growth had a negative effect on NPL, although not significantly. Another important study was a study conducted on regional development banks in Indonesia, which found that increasing the percentage of long-term loans (including infrastructure loans) can help regional development banks reduce their NPL (Karamoy & Tasik, 2020). As the direction of the relationship between the two variables is not clear in the scope of regional development banks in Indonesia, the first hypothesis proposed is as follows:

H1. There is a relationship between credit growth (GRLO) and NPL.

The second microeconomic factor is Return on Assets (ROA) which reflects profitability. Profitability has been shown to have a negative effect on NPL at the cross-country level (Bolat & Isik, 2016; Ciukaj & Kil, 2020; Makri et al., 2014; Riyazahmed & Baranwal, 2021; Wood & Skinner, 2018) and Indonesia (Prawira & Wiryono, 2020; Shonhadji, 2020). Higher ROA for each bank indicates strong financial performance and a healthy financial system. Banks with high profitability are less willing to take part in riskier projects that could result in loan default.

This differs from the findings in Italy (Barra & Ruggiero, 2021), Nepal (Singh et al., 2021), and regional development banks in Indonesia (Alexandri & Santoso, 2015) which showed a positive influence of ROA on the increase in NPL. This shows as an indication that the increase in ROA reflects bank management's efforts to increase income by taking higher risks. As a result, this might lead to more bad debts in the future (Fiordelisi et al., 2011). The direction of the relationship between the two variables is not clear in the scope of regional development banks in Indonesia. Thus, another nondirectional hypothesis proposed is as follows:

H2. There is a relationship between profitability (ROA) and NPL.

Capitalisation, measured by the ratio of total equity to total assets (ETA), is the third microeconomic factor to be examined. While examining the relationship between capitalisation and NPL, some studies have conflicting findings. Some studies found a positive impact of capitalisation on the rate of NPL (Bolat & Isik, 2016; Ćurak et al., 2013; Ghosh, 2015). In other words, a higher capital ratio is related to a higher rate of NPL, not supporting the moral hazard concept that a bank with little capital may have a high NPL. This moral hazard incentive for managers resulted in a high level of risk and a rise in the number of NPLs. This contradicts findings from other studies which found that ETA has a significant negative effect on NPL, especially when covering a certain area (Barra & Ruggiero, 2021). Based on the conflicting findings from the previous research, another nondirectional hypothesis proposed is as follows:

H3. There is a relationship between capitalisation (ETA) and NPL.

The fourth microeconomic factor is capital adequacy. Several studies related to the relationship between capital adequacy and NPL in Indonesia, which examined the relationship between the Capital Adequacy Ratio (CAR) and NPL, found a positive effect on NPL across Indonesia (Yulianti et al., 2018) and cross-country level (Wood & Skinner, 2018). Other studies also found this positive relationship, although not significant (Alexandri & Santoso, 2015; Suryanto, 2015). Banks with high CARs prefer to give a loan easily because management believes that the bank will not go bankrupt or fail as a result of these loans; as a result, banks are heavily invested in the practice of doubtful loan activities, indicating a positive relationship between NPL and bank capital.

Other findings found that CAR has a negative effect on NPL in Indonesia and regional development banks in particular (Ramli & Kristian, 2019). Cross-country studies also found the same relationship (Jameel, 2014; Rahman et al., 2016). Meanwhile, a study that covers conventional banks in Indonesia found that CAR does not significantly affect NPL (Juliani, 2022). The direction of the relationship between the two variables is not clear in the scope of regional development banks in Indonesia. Thus, the fourth hypothesis proposed is as follows:

H4. There is a relationship between capital adequacy (CAR) and NPL.

Bank size is the fifth microeconomic factor to be examined. Regarding bank size, measured by total assets, several studies found that total assets have a positive impact on NPL (Abid et al., 2014; EL-Maude et al., 2017; Juliani, 2022; Margaretha & Kalista, 2018). Banks with larger sizes tend to be compelled to take excessive risks by increasing their leverage under the assumption of being 'too big to fail' and this will lead to high NPL values. This happens because of the belief that the government can help big banks that are at risk so it will not have an impact on the country's economy.

This finding contradicts findings found in studies conducted on a cross-country level (Ćurak et al., 2013; Singh et al., 2021) and in Indonesia (Dewi & Ramantha, 2015; Ramli & Kristian, 2019; Yulianti et al., 2018) which found a negative relationship between bank size and NPL. The larger the bank size, the greater the possibility of high diversification, which leads to a lower-risk proxy through NPL. Meanwhile, some studies have found that bank size does not have a significant effect on NPL (Alexandri & Santoso, 2015; Barra & Ruggiero, 2021; Suryanto, 2015). The conflicting findings from previous research on bank size lead to the fifth hypothesis:

H5. There is a relationship between bank size (TA) and NPL.

The sixth microeconomic factor examined is credit volume, measured through the ratio of total loans to total assets (loans to assets or LTA) which was found to negatively affect NPL at the cross-country level (Barra & Ruggiero, 2021; Ciukaj & Kil, 2020; Kingu et al., 2017). This implies that banks tend to give large credit to a few established borrowers; corporate customers, due to the small size of the banking market and a highly competitive environment made up of few borrowers. Those borrowers have an excellent track record, which lowers the risk of a rise in the default rate. This finding supports a study on conventional banks in Indonesia (Martina & Prastiwi, 2014).

However, another study found that credit volume has a positive effect on NPL in Indonesia (Musta'da & Pramono, 2022) and Europe (Klein, 2013). Excessive levels of lending lead to an increase in the NPL ratio in banks. An increase in bank lending activity is often associated with lower standards when providing loans which increase the outstanding loan amount. Based on the controversies from the previous research, the hypothesis is structured as follows.

H6. There is a relationship between credit volume (LTA) and NPL.

The next factor to be examined is bank liquidity. In Indonesia, banks use a ratio called loans to deposit ratio (LDR) to reflect the bank's liquidity. LDR is the ratio of total credit to total third-party funds. Apart from being an intermediation indicator, this ratio also reflects the level of aggressiveness of banks in providing credit. The higher this ratio, the lower the liquidity of the bank. LDR was found to have a significant positive relationship with NPL in regional development banks and conventional banks in general, respectively (Kartikasary et al., 2020; Suryanto, 2015). Similar to the explanation regarding credit volume, rapid credit expansion may not be an issue in and of itself, however, it does lead to poor screening and lending to low-quality borrowers while deposits are quite stagnant, or even slightly decrease. The findings in cross-country studies also support that LDR has a significant positive relationship with NPL (EL-Maude et al., 2017; Rahman et al., 2016; Wood & Skinner, 2018).

Similar to LTA, some studies also found that LDR negatively affects NPL in Indonesia (Dewi & Ramantha, 2015) and India (Ranjan & Dhal, 2003). Meanwhile, Juliani (2022) states that LDR does not significantly affect NPL. Considering the contradicting previous findings mentioned above, the hypothesis proposed is as follows:

H7. There is a relationship between bank liquidity (LDR) and NPL.

The last microeconomic factor is operational inefficiency. At the cross-country level, cost inefficiency, measured by the ratio of operating costs to total assets in the research of Riyazahmed and Baranwal (2021) and Barra and Ruggiero (2021), was found to have a positive effect on NPL. Other studies that measured operational inefficiency through the ratio of operating costs to operating income or *Biaya Operasional dan Pendapatan Operasional* (BOPO) in Indonesia also found a positive relationship between operational inefficiency and NPL (Abid et al., 2014). This finding supports the result of a study conducted on regional development banks in Indonesia (Suryanto, 2015). The bad management hypothesis, first proposed by Berger and DeYoung (1997), states that in response to an increase in NPL caused by adverse selection, bank management tends to devote more resources to managing and monitoring bad loans, resulting in an increase in operating expenses over interest income in the long run. The higher the BOPO, the less efficient the operation of the bank is since the management cannot effectively manage operational costs. Meanwhile, Juliani (2022) states that BOPO does not significantly affect NPL. Considering the findings from previous research, the hypothesis of this study will be formulated as follows.

H8. There is a negative influence of operational inefficiency (BOPO) on NPL.

2.2.2. Macroeconomic Factors
Various studies have shown that macroeconomic factors can affect bank credit risk. Gross Domestic Product (GDP) growth has been shown to have a significant negative impact on NPL because macroeconomic developments have increased the ability of economic actors to repay their debts (Abid et al., 2014; Barra & Ruggiero, 2021; Bolat & Isik, 2016; Ćurak et al., 2013; Jameel, 2014; Makri et al., 2014; Singh et al., 2021; Wood & Skinner, 2018; Yurdakul, 2014). This finding is consistent with findings found in the conventional banks in Indonesia that show a negative significant relationship between GDP growth and NPL (Kusmayadi et al., 2018). However, research conducted by Shonhadji (2020) in conventional banks in Indonesia showed that GDP growth does not have a significant influence on NPL, supporting a study conducted by Alexandri and Santoso (2015) in regional development banks in Indonesia.

Considering that this study focuses on regional development banks, the Gross Regional Domestic Product (GRDP) growth rate of each province is used to reflect the aggregate measurement of economic activity in a particular province according to the operational area of each bank. A study, which is focusing on regional developments bank in Indonesia, has found that the growth of GRDP negatively affected NPL (Rokhim & Yanti, 2014), in accordance with the GDP impact from other previous studies on the cross-country and national levels. Based on the previous findings mentioned above, the hypothesis proposed is as follows:

H9. There is a negative influence of regional economic growth (GRGRDP) on NPL.

In addition to the GRDP of each province, this study will use several variables used by Barra and Ruggiero (2021) to measure the effect of high heterogeneity in terms of both financial development and credit risk-taking tendencies, when researching banks in Italy while considering the differences between geographical areas. Barra and Ruggiero (2021) find that a higher DD tends to improve credit risk in non-cooperative banks in Italy, which means lowering the percentage of NPL. There is a different finding with cooperative banks in Italy, as a higher DD determines an increase in the interest rate that the bank must pay and the credit risk it bears. Considering the conflicting findings, the hypothesis proposed is as follows:

H10. There is a relationship between DD and NPL.

This study also discovered that as banks grow their branch networks, they become less efficient, resulting in an overabundance of branches. More inefficiency is reflected in a higher number of NPLs (Berger & DeYoung, 1997), in this case, the deposits per branch (DB) have a negative impact on NPL. Considering the findings, the hypothesis proposed is as follows:

H11. There is a negative influence of DB on NPL.

Increased specialisation of banks has been found to have a negative impact on credit quality (Barra & Ruggiero, 2021). As banks grow more specialised, expanding the number of branches in the respective area, they become more aggressive lenders and embark on hazardous projects, resulting in an increase in the percentage of NPL. Considering the findings, the hypothesis proposed is as follows:

H12. There is a positive influence of the SI on NPL.

2.2.3. Effects of COVID-19 Pandemic

The effect of COVID-19 on the banking sector in Indonesia has been conducted in some studies (Krisetiawati, 2021; Musta'da & Pramono, 2022; Siska et al., 2021). However, none of these studies have examined the effect of the COVID-19 pandemic on regional development banks' NPLs. Research conducted by Siska et al. (2021) does show that there is a significant difference in credit risk or NPL of commercial banks in Indonesia before and after the COVID-19 pandemic. However, is it true that the COVID-19 crisis significantly affects the NPL of regional development banks?

This research defines a dummy variable (COVID) to examine and assess the effects of the COVID-19 pandemic on the NPL of regional development banks. This study expects a positive relationship between the dummy variable and NPL. Hence, the hypothesis proposed is as follows:

H13. There is a positive influence of the COVID-19 pandemic (COVID) on NPL.

3. METHODOLOGY

3.1. Data and Variable

The microeconomic data used in this study were obtained from the quarterly financial reports of commercial banking in Indonesia disseminated on the website of the Indonesia Financial Services Authority or *Otoritas Jasa Keuangan* (OJK) and each bank's website. The NPL data for representing the regional development banks' risk-taking behaviour before the COVID-19 crisis will use NPL data from Q1 2019 until Q1 2020, while NPL data from Q3 2020 until Q3 2021 will represent the regional development banks' risk-taking behaviour after the COVID-19 crisis. As this study uses the lagged level of any independent variables included in the analysis, the bank-specific variables data or the microeconomic factors from Q4 2018 until Q4 2019 are used to represent the regional development banks' performance before the COVID-19 crisis, meanwhile, the data from Q2 2020 until Q2 2021 are used to represent the regional development banks' performance after the COVID-19 crisis.

To determine whether the distinct and limited operational areas might also somehow affect the regional development banks' risk-taking behaviour, the object of this research is limited to regional development banks which only operate in one particular province and do not have branches in other provinces, or only have a maximum of 5% branch offices outside the respected province out of all the total branch offices owned. Of 27 regional development banks in Indonesia, only 10 of them fall under the category.

A detailed explanation of the variables that will be tested in this study is provided in Table 12.1.

3.2. Regression Model

Benchmarked against a study in Italy conducted by Barra and Ruggiero (2021), all independent variables are lagged because this study expects that the variables do not affect NPL immediately. The model is specified as follows:

$$
\begin{aligned}
NPL_{i,t} = {} & \beta_0 + \beta_1 GRLO_{i,t-1} + \beta_2 ROA_{i,t-1} + \beta_3 ETA_{i,t-1} + \beta_4 CAR_{i,t-1} \\
& + \beta_5 TA_{i,t-1} + \beta_6 LTA_{i,t-1} + \beta_7 LDR_{i,t-1} + \beta_8 BOPO_{i,t-1} \\
& + \beta_9 GRGRDP_{i,t-1} + \beta_{10} DD_{i,t-1} + \beta_{11} DB_{i,t-1} + \beta_{12} SI_{i,t-1} \\
& + COVID + \varepsilon_{i,t}
\end{aligned}
\tag{3.1}
$$

Table 12.1. Description of Variables.

Variable	Measurement	Labels	Expected Result
Dependent Variable: Bank credit risk, measured by NPLs to total loans.			
Independent Variables (Microeconomic Factors)			
Credit growth	Growth of total loans	GRLO	(+)/(−)
Profitability	Profit to total assets	ROA	(+)/(−)
Capitalisation	Equity to total assets	ETA	(+)/(−)
Capital adequacy	Capital to Risk-Weighted Assets	CAR	(+)/(−)
Bank size	Natural logarithm of total assets or Ln(Total assets)	TA	(+)/(−)
Credit volume	Bank loans to total assets	LTA	(+)/(−)
Bank liquidity	Loan to deposits	LDR	(+)/(−)
Operational inefficiency	Operating cost to operating income	BOPO	(−)
Independent Variables (Macroeconomic Factors)			
Regional economic growth	Growth of gross regional domestic product	GRGRDP	(−)
Deposit density	Natural logarithm of total aggregate deposits per province per km² (towards province area) or Ln(Deposit density)	DD	(+)/(−)
Deposits per branch	Natural logarithm of total aggregate deposits to number of branches or Ln(Deposits per branch)	DB	(−)
Specialisation index	Natural logarithm of the number of bank branches to the total of aggregate loans and deposits or Ln(Specialisation index)	SI	(+)
Dummy Variable			
Effects of COVID-19	$D=1$ represents the time after COVID-19 and $D=0$ represents the time before COVID-19	COVID	(+)

In the equation above, subscript i denotes the observation that belongs to the ith regional development bank and subscript t denotes the time period. NPL as the dependent variable represents the credit risk of bank i over the time period t is regressed on various possible NPL determinants. In addition, β_0, β_i, and $\epsilon_{i,t}$, represent the intercept term of the multiple regression, the slope coefficient for the ith independent variables, and the error term for the ith observation in the period t, respectively.

4. RESULT AND DISCUSSION

4.1. Descriptive Statistics

The descriptive statistics of the variables used in this research are presented in Table 12.2.

4.2. Regression Result

The models to estimate the data are expressed as follows:
Model 1

$$\begin{aligned}
NPL_{i,t} = {} & \beta_0 + \beta_1 GRLO_{i,t-1} + \beta_2 ROA_{i,t-1} + \beta_3 ETA_{i,t-1} \\
& + \beta_4 CAR_{i,t-1} + \beta_5 TA_{i,t-1} + \beta_6 LTA_{i,t-1} + \beta_7 LDR_{i,t-1} \\
& + \beta_8 BOPO_{i,t-1} + \beta_9 GRGRDP_{i,t-1} + \beta_{10} DD_{i,t-1} + \beta_{11} DB_{i,t-1} \\
& + COVID + \varepsilon_{i,t}
\end{aligned} \tag{4.1}$$

Table 12.2.   Descriptive Statistics.

Variables	Labels	Obs	Mean	Std. Dev	Min	Max
Credit risk	NPL	100	0.0221	0.0154	0.0029	0.0635
Credit growth	GRLO	100	0.0302	0.0298	−0.0485	0.1637
Profitability	ROA	100	0.0291	0.0072	0.0141	0.0515
Capitalisation	ETA	100	0.1390	0.0166	0.1057	0.1915
Capital adequacy	CAR	100	0.2382	0.0254	0.1890	0.2996
Bank size	TA	100	20,600,000	20,300,000	6,042,682	95,500,000
Credit volume	LTA	100	0.6212	0.0783	0.4461	0.7915
Bank liquidity	LDR	100	0.8202	0.1405	0.5225	1.2142
Operational inefficiency	BOPO	100	0.7390	0.0579	0.5935	0.9273
Regional economic growth	GRGRDP	100	0.0397	0.0428	−0.0688	0.2008
Deposits density	DD	100	606.27	1,033.84	39.76	4,502.19
Deposits per branch	DB	100	711,071.70	410,156.30	245,833.00	2,015,148.00
Specialisation index	SI	100	0.0000010	0.0000005	0.0000003	0.0000021

Model 2

$$\begin{aligned}
\text{NPL}_{i,t} = {}& \beta_0 + \beta_1 \text{GRLO}_{i,t-1} + \beta_2 \text{ROA}_{i,t-1} + \beta_3 \text{ETA}_{i,t-1} \\
& + \beta_4 \text{CAR}_{i,t-1} + \beta_5 \text{TA}_{i,t-1} + \beta_6 \text{LTA}_{i,t-1} + \beta_7 \text{LDR}_{i,t-1} \\
& + \beta_8 \text{BOPO}_{i,t-1} + \beta_9 \text{GRGRDP}_{i,t-1} + \beta_{10} \text{DD}_{i,t-1} + \beta_{11} \text{SI}_{i,t-1} \\
& + \text{COVID} + \varepsilon_{i,t}
\end{aligned} \tag{4.2}$$

The null hypothesis in Chow and Hausman tests are both rejected at a 0.01 significance level (p-value < 0.01), which means that the fixed effect model is selected. All models are using the fixed effect model with robust standard error to overcome heteroscedasticity.

From the results obtained as shown in Table 12.3, the probability of the F-statistic from all models is zero. Thus, the null hypothesis in all models is rejected. These results indicate that there is a joint effect between the independent variables with the dependent variable in all models.

From Table 12.3, this study finds out that among eight microeconomic factors examined in this study, only credit volume has a significant influence on the next quarter's NPL in all models. Meanwhile, there are three macroeconomic factors that have a significant influence on the next quarter's NPL. The COVID-19 pandemic proved to have a significant influence on NPL in all models.

Credit volume, measured by LTA, is the only microeconomic factor that has a significant relationship with the next quarter's NPL in all models. In Models 1 and 2, credit volume has a significant negative relationship with the next quarter's NPL at a 0.05 significance level and 0.10 significance level, respectively.

DD shows a significant positive impact on next quarter's NPL at a 0.05 significance level in all models. Meanwhile, DB have a significant negative influence on the next quarter's NPL at a 0.10 significance level. SI shows a significant positive impact on the next quarter's NPL at a 0.10 significance level.

Last variable which shows a significant impact on regional development banks' NPL is the COVID-19 pandemic. All models show that the COVID-19 pandemic has a significant positive influence on NPL at a 0.10 significance level, indicating the presence of the COVID-19 pandemic increases the value of NPL.

The coefficient of determination (R-squared) of Models 1 and 2 are 0.1738 and 0.1779, respectively. It means that in Models 1 and 2, 17.38% and 17.79% of the variation of regional development banks' next period's NPL is influenced by the current quarter's microeconomic and macroeconomic factors, and the effects of COVID-19, respectively. The remaining 82.62% and 82.21% are determined by other factors outside the research model.

4.3. Discussion

In this study, the regression result shows that credit volume has a negative effect on the next quarter's NPL. This finding supports the previous studies which found that credit volume negatively affects NPL in Indonesia (Martina & Prastiwi, 2014) and cross-country level (Barra & Ruggiero, 2021; Ciukaj & Kil, 2020; Kingu et al., 2017). However, this research contradicts the previous studies which found a

Table 12.3. Regression Result.

| | | Dependent variable: NPL_t | |
| Variables | Labels | Coefficient (Robust std. errors) | |
		Model 1	Model 2
Microeconomic Factors			
Credit growth	$GRLO_{t-1}$	−0.004138	−0.0030084
		(0.0124558)	(0.0123668)
Profitability	ROA_{t-1}	−0.4658661	−0.4857728
		(0.4266582)	(0.4340186)
Capitalisation	ETA_{t-1}	0.3772907	0.3758534
		(0.260427)	(0.2612327)
Capital adequacy	CAR_{t-1}	−0.2408441	−0.2412464
		(0.1626647)	(0.162286)
Bank size	TA_{t-1}	−0.0516485	−0.0315619
		(0.0304515)	(0.0363604)
Credit volume	LTA_{t-1}	**−0.1546786****	**−0.1234762***
		(0.0561473)	**(0.0595606)**
Bank liquidity	LDR_{t-1}	0.0379868	0.0388613
		(0.0301896)	(0.0297493)
Operational inefficiency	$BOPO_{t-1}$	−0.0371942	−0.0389739
		(0.037488)	(0.0383241)
Macroeconomic Factors			
Regional economic growth	$GRGRDP_{t-1}$	0.0021285	0.0025883
		(0.0209022)	(0.0207409)
Deposits density	DD_{t-1}	**0.0647308****	**0.050611****
		(0.0229807)	**(0.0225735)**
Deposits per branch	DB_{t-1}	**−0.0390043***	
		(0.0193816)	
Specialisation index	SI_{t-1}		**0.045994***
			(0.0249084)
Effects of COVID-19	COVID	**0.0045425***	**0.0047268***
		(0.0023655)	**(0.0023717)**
Constant		**1.151241*****	**0.999008****
		(0.3436007)	**(0.3467412)**
N		100	100
Probability (F-statistic)		0.00	0.00
R-squared within		0.1738	0.1779
R-squared between		0.0646	0.1027
R-squared overall		0.0577	0.0923

Notes: The table shows the coefficient estimates. Robust standard errors are in parentheses. To overcome heteroscedasticity, this study used robust standard error. Coefficients in boldface are significant. *, **, and *** denote statistical significance levels at 0.10, 0.05, and 0.01, respectively.

significant positive influence of credit volume on NPL in Indonesia (Musta'da & Pramono, 2022) and Europe (Klein, 2013).

This rather contradictory result may be due to the small market nature of regional development banks, coupled with a highly competitive but narrow regional environment that consists of few borrowers (Kingu et al., 2017), regional development banks tend to extend large loans to a few existing borrowers; corporate customers, government agencies, and investment projects related to regional development. Regional development banks manage to raise third-party funds and distribute them in the form of credit in relatively large amounts, either to individual customers, companies, or other institutions in their region. The finding of the negative influence of credit volume on regional development banks' NPL shows that regional development banks' management can manage proper lending criteria to select qualified borrowers to reduce the likelihood of bad debts.

The negative impact of credit volume in NPL also implies that borrowers attach great importance to relatively more credit (customer) oriented banks (Ranjan & Dhal, 2003). Regional development banks, as relatively more customer-friendly banks for the regional economy, are most likely to face lower defaults as the borrower will expect to turn back to the bank for further financing requirements related to regional economic development.

In case regional development banks in Indonesia experience a decrease in lending and an increase in the total assets at the same time, it will result in a decrease in credit volume (LTA). As the main role of regional development banks is to provide funds for investment purposes, expansion, and renewal of regional development projects in the region concerned, thus, when the regional investment projects are delayed or even annulled due to the COVID-19 pandemic, there will be a decrease in lending provided by regional development banks.

Since the NPL is the ratio of aggregate NPLs to total loans, of course, NPL tends to increase if there is a stagnant amount of total loans or even a decrease in total loans. The magnitude of this effect will be even greater if it is backed by an increase in bad debts, even with the tight credit criteria. Hence, this finding indicates the need for guidelines for the proper amount of credit volume as it shows that increasing credit volume can negatively influence the next period's credit risk in regional development banks, with consideration of good credit criteria.

DD positively influences regional development banks' NPL in the next quarter, supporting the finding found in cooperative banks in Italy (Barra & Ruggiero, 2021). The higher the number of deposits in a bank, the higher the ratio of DD, and vice versa. The narrower the operational area of a bank the higher the ratio of DD, and vice versa. The higher the number of deposits per km^2 can increase the percentage of the next period's NPL.

This relationship indicates that regional development banks that cover a narrow area of the province but have a fairly high deposit must be vigilant and monitor their DD because it has a significant positive impact on the next period's NPL. It is related to how well regional development banks can manage the third-party funds in their operational area and manage their efficiency by utilising the third-party funds to increase lending for qualified borrowers so that they can improve the quality of their credit risk in the next period.

The next macroeconomic factor is DB that are found to have a significant negative influence on the next quarter's NPL. This evidence also supports the research conducted by Barra and Ruggiero (2021) who also discovered that as banks grow their branch networks, they become less efficient, resulting in an overabundance of branches. The finding seems to support research conducted by Pham et al. (2022) which found that branch-closing activities increase bank profitability in general.

The operation of regional development banks throughout Indonesia influences its respective regional financial markets. If regional development banks manage to raise third-party funds while keeping in check their efficiency (meaning that avoid over-expansion of their branches) and are able to distribute the deposits in the form of credit, either to high-quality borrowers, targeting regional development investment projects, and improving regional economy, it can help to improve the quality of credit risk which means reducing the percentage of NPL in the next period.

Another macroeconomic factor that is found to be significant is the SI. This finding of SI is in line with Barra and Ruggiero (2021) who found that increasing bank specialisation worsens credit quality, leading to an increase in the next period's NPL. Banks that have a high SI indicate a large number of branch offices that cover a fairly small total aggregate loans and deposits in an area. The higher the SI of a bank, the more the bank focuses its operations in an area by providing dense branch offices without concern about how many total aggregate deposits and loans it has. On the other hand, banks with low specialisation have relatively few branch offices but can cover a fairly huge amount of total aggregate loans and deposits in an area.

In the case of regional development banks, the increase in specialisation indicates either a decrease in total aggregate deposits and loans in a region or an increase in the number of branch offices in a region. This can increase the possibility of insolvency and lead to higher risk-taking from a decrease in bank efficiency due to careless branch expansion. Supporting moral hazard theory, bank managers under the circumstances can become more aggressive lenders and undertake risky projects.

The decrease in specialisation indicates either an increase in the total aggregate deposits and loans in a region; or the closing of the number of branch offices in a region. Of course, this can improve the quality of credit risk or decrease the NPL rate in the next period because regional development banks can improve efficiency and allocate resources to better credit quality. When regional development banks in Indonesia experienced a decrease in specialisation, it may be caused by the increase in deposits whose magnitude was greater than the decrease in total loans. Considering this relationship, the management of regional development banks should carefully consider the decision to open a new branch.

The last finding is that there is evidence that the effects of COVID-19 significantly increase the rate of NPL in regional development banks in Indonesia. This supports findings found by Siska et al. (2021) that show there is a significant difference in credit risk or NPL of commercial banks in Indonesia before and after the COVID-19 pandemic. This depicts that regional development banks must be ready for the next future crisis because the crisis caused by the COVID-19 pandemic has been proven to significantly increase NPL.

5. CONCLUSIONS AND RECOMMENDATIONS

By examining the influence of microeconomic and macroeconomic factors on regional development banks' NPL in Indonesia and how regional development banks' risk-taking behaviour reacted to the adverse shock caused by the financial crisis caused by the COVID-19 pandemic, this study finds that: (a) credit volume is the only microeconomic factor that significantly influences regional development banks' risk-taking behaviour; meanwhile, DD, DB, and SI are the macroeconomic factors that significantly influence regional development banks' risk-taking behaviour; (b) the effects of the COVID-19 pandemic significantly influence regional development banks' risk-taking behaviour.

Bank management can prepare to face the future financial crisis in the next period, by paying attention to and monitoring significant factors in the current period, in this case: credit volume, DD, deposit per branch, and SI. Appropriate credit culture, operational efficiency, and lending policy from regional development banks, which incorporates key regional economic and financial variables in terms of credit, will have a substantial impact on stabilising NPL in regional development banks.

Considering the diversity of opinions and controversy among researchers about the relationship between NPL determinants researched in this study, authorities in Indonesia may consider monitoring the LTA (loan-to-total assets ratio) variable and establishing an upper and lower threshold of ideal credit volume. Regulatory authorities also can try to establish and monitor new macroeconomic indicators to measure the health of credit risk. To manage the macroeconomic factors, authorities can monitor regional development banks' DD, set a limit on the number of branches that can operate in a certain area to minimise inefficient branch proliferation, and monitor banks' specialisation activities to increase financial stability.

ACKNOWLEDGEMENTS

This research has benefited from the financial support of *Program Bantuan Penelitian* Bank Indonesia Institute (BINS), a research grant program from the Central Bank of Indonesia research institute.

BIBLIOGRAPHY

Abid, L., Ouertani, M. N., & Zouari-Ghorbel, S. (2014). Macroeconomic and bank-specific determinants of household's non-performing loans in Tunisia: A dynamic panel data. *Procedia Economics and Finance, 13*(December), 58–68. https://doi.org/10.1016/s2212-5671(14)00430-4

Agustin, H., Rus, R. M., & Mohd, K. N. T. (2013). Financial performance and ownership structure: A comparison study between community development banks, government banks and private banks in Indonesia. *International Journal of Academic Research in Business and Social Sciences, 3*(12), 38–49. https://doi.org/10.6007/ijarbss/v3-i12/410

Akdogu, S. K., & Umutlu, M. (2014). The link between financial system and economics: Functions of the financial system, financial crises, and policy implications. *International Journal of Financial Research*, 5(4), 52–66. https://doi.org/10.5430/ijfr.v5n4p52

Alexandri, M. B., & Santoso, T. I. (2015). Non performing loan: Impact of internal and external factor (Evidence in Indonesia). *International Journal of Humanities and Social Science Invention*, 4(1), 87–91.

Altman, D. G., & Bland, J. M. (1995). Statistics notes: The normal distribution. *BMJ (Clinical research ed.)*, 310(6975), 298. https://doi.org/10.1136/bmj.310.6975.298

Barra, C., & Ruggiero, N. (2021). Do microeconomic and macroeconomic factors influence Italian bank credit risk in different local markets? Evidence from cooperative and non-cooperative banks. *Journal of Economics and Business*, 114(December 2020), 105976. https://doi.org/10.1016/j.jeconbus.2020.105976

Baum, C. F. (2001). Residual diagnostics for cross-section time series regression models. *The Stata Journal*, 1(1), 101–104. https://doi.org/10.1177/1536867X0100100108

Berger, A. N., & DeYoung, R. (1997). Problem loans and cost efficiency in commercial banks. *Journal of Banking and Finance*, 21(6), 849–870. https://doi.org/10.1016/S0378-4266(97)00003-4

Bolat, S., & Isik, O. (2016). Determinants of non-performing loans of deposit banks in Turkey. *Pressacademia*, 5(4), 341–350. https://doi.org/10.17261/pressacademia.2017.356

Ciukaj, R., & Kil, K. (2020). Determinants of the non-performing loan ratio in the European Union banking sectors with a high level of impaired loans. *Economics and Business Review*, 6(20), 22–45. https://doi.org/10.18559/ebr.2020.1.2

Creel, J., Hubert, P., & Labondance, F. (2015). Financial stability and economic performance. *Economic Modelling*, 48, 25–40. https://doi.org/10.1016/j.econmod.2014.10.025

Ćurak, M., Pepur, S., & Poposki, K. (2013). Determinants of non-performing loans – Evidence from Southeastern European banking systems. *Banks and Bank Systems*, 8(1), 45–53.

Dancey, C. P., & Reidy, J. (2020). *Statistics without maths for psychology*. Pearson Education Limited.

Dewi, K. P., & Ramantha, I. W. (2015). Pengaruh loan deposit ratio, Suku Bunga Sbi, Dan Bank Size Terhadap Nonperforming Loan. *E-Jurnal Akuntansi Universitas Udayana*, 11(3), 909–920.

Drukker, D. (2003). Testing for serial correlation in linear panel data models. *Stata Journal*, 3, 168–177. https://doi.org/10.1177/1536867X0300300206

EL-Maude, J. G., Abdul-Rahman, A., & Ibrahim, M. (2017). Determinants of non-performing loans in Nigerias Deposit Money Banks. *Archives of Business Research*, 5(1), 74–88. https://doi.org/10.14738/abr.51.2368

Fiordelisi, F., Marques-Ibanez, D., & Molyneux, P. (2011). Efficiency and risk in European banking. *Journal of Banking & Finance*, 35(5), 1315–1326. https://doi.org/10.1016/J.JBANKFIN.2010.10.005

Gambo, E.-M. J., Abdul-Rahman, A., & Ibrahim, M. (2017). Determinants of non-performing loans in Nigerias Deposit Money Banks. *Archives of Business Research*, 5(1). https://doi.org/10.14738/abr.51.2368

Georgiou, M. N. (2012). Credit expansion and NPLs: A panel data analysis for Western Europe and the United States. *SSRN Electronic Journal* [Preprint], (70). https://doi.org/10.2139/ssrn.1977675

Ghasemi, A., & Zahediasl, S. (2012). Normality tests for statistical analysis: A guide for non-statisticians. *International Journal of Endocrinology and Metabolism*, 10(2), 486–489. https://doi.org/10.5812/ijem.3505

Ghosh, A. (2015). Banking-industry specific and regional economic determinants of non-performing loans: Evidence from US states. *Journal of Financial Stability*, 20, 93–104. https://doi.org/10.1016/j.jfs.2015.08.004

Gregorich, M. et al. (2021). Regression with highly correlated predictors: Variable omission is not the solution. *International Journal of Environmental Research and Public Health*, 18(8), 4259. https://doi.org/10.3390/ijerph18084259

Gujarati, D., & Porter, D. (2009). *Basic econometrics* (5th ed.). McGraw-Hill/Irwin.

Hair Jr, J. F. et al. (2018). *Multivariate data analysis* (8th ed.). Cengage Learning EMEA.

Herdhayinta, H., & Supriyono, R. A. (2019). Determinants of bank profitability: The case of the Regional Development Bank (BPD Bank) in Indonesia. *Journal of Indonesian Economy and Business*, 34(1), p. 1. https://doi.org/10.22146/jieb.17331

Jameel, K. (2014). Crucial factors of nonperforming loans evidence from Pakistani banking sector. *International Journal of Scientific & Engineering Research*, 5(7), 704–710. http://www.ijser.org

Juliani, M. (2022). Analisis Faktor Spesifik Bank Terhadap Non Performing Loan Pada Bank Umum Konvensional Yang Terdaftar Di Bursa Efek Indonesia. *Owner: Riset & Jurnal Akuntansi*, 6(1), 43–55. https://doi.org/10.33395/owner.v6i1.569

Karamoy, H., & Tasik, H. H. D. (2020). The role of infrastructure loan in the Regional Development Bank. *Jurnal Ekonomi Malaysia*, 54(3), 77–87. https://doi.org/10.17576/jem-2020-5403-6

Karamoy, H., & Tulung, J. (2020). The impact of banking risk on regional development banks in Indonesia. *Banks and Bank Systems*, 15(2), 130–137. https://doi.org/10.21511/bbs.15(2).2020.12

Kartikasary, M. et al. (2020). Factors affecting the non-performing loans in Indonesia. *Accounting*, 6(2), 97–106. https://doi.org/10.5267/j.ac.2019.12.003

Katadata. (2021). *Rasio Kredit Bermasalah Sektor Pertambangan Tertinggi pada Kuartal II-2021*. Retrieved October 12, 2021, from https://databoks.katadata.co.id/datapublish/2021/10/07/rasio-kredit-bermasalah-sektor-pertambangan-tertinggi-pada-kuartal-ii-2021

Kingu, P. S., Macha, S., & Gwahula, R. (2017). Determinants of non-performing loans: Evidence from commercial banks in Tanzania. *The International Journal of Business & Management*, 5(12), 18–28. www.theijbm.com

Klein, N. (2013). *Non-Performing Loans in CESEE: Determinants and impact on macroeconomic performance*. http://www.imf.org/external/pubs/cat/longres.aspx?sk=40413

Krisetiawati, I. S. (2021). The performance of regional development banks during Covid-19 pandemic. *Efficient: Indonesian Journal of Development Economics*, 4(3), 1337–1349. https://doi.org/https://doi.org/10.15294/efficient.v4i3.46962

Kusmayadi, D., Firmansyah, I., & Badruzaman, J. (2018). The impact of macroeconomic on nonperforming loan: Comparison study at conventional and Islamic banking. *Iqtishadia*, 10(2), 59. https://doi.org/10.21043/iqtishadia.v10i2.2864

Makri, V., Tsagkanos, A., & Bellas, A. (2014). Determinants of non-performing loans: The case of Eurozone. *Panoeconomicus*, 61(2), 193–206. https://doi.org/10.2298/PAN1402193M

Margaretha, F., & Kalista, V. (2018). Faktor Yang Mempengaruhi non performing loan Pada Bank Di Indonesia. *Jurnal Kesejahteraan Sosial*, 3(01), 65–80. https://doi.org/10.31326/jks.v3i01.170

Martina, E., & Prastiwi, D. (2014). Pengaruh Inflasi, gross domestic product, Suku Bunga Kredit, Loan to Asset Ratio, dan Kualitas Aktiva Produktif terhadap non performing loan. *Jurnal Ilmu Manajemen*, 2(2), 513–524.

Mishra, P. et al. (2019). Descriptive statistics and normality tests for statistical data. *Annals of Cardiac Anaesthesia*, 22(1), 67–72. https://doi.org/10.4103/aca.ACA_157_18

Musta'da, N., & Pramono, N. H. (2022). Non performing loan: analisis kredit bermasalah di masa pandemi Covid 19. *Journal of Accounting and Digital Finance*, 2(1), 1–15. https://doi.org/10.53088/jadfi.v2i1.335

Nandy, S., & Sussan, F. (2022). COVID emergency declaration and fintech digital payment companies' Performance. *Review of Integrative Business and Economics Research*, 11(1), 51–62.

O'Brien, R. M. (2017). Dropping highly collinear variables from a model: Why it typically is not a good idea. *Social Science Quarterly*, 98(1), 360–375. https://doi.org/10.1111/ssqu.12273

Otoritas Jasa Keuangan. (2020). *The Indonesian financial services sector master plan to recover the national economy and enhance the financial services sector resiliency and competitiveness 2021–2025*. https://ojk.go.id/id/berita-dan-kegiatan/publikasi/Documents/Pages/Master-Plan-Sektor-Jasa-Keuangan-Indonesia-2021-2025/The Indonesian Financial Services Sector Master Plan 2021-2025.pdf

Pham, D. J. et al. (2022). The decline of branch banking and the transformation of bank accessibility. *Review of Integrative Business and Economics Research*, 11(3), 1–19.

Prawira, R., & Wiryono, S. K. (2020). Determinants of non-performing loans in state-owned banks. *Jurnal Akuntansi & Auditing Indonesia*, 24(2), 159–166. https://doi.org/10.20885/jaai.vol24.iss2.art9

Putra, I. G. C. et al. (2021). The influence of macroeconomic indicators on profitability: A case study of regional development banks in Indonesia. *Journal of Asian Finance, Economics and Business*, 8(6), 79–87. https://doi.org/10.13106/jafeb.2021.vol8.no6.0079

Rahman, Md. A., Asaduzzaman, Md., & Hossin, Md. S. (2016). Impact of financial ratios on non-performing loans of publicly traded commercial banks in Bangladesh. *International Journal of Financial Research*, 8(1), 181. https://doi.org/10.5430/ijfr.v8n1p181

Ramli, I., & Kristian, E. (2019). Dinamika Risiko Kredit Bank Pembangunan Daerah Di Indonesia Periode 2011-2016. *Jurnal Muara Ilmu Ekonomi dan Bisnis*, *3*(2), 219. https://doi.org/10.24912/jmieb.v3i2.1592

Ranjan, R., & Dhal, S. C. (2003). Non-performing loans and terms of credit of public sector banks in India: An empirical assessment. *Reserve Bank of India Occasional Papers*, *24*(3), 81–121.

Ratner, B. (2009). The correlation coefficient: Its values range between +1/−1, or do they? *Journal of Targeting, Measurement and Analysis for Marketing*, *17*(2), 139–142. https://doi.org/10.1057/jt.2009.5

Riyazahmed, K., & Baranwal, G. (2021). Determinants of credit risk. *International Journal of Accounting & Finance Review*, *6*(1), 53–71. https://doi.org/10.46281/ijafr.v6i1.1005

Rokhim, R., & Yanti, M. I. S. M. (2014). Risiko NPL Kredit Bank Pembangunan Daerah sebagai Regional Champion. *Jurnal Keuangan dan Perbankan*, *18*(1), 120–129. http://jurnal.unmer.ac.id/index.php/jkdp/article/view/783

Shonhadji, N. (2020). What most influence on non-performing loan in Indonesia? Bank accounting perspective with Mars analysis. *Journal of Accounting and Strategic Finance*, *3*(2), 136–153. https://doi.org/10.33005/jasf.v3i2.85

Singh, S. K., Basuki, B., & Setiawan, R. (2021). The effect of non-performing loan on profitability: Empirical evidence from Nepalese Commercial Banks. *Journal of Asian Finance, Economics and Business*, *8*(4), 709–716. https://doi.org/10.13106/jafeb.2021.vol8.no4.0709

Sintha, L. (2018). Financial performance banking model in Indonesia before and after implementation of PBI No. 13/1/PBI/2011: Risk Profile Bank Regional Development. In *The 2nd International Conference on Vocational Higher Education Page 937 (ICVHE) 2017 "The Importance on Advancing Vocational Education to Meet Contemporary Labor Demands*, pp. 937–951. https://doi.org/10.18502/kss.v3i11.2818

Siska, E. et al. (2021). Analysis impact of Covid-19 outbreak on performance of commercial conventional banks: Evidence from Indonesia. *International Journal of Social and Management Studies*, *2*(6), 8–16.

Suryanarayana, A. (2022). Perceived HRM practices and organizational commitment in Nepali Banking Sector: Mediating role of person-organization fit. *Review of Integrative Business and Economics Research*, *11*(1), 1–29.

Suryanto. (2015). Non performing loans on regional development bank in Indonesia and factors that influence. *Mediterranean Journal of Social Sciences*, *6*(4), 280–287. https://doi.org/10.5901/mjss.2015.v6n4p280

Vithessonthi, C. (2016). Deflation, bank credit growth, and non-performing loans: Evidence from Japan. *SSRN Electronic Journal* [Preprint], (March). https://doi.org/10.2139/ssrn.2624275

Wood, A., & Skinner, N. (2018). Determinants of non-performing loans: Evidence from commercial banks in Barbados. *The Business and Management Review*, *9*(3), 44–64.

Yulianti, E., Aliamin, A., & Ibrahim, R. (2018). The effect of capital adequacy and bank size on non-performing loans in Indonesian Public Banks. *Journal of Accounting Research, Organization and Economics*, *1*(2), 205–214. https://doi.org/10.24815/jaroe.v1i2.11709

Yurdakul, F. (2014). Macroeconomic modelling of credit risk for banks. *Procedia – Social and Behavioral Sciences*, *109*, 784–793. https://doi.org/10.1016/j.sbspro.2013.12.544

CHAPTER 13

APPLICATION OF TECHNOLOGY ACCEPTANCE MODEL (TAM) ON DIGITAL PROMOTION MEDIA FOR TOURISM IN PONTIANAK CITY

Jessica Christella Hidayat and Taufik Faturohman

Institut Teknologi Bandung, Indonesia

ABSTRACT

Pontianak City, the capital of West Kalimantan, has a unique characteristic that is rarely found in other cities. Therefore, Pontianak needs to develop tourist attractions that provide tourism-supporting facilities and improve its promotional media to spread its tourism potential. This study aims to find the factors influencing the behavioural intention of using digital catalogues which will contribute to the literature in tourism marketing to advance the unexplored tourism potential with the help of digital catalogues. It was found that perceived usefulness, perceived ease of use, and the amount of information significantly influence behavioural intention to use digital catalogues.

Keywords: Digital catalogue; tourism; technology acceptance model; behavioural intention; Indonesia

JEL Code: Z32 tourism and development

The Finance-Innovation Nexus: Implications for Socio-Economic Development
International Symposia in Economic Theory and Econometrics, Volume 34, 195–203
Copyright © 2025 by Emerald Publishing Limited
All rights of reproduction in any form reserved
ISSN: 1571-0386/doi:10.1108/S1571-038620240000034015

1. INTRODUCTION

Pontianak, the capital of West Kalimantan, has a unique characteristic that is rarely found in other cities. Equator city, the nickname of Pontianak, is also called the city of water because it has hundreds of ditches or tributaries. The city is traversed by two major rivers: the Kapuas and the Landak. Pontianak also has a rich history, which originated from the banks of the Kapuas River, namely, the establishment of the centre of government/kingdom of the Kadariyah Palace, which is located on the banks of the Kapuas River. Therefore, Pontianak needs to develop tourist attractions that provide tourism-supporting facilities and improve its promotional media to spread its tourism potential.

In the era of digitisation, the use of the internet as an effort to advance tourist attractions can be an effective way. Digital promotion media in the form of a digital catalogue is one example of the use of technology in the tourism sector. It provides information related to attractions and tourist activities offered by the organisers, accommodation, transportation, and other important information in the form of online booklets.

Based on this description, further research is needed regarding the public acceptance of digital catalogues as a response to post-COVID-19 economic recovery and it could contribute to the literature in tourism marketing to advance the unexplored tourism potential with the help of digital catalogue. This study used the TAM model to assess the possible determinants associated with digital catalogue acceptance. The findings of this study may help the central or local government to choose the most suitable strategy to promote Pontianak tourism through digital catalogues.

2. LITERATURE REVIEW

2.1. Technology Acceptance Model

Since the digital catalogue is considered a technology, the technology acceptance model or TAM is more applicable compared to the theory of planned behaviour or the theory of reasoned action (TRA). The TAM was developed by Davis (1989) and is widely used in predicting the acceptance of information systems and technology. In TAM, two factors influence the acceptance and use of technology, namely, perceived ease of use and perceived usefulness, which affect a person's intention to use the technology (Fig. 13.1).

Perceived ease of use measures one's belief in a technology that is easy to understand and use. In comparison, perceived usefulness is a measure of where technology is believed to bring benefits to the people who use it. At the same time, behavioural intention to use is defined as a tendency to act towards certain activities or situations accompanied by feelings of pleasure. Another factor that might influence the behavioural intention to use is the amount of information related to the technology.

Several previous studies were conducted by Waluyani et al. (2018) to discover student interest in using online travel agents with TAM and influenced

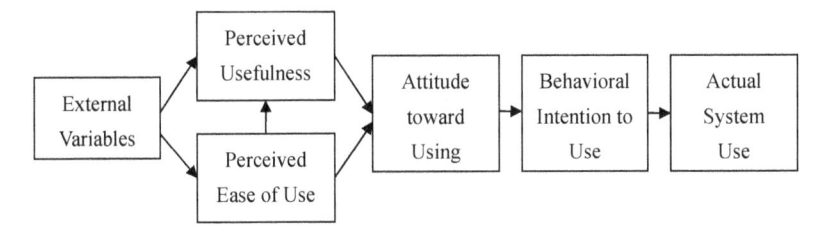

Fig. 13.1. Model of Technology Acceptance Model.

by perceived usefulness, perceived convenience, attitude, electronic trust, personal innovation, and communication. Faturohman et al. (2021) examined what factors influence the acceptance of the COVID-19 vaccine in Indonesia using TAM, and it was found that perceived usefulness influenced acceptance. Perceived usefulness was influenced by perceived convenience. The use of TAM in understanding interactive multimedia-based learning media was also developed by Syafrizal et al. (2015) to seek the acceptance of using information technology in learning activities.

3. METHODS

3.1. The Model and Statistical Analysis

In our proposed TAM model, we include three explanatory variables: (1) perceived usefulness, (2) perceived ease of use, and (3) amount of information that might affect the behavioural intention to use digital catalogues. This study also sought to assess whether perceived ease of use influenced perceived usefulness. The constructs of the proposed TAM model are presented in Fig. 13.2 and consist of four hypotheses:

H1. Perceived usefulness influences behavioural intention to use digital catalogues.

H2. Perceived ease of use influences behavioural intention to use digital catalogues.

H3. Amount of information influences behavioural intention to use digital catalogues.

H4. Perceived ease of use influences perceived usefulness.

The partial least square structural equation model (PLS-SEM) was used in this study to model the relationship between the variables. The goodness of fit of the PLS-SEM model was measured using several measurements, such as (1) SRMR, which is defined as the difference between the observed correlation and the model implied correlation matrix; (2) Bentler–Bonett's normed fit index (NFI); and (3) R square and adjusted R square. Hu and Bentler (1999) stated that the acceptable range for the SRMR index is between 0 and 0.08. For NFI, values above 0.9 usually represent an acceptable fit.

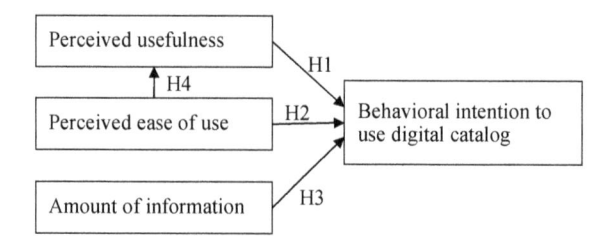

Fig. 13.2.   Proposed Model of the Relationship Between Perceived Usefulness, Perceived Ease of Use, Amount of Information and Behavioural Intention.

3.2. Study Design, Instrument, and Variables

This study conducted an online survey through Populix around May 2022. Populix is a start-up company that is a consumer insights service provider which connects the surveyor with a collection of qualified and targeted respondents throughout Indonesia. The target population was Indonesians who were 18 years old or older, and before they filled in the questions, a sample of the digital catalogue was provided for them to look at and study the content.

PLS is used in the data processing of this study, which is a variant-based SEM (structural equation analysis) that can simultaneously test the measurement and structure of the built model. In addition, according to Ghozali's (2006) explanation, PLS analysis also does not assume that the data must follow a particular measurement scale so that the number of samples required is not too large (less than 100). Data analysis is divided into two stages, the first is the evaluation of the measurement model, and the second is the evaluation of the structural model.

A questionnaire in Bahasa Indonesia (the national language) was developed based on previous studies and information related to the digital catalogue. The questionnaire consisted of several sections: sociodemographic data, behavioural intention to use digital catalogues, and some explanatory variables. The explanatory variables were perceived usefulness (three questions), perceived ease of use (four questions), and the amount of information on the digital catalogue (two questions). The responses were provided on a Likert scale from strongly disagree (score as one) to strongly agree (scored as five). The questionnaire also collected age, gender, domicile, educational attainment, type of occupation, travel experience to Pontianak, and preferred tourism attractions. The detailed questions used to assess each variable are presented in Table 13.1.

The average variance extracted (AVE), composite reliability, factor loading, and Cronbach's alpha were measured for each domain of the variables to assess the validity and reliability of the questionnaire. Based on Table 13.1, the question within the domain is valid, indicated by the value of standard loadings and AVE were both higher than 0.5, and the reliability of items within the domain is indicated by composite reliability and a Cronbach's alpha greater than 0.7 (Ghozali & Latan, 2015).

Table 13.2 shows that the correlation between the variable itself is higher than the correlation with other variables, which means that each variable's statements are acceptable and that all variables can be used for a more detailed analysis.

Table 13.1. Statements or Questions Used to Assess Each Domain and the Validity and Reliability Test of the Questionnaire.

Variable	Code	Statement	Standard Loading (>0.5)	AVE (>0.5)	Composite Reliability (>0.7)	Cronbach's Alpha (>0.7)
Behavioural intention to use	BI1	I predict to use a digital catalogue to plan my trip	0.927	0.814	0.929	0.886
	BI2	I will recommend a digital catalogue to people around me	0.913			
	BI3	I would be happy to use a digital catalogue instead of looking for travel information on my own	0.865			
Perceived usefulness	USE1	I think using a digital catalogue can help me organise my travel plans	0.936	0.839	0.940	0.904
	USE2	I think using a digital catalogue will make the time I spend planning trips more efficient	0.938			
	USE3	I think the products provided in the digital catalogue are complete	0.872			
Perceived ease of use	EASE1	I find it easy to organise travel plans with a digital catalogue	0.929	0.860	0.961	0.946
	EASE2	I think it is easier to find travel information through the digital catalogue	0.938			
	EASE3	I think it is easy to access the digital catalogue	0.904			
	EASE4	I think it is easy for me to understand the contents of the digital catalogue	0.937			
Amount of information	INFO1	I often receive information about the digital catalogue	0.864	0.802	0.890	0.758
	INFO2	I obtained enough information to plan my travel from the digital catalogue	0.927			

Table 13.2.   Results of Discriminant Validity.

	Amount of Information	Behavioural Intention	Perceive Ease of Use	Perceive Usefulness
Amount of information	**0.896**			
Behavioural intention	0.751	**0.902**		
Perceive ease of use	0.727	0.864	**0.927**	
Perceive usefulness	0.712	0.850	0.914	**0.916**

4. RESULTS AND DISCUSSION

As a result, we received 231 respondents and included them in the analysis. Of the total respondents, the majority were female and more than half were aged between 18 and 24 years old. Almost two-thirds of the respondents live in Java, while more than half of the respondents had no degree and are mostly students. As a comparison, the ratio of respondents who had experience travelling to Pontianak is around 1:4. Also, our respondents chose social media as the preference to access the digital catalogue, such as Instagram, Facebook, or Twitter, while an application is the second preference. This gives an essential insight for tourism businesses in Pontianak to make social media accounts or applications for them to share their digital catalogues (Table 13.3).

The result of the PLS-SEM model is shown in Fig. 13.3. The relation between each variable is measured in Table 13.4. It indicates that perceived usefulness,

Table 13.3.   Demographic Characteristics of Respondents ($n = 231$).

Demographic Variable	Number (%)
Gender	
Male (*R*)	30 (13.0)
Female	201 (87.0)
Age group (year)	
18–24 (*R*)	123 (53.2)
25–35	84 (36.4)
35–55	24 (10.4)
Domicile	
Java (*R*)	140 (60.6)
Sumatera	34 (14.7)
Sulawesi	14 (6.1)
Kalimantan	32 (13.9)
Bali, NTT, and NTB	11 (4.7)
Education attainment	
Had no degree (*R*)	134 (58.0)
University bachelor	87 (37.7)
Post-graduate	10 (4.3)
Type of occupation	
Students (*R*)	92 (39.8)
Employee	78 (33.8)
Entrepreneur	20 (8.6)
Others	41 (17.8)

(*Continued*)

Table 13.3. (*Continued*)

Demographic Variable	Number (%)
Had experience travelling to Pontianak	
Yes (*R*)	49 (21.2)
No	182 (78.8)
Preferences for accessing the digital catalogue	
Application	107 (46.3)
Social media (Instagram, Facebook, Twitter)	116 (50.2)
Travel agent	8 (3.5)

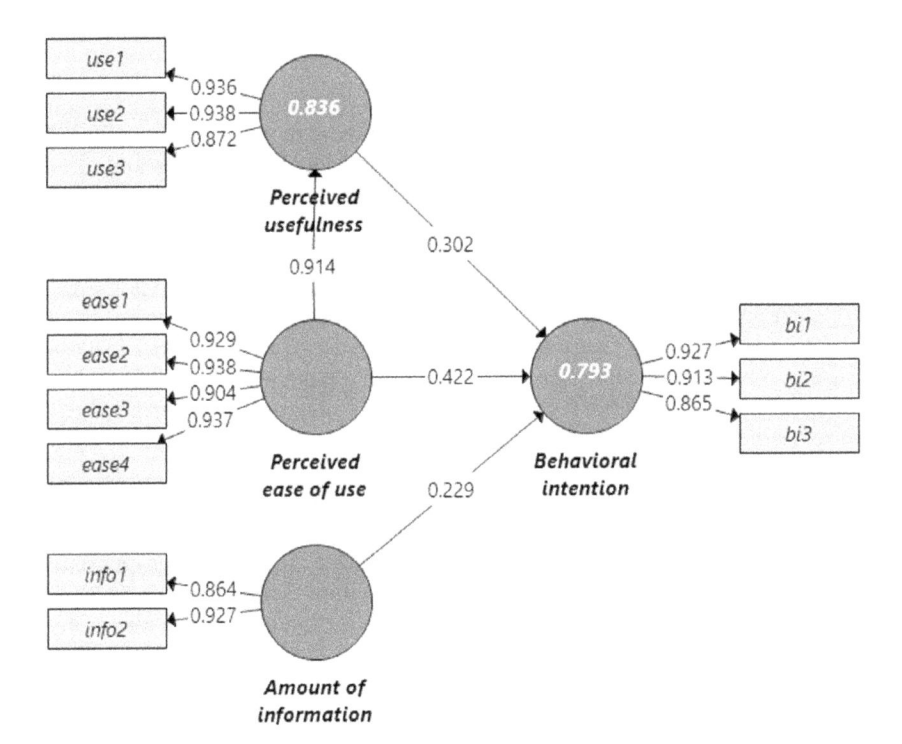

Fig. 13.3. Loading Factor Diagram and PLS-SEM Simulation Results.

Table 13.4. Result of PLS-SEM Analysis of the Proposed Model.

	Hypothesis	Original Sample	Simple Mean	Standard Deviation	*T*-statistics	*p*-Value	Supported
USE → BI	*H1*	0.302	0.298	0.085	3.543	0.000	Yes
EASE → BI	*H2*	0.422	0.423	0.091	4.624	0.000	Yes
INFO → BI	*H3*	0.229	0.230	0.058	3.913	0.000	Yes
EASE → USE	*H4*	0.914	0.912	0.017	52.876	0.000	Yes

Table 13.5. Goodness-of-fit Result of the Proposed PLS-SEM Model.

	Saturated Model	Estimated Model
SRMR	0.077	0.077
NFI	0.862	0.863

Table 13.6. R Square of the Proposed PLS-SEM Model.

	R Square	Adjusted R Square
Behavioural intention	0.793	0.791
Perceived usefulness	0.836	0.835

perceived ease of use, and amount of information have path coefficients of 0.302, 0.422, and 0.229 for behavioural intention to use digital catalogues and all of them have p-value greater than 0.01. It means perceived usefulness has a direct effect on behavioural intention to use digital catalogues of 0.302, while perceived ease of use has a direct effect of 0.422 and the amount of information has a direct effect of 0.229. Among the three variables, perceived ease of use has the biggest effect on behavioural intention to use digital catalogues which means digital catalogues must be easy to use for the tourists. On the other path, perceived ease of use also has a path coefficient value of 0.914 for perceived usefulness and the p-value is greater than 0.01. It means that the data suggested that perceived ease of use is significantly affecting perceived usefulness. The result of the goodness of fit of our model is presented in Table 13.5.

The R square value for behavioural intention and perceived usefulness are 0.793 and 0.836, respectively (Table 13.6). It means the model for behavioural intention to use digital catalogues is explained 79.3% of the variance by perceived usefulness, perceived ease of use, and amount of information. In comparison, 20.7% of the variables were not included in the study. While the model for perceived usefulness is also explained with perceived ease of use by 86.2% and 13.8% by the others. The values of R square on both models indicate that the model is good.

5. CONCLUSION AND RECOMMENDATIONS

From this study, we suggest that behavioural intention to use a digital catalogue is influenced by perceived usefulness, where a person believes that using a digital catalogue will give them benefit, compared to not using the digital catalogue; perceived ease of use, where a person believes that using a digital catalogue will be effortless or easy to use; and the amount of information available on digital catalogues. Our study also suggests that perceived ease of use also influences perceived usefulness.

Besides that, Kamenidou and Stavrianea (2022) were found that memorable tourism experience will attract and retain customers, which might be additional variables to increase the behavioural intention to use digital catalogue, where the digital catalogue might provide the early experience for the tourist that will attract them to visit the place. Also, Muljadi and Rauf (2022) showed that social media marketing and product reviews have a positive effect on purchase decisions where in tourism sector could be implemented on the digital catalogue marketing on social media and the tourists could give their review for the others tourist who planning their trip.

In conclusion, to increase tourism activities in Pontianak through digital catalogue promotion, perceived usefulness, perceived ease of use, and amount of information influence the behavioural intention to use it.

REFERENCES

Davis, F. D. (1989). Perceived usefulness, perceived ease of use, and user acceptance of information technology. *MIS Quarterly, 13*, 319–340.

Faturohman, T., Kengsiswoyo, G. A. N., Harapan, H., Zailani, S., Rahadi, R. A., & Arief, N. N. (2021). Factors influencing COVID-19 vaccine acceptance in Indonesia: An adoption of technology acceptance model. *F1000Research, 10*, e476.

Ghozali, I. (2006). Analisis multivariate lanjutan dengan program SPSS. Semarang: Badan Penerbit Universitas Diponegoro, 105.

Ghozali, I., & Latan, H. (2015). *Konsep, teknik, aplikasi menggunakan Smart PLS 3.0 untuk penelitian empiris*. BP Undip, Semarang.

Hu, L. T., & Bentler, P. M. (1999). Cutoff criteria for fit indexes in covariance structure analysis: Conventional criteria versus new alternatives. *Structural Equation Modeling, 6*, 1–55.

Kamenidou, I., & Stavrianea, A. (2022). Profiling monastery tourists based on memorable experiences, place identity, satisfaction, intention to revisit and intention to recommend. *Review of Integrative Business & Economics Research, 11*(1), 86–110.

Muljadi, W. I., & Rauf, A. (2022). Analysis of social media marketing and product review on the marketplace shopee on purchase decisions. *Review of Integrative Business & Economics Research, 11*(1), 274.

Syafrizal, A., Ernawati, E., & Dwiandiyanta, B. Y. (2015). Penerapan model technology acceptance model (TAM) untuk Pemahaman Media Pembelajaran Berbasis Multimedia Interaktif. *Scientific Journal of Informatics, 2*(1), 9–14.

Waluyani, R. C., Subroto, B., & Purnomosidhi, B. (2018). Effect of external factors of technology acceptance model toward technology acceptance of online travel agent. *Journal Economia, 14*(2), 158–176.

CHAPTER 14

RELATIONSHIP BETWEEN FINANCIAL LITERACY AND GREEN MICROFINANCE: AN INVESTIGATION OF PARTIAL LEAST SQUARES-MULTIGROUP ANALYSIS

Min-Sun Kim[a] and Andrian Dolfriandra Huruta[b, *]

[a]Chung Yuan Christian University, Republic of China
[b]Satya Wacana Christian University, Indonesia
*Corresponding author

ABSTRACT

The aim of this research is to attempt to identify the impact of gender in the relationship between financial literacy and green microfinance practice in rural area. This research was set to add a comprehensive view to existing studies of green microfinance by observing gender. This research employed non-probability purposive sampling to collect samples from women microfinance group in East Sumba, Indonesia. This research used partial least squares-multigroup analysis (PLS-MGA) for analysis. This research presents empirical evidence to support that financial literacy is positively linked to green microfinance. In the meantime, this research shows the impact of gender in the relationship between financial literacy and green microfinance. The findings suggest that a female has a bigger role than a male in the relationship between financial

The Finance-Innovation Nexus: Implications for Socio-Economic Development
International Symposia in Economic Theory and Econometrics, Volume 34, 205–214
Copyright © 2025 by Emerald Publishing Limited
All rights of reproduction in any form reserved
ISSN: 1571-0386/doi:10.1108/S1571-038620240000034017

literacy and green microfinance. It is a significant step forward in our understanding of green microfinance.

Keywords: Green microfinance; financial literacy; gender; women microfinance group; rural development; PLS-MGA

JEL Classification: F63; G21; G28

INTRODUCTION

Green microfinance is a topic which fits nowadays environmental concern (Abdur Rouf, 2012). There has been quite a bit scholarly effort aiming to understand the role of gender on microfinance (Atahau et al., 2021; Lee & Huruta, 2022). Atahau et al. (2021) found that green microfinance casts itself in the role of empowering females. Most research papers featuring microfinance in rural area targeted its effect on females (Atahau et al., 2021; Lee & Huruta, 2022; Nawaz, 2015). Furthermore, some research papers tried to identify women empowerment on green microfinance (Agier & Szafarz, 2013; Lee & Huruta, 2022). Green microfinance is facilitated by financial literacy (Lee & Huruta, 2022). A financially literate person has an eye for economic potential in one's surroundings and propels the potential into realisation (Lee & Huruta, 2022). Financial literacy awards more choices in investment (Brent & Ward, 2018). And it also brings discernment in selecting a right choice (Brent & Ward, 2018). Financial knowledge guides a financially literate person to evaluate each financial choice (Arena et al., 2023). It helps the person get the best option. In rural area, the business potential can be boosted by microfinance (Abdur Rouf, 2012). The business potential is possible to be encouraged by green microfinance, in the case the idea is eco-friendly. This research addresses the relationship between green microfinance and financial literacy in rural areas. And it places gender at its analytic centre. In India, literate females are empowered to make decisions, and its impact is linked to their business positively (Banerjee et al., 2023). In Iran, personal traits out of gender affect the way of evaluating investment and making decisions in finance (Cude et al., 2021). This research does not only put an emphasis on female side but considers both genders in the relationship between financial literacy and green microfinance. The aim of this research is to add a comprehensive perspective to existing literature by examining gender in the relationship. Accordingly, this research is first to make clear the relationship among three factors, then to develop a structural model, and finally to suggest how the model would be understood. It would provide meaningful information for policymakers in developing a business framework in rural area.

LITERATURE REVIEW
Financial Literacy and Green Microfinance

Rural area in which limited resources and infrastructures for business are given does normally not allow much business ideas (Tabares et al., 2022). Accordingly, substantial rural businesses depend much on natural resources (Tabares et al., 2022). Increasing environmental concerns require government to restrain destructing natural environment in doing business and to encourage doing green way (Abdur Rouf, 2012). That situation calls for green microfinance. It is a loan for the person managing a small business in a sustainable way (Abdur Rouf, 2012). Lee and Huruta (2022) proved that financial literacy is positively associated with green microfinance. Generally speaking, enhanced financial understanding enables access to financial resources (Bongomin et al., 2015; Lee & Huruta, 2022). Financial literacy gives discernment of evaluating financial utility among diverse financial products and services (Bongomin et al., 2015). A financially literate person knows how to manage risk in doing business (Bongomin et al., 2015). Bongomin et al. (2015) suggested that a financial literateness leads people in rural areas to a right financial product. The improvement in financial literacy is significantly related to a better financial management (Bongomin et al., 2015). Financial literacy features a right financial decision, and it is linked to microfinance in rural area (Bongomin & Munene, 2019).

The Impact of Financial Literacy on Green Microfinance Based on Gender's Role

A distinctive role between a male and a female affects the application of green microfinance (Atahau et al., 2021). Atahau et al. (2021) noted that the utility of green microfinance attracts females and that it empowers females to be more productive (Lee & Huruta, 2022). Green business in rural areas utilises natural resources being easily given from surroundings so that its concept allows females to engage in green business (Dorfleitner et al., 2020). A rural area in which local wisdom and its specific custom specially affect social activities gives female restriction in doing business (Lee & Huruta, 2022). Agier and Szafarz (2013) addressed the size of microfinance on gender difference. They found that stereotype on gender causes discrimination in loan size and that it negatively impacts female entrepreneurs planning a big project (Agier & Szafarz, 2013). Lee and Huruta (2022) observed that green microfinance gives females an access to financial resource. In that sense, green microfinance devotes itself to achieving equality in distribution. Financially literate females know how to get financial resource such as green microfinance and, furthermore, make profit by managing the resource (Lee & Huruta, 2022). Financial literacy empowers females to engage in economic activity (Lee & Huruta, 2022). The empowerment gives females an opportunity to develop their social status (Lee & Huruta, 2022). Warnecke (2015) noted that green microfinance contributes to gender equity. Green microfinance lowers economic vulnerability in household (Warnecke, 2015). Clean energy efficiency which green microfinance supports enables females to save energy cost in household, and it becomes an additional income to females (Warnecke, 2015).

From the point of view, it is highly probable that gender takes on a critical role in which financial literacy embodies green microfinance. As mentioned before, this research does not only put a stress on female as most related research did. Thus, this research hypothesises as below.

H1. A female has a bigger role than a male in the relationship between financial literacy and green microfinance.

METHODOLOGY

This research employed a purposive sampling to collect samples at Tapa Walla Badi women microfinance group in East Sumba, Indonesia. Statistical power and pointing arrows were used to verify the sample size of 50 respondents for analysis. Statistical power and pointing arrows are important factors in determining the sample size (Cohen, 1992). The minimum sample size with a statistical power of 80% and one pointing arrow (R^2 value is at least 0.5; probability of error is 5%) is 33. The number was decided based on the sample size for the PLS-SEM (Hair et al., 2017). PLS-SEM first defines constructs. This process lays groundwork for designing individual indicators (Hair et al., 2018). Each indicator was measured with the 5-point Likert scale (1 = strongly disagree to 5 = strongly agree). Each indicator was set to be capable of representing a corresponding latent construct in Table 14.1.

Based on constructs and indicators formulated, this research developed a research framework as follows:

Fig. 14.1 illustrates the relationship between constructs. It also shows the relationship corresponding to the hypothesis. The PLS-SEM begins by defining constructs. This procedure establishes its foundation for developing individual indicators. On a Likert scale, each scale indication was evaluated. Each scale was subdivided into 0.8 intervals in Table 14.2.

Table 14.1. Constructs and Indicators.

Constructs	Indicators
Green microfinance	1. MFIs offer soft loans for eco-friendly businesses
	2. Live pharmacy is encouraged by MFIs
	3. MFI members follow the principle of affordability by performing tasks efficiently
	4. MFIs help reduce grassland and forest fires
	5. In MFIs, utensils are used repeatedly
	6. MFIs have a recycling policy
Financial literacy	1. My business will be benefitted by a low-interest loan
	2. It is necessary to set up funds for unplanned expenses
	3. Purchasing life insurance will protect you from risks of accidents and other disasters
	4. Debit side records incoming funds, while credit side records outgoing funds
	5. Making a financial budget is important for determining funding priorities
	6. Saving money in a variety of assets reduces the risk of losing money

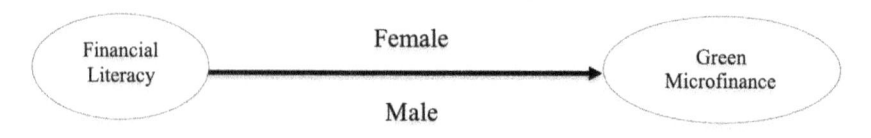

Fig. 14.1. Research Framework.

Table 14.2. Response Category of Indicators.

Scale	Interval	Category
1	1.00–1.80	Very low
2	1.81–2.60	Low
3	2.61–3.40	Medium
4	3.41–4.20	High
5	4.21–5.00	Very high

Notes: $I = (\text{max}-\text{min})/k$. I represents an interval, max denotes the largest response, min defines the lowest response, and k indicates categorisation.

Respondent responses were scored on a 5-point Likert scale, 5 representing very high, 4 representing high, 3 representing medium, 2 representing low, and 1 representing very low (Atahau et al., 2021). Constructs are examined in indicator reliability and construct validity. Outer loadings assess individual indicator reliability. The value of greater than 0.6 is considered reliable (Hair et al., 2017). Construct validity is assessed in three criteria: Cronbach's alpha, average variance extracted, and composite reliability (CR). An alpha level of greater than 0.7 is typically considered acceptable (Taber, 2018; Tavakol & Dennick, 2011). An AVE of 0.5 or higher suggests an adequate convergence (Hair et al., 2018). A CR value of higher than 0.7 indicates that internal consistency exists (Bacon et al., 1995; Brunner & Süß, 2005; Chau, 1999; Fornell & Larcker, 1981). After construct validity being examined, it shifts focus to build a specific model. It involves assessing the overall model fit and path between constructs (Hair et al., 2018).

Furthermore, the PLS-MGA allows to test whether pre-defined data groups (female and male) have significant differences in their group-specific parameter estimates. SmartPLS provides outcome from bootstrapping results of every group (Hair et al., 2018).

EMPIRICAL RESULTS

The empirical result consists of several parts, such as statistics of frequency (Table 14.3), descriptive statistics for respondent's profile (Table 14.4), descriptive statistics for indicators (Table 14.5), reflective measurement (Table 14.6), PLS-MGA paths (Fig. 14.2), and hypothesis testing (Table 14.7).

All constructs and indicators have been already examined by the PLS-MGA in SmartPLS. It can be seen in Table 14.6.

PLS-MGA paths and hypothesis testing are shown in Fig. 14.2 and Table 14.7.

Fig. 14.2 and Table 14.7 show that β female (0.773) is bigger than β male (0.765). It denotes that females' role is bigger than males' in the relationship between financial literacy and green microfinance. It indicates that *H1* is supported by this empirical result.

Table 14.3. Frequency of Respondents' Profile.

	Frequency	%	Cumulative %
Age			
20–35	26	52	52
36–44	9	18	70
45–54	2	4	74
55–64	7	14	88
65+	6	12	100
Total	50	100	
Gender			
Male	24	48	48
Female	26	52	100
Total	50	100	
Education			
Did not finish elementary school	2	4	4
Elementary school	30	60	64
Junior high school and equivalent	8	16	80
Senior high school and equivalent	6	12	92
Diploma/bachelor degree	4	8	100
Total	50	100	
Occupation			
Teacher	3	6	6
Housewife	18	36	42
Entrepreneur	2	4	46
Farmer	27	54	100
Total	50	100	
Income			
≤IDR 1,000,000	37	74	74
>IDR 1,000,000–5,000,000	9	18	92
>IDR 5,000,000	4	8	100
Total	50	100	

Table 14.4. Descriptive Statistics for Respondent's Profile.

Constructs	Min	Max	Mean	S.D.
Gender	1	2	1.52	0.505
Education	1	5	2.6	1.03
Occupation	1	9	5.96	3.54
Income	1	3	1.34	0.626

DISCUSSION

The result is in line with the empirical evidence of Lee and Huruta (2022) that green microfinance plays an intermediary role in distributing resources to poor people, particularly to females. Females who are financially literate know how to get to financial resources like green microfinance and how to make profits managing such resources. Green microfinance enables females to access to financial resources. In this manner, achieving gender equality is one of contributions of green microfinance. Microfinance could effectively empower female to improve their economic position and power relationships (Nawaz, 2015). Atahau et al.

Table 14.5. Descriptive Statistics for Indicators.

Indicators	Mean	Min	Max	S.D.	Exc. Kurtosis	Skewness
FL1	3.98	2	5	0.883	−1.351	−0.14
FL2	4.42	2	5	0.777	1.945	−1.439
FL3	3.94	2	5	0.81	0.132	−0.585
FL4	4.06	2	5	0.81	−0.805	−0.346
FL5	3.9	2	5	0.985	−0.661	−0.57
FL6	3.72	1	5	1.059	−0.579	−0.448
Financial literacy	4.00			High		
GM1	4	2	5	0.775	0.13	−0.533
GM2	4.16	1	5	0.833	2.489	−1.172
GM3	4.34	2	5	0.681	1.342	−0.955
GM4	4.36	2	5	0.656	1.827	−0.991
GM5	4.46	2	5	0.78	2.2	−1.558
GM6	4.14	2	5	0.749	0.98	−0.831
Green microfinance	4.24			Very high		

Table 14.6. Validity and Reliability Results of PLS-MGA.

Indicators	Outer Loadings		Cronbach's Alpha		CR		AVE	
	Female	Male	Female	Male	Female	Male	Female	Male
FL1	0.624	0.740						
FL2	0.724	0.673						
FL3	0.771	0.787	0.838	0.846	0.878	0.887	0.548	0.570
FL4	0.816	0.614						
FL5	0.824	0.798						
FL6	0.659	0.885						
GM1	0.653	0.654						
GM2	0.687	0.640						
GM3	0.888	0.789	0.860	0.808	0.897	0.861	0.594	0.510
GM4	0.747	0.823						
GM5	0.836	0.664						
GM6	0.787	0.695						

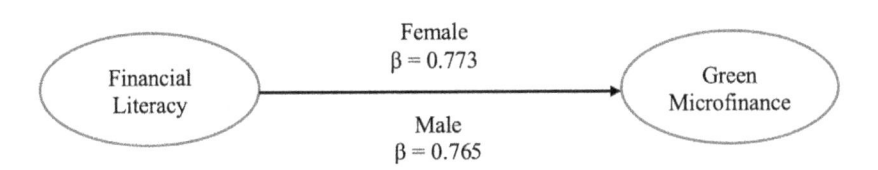

Fig. 14.2. PLS-MGA Paths.

(2021) also stated that the financial literacy of female entrepreneurs determines their success in establishing rural entrepreneurship.

　　Financial literacy serves as a catalyst for microfinancing (Brent & Ward, 2018). It makes business possibility a real business (Brent & Ward, 2018). Green microfinance is one of choices financing one's business, and financial literacy takes a role in connecting entrepreneur to financing sources such as green microfinance.

Table 14.7. Hypothesis Testing of PLS-MGA.

β Female ($n = 26$)	STDEV (Female)	t-Value (Female)	p-Value (Female)	β Difference
0.773	0.051	15.130	0.000	
β Male ($n = 24$)	STDEV (Male)	t-Value (Male)	p-Value (Male)	0.008
0.765	0.092	8.271	0.000	

Green loans are given to female farmers in a diverse form: a yarn for weaving, a biogas equipment, an organic fertiliser, a micro-hydropower plant, a waste bank, and other items (Atahau et al., 2021). Female's empowerment would be a powerful tool to support green microfinance as long as financial literacy accompanies. Banerjee et al. (2023) noted that a literate female weans herself off being dependent and is empowered to make decisions by herself. By extension, it would be associated with female entrepreneurship on green microfinance. This is in line with previous researches that financial literacy has an impact on female's empowerment and access to microfinance (Atahau et al., 2021; Lee & Huruta, 2022; Lindahl & Mokvist, 2020). Atahau et al. (2022) noted that some male respondents were also found in women farmer group. It indicates that management of the group needs men to take part in.

CONCLUSION

This research advocates that financial literacy takes on a substantial role over green microfinance. The findings corroborate that financial literacy propels those who have it into economic activity. Green microfinance would be a chance to those who are able to catch business potential from their financial understanding. Furthermore, the understanding allows people to choose a fit microfinance and build a plan for the loan. Green microfinance would be a precious chance to people in rural area in which there are not much business chances. Thus, it definitely hinges on the awareness of it. The awareness of green microfinance is from a full understanding of its utility, and the understanding is built on financial knowledge. This research is concerned with the role of gender. As suggested before, the research attempted to address both genders in analysis beyond existing studies. It proved that females cast themselves in the major role in comparison with males. In general terms, it is apparent that both genders have impact in the relationship between financial literacy and green microfinance and that female's impact is bigger than males. The findings broaden the horizon of understanding of genders' roles on green microfinance.

ACKNOWLEDGEMENT

We would like to sincerely thank for Chung Yuan Christian University that support the research funding.

REFERENCES

Abdur Rouf, K. (2012). Green microfinance promoting green enterprise development. *Humanomics*, *28*(2), 148–161. https://doi.org/10.1108/08288661211228906

Agier, I., & Szafarz, A. (2013). Microfinance and gender: Is there a glass ceiling on loan size? *World Development*, *42*, 165–181. https://doi.org/10.1016/j.worlddev.2012.06.016

Arena, C. M. R., Batac, A. A. S., Religioso, A. M. A., Magbata, E. V. S., & Mandigma, M. B. S. (2023). Influences on the stock market investing of tertiary students in the national capital region, Philippines. *Review of Integrative Business and Economics Research*, *12*(2), 148–166. https://sibresearch.org/uploads/3/4/0/9/34097180/riber_12-2_13_t23-043_148-166.pdf

Atahau, A. D. R., Lee, C.-W., Kesa, D. D., & Huruta, A. D. (2022). Developing social entrepreneurship in rural areas: A path mediation framework. *International Sociology*, *37*(4), 475–495. https://doi.org/10.1177/02685809221095912

Atahau, A. D. R., Sakti, I. M., Huruta, A. D., & Kim, M.-S. (2021). Gender and renewable energy integration: The mediating role of green-microfinance. *Journal of Cleaner Production*, *318*, 128536. https://doi.org/10.1016/j.jclepro.2021.128536

Bacon, D. R., Sauer, P. L., & Young, M. (1995). Composite reliability in structural equations modeling. *Educational and Psychological Measurement*, *55*(3), 394–406. https://doi.org/10.1177/0013164495055003003

Banerjee, S., Alok, S., Kumar, R., & George, B. (2023). Intrahousehold personal decision-making power as a measure of women empowerment and its effect on children's education – A study of rural India. *Review of Integrative Business and Economics Research*, *12*(2), 118–135. http://buscompress.com/uploads/3/4/9/8/34980536/riber_12-2_11_t22-043_118-135.pdf

Bongomin, G. O. C., & Munene, J. C. (2019). Examining the role of institutional framework in promoting financial literacy by microfinance deposit-taking institutions in developing economies. *Journal of Financial Regulation and Compliance*, *28*(1), 16–38. https://doi.org/10.1108/jfrc-12-2018-0158

Bongomin, G. O. C., Ntayi, J. M., Munene, J. C., & Nabeta, I. N. (2015). Financial inclusion in rural Uganda: Testing interaction effect of financial literacy and networks. *Journal of African Business*, *17*(1), 106–128. https://doi.org/10.1080/15228916.2016.1117382

Brent, D. A., & Ward, M. B. (2018). Energy efficiency and financial literacy. *Journal of Environmental Economics and Management*, *90*, 181–216. https://doi.org/10.1016/j.jeem.2018.05.004

Brunner, M., & Süß, H. M. (2005). Analyzing the reliability of multidimensional measures: An example from intelligence research. *Educational and Psychological Measurement*, *65*(2), 227–240. https://doi.org/10.1177/0013164404268669

Chau, P. Y. K. (1999). On the use of construct reliability in MIS research: A meta-analysis. *Information and Management*, *35*(4), 217–227. https://doi.org/10.1016/S0378-7206(98)00089-5

Cohen, J. (1992). A power primer. *Psychological Bulletin*, *112*(1), 155–159. https://doi.org/10.1037/0033-2909.112.1.155

Cude, B. J., Chatterjee, S., & Tavosi, J. (2021). Investment strategies, personality traits, and overconfidence: Evidence from Iran. *Review of Integrative Business and Economics Research*, *10*(3), 83–107. https://www.sibresearch.org/uploads/3/4/0/9/34097180/riber_10-3_05_m19-123_83-107.pdf

Dorfleitner, G., Forcella, D., & Nguyen, Q. A. (2020). Microfinance and green energy lending: First worldwide evidence. *Credit and Capital Markets-Kredit und Kapital*, *53*(4), 427–460. https://doi.org/10.3790/ccm.53.4.427

Fornell, C., & Larcker, D. F. (1981). Evaluating structural equation models with unobservable variables and measurement error. *Journal of Marketing Research*, *18*(1), 39–50.

Hair, J. F., Black, W. C., Babin, B. J., & Anderson, R. E. (2018). *Multivariate data analysis* (8th ed.). Cengange Learning.

Hair, J. F., Hult, G. T. M., Ringle, C. M., & Sarstedt, M. (2017). *A primer on partial least squares structural equation modeling (PLS-SEM)* (2nd ed.). Sage.

Hair, J. F., Sarstedt, M., Ringle, C. M., & Gudergan, S. P. (2018). *Advanced issues in partial least squares structural equation modeling (PLS-SEM)*. Sage.

Lee, C.-W., & Huruta, A. D. (2022). Green microfinance and women's empowerment: Why does financial literacy matter? *Sustainability*, *14*(5), 3130. https://doi.org/10.3390/su14053130

Lindahl, P., & Mokvist, L. (2020). *Accessing microfinance through financial literacy: A case study of hand in hand eastern Africa's operations in Kenya* [Umeå University]. https://www.diva-portal.org/smash/record.jsf?pid=diva2:1444775

Nawaz, F. (2015). Microfinance, financial literacy, and household power configuration in rural Bangladesh: An empirical study on some credit borrowers. *VOLUNTAS: International Journal of Voluntary and Nonprofit Organizations*, *26*(4), 1100–1121. https://doi.org/10.1007/s11266-015-9585-z

Tabares, A., Londoño-Pineda, A., Cano, J. A., & Gómez-Montoya, R. (2022). Rural entrepreneurship: An analysis of current and emerging issues from the sustainable livelihood framework. *Economies*, *10*, 142. https://doi.org/10.3390/economies10060142

Taber, K. S. (2018). The use of Cronbach's alpha when developing and reporting research instruments in science education. *Research in Science Education*, *48*(6), 1273–1296. https://doi.org/10.1007/s11165-016-9602-2

Tavakol, M., & Dennick, R. (2011). Making sense of Cronbach's alpha. *International Journal of Medical Education*, *2*, 53–55. https://doi.org/10.5116/ijme.4dfb.8dfd

Warnecke, T. (2015). "Greening" gender equity: Microfinance and the sustainable development agenda. *Journal of Economic Issues*, *49*(2), 553–562. https://doi.org/10.1080/00213624.2015.1042803

CHAPTER 15

ASSESSING THE IMPACT OF ORGANIZATIONAL EFFECTIVENESS AND EFFICIENCY RESULTING FROM MIS USAGE IN TERMS OF CUSTOMER SATISFACTION, OPERATIONAL MANAGEMENT, AND FINANCIAL INVESTMENT: THE CASE OF JDI COMPANY

Harvey T. Ong

De La Salle University-Manila, Philippines

ABSTRACT

This study identifies the effectiveness and efficiency resulting from management information system (MIS) use. Organisational effectiveness and efficiency can be assessed by examining customer service, financial management, and operations management. For the case of JDI company, in terms of customer service, MIS has increased the output of the users, which is easily accessed and produced; it delivers reliable output for its users and has a friendly interface, and users have minimal difficulty in using the MIS. In terms of operations management, their

The Finance-Innovation Nexus: Implications for Socio-Economic Development
International Symposia in Economic Theory and Econometrics, Volume 34, 215–225
Copyright © 2025 by Emerald Publishing Limited
All rights of reproduction in any form reserved
ISSN: 1571-0386/doi:10.1108/S1571-038620240000034018

MIS can deliver accurate data, and information is easily accessed by its users. Employees can organise their work and time more efficiently, as their idle time is significantly distressed. About financial investment, their MIS also paved the way to create a better understanding regarding the company's financial data; it has more benefits than costs and has helped in making better decisions.

Keywords: Organisational effectiveness; organisational efficiency; customer satisfaction; operational management; financial investment; management information systems

JEL Codes: O11; Q01; Q5

1. INTRODUCTION

1.1. Background of the Study

MISs contribute to the effectiveness and efficiency of organisations. This is supported by the study of Adonie et al. (2007), which found that relevant information using MIS can provide recommendations to enhance products and allow organisations to gain a competitive advantage in this rapidly changing environment. The effects of MIS can be seen from the perspective of customer service and the financial and operations management of firms. De Queiroz and Olveria (2014) also support this, stating that companies such as clothing retail businesses are searching for technology that gives them more flexibility and smoothens operations, as well as gives them a competitive advantage over their current competitors and soon-to-be competitors. Many scholars have also confirmed the importance of innovation factors in the competitive capacity of emerging economies in the international market (Phuong et al., 2023).

The online-to-offline (O2O) business model involves bringing customers from online to offline sales platforms. Adopting the O2O business model is not only a 'future trend' but also a 'current progression'. The click-and-mortar business model and e-commerce will each become dominant consumption modes. Firms' market shares are subject to the fact that the pie is enlarging while a multitude of competitors are diluting each individual firm's sales (Cho & Lai, 2023).

We chose JDI as the company to be studied. The results of this research study could serve as a benchmark for the other top corporations in the Philippines and would be able to apply what JDI did in terms of MIS usage.

1.2. Objectives of the Study

The MIS is a system that collects and processes data and provides it to managers at all levels for decision-making, planning, and implementation (Michalek, 2006). It has been perceived to have many benefits, both tangible and intangible. The purpose of this research is to discover the extent of the contribution of JDI's MIS to organisational efficiency and effectiveness in terms of customer satisfaction, operational management, and financial investment.

2. FRAMEWORK

2.1. Theoretical Framework

2.1.1. Types of MISs

The four categories of MISs are based on the level of support that the information system provides in the process of decision-making. The Databank Information System is responsible for observing, classifying, and storing any data item that can potentially be useful to the decision-maker. The predictive information system provides data and information as well as predictions and inferences. Finally, the decision-making information system is where the information and the decision-maker are the same.

2.1.2. Operational Management

When comparing old and new systems, the costs and benefits of creating that system are to be weighed to determine the viability. Cost–benefit analysis (CBA) can be used to assess system performance. If the system is not performing well, further alternatives have to be explored to make the system efficient (Picus et al., 2010).

The CBA has four aspects:

(1) Operational analysis

This analysis checks if (a) the organisational performance is adequate, (b) the system provides accurate and useful information, (c) the operations provide cost-effective information, (d) the system data are secured, (e) the operations maximise resources, and (f) the system provides reliable service.

(2) Technical analysis

This analysis looks at the proposed or other practical forms of technology. Appropriate technology and users who can handle them are required in tandem.

(3) Economic analysis

This analysis studies the economic feasibility of the alternatives provided.

(4) Schedule analysis

This analysis checks if the time allotted for the proposed system is sufficient and if the necessary skills do not take too long to learn. It is also used to assess whether the proposed system reached the deadline.

2.2. Operational Framework

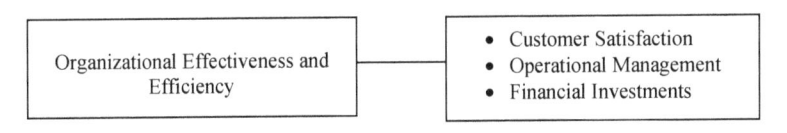

2.3. Operational Definition of Terms

- *Customer satisfaction* – how the organisation's offerings meet customer expectations, needs, and wants.

- *Human resources* – a group of people who make up an organisation's workforce.
- *Organisational effectivity* – how effective an organisation is in achieving intended outputs.
- *Organisational efficiency* – the ability to implement plans using the least amount of resources.

3. RESEARCH METHODOLOGY

3.1. Research Design

The survey was used in the study because it can gather data from a large population in a relatively convenient and efficient manner. Surveys are systematic, self-monitoring, and representative, as they are often used in research studies (Burton, 2007). Burton (2007) defined participant observation as the systematic description of behaviours in a social setting of a chosen study. Furthermore, survey forms were also deployed to assess the MIS efficiency and effectiveness in an organisation. The researcher also chose to do fieldwork for this study since it is often used to monitor human behaviours in natural conditions of their daily life (Basinska, 2012). Hence, the researcher is closer to the real world and, thus, gains from immediate contact with the respondents. It is one of the best ways to discover the information required and to answer research problems.

Basinska (2012) emphasised the importance of fieldwork, especially in data gathering in different organisations, as it allows the researcher to interact, understand the people in the company, and see problems that cannot be extracted from interviews. With the data from the surveys and interviews, the proponent used three major methods of analysis for this study, namely, descriptive analysis, cross-tabulation, and correlational analysis.

3.2. Sampling Plan

According to Robert Yin (2014), the embedded case study involves more than one unit of analysis. The research studied JDI company, which is in the home and garden industry of the home improvement category. The company was screened to ensure that they have been using MIS for at least three years to account for the lag effect in innovation. The chosen company was given surveys to be answered by both internal and external users to determine the effect MIS has on employees and their customers. The internal respondents refer to the employees that use the MIS and the external users refer to the long-term (5–10 years) clients of the companies.

4. RESEARCH FINDINGS

4.1. Initial Analysis

As mentioned in the previous chapter, the researcher used self-administered questionnaires to gather data from both the staff and customers of Marswin marketing. Afterwards, in-depth interviews were conducted with the IT heads of the company so that their insights could be gathered. Both quantitative and qualitative data were collected, and internal customers from the respondent companies were invited to answer the survey on organisational capabilities, organisational effectiveness, and efficiency.

4.2. Demographic Profile

4.2.1. Company Respondents Profiling

As the company backgrounds have already been established in the previous chapter, Table 15.1 shows the demographic profile of respondents from each company. The table also includes the profile of each IT manager (or its equivalent) who was selected for the interview. The internal respondents of the study were the IT managers of the respective companies and the users of the MIS, while the external respondents of the study were the customers who avail themselves of each company's products and/or services. See also Tables 15.2 and 15.3.

4.2.2. Organisational Effectiveness and Efficiency

Internal

The mean score of questions under the customer metric showed a score of 4.35 and a mode of 4, which means that the users are very pleased with their system. As seen in Table 15.3, all of the questions generated similar mean scores that fell under the response category of agree. This indicates that respondents concur that the MIS has reduced the workload and increased the output of the users. Furthermore, the employees also agree that the system delivers consistent and reliable output and has improved the working environment in the company. The employees also agree that the MIS has a user-friendly interface and has made the users engaged and motivated in their jobs.

Table 15.1. JDI Respondent Profile.

Jardine	Freq. Count	% Share	Freq. Count	% Share
Location				
Warehouse	12	26.67%	N/A	N/A
Office	33	73.33%	N/A	N/A
Age				
18–25	4	8.89%	0	0%
26–30	10	22.22%	5	22.73%
31–35	12	26.67%	6	27.27%
36–40	10	22.22%	5	22.73%
41–45	3	6.67%	6	27.27%
46–50	3	6.67%	0	0%
51–55	2	4.44%	0	0%
56–60	1	2.22%	0	0%
Gender				
Male	35	77.78%	20	90.91%
Female	10	22.22%	2	9.09%
Jardine	Name		Rank	
IT representative	Susan Dizon		IT Manager	

Table 15.2.   MIS Initial Analysis.

	JDI
Website	http://jardinedistribution.com/about-us/
Types of MIS	Inventory, transactional, and human resource
MIS developer	Third party vendor (undisclosed), SAP, and in-house IT
Investment in the MIS	Approx. Php 2,000,000 initial investment
Manages maintenance of MIS	Stephen Jones Sumulong – IT manager
Operations of MIS	24 h a day for 7 days a week
Number of users	45
Number of IT personnel	9
Accounting MIS	✓
Manufacturing MIS	✓
Human resources MIS	✓
Marketing MIS	✓

Table 15.3.   Organisational Effectiveness and Efficiency Summary.

Organisational Effectiveness and Efficiency	Respondents	Jardine Distributions Inc.
Customer satisfaction	Internal	Mean: 4.35
	External	Mode: 4

External

The mean score of questions under the customer metric showed a score of 3.63 and a mode of 4, which means that the customers are happy with their system. All the questions revealed similar mean scores, which generally indicate a neutral response. However, the scores also tend to lean more towards the agree-on response category, which may mean that the company's clients can experience some positive effects from the system.

4.2.3. Operational Management

Operational

The mean score for the questions under the operational metric showed a score of 4.17 and a mode of 5 (see Table 15.4). The first question, *the user can deliver at maximum productivity levels in terms of reducing workload*, generated a mean score of 4.20, which falls on the agreed response answer. This result implies that the average employee thinks and agrees that the users can deliver at the maximum level in terms of reducing the workload. The second question, *the user can deliver at maximum productivity levels in terms of timeliness of output*, and the third question, *the user can deliver at maximum productivity levels in terms of retrieving accurate data*, also have similar scores, which are 4.61 and 4.84, respectively. This indicates that the output is timely and that the system retrieves accurate data. At the same time, the fourth question, *the processed information is easily accessed*, has a mean score of 4.78, which corresponds to the response of agree. This indicates ease of access to processed information by employees. The fifth question,

Table 15.4. Operational Management Summary.

Operational Management	Jardine Distributions Inc.
Operational	Mean: 4.18
Technological	Mode:5
Economic	Mean: 3.37
Scheduling	Mode:4

the workforce has been reduced due to the implementation of MIS, has a mean score of 2.85, which is a response of disagree. It shows that the users disagree that employees were retrenched due to the MIS implementation. In the sixth question, *the user has minimal difficulty in utilising MIS* and has a score of 3.72, showing a neutral response but leaning more on the agree side. The employees agree that the user has minimal difficulty in using the system. The last question, *the user is confident about the security of the data uploaded into MIS*, has a mean score that indicates a response of agree; thus, it is inferred that the users are confident about the data security of MIS.

Technological

The mean score for the questions under the technological metric showed a score of 3.36 and a mode of 4. As shown in Table 15.4, the first question has a mean score of 3.43, which falls between neutral and agree on response answers but leans slightly more towards the agree response. This implies that the employees somewhat agree that the users are familiar with every aspect of the MIS. The second and third questions have the same mean score of 4.33, which means that the employees agree that they are familiar with the process and that the MIS is using up-to-date technology. The fourth question has a mean score of 2, which indicates a response of disagree. The employees disagree that the current MIS crashes and experiences traffic. The fifth question has a score that also shows a disagree response. The employees disagree that the MIS requires constant updates to function.

Economic

The mean score for the questions under the economic metric showed a score of 3.73 and a mode of 4. The first question has a mean score of 3.87, which falls between neutral and agree; however, it leans more towards the agree response. This result indicates that the average employee agrees that the acquisitions and installation of hardware and software incurred high costs. The second and third questions have similar scores but lean more on the neutral side. The employees choose to be neutral whether the operational fixed and variable costs being incurred are high. The fourth question has a score of 4.48, which is a response to the agreement. The employees do not experience stress when using the MIS. The fifth question has a mean score of 2.41, which indicates a level of disagreement. The employees disagree that the operations of the MIS incurred unnecessary costs. The sixth and seventh questions have a mean score that shows that the respondents agree more than they disagree with the item. The employees agree that the MIS is more time efficient and cost-effective and that it has established strong relations with other participants.

Scheduling

The mean score for the scheduling metric showed a score of 4.01 and a mode of 4. The first question, *training in the usage of the MIS required minimal time and effort*, has a score of 3.76, which is neutral but leans more on the agree side. The employees agree that the training required minimal effort and time. The second question's, *it took a while for MIS to be implemented and used in the workplace*, score leans more on the neutral side. The employees have a neutral response, indicating that they have chosen to be neutral whether the implementation of the system took a while. The mean score of the third question, *idle time, was removed with the use of MIS*, the fourth question, *employees can organise their work and time more efficiently*, and the fifth question, *the MIS helped the users achieve their work efficiently*, showed an agreed response. This depicts that the employees agree that the idle time was removed in using the MIS and that the system helped the users organise their work and time more efficiently.

4.2.4. Financial Investment

As illustrated in Table 15.5, the mean score of the results for each question under the financial management evaluation criteria showed a score of 4.58 and a mode of 4, which means that the current system exceeds its expectations of it. The first question, *the benefits of installing an MIS outweigh the costs*, was able to generate a mean score of 4.67, which falls between agree and strongly agree on response answers. This result infers that the average employee of Jardine Distributions Inc. agrees that the benefits of installing an MIS outweigh the costs. At the same time, the second question, *the MIS, significantly improved the company's budgeting* and had a mean score of 4.54, which also falls between agree and strongly agree on responses. This indicates that the average employee in the company does feel that the MIS significantly improved the company's budgeting. Subsequently, the third question, *the MIS helps the company minimise operating expenses*, for the metric was able to garner a mean score of 4.43 which at the same time falls right in between agree and strongly agree on responses. A mean score of 4.43 indicates that the average employee feels that the MIS helps the company minimise operating expenses. The fourth, *the MIS, has made the company make better decisions regarding financial matters*, and the fifth question, *the MIS, allowed the users to have a better understanding of the company's financial data*, for the metric was able to generate mean scores of 4.61 and 4.63, respectively, both of which also fall between agree and strongly agree. This indicates that the employees agree on average when asked whether the MIS has made the company make better decisions regarding financial matters and that the MIS allowed the users to have a better understanding of the company's financial data.

Table 15.5. Financial Investment Summary.

Financial Investment	Jardine Distributions Inc. Mean: 4.58

4.3. Organisational Effectiveness and Efficiency Cross-case Analysis

Customer satisfaction

The IT manager believes that the MIS has increased the output of the users, which is easily accessed and produced. At the same time, the MIS delivers reliable output for its users and has a friendly interface; thus, the users have minimal difficulty in using the MIS. The MIS has helped users reduce their workload as it has increased their output. It also improved the employees' working environment, as they became more engaged and motivated in their work. See Table 15.6.

Operational management

The MIS can deliver accurate data, and information is easily accessed by its users. The MIS goes through updates to improve the present version. With the use of MIS, efficient output was produced. The employees agree that the information is easily accessed and tracked through the system, and they experienced minimal difficulty in operating the system. Moreover, they agree that the MIS uses up-to-date technology and experiences only a few to zero crashes and traffic. With the use of the system, employees can organise their work and time more efficiently, as their idle time is significantly distressed.

Financial investment

The MIS has helped make better decisions about their finances since better analysis and balance sheets are created with the use of the system. The MIS also paved the way to create a better understanding of the company's financial data.

Table 15.6. Organisational Effectiveness and Efficiency Cross-case Analysis.

	JDI		
	Survey	Interview with IT Manager	Company Documents
Organisational effectiveness and efficiency	Mean: 4.25 Mode: 4	The MIS has increased the output of the users. There is also reliable output for users There is minimal difficulty in using the system	The timesheet of the employees shows less over time as compared to the prior implementation of MIS, and their turnover rate has been lowered as well
Customer satisfaction	Mean: 4.35 Mode: 4	The users are satisfied with the system since it is regularly updated due to their maintenance agreement with the vendor	No company documents are available
Operational management	Mean: 3.83 Mode: 4	The users have no complaints about how the system affects their work	No company documents are available

The MIS has more benefits than costs and has helped in making better decisions regarding the financial mayors of the company.

Correlational analysis

The researcher used a correlation analysis to determine whether organisational slack significantly relates to innovation in Jardine Distributions Inc.\ Organisational slack is divided into absorbed and unabsorbed slack, while innovation is divided into organisational, marketing, process, product, behavioural, and strategic slack. See Table 15.7.

Table 15.7.   Correlational Analysis.

Propositions	Slack	Jardine	
		Survey	Survey
Organisational slack can help create innovation models in the companies under study	Absorbed	Organisational Pearson $R = -0.295$ P-value $= 0.046^*$	Organisational Pearson $R = -0.761$ P-value$=0.000^{**}$
		Marketing Pearson $R = 0.031$ P-value $= 0.428$	Marketing Pearson $R = -0.251$ P-value $= 0.031^*$
		Process Pearson $R = 0.168$ P-value $= 0.176$	Process Pearson $R = 0.025$ P-value $= 0.435$
		Product Pearson $R = 0.030$ P-value $= 0.434$	Product Pearson $R = -0.226$ P-value $= 0.067$
		Behavioural Pearson $R = 0.155$ P-value $= 0.194$	Behavioural Pearson $R = -0.404$ P-value $= 0.003^{**}$
		Strategic Pearson $R = 0.334$ P-value $= 0.029^*$	Strategic Pearson $R = -0.607$ P-value $= 0.000^{**}$
	Unabsorbed	Organisational Pearson $R = 0.328$ P-value $= 0.031^*$	Organisational Pearson $R = -0.230$ P-value $= 0.064$
		Marketing Pearson $R = 0.205$ P-value $= 0.127$	Marketing Pearson $R = -0.151$ P-value $= 0.161$
		Process Pearson $R = 0.181$ P-value $= 0.157$	Process Pearson $R = -0.450$ P-value $= 0.001^{**}$
		Product Pearson $R = -0.035$ P-value $= 0.425$	Product Pearson $R = -0.508$ P-value $= 0.000^{**}$
		Behavioural Pearson $R = -0.290$ P-value $= 0.051$	Behavioural Pearson $R = 0.110$ P-value $= 0.236$
		Strategic Pearson $R = 0.047$ P-value $= 0.398$	Strategic Pearson $R = 0.376$ P-value $= 0.005^{**}$

5. CONCLUSION

Based on the information gathered from interviews, it can be concluded that JDI has the appropriate organisational capability to run the MIS. Physically, JDI ensured that the system was running on compatible hardware. The MIS managed to bring about improvements in the business processes of JDI in terms of customer satisfaction, operational management, and financial investment. The MIS also increased the motivation of their employees, as it reduced the burden due to the heavy workload. The customers are satisfied with the use of the information system. Among the survey participants, none demonstrated dissatisfaction with its information system. Moreover, the system was revealed to deliver consistent and reliable data. The data produced by the system are also reported to be accurate. The MIS of JDI can deliver maximum productivity since it produces timely and accurate data. The information stored can easily be accessed, and it has a friendly interface. In terms of the system's financial management, the MIS increased JDI's effectiveness and efficiency by streamlining the task of budgeting since the data retrieved are accurate and up to date.

REFERENCES

Adonie, R. J., Russo, E., & Dean, R. (2007). Crossing the Rubicon: A generic intelligent advisor [Abstract]. *International Journal of Computers, Communications & Control, 1*, 20.

Basinska, A. (2012). *Higher school of humanities and journalism.* http://www.crest.fr/congres-afs/basinska.pdf

Burton. (2007). *Survey research: Choice of instrument, sample.* School of Public Health. Retrieved from http://ocw.jhsph.edu/courses/hsre/pdfs/hsre_lect11_burton.pdf

Cho, H.-K., & Lai, W.-H. (2023). Analyzing the influential factors of O2O business using the technology acceptance model. *Review of Integrative Business and Economics Research, 10*(4), 1–17.

De Queiroz, J. P., & Oliveira, B. (2014). Benefits of the marketing information system in the clothing retail business. *Journal of Information Systems and Technology Management: JISTEM, 11*(1), 153–168. Retrieved from http://search.proquest.com/docview/153008 2808?accountid=2854

Michalek, D. (2006). Benefits of management information systems and important conditions for successful implementation and running [Abstract]. *Journal of Information Systems and Operation Management.*

Phuong, N., Thuong, P., Hoa, T., Long, L., & Khoa, T. (2023). Opportunities and challenges for developing a sustainable software city: Lessons from Quang Trung Software City in Vietnam. *Review of Integrative Business and Economics Research, 11*(3), 38–60.

Picus, L., Adamson, F., Montague, W., & Owens, M. (2010). *A new conceptual framework for analyzing the costs of performance assessment.* http://edpolicy.stanford.edu/sites/default/files/publications/new-conceptual-framework-analyzing-costs-performance-assessment_0.pdf

Yin, R. (2014). *Case Study Research Design and Methods* (5th ed.). Sage Publications, Inc.

CHAPTER 16

TERM STRUCTURE OF INTERBANK INTEREST RATES IN JAPAN UNDER DIFFERENT REGIMES OF NON-TRADITIONAL MONETARY POLICY

Takayasu Ito

Meiji University, Japan

ABSTRACT

This chapter presents comparative analyses of the term structure of interbank interest rates in Japan under different regimes of non-traditional monetary policy. The yield curve under a 'quantitative and qualitative easing policy' is driven by three common trends and driven by two common trends under a 'negative interest rate policy'. Market practitioners assumed that there was little room for interbank interest rates to be lowered because of the zero lower bound restriction under 'a quantitative and qualitative easing policy'. But after the BOJ introduced 'a negative interest rate policy', the zero lower bound restriction was lifted. This is why the market function of interbank interest rate began to recover.

Keywords: Interbank interest rate; negative interest rate; quantitative and qualitative easing; term structure; Japan

JEL Classifications: E43; G12

The Finance-Innovation Nexus: Implications for Socio-Economic Development
International Symposia in Economic Theory and Econometrics, Volume 34, 227–236
Copyright © 2025 by Emerald Publishing Limited
All rights of reproduction in any form reserved
ISSN: 1571-0386/doi:10.1108/S1571-038620240000034019

1. INTRODCUTION

This chapter focuses on the term structure of interbank interest rates in Japan under different monetary policy regimes. It investigates the number of common trends as driving forces of the yield curve by making comparisons of a 'quantitative and qualitative easing policy' and a 'negative interest rate policy'.

The Bank of Japan (2013) stated that 'The BOJ (Bank of Japan) adopted a quantitative and qualitative easing policy during the period from April 4, 2013 to January 28, 2016'. The pillars of a 'quantitative and qualitative easing policy' are as follows: '(1) The adoption of monetary base control, (2) An increase in JGB (Japanese Government Bond) purchases and their maturity, (3) An increase in ETF (Exchange Traded Fund) and J-REIT (Real Estate Investment Fund) purchases, (4) A continuation of quantitative and qualitative monetary easing to achieve the price stability target of 2 percent'.

The BOJ adopted a 'negative interest rate policy' from 29 January 2016. According to the Bank of Japan (2016), 'they apply a negative interest rate of minus 0.1 percent to the policy-rate balances in current accounts held by financial institutions at the Bank. They purchase JGBs so that 10-year JGB yield remains more or less at the current level (around zero percent)'.

This chapter makes several original contributions to related literature, mentioned below. It is the first to analyse the term structure of interbank interest rates for about seven years under a 'negative interest rate policy' in Japan. In addition, it gets an implication of the recovery of market function in comparison with the results of Ito (2023) analysing Treasury Bill (TB) market.

Related studies, such as Andresen et al. (2015), Jackson (2015), Arteta et al. (2016), Bech and Malkhozov (2016), Turk (2016), Ito (2017), Ito (2019), and Ito (2023), analyse short-term money markets under 'non-traditional monetary policies such as negative interest rate policy'.

Andresen et al. (2015) concluded that 'the reduction of the certificate of deposit (CD) rate has increased the spread between the current account rate and the CD rate and thus the scope for fluctuations in overnight money market rates in Denmark'. Jackson (2015) outlined 'the concerns associated with negative interest rates, provides an overview of the international experience with negative policy rates so far, and sets out some general observations based on this experience'.

Arteta et al. (2016) reported that 'monetary transmission channels under a negative interest rate policy are conceptually analogous to those under a conventional monetary policy, but a negative interest rate policy presents complications that could limit policy effectiveness'. Bech and Malkhozov (2016) concluded that, 'for the most part, modestly negative policy rates transmit through to money markets and other interest rates in the same way as positive rates do'. Turk (2016) analysed 'the profitability of Danish and Swedish banks under a negative interest rate policy'.

Ito (2017) concluded that 'in Denmark, monetary policy expectations have some impact on the interbank interest rates in the maturities of one, three, and six months'. Ito (2019) concluded that 'monetary policy expectations are not fully transmitted to the yield curve end of the short-term money market under a quantitative and qualitative easing policy or a negative interest rate policy'. Ito (2023) reported that the 'TB yield curve under a negative interest rate policy is driven by a single common trend with mutual causalities in all maturities. In other words, normal transmission function of TB yield curve recovered by the introduction of a "negative interest rate policy"'.

2. DATA

Daily data of interbank interest rates with maturities of 3, 6, and 12 months provided by Datastream are used for the analyses. The sample period is from 4 April 2013 to 30 March 2023. It is divided into two sub-sample periods. The first period, from 4 April 2013 to 28 January 2016, is named Sample A. The BOJ adapted a 'quantitative and qualitative easing policy'. The second period, from 29 January 2016 to 30 March 2023, is Sample B. They adapted a 'negative interest rate policy'. The movements of interbank interest rates are shown in Fig. 16.1. The descriptive statistics are provided in Table 16.1.

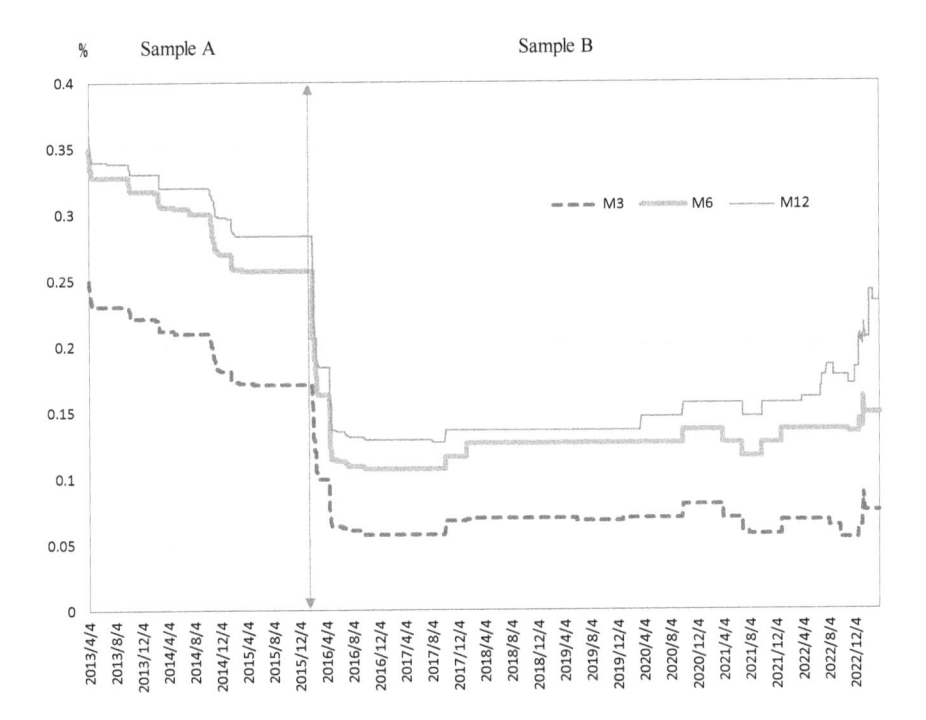

Fig. 16.1. Movement of Interbank Interest Rate. *Notes*: Sample A is from 4 April 2013 to 28 January 2016. Sample B is from 29 January 2016 to 30 March 2023. M3 is interbank interest rate 3 month. M6 is interbank interest rate 6 month. M12 is interbank interest rate 12 month. Date source is Datestream.

Table 16.1.   Descriptive Statistics.

Variable	Average	SD	Min	Max	Median
Sample A					
M3	0.20	0.02	0.17	0.25	0.21
M6	0.29	0.03	0.26	0.35	0.30
M12	0.31	0.02	0.28	0.36	0.32
Sample B					
M3	0.07	0.01	0.05	0.17	0.07
M6	0.13	0.01	0.11	0.26	0.13
M12	0.15	0.02	0.13	0.28	0.14

Notes: Sample A is from 4 April 2013 to 28 January 2016.
Sample B is from 29 January 2016 to 30 March 2023.
M3 is interbank interest rate 3 month. M6 is interbank interest rate 6 month.
M12 is interbank interest rate 12 month.

3. METHODOLOGY

3.1. Unit Root Test

The augmented Dickey–Fuller (ADF) test and the Kwiatowski–Phillips–Schmidt–Shin (KPSS) test are used. According to Dickey and Fuller (1979, 1981), 'the ADF test defines the null hypothesis as unit roots exist and the alternative hypothesis as unit roots do not exist'. Fuller (1976) provided 'a table for the ADF test'. According to Kwiatkowski et al. (1992), 'the KPSS test defines the null hypothesis as unit roots do not exist and the alternative hypothesis as unit roots exist'. Following Ito (2019), 'first, the original data are checked to verify whether they contain unit roots'. 'Next, the data with first difference are analyzed to determine whether they have unit roots to confirm that they are I (1) process'.

3.2. Johansen Cointegration Test

As described in Ito (2023), 'the Johansen cointegration test is applied in the way detailed below after it is confirmed that the data used for analysis are non-stationary I (1) variables'. Johansen (1988) suggested 'an analysis with the k order VAR model'. Here, 'the VAR model is presented with k order against vector X_t with p variables'. Trace and maximal Eigen value tests are conducted to analyse interbank interest rates in maturities of 3, 6, and 12 months. 'The critical values at the 5% level provided by Osterwald-Lenum (1992)' are used, as in Ito (2023).

$$X_t = \Pi_1 X_{t-1} + \ldots + \Pi_k X_{t-k} + \lambda + u_t \qquad (1)$$

According to Johansen (1988), 'all the p elements of X_t are considered to be I (1) variables. u_t is an error term with a zero mean. λ is a constant term'.

As Stock and Watson (1988) showed, 'an alternative interpretation of the cointegration among yields of different maturities arises from the relationship between cointegration and common trends'. They conclude that 'when there are $(n - p)$ linearly independent cointegration vectors for a set of n I (1) variables, then each of these n variables can be expressed as a linear combination of p I (1) common trends and $(n - p)$ I (0) components'.

Applying the result to this study, Stock and Watson (1988) mentioned that 'there will be a couple of non-stationary common trends in the yield curve of different maturities'. Hall et al. (1992) is relevant to this part of the analysis. They conducted 'the Johansen cointegration test using the monthly data of the US Treasury bill data (11 series: one month through to 11 months) from 1970 through to 1988' and found that 'the entire series comprises 10 cointegration vectors and one common trend'. They also stated that 'denoting the I (1) common trends by $W(t_1)$ ... $W(t_n)$, a simple representation of how they link the yield curve is given by

$$R(1,t) = A(1,t) + b_1 W(t_1)$$

$$R(2,t) = A(2,t) + b_2 W(t_1) + b_2 W(t_2)$$

$$\text{.......}$$

$$R(n,t) = A(n,t) + b_n W(t_1) + b_n W(t_2) \text{ .... } b_n W(t_n)$$

where $A(i,t)$ are I (0) variables'. 'Since $W(t_n)$ is I (1) and $A(i,t)$a are I (0), the observed long-run movement in each yield is mainly due to the common trend(s)'. Stock and Watson (1988) concluded that '$W(t_n)$ drives the time-series behavior of each yield and determines how the entire yield curve changes over time'. According to Hall et al. (1992), '$W(t_n)$ is considered as something exogenous to the yield curve system'. As Ito (2019) pointed out, 'when a single trend is found by the Johansen cointegration test, the yield curve is assumed to be moving as a result of a single trend caused by monetary policy expectations'. The term structure up to 12 months is moved by a single common trend under a normal monetary policy regime of interest rate targeting, as reported in Hall et al. (1992).

3.3. Granger Causality Test

Granger causality tests are utilised to check the causalities among three interbank yields. According to Toda and Yamamoto (1995), 'the original data are usually transformed into the change ratio to avoid the problem of spurious regression, but using these data is considered to cause an error'. They, therefore, developed 'the Granger causality test in which non-stationary data are used directly'. The Granger causality test was originally proposed by Granger (1980).

In their method, 'the null hypothesis is tested by adding trend term t and $p + 1$ (original lag plus one) for the estimation of the three equations mentioned below'. These three equations are used to test three interbank interest rates: for example, equation (2) shows whether interbank interest rates of 6 and 12 months cause interbank interest rate of 3 months. As in Ito (2023), 'the AIC (Akaike information criterion) standard is used for the determination of original number of lags'.

$$\text{IR}\,3\,M = \kappa_0 + \lambda t + \sum_{i=1}^{p+1} \alpha_i \text{IR}\,6\,M_{t-1} + \sum_{i=1}^{p+1} \beta_i \text{IR}\,12\,M_{t-1} + u_t \tag{2}$$

$$IR6\ M = \kappa_0 + \lambda t + \sum_{i=1}^{p+1} \alpha_i IR3\ M_{t-1} + \sum_{i=1}^{p+1} \beta_i IR12\ M_{t-1} + u_t \qquad (3)$$

$$IR12\ M = \kappa_0 + \lambda t + \sum_{i=1}^{p+1} \alpha_i IR3\ M_{t-1} + \sum_{i=1}^{p+1} \beta_i IR6\ M_{t-1} + u_t \qquad (4)$$

4. RESULTS

4.1. Unit Root Test

The results of the ADF and KPSS tests show that the original series have unit roots except for ADF test without trend (maturity of 12 months in Sample A) and with trend (all maturities in Sample B). The results are shown in Tables 16.2 and 16.3.

All results of the ADF and KPSS tests, except for the KPPS test for Sample B, show that the first-differenced series do not have unit roots. Taking into account the results of both ADF and KPSS tests, I can conclude that all data used for the analyses are non-stationary I (1) variables. The results are shown in Tables 16.4 and 16.5.

4.2. Johansen Cointegration Test

The results for Sample A indicate that the series have no cointegration vector and three common trends. The results for Sample B show that the series have one cointegration vector and two common trends. As Ito (2019) pointed out, 'when a single trend is found by the Johansen cointegration test, the entire yield curve is assumed to be moving as a result of a single trend'.

Table 16.2. ADF Test – Original Series.

Variable	Without Trend	With Trend
Sample A		
M3	−2.027	−2.071
M6	−2.353	−1.493
M12	−2.924*	−1.436
Sample B		
M3	−1.005	−4.627*
M6	−0.464	−4.893*
M12	0.191	−3.466*

Notes: * indicates significance at the 5% level.
5% critical values are −2.86 (Without Trend) and −3.41 (With Trend)
Sample A is from 4 April 2013 to 28 January 2016.
Sample B is from 29 January 2016 to 30 March 2023.
M3 is interbank interest rate 3 month. M6 is interbank interest rate 6 month.
M12 is interbank interest rate 12 month.

Table 16.3. KPSS Test – Original Series.

Variable	Lag = 4		Lag = 12	
	$\eta\mu$	$\eta\tau$	$\eta\mu$	$\eta\tau$
Sample A				
M3	13.359*	1.082*	5.190*	0.428*
M6	13.482*	1.204*	5.234*	0.476*
M12	13.358*	1.015*	5.192*	0.403*
Sample B				
M3	0.926*	0.978*	0.381*	0.402*
M6	7.929*	0.879*	3.202*	0.362*
M12	14.631*	3.333*	5.812*	1.351*

Notes: * indicates significance at the 5% level.
5% critical values are 0.463 (level stationary), 0.146 (trend stationary).
$\eta\mu$ indicates level stationarity. $\eta\tau$ indicates trend stationary.
Sample A is from 4 April 2013 to 28 January 2016.
Sample B is from 29 January 2016 to 30 March 2023.
M3 is interbank interest rate 3 month. M6 is interbank interest rate 6 month.
M12 is interbank interest rate 12 month.

Table 16.4. ADF Test – First Differenced Series.

Variable	Without Trend	With Trend
Sample A		
ΔM3	−10.057*	−24.907*
ΔM6	−9.605*	−12.567*
ΔM12	−11.587*	−28.107*
Sample B		
ΔM3	−7.854*	−24.728*
ΔM6	−9.578*	−12.564*
ΔM12	−7.904*	−27.833*

Notes: * indicates significance at the 5% level.
5% critical values are −2.86 (without trend) and −3.41 (with trend)
Sample A is from 4 April 2013 to 28 January 2016.
Sample B is from 29 January 2016 to 30 March 2023.
M3 is interbank interest rate 3 month. M6 is interbank interest rate 6 month.
M12 is interbank interest rate 12month.

Table 16.5. KPSS Test – First Differenced Series.

Variable	Lag = 4		Lag = 12	
	$\eta\mu$	$\eta\tau$	$\eta\mu$	$\eta\tau$
Sample A				
ΔM3	0.440	0.139	0.231	0.089
ΔM6	0.378	0.137	0.249	0.091
ΔM12	0.323	0.114	0.238	0.084

(Continued)

Table 16.5. (*Continued*).

Variable	Lag = 4		Lag = 12	
	η_μ	η_τ	η_μ	η_τ
Sample B				
ΔM3	1.060*	0.403*	0.781*	0.301*
ΔM6	1.335*	0.463*	0.920*	0.324*
ΔM12	1.662*	0.300*	1.220*	0.228*

Notes: * indicates significance at the 5% level.
5% critical values are 0.463 (level stationary), 0.146 (trend stationary).
η_μ indicates level stationarity. η_τ indicates trend stationary.
Sample A is from 4 April 2013 to 28 January 2016.
Sample B is from 29 January 2016 to 30 March 2023.
M3 is interbank interest rate 3 month. M6 is interbank interest rate 6 month.
Ml2 is interbank interest rate 12 month.

Table 16.6. Johansen Cointegration Test.

Null	Alternative	Test Statistics	5% Value	10% Value	Test Statistics	5% Value	10% Value
Sample A		Maximal Eigen Value Test			Trace Test		
$r = 0$	$r = 1$	13.683	22.00	19.77	25.421	34.91	32.00
$r \leqq 1$	$r = 2$	9.147	15.67	13.75	11.739	19.96	17.85
$r \leqq 2$	$r = 3$	2.59	9.24	7.52	2.592	9.24	7.52
Sample B							
$r = 0$	$r = 1$	24.059*	22.00	19.77	34.010**	34.91	32.00
$r \leqq 1$	$r = 2$	7.468	15.67	13.75	9.996	19.96	17.85
$r \leqq 2$	$r = 3$	2.495	9.24	7.52	2.495	9.24	7.52

Notes: *,** indicates significance at thr 5% and 10% levels.
Critical values are cited from Osterwald-Lenum (1992).
Sample A is from 4 April 2013 to 28 January 2016.
Sample B is from 29 January 2016 to 30 March 2023.
M3 is interbank interest rate 3 month. M6 is interbank interest rate 6 month.
M12 is interbank interest rate 12 month.

Thus, the yield curve of interbank interest rates in Sample A is driven by three common trends, but the yield curve of interbank interest rates in Sample B is driven by two common trends. As Stock and Watson (1988) mentioned, 'they are exogenous to yield curve, and are caused by an expectation regarding monetary policy and another trends' (see also Ito 2023). The results are shown in Table 16.6.

4.3. Granger Causality Test

The results for Samples A and B show that there are mutual causalities in all combinations of interbank interest rates. The results are shown in Table 16.7.

Table 16.7. Granger Causality Test.

Variables	Test Statistics	Variables	Test Statistics
Sample A		Sample B	
M3 → M6	6.937*	M3 → M6	10.855*
M3 → M12	8.786*	M3 → M12	3.875*
M6 → M3	3.024*	M6 → M3	28.793*
M6 → M12	4.167*	M6 → M12	4.236*
M12 → M3	4.575*	M12 → M3	7.297*
M12 → M6	2.713*	M12 → M6	4.297*

Notes: * indicates significance at the 5% level.
As for the number of lags, one is added to AIC selection.
Sample A is from 4 April 2013 to 28 January 2016.
Sample B is from 29 January 2016 to 30 March 2023.
M3 is interbank interest rate 3 month. M6 is interbank interest rate 6 month.
M12 is interbank interest rate 12 month.

5. CONCLUSION

The purpose of this chapter is to present comparative analyses of the term structure of interbank interest rates in Japan under different regimes of non-traditional monetary policy. It has been found that the yield curve under a 'quantitative and qualitative easing policy' is driven by three common trends, while the yield curve under a 'negative interest rate policy' is driven by two common trends.

The results of this chapter have a similarity but also present a difference to those of Ito (2023). It concludes that 'the TB yield curve' under a 'quantitative and qualitative easing policy' is driven by two common trends, whereas the TB yield curve under 'a negative interest rate policy' is driven by a single common trend. This is a difference. The similarity is that the market function improved in both TB and interbank markets after the introduction of a 'negative interest rate policy'.

Market practitioners assumed that there was little room for interbank interest rates to be lowered because of the zero lower bound restriction under 'a quantitative and qualitative easing policy'. But after the BOJ introduced 'a negative interest rate policy', the zero lower bound restriction was lifted. This is why the market function of interbank interest rates began to recover, but not as quickly as the TB market. Practitioners of the interbank money market are limited to financial institutions, but those of the TB market are open to both financial institutions and non-financial institutions. This is why the market function recovered earlier in the TB market than in the interbank money market.

This chapter has analysed the interbank market in Japan. There is room to expand this research to analyse market structure of the money market including both TB and interbank interest rates in Japan.

ACKNOWLEDGEMENTS

This research is supported financially by Institute of Social Sciences Meiji University. The author would like to express an appreciation for the support.

REFERENCES

Andresen, M. M., Kristoffersen, M. S., & Risbjerg, L. (2015). *The money market at pressure on the Danish Krone and negative interest rates*. Danmarks National Bank Monetary Review.

Arteta, C., Kose, A., Stocker, M., & Taskin, T. (2016). *Negative interest rate policies: Sources and implications*. Centre for Economic Policy Research DP11433.

Bank of Japan. (2013). http://www.boj.or.jp/en/announcements/release_2013/k130404a.pdf.

Bank of Japan (2016). http://www.boj.or.jp/en/announcements/release_2016/k160129a.pdf.

Bech, M., & Malkhozov, A. (2016, March). How have central banks implemented negative policy rates? *BIS Quarterly Review*, 31–44.

Dickey, D. A., & Fuller, W. A. (1979). Distribution of the estimators for autoregressive time series with a unit root. *Journal of the American Statistical Association*, *74*(366), 427–431.

Dickey, D. A., & Fuller, W. A. (1981). Likelihood ratio statistics for autoregressive time series with a unit root. *Econometrica*, *49*(4), 1057–1072.

Fuller, W. A. (1976). *Introduction to statistical time series*. John Wiley & Sons, Inc.

Granger, C. W. J. (1980). Testing for causality: A personal viewpoint. *Journal of Economic Dynamics and Control*, *2*, 329–352.

Hall, A. D, Anderson, H. M., & Granger, C. W. J. (1992). A cointegration analysis of treasury bill yields. *Review of Economics and Statistics*, *74*, 116–126.

Ito, T. (2017). Do monetary policy expectations influence the transmission mechanism in the Danish interbank market under a negative interest rate policy? *International Journal of Bonds and Derivatives*, *3*(3), 223–234.

Ito, T. (2019). Transmission of monetary policy expectations on the money markets: Comparative analysis of non-traditional monetary policy regimes in Japan. *Journal of Corporate Accounting and Finance*, *30*(4), 48–53.

Ito, T. (2023). Yield curve of treasury bills in Japan under different regimes of non-traditional monetary policy. *Journal of Corporate Accounting and Finance*, *34*(3), 337–342.

Jackson, H. (2015). *The international experience with negative policy rates* [Bank of Canada Staff discussion paper].

Johansen, S. (1988). Statistical analysis of cointegrated vectors. *Journal of Economic Dynamics and Control*, *12*(2–3), 231–254.

Kwiatkowski, D., Phillips, P. C. B., Schmidt, P., & Shin, Y. (1992). Testing the null hypothesis of stationarity against the alternative of a unit root. *Journal of Econometrics*, *54*(1–3), 159–178.

Osterwald-Lenum, M. (1992). Practitioners' corner: A note with quantiles of the asymptotic distribution of the maximum likelihood cointegration rank test statistics. *Oxford Bulletin of Economics and Statistics*, *54*(3), 169–210.

Stock, J. H., & Watson, M. W. (1988). Testing for common trends. *Journal of the American Statistical Association*, *83*(404), 1097–1107.

Toda, H. Y., & Yamamoto, T. (1995). Statistical inference in vector autoregressions with possibly integrated processes. *Journal of Econometrics*, *66*(1–2), 225–250.

Turk, R. A. (2016). Negative interest rates: How big a challenge for large danish and swedish banks? [IMF working paper WP/16/198].

CHAPTER 17

THE ROLE OF ORGANISATIONAL CAPABILITIES IN THE RELATIONSHIP BETWEEN ENTREPRENEURSHIP AND TECHNOLOGICAL INNOVATION IN SMEs

Su-Jung Hwang[a] and Jae-Hyeok Choi[b]

[a]Keimyung University, Daegu, South Korea
[b]Bina Nusantara University, Jakarta, Indonesia

ABSTRACT

Technological innovation is crucial for businesses to achieve development and profitability through enhancing core capabilities and differentiating competitive advantages. The key to organisational survival is boosting innovation performance focused on technological innovation, as SMEs lack resources and competencies compared to large companies. Entrepreneurship is a topic of active research to overcome SMEs' resource and size limits. This is because entrepreneurs' capabilities are considered more important in small and medium-sized enterprises closely related to corporate success than in large enterprises that can receive organisational support. In addition, a company's holding capacity is a direct driver of creating differentiated competitiveness because it can pursue product differentiation through high levels of market capabilities and technology capabilities. Therefore, this study attempts to demonstrate

The Finance-Innovation Nexus: Implications for Socio-Economic Development
International Symposia in Economic Theory and Econometrics, Volume 34, 237–254
Copyright © 2025 by Emerald Publishing Limited
All rights of reproduction in any form reserved
ISSN: 1571-0386/doi:10.1108/S1571-038620240000034020

entrepreneurship and technological innovation for SMEs. Reviewing previous studies, the authors derive the organisational capabilities needed by the organisation for innovation and examine how these organisational capabilities (technological, market, and operational capabilities) relate to entrepreneurship and technological innovation.

Keywords: Entrepreneurship; organisational capabilities; technological innovation; SMEs; South Korea

JEL Classification Code: 'M00 General'

1. INTRODUCTION

In a rapidly changing business environment, corporate innovation is essential for continued survival and long-term growth. Corporate innovation is necessary for companies to create a differentiated competitive advantage by strengthening their core competencies and achieving growth and profitability. In particular, since small and medium-sized enterprises lack internal and external resources compared to large companies, enhancing innovation performance centred on technological innovation is the key to corporate survival (Adams et al., 2006).

Moreover, for SMEs to systematically achieve corporate innovation and lead to corporate performance, they must establish and strengthen their innovation capabilities, such as a good understanding of innovation, establishing clear innovation strategies, continuous investment in innovation systems, participation of all members, and spreading innovative culture (Drucker, 2006). However, prior research conducted on small and medium-sized enterprises does not provide guidance on the drivers or results of innovation due to a lack of systematic research. It has limitations because it does not provide a relationship with management performance from an integrated perspective of technology and organisation (Weerawardena, 2003).

Meanwhile, research on entrepreneurship in the field of organisational and strategic management is steadily spreading (Dess et al., 2003; Zahra et al., 2000). Furthermore, entrepreneurship is also active as a factor that overcomes the limitations of size and resource constraints of small and medium-sized enterprises (Rialp et al., 2005). This is because the competence of entrepreneurs is considered more important in SMEs that are closely related to corporate success than in large companies that can receive organisational support. Also, entrepreneurship allows companies to respond quickly to rapidly changing business environments, develop niche markets by contacting customers more closely (Yang et al., 2017), and enable activities that exceed the restrictions of controllable resources held by small and medium-sized enterprises (Cho, 2010).

In particular, the importance of entrepreneurship is becoming more prominent due to the recent global business environment that requires higher adaptability and value-added creation than ever before (Dess et al., 2003; Zahra et al., 2000; Zhou et al., 2007). However, due to the underestimation of top management's role, research on management's impact on corporate innovation is still lacking (O'Regan et al., 2006), and empirical research on entrepreneurship for small and medium-sized enterprises in Korea is also insufficient.

A study by Christensen et al. (2004) identified that SMEs have strengths in implementing entrepreneurial behaviour compared to large companies. This is because SMEs, which have less complex organisational structures than large companies, have the advantage of being able to respond more flexibly to environmental changes. Research on entrepreneurship can be an essential research task for small and medium-sized enterprises because SMEs that have been established for a long time often tarnish entrepreneurship and need to seek new changes (Moreno & Casillas, 2008; Simsek, 2007).

Therefore, this study aims to empirically analyse the relationship between entrepreneurship and technological innovation for SMEs. Specifically, prior research will derive the capabilities necessary for innovation and examine how these organisational capabilities (technological, market, and operational capabilities) relate to entrepreneurship and technological innovation.

2. LITERATURE REVIEW

2.1. Innovation

Innovation is essential for companies to gain a competitive advantage or enter a new market in today's competitive environment (Stock & Watson, 2002). Linder et al. (2003) defined innovation as implementing new ideas that create value. This conceptualisation encompasses various forms of innovation, such as new product development, new process technology, or management innovation (Zott, 2003). From a practical point of view, it means introducing new products or processes to improve corporate competitiveness and profitability by satisfying customer needs (Zahra et al., 1999).

Moreover, innovation also affects sustainable growth, as it enables cost-effectiveness and the development of new products to meet customers' needs (McEvily et al., 2004). According to Hitt et al. (2001), innovation is crucial in strengthening SMEs' competitiveness in domestic and foreign markets, and Lee et al. (2010) also mentioned the importance of innovation for SMEs. Innovation contributes to performance improvement in many industries (Zahra et al., 1999), especially in enhancing the competitive advantage of companies (Prahalad & Ramaswamy, 2003). According to Kanter (1999)'s argument, in today's competitive environment, small and medium-sized enterprises cannot survive the competition without innovation, and only innovative companies can enjoy a first-mover advantage.

Small and medium-sized enterprises with high creativity and the ability to develop new products can innovate more effectively than large enterprises (Vossen, 1998). Unfortunately, however, many small and medium-sized enterprises do not have such capabilities. Thus, SMEs with the ability to innovate quickly can gain a continuous competitive advantage. Therefore, effective technological innovation means that SMEs maximise their creative resources (Nonaka & Takeuchi, 1995). Many studies have discussed that innovation is essential for improving performance and gaining a competitive advantage (Banbury & Mitchell, 1995).

Meanwhile, innovation allows SMEs to create employment and achieve economic growth (Keizer et al., 2002). Small and medium-sized enterprises are well known as catalysts for employment and growth. The most important way of implementing this is the ability of small and medium-sized enterprises to innovate.

2.2. Technological Innovation

Technological innovation is the introduction of new products or new processes to improve a company's competitiveness and profitability by satisfying customer needs (Zahra et al., 2000). It has also been defined as a set of all activities to develop new products or improve existing products to create new markets (Song et al., 2006) and customers or increase market share and introduce new ideas or elements in the production process (Song & Dyer, 1995). In addition, technological innovation positively impacts corporate performance, and the company's internal capabilities and external environment are important factors in enhancing corporate innovation (Wang et al., 2022). In other words, technological innovation is the development of new products, services, and processes and improving products, services, and processes. In addition, technological innovation has a meaning as a new output, but rather as a process to create it. Technological innovation is exploring and utilising opportunities for new or improved products, services, and processes (Lee & Nawata, 2021; Pavitt et al., 1989).

2.3. Entrepreneurship

Entrepreneurship is the exploration and action of a company to create something new (Baron & Shane, 2007). In addition, it is defined as progressive behaviour in response to changes in the environment or organisation (Covin & Slevin, 1991) and behaviour for corporate growth rather than the psychological characteristics of invisible entrepreneurs (Sexton & Bowman, 1985). Although it is difficult to generalise entrepreneurship into a definition, it can be seen as creating a new business and pursuing innovation (Baron & Shane, 2007).

This concept of entrepreneurship is not only applicable to technology-oriented high-tech industries or large companies but can also be applied to small and medium-sized enterprises, venture companies, and public organisations (Yang et al., 2017). In addition, entrepreneurship appears in individuals, all societies, and companies of all sizes and forms (Davis et al., 1991). In recent years, entrepreneurship has been deeply related to strategic management rather than a spirit related to small businesses with a simple organisational structure. It has been studied as a necessary factor in identifying strategies (Sul, 2002).

Meanwhile, entrepreneurship is also being studied steadily in the field of organisational and strategic management (Dess et al., 2003; Zahra et al., 2000). Entrepreneurship is understood as a driver of a company's new business that can be achieved through internal innovation, joint ventures, or acquisitions. Existing studies include strategic transformation (Hitt et al., 1999), product, process, and organisational innovation (Zahra et al., 2000), and diversification (Burgelman, 1991), as well as the process of individual ideas developing into collective action through uncertainty management (Chung & Gibbons, 1997).

Entrepreneurial activities bring economic development and increase individual organisations' economic performance (Dornbusch et al., 2000). Moreover, entrepreneurial capabilities are considered more important in small and medium-sized enterprises closely related to corporate success than in large companies that can receive organisational support. In addition, companies can respond fast to rapidly changing business environments and develop niche markets by contacting customers more closely (Yang et al., 2017). Therefore, more active entrepreneurial activities at the corporate level are required for companies to maintain a competitive advantage in the rapidly changing environment (Zahra et al., 2000).

In addition, entrepreneurship is a concept related to various forms of novelty and plays an important role in the growth, survival, and performance of an organisation (Dess et al., 2003; Kazanjian et al., 2017; Kuo et al., 2022; Zahra & Nielsen, 2002). From a resource-based perspective, entrepreneurship is crucial in accumulating, transforming, and leveraging resources to achieve competitive advantage (Floyd & Wooldridge, 1999). In particular, it is reported to positively affect product, process, and organisational innovation to revitalise corporate organisations and improve market status (Zahra et al., 2000).

Considering the impact of the characteristics of founders and managers on startups, the importance of entrepreneurship on competitive strategies or holding capabilities of small and medium-sized enterprises can also be seen (McDougall & Oviatt, 2003). Entrepreneurship is one of the most influential factors in enhancing the performance of SMEs with resource constraints (McDougall & Oviatt, 2003). These characteristics can also be found in active behaviour (Spence & Crick, 2009). Active behaviour is related to the tendency to find various possibilities. Entrepreneurial activity goes beyond a pessimistic perception of one's situation and aims for more positive possibilities. Therefore, the expression of active can be seen as an opening to possibilities.

2.4. Organisational Capabilities

Based on existing studies, the capabilities required by the organisation to implement innovation are summarised in Table 17.1. Therefore, in this study, technological capabilities, market capabilities, and operational capabilities are presented as components of organisational capabilities.

In this study, the technological capabilities include technology environment (competitor) analysis ability, activity and response-ability to new technology development, technology portfolio management ability, and resource allocation ability. Market capabilities are regarded as marketing capabilities that commercially succeed innovative products, and operational capabilities are regarded as an organisational culture that promotes organisational innovation.

2.5. Entrepreneurship and Organisational Capabilities

Entrepreneurship is closely related to organisational capabilities and active adaptation, response, and innovation necessary for the changing environment (McDougall & Oviatt, 2003). In addition, high entrepreneurship is the basis for various activities of companies to create a final competitive advantage (Knight &

Table 17.1.   Prior Research and Derivation of Organisational Capabilities.

Organisational Capabilities	Siguaw et al. (2006)	Yam et al. (2004)	Jo et al. (2016)	Jung and Lee (2013)
Technological Capabilities	Technological capabilities — Explore, develop, acquire, and utilise new technologies	R&D capabilities — Innovation strategy, project execution, portfolio management, R&D investment	Technological capabilities	Technological innovation capabilities — R&D capability, technology accumulation capability, technology innovation system
	Resource allocation capabilities — Capital, tools, human resources, funds	Resource allocation capabilities — Human resource, capital, technology	Learning competency	
	Employee capabilities — Openness, autonomy, ideas, cooperation	Learning competency		
		Strategic planning capabilities		
Market Capabilities	Market capabilities — Collection of market information and internal adjustment	Production capabilities — Commercialisation	Marketing capabilities	Technology commercialisation capability — Commercialisation, production, and marketing capabilities
		Marketing capabilities		
Operational Capabilities	Production operation capabilities — Management-control activities, organisational structure, organisational culture	Organisational capabilities — Cultivate organisational culture		

Cavusgil, 2004). In particular, it will be more so if the company's size is small. SMEs need specific capabilities beyond vague behaviour to overcome weaknesses (Knight & Cavusgil, 2004), and it is essential to form an organisational culture that emphasises the retention of these capabilities (McDougall & Oviatt, 2003). Especially the formation of organisational culture will be most influenced by entrepreneurs depending on its size.

Furthermore, entrepreneurship recognises problems and trends and reorganises the management of resources, organisational structures, and systems to create opportunities to utilise technology while keeping customer needs in mind. Teece (2007) emphasised the importance of entrepreneurship in that it strengthens organisational capabilities. Not only is entrepreneurship highly associated with recognising new opportunities and combining market activities in newer ways, but it also affects creatively coordinating combinations of interrelated factors internally. As a result, it was argued that it consequently affects organisational capabilities that require integrating, coordinating, and relocating various resources.

2.6. Organisational Capabilities and Technological Innovation

In order to strengthen technological innovation activities, the ability to efficiently combine and utilise resources along with internal resources is important (Eisenhardt & Martin, 2000; Frost et al., 2002), and internal factors are more important than external factors (Hall & Bagchi-Sen, 2002). Efficient use of internal capabilities plays a vital role in the growth of small and medium-sized enterprises in the market, which are relatively lacking in size and resources compared to large companies. Grant (2008) argued that a company's internal capabilities are directly related to the survival and competitiveness of the company, so it is necessary to continuously develop capabilities such as R&D, production, marketing, and sales and distribution.

3. RESEARCH MODEL AND HYPOTHESES

3.1. Research Model

The proposed research model is shown in Fig. 17.1.

3.2. Research Hypotheses

3.2.1. Relationship Between Entrepreneurship and Technology Capabilities

Entrepreneurship can be seen as having an active impact on activities with competitive capabilities (Liu et al., 2010). In other words, managers with high entrepreneurship will try to achieve higher performance through competitive competencies (Zhou et al., 2007). Organisational capabilities directly drive differentiated competitiveness, and product differentiation can be pursued through high technological or marketing capabilities. This differentiation gives good cognition to customers (Khavul et al., 2010) and affects the repetitive purchase behaviour of products (McDougall & Oviatt, 2003). The following hypothesis is advanced based on the preceding discussions:

H1. Entrepreneurship has a positive effect on technology capabilities.

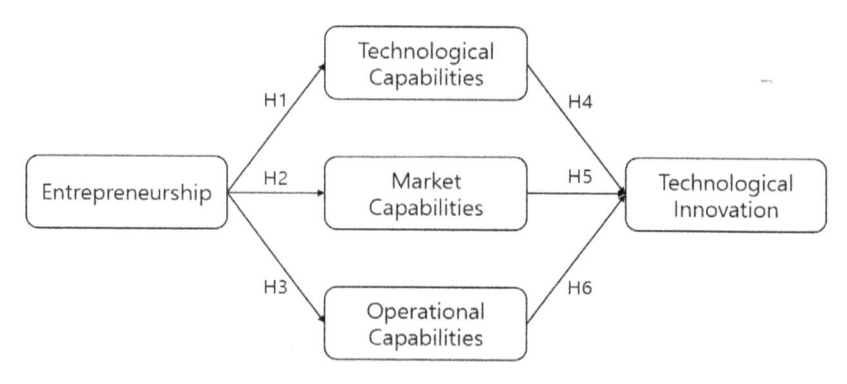

Fig. 17.1.   Proposed Model.

3.2.2. *Relationship Between Entrepreneurship and Market Capabilities*

According to Knight's (2000) study, entrepreneurship directly affects a company's marketing strategy. Similarly, a study by Hills and LaForge (1992) argued that companies strive to meet customers' needs in a competitive environment. In addition, Yoon (2015) also concluded that entrepreneurship directly affects marketing capabilities rather than directly affecting management performance. Accordingly, the following hypothesis is proposed:

H2. Entrepreneurship has a positive effect on market capabilities.

3.2.3. *Entrepreneurship and Operational Capabilities*

Entrepreneurship provides a foundation for effectively innovating companies, improving external competitiveness, enhancing employee morale and productivity, and increasing firm performance (Drucker, 1970; Stevenson & Gumpert, 1985). The reason is that entrepreneurship affects the behaviour of organisational members and is directly or indirectly related to organisational culture as a part of organisational characteristics. In particular, in the case of small and medium-sized enterprises, the overall corporate management often changes depending on the characteristics of managers (Hornsby & Kuratko, 1990) and because the personal characteristics of CEOs affect the structure and strategy (Garand & Fabi, 1991).

Moreover, managers with high entrepreneurship do not consider their constraints as weaknesses (Teece, 2007). They focus on overseas markets for more diverse possibilities and develop the necessary capabilities (Zhou et al., 2007). In other words, entrepreneurship becomes a fundamental engine for forming organisational culture. These engines build more diverse tangible and intangible resources, and these tangible and intangible resources affect corporate performance (McDougall & Oviatt, 2003). Consequently, the following hypothesis is established:

H3. Entrepreneurship has a positive effect on operational capabilities.

3.2.4. Relationship Between Technological Capabilities and Technological Innovation

Although technology is not the primary factor in improving productivity (Mavondo & Farrell, 2003), it has been found that corporate technology choices have a significant impact on a company's innovation success rate (Gatignon & Xuereb, 1997; Han et al., 1998). Innovation-oriented companies actively search, develop, acquire, and utilise new technologies for innovation (Grupp, 1998; Lee & Le, 2021). Han and Zhang (2021) also stated that very innovative companies tend to select and allocate resources for developing, acquiring, and utilising new technologies, organisational processes, and R&D. Therefore, the following hypothesis is established:

H4. Technology capabilities have a positive effect on technological innovation.

3.2.5. Relationship Between Market Capabilities and Technological Innovation

Marketing capabilities establish a competitive advantage by differentiating corporate images or products in the market (Cavusgil, 1980) and are an important determinant in improving corporate performance. The ability to market new products and services is also critical for successful innovation. This marketing ability has been shown to affect technological innovation by exploring the market environment, developing new products, and identifying customer demand required to improve existing products in the process of innovation (Rothwell, 1992). For SMEs to compete successfully in the market, they must be able to build capabilities in the marketing sector and connect them to competitive advantage factors (Knight, 2000). Accordingly, companies can build a competitive advantage due to superior marketing capabilities (Katsikeas et al., 1997). Accordingly, the following hypothesis is proposed:

H5. Market capabilities have a positive effect on technological innovation.

3.2.6. Relationship Between Operational Capabilities and Technological Innovation

In order to continuously implement technological innovation, an organisational culture that encourages innovation is most important. Organisational culture is shared by members of an organisation, which means values, beliefs, or fundamental assumptions (Oshima & Toma, 2023; Schein, 1985). Accordingly, organisational culture strongly influences the behaviour of members and creates norms that define the behaviour of individuals and groups. Also, organisational culture plays an essential role in improving organisational performance, and innovation-oriented organisational culture contributes to the organisation's various external resources and internal efforts for innovation, leading to technological innovation performance (Ma et al., 2021; Sackmann, 2011). A study by Moon (2009) also proved that innovation-oriented organisational culture has a positive relationship with the innovative behaviour of organisational members. A culture that fosters employees' challenges and experimental spirit enables innovation, especially innovation-oriented companies should create an environment where employees can explore freely without fear of punishment (Dundon, 2002). Thus, the following hypothesis is proposed:

H6. Operational capabilities have a positive effect on technological innovation.

4. RESEARCH METHODOLOGY

4.1. Sample and Data Collection

This study collected data from SMEs in major strategic industries during 2018 and 2019 in Daegu and Gyeongsangbuk-do Province in South Korea. Among 501 firms collected, 360 were selected for the analysis through preliminary verification, excluding 141 data representing low reliability. In order to increase the reliability of the survey results, the survey respondents were requested as CEOs or middle managers or higher. If responding is difficult, a working-level person with sufficient knowledge of the entire company should respond.

4.2. Measurement of Variables

Entrepreneurship. This research used four items (5-point Likert scale) to measure entrepreneurship by Covin and Slevin (1991).

Technological Capabilities. It is measured in six items (5-point Likert scale), such as the level of exploration, development, acquisition, and utilisation of technology by Grupp (1998) and the Ministry of SMEs and Startups (2007).

Market Capabilities. It is measured in five items (5-point Likert scale) by referring to Song and Parry (1996), and Verhaeghe and Kfir (2002) as marketing capabilities that commercially succeed innovative products.

Operational Capabilities. It is measured as a cultural characteristic that promoted the organisation's innovation orientation and was measured in seven items (5-point Likert scale) by referring to Denison and Mishra (1995).

Technological Innovation. It is measured by the proportion of new products in total sales over the past three years (Raymond & St-Pierre, 2010).

To solve the endogeneity issue, the firm size and firm age, suggested as factors that can affect technological innovation in existing studies, are introduced as control variables.

Firm Size. According to Cosh and Hughes (2000) study, firm size significantly affects technological innovation. Thus, in this study, firm size is controlled. The total number of employees was measured on the scale, and a natural log was taken and used for analysis.

Firm Age. Compared to old firms, young firms are more innovative. However, the longer the establishment period, the more access to external sources can be active (Mosakowski, 1991), and the more new products are produced, and patents are obtained (Deeds & Hill, 1996). Therefore, firm age is introduced as a control variable in this study, and the measurement was the number of years elapsed from the year of establishment to the present point.

4.3. Empirical analysis

4.3.1. Reliability and Validity

In this study, the construct validity of these data was verified by factor analysis by Varimax rotating four items for entrepreneurship measurement, six for technological capabilities measurement, five for market capabilities measurement, and six for operation capabilities measurement. As a result of the initial factor analysis, the factor analysis was conducted again because the first item measuring technological capabilities and the first item measuring operational capabilities were not significantly loaded. As a result, five factors were found. Furthermore, to review the data's reliability, Cronbach alpha values for each type were determined for the above questions. As a result, entrepreneurship 0.891, technological capabilities 0.926, market capabilities 0.830, and operational capabilities 0.877 were found to be reliable. These results are presented in Table 17.2.

4.3.2. Reliability and Validity

The mean, standard deviation, and correlation of each variable of the measurement variables are as shown in Table 17.3. Entrepreneurship was found to have a positively significant relationship with technological capabilities, market capabilities, operational capabilities, and technological innovation. In addition, technological innovation was found to have a positively significant relationship with entrepreneurship, technological capabilities, market capabilities, and operational capabilities.

Table 17.2. Results of Factor Analysis and Reliability.

Variable	Contents	1	2	3	4	Cronbach's α
Entrepreneurship	ENT1	0.317	0.326	0.183	**0.672**	0.891
	ENT2	0.219	0.206	0.070	**0.799**	
	ENT3	0.260	0.214	0.099	**0.827**	
	ENT4	0.271	0.243	0.125	**0.814**	
Technological Capabilities	TC1	0.195	**0.767**	0.202	0.220	0.926
	TC2	0.136	**0.795**	0.214	0.227	
	TC3	0.237	**0.815**	0.218	0.196	
	TC4	0.234	**0.832**	0.127	0.192	
	TC5	0.224	**0.836**	0.128	0.181	
Market Capabilities	MC1	0.055	0.230	**0.702**	0.024	0.830
	MC2	0.287	0.039	**0.563**	0.174	
	MC3	0.065	0.083	**0.824**	0.092	
	MC4	0.001	0.193	**0.802**	0.083	
	MC5	0.115	0.167	**0.826**	0.052	
Operational Capabilities	OC1	**0.714**	0.284	0.111	0.204	0.877
	OC2	**0.761**	0.216	0.118	0.142	
	OC3	**0.784**	0.164	0.137	0.154	
	OC4	**0.766**	0.098	0.163	0.116	
	OC5	**0.714**	0.138	0.036	0.243	
	OC6	**0.681**	0.163	α0.013	0.269	
Eigen value		8.186	2.468	1.787	1.339	
Percentage of variance (%)		40.930	12.339	8.936	6.694	
Percentage of cumulative variance (%)		40.930	53.270	62.205	68.900	

Table 17.3. Correlation Analysis.

	Mean	SD	1	2	3	4	5	6
1. Age	20.47	9.66						
2. Size(Log)	1.47	0.41	0.297**					
3. Entrepreneurship	3.97	0.72	−0.133*	0.098				
4. Technological Capabilities	3.46	0.68	−0.117*	0.004	0.561**			
5. Market Capabilities	3.34	0.63	0.030	0.084	0.325**	0.409**		
6. Operational Capabilities	3.70	0.63	−0.242**	−0.015	0.578**	0.504**	0.307**	
7. Technological Innovation	2.68	0.07	−0.205**	−0.129*	0.169**	0.281**	0.129**	0.238**

$*p < 0.05$, $**p < 0.01$.

4.3.3. Hypotheses Test

This study analysed the relationship between entrepreneurship, technological, market, and operational capabilities while age and size were controlled. Model 2 in Table 17.4 introduced entrepreneurship with age and size as control variables with technological capabilities as dependent variables, and the research model was significant ($F = 55.991$, $p < 0.01$), and R^2 also increased significantly compared to Model 1 ($\Delta R^2 = 0.303$, $p < 0.01$). Entrepreneurship has a significant and positive relationship with technological capabilities ($\beta = 0.561$, $p < 0.01$) (*H1*, supported).

Also, Model 4 determined entrepreneurship with age and size as control variables using market capabilities as dependent variables, and the research model was significant ($F = 15.011$, $p < 0.01$), and R^2 also increased significantly compared to Model 3 ($\Delta R^2 = 0.105$, $p < 0.01$). Entrepreneurship significantly and positively affects market capabilities ($\beta = 0.331$, $p < 0.01$) (*H2*, supported). Moreover, Model 6 was analysed with age and size as control variables using operational capabilities as dependent variables, and the research model was significant ($F = 67.518$, $p < 0.01$), and R^2 was also significantly increased compared to Model 5 ($\Delta R^2 = 0.301$, $p < 0.01$). Entrepreneurship has a positive and significant effect on operational capabilities ($\beta = 0.559$, $p < 0.01$) (*H3*, supported).

Table 17.4. Regression Analysis Results 1.

Variable	Model 1	Model 2	Model 3	Model 4	Model 5	Model 6
		Technological Capabilities	Market Capabilities		Operational Capabilities	
Age	−0.130*	−0.030	0.006	0.065	−0.260**	−0.161
Size	0.043	−0.042	0.082	0.032	0.063	−0.022
Entrepreneurship	–	0.561**	–	0.331**	–	0.559**
F	2.800	55.991**	1.262	15.011**	11.790**	67.518**
R^2	0.015	0.312	0.001	0.105	0.062	0.363
Adjusted R^2	0.010	0.303	0.380	0.380	0.057	0.357
ΔR^2 with Model 1	–	0.303**	–	0.105**	–	0.301*

$*p < 0.05$, $**p < 0.01$.

In Table 17.5, Model 2 used technological capabilities with age and size as control variables with technological innovation as a dependent variable, and the research model was significant ($F = 15.648$, $p < 0.01$), R^2 also increased significantly compared to Model 1 ($\Delta R^2 = 0.069$, $p < 0.01$). Technological capabilities have a significant and positive relationship with technological innovation ($\beta = 0.264$, $p < 0.01$) (*H4*, supported).

Furthermore, Model 3 analysed technological innovation as a dependent variable, age and size as control variables, and the research model was significant ($F = 8.570$, $p < 0.01$), R^2 also increased significantly compared to Model 1 ($\Delta R^2 = 0.020$, $p < 0.05$). There is a positive and significant relationship between market capabilities and technological innovation ($\beta = 0.142$, $p < 0.01$) (*H5*, supported). Also, Model 4 was significant ($F = 11.294$, $p < 0.01$), R^2 also increased significantly compared to Model 1 ($\Delta R^2 = 0.040$, $p < 0.01$). Operational capabilities have a significant and positive effect on technological innovation ($\beta = 0.205$, $p < 0.01$) (*H6*, supported).

5. EMPIRICAL RESULTS

5.1. Discussion and Implications

For SMEs to overcome the risk of market failure and secure a continuous competitive advantage, they must be able to achieve innovative results based on technological innovation. In the face of a lack of empirical research on entrepreneurship and technological innovation of domestic SMEs, this study will provide meaningful theoretical and practical implications for local SMEs. Furthermore, organisational capabilities (technological capabilities, market capabilities, and operational capabilities) derived from previous studies will be affected by entrepreneurship and can be used as primary data for policy support. The results of this study are as follows.

Table 17.5. Regression Analysis Results 2.

Variable	Dependent Variable: Technological Innovation				
	Model 1	Model 2	Model 3	Model 4	Model 5
Age	−0.183**	−0.149*	−0.184**	−0.130*	−0.133*
Size	−0.075	−0.086	−0.086	−0.088	−0.092
Technological Capabilities	–	0.264**	–	–	0.209**
Market Capabilities	–	–	0.142**	–	0.028
Operational Capabilities	–	–	–	0.205**	0.091
F	8.863**	15.565**	8.570**	11.294**	9.934**
R^2	0.047	0.116	0.067	0.087	0.123
Adjusted R^2	0.042	0.109	0.059	0.079	0.111
ΔR^2 with Model 1	–	0.069**	0.020*	0.040**	0.076**

*$p < 0.05$, **$p < 0.01$.

First, entrepreneurship has a positively significant relationship with technological, market, and operational capabilities, supporting the results of previous studies (Liu et al., 2010; Zhou et al., 2007). In particular, in the case of small and medium-sized companies, the CEO's influence greatly affects the entire organisation, so efforts should be made to strengthen internal capabilities and improve competitiveness through efforts to develop technologies based on entrepreneurship and actively respond to changes.

Second, it is found that technological, market, and operational capabilities have a positive relationship with technological innovation. These findings support previous studies that the ability to combine and utilise internal resources for technological innovation performance efficiently (Eisenhardt & Martin, 2000; Makumbe, 2022) and that the selection, development, and utilisation of new technologies are essential for technological innovation performance (Han & Zhang, 2021). In addition, marketing capabilities are important for the success of new product performance of SMEs (Knight, 2000).

For the continuous implementation and success of technological innovation, it is judged that it is important to establish an organisational culture that affects organisational members and the entire organisation. In particular, it is crucial to strengthen internal capabilities and manage innovation performance based on them in the case of small and medium-sized companies that lack spare resources.

Finally, policy implications are derived from the results of this study. This study confirms the validity of the previous research results, which are analysed without focusing on the innovation process while providing a useful basis for CEOs and policymakers to monitor and improve the innovation process.

In addition, regional industrial performance will increase by enhancing SMEs' innovation capabilities, and as a result of this, it will contribute to regional growth. It also presents a direction for SMEs to achieve successful technological innovation performance in an uncertain business environment where the need for business diversification and pressure for business conversion is increasing.

5.2. Limitations and Future Research Recommendations

In spite of the important results aforementioned, this study has the following limitations. First, in this study, technological innovation performance was measured as the proportion of new products in total sales over the past three years. Recently, as the importance of intellectual property rights increases, patents and trademarks need to be considered, and process innovation such as process development and process improvement may play an important role depending on the industry. Second, since the technological innovation process tends to take place over a long time, the need for long-term research using panel data should also be considered because differences in research results and implications depend on the research sample.

REFERENCES

Adams, R., Bessant, J., & Phelps, R. (2006). Innovation management measurement: A review. *International Journal of Management Reviews*, 8(1), 21–47.

Banbury, C. M., & Mitchell, W. (1995). The effect of introducing important incremental innovations on market share and business survival. *Strategic Management Journal*, 16(1), 161–182.

Baron, R. A., & Shane, S. (2007). Entrepreneurship: A process perspective. *The Psychology of Entrepreneurship*, 19–39.

Burgelman, R. A. (1991). Intraorganizational ecology of strategy making and organizational adaptation: Theory and field research. *Organization Science*, 2(3), 239–262.

Cavusgil, S. T. (1980). On the internationalization process of the firm. *European Research*, 6, 273–281.

Cho, A. (2010). *The jazz process: Collaboration, innovation, and agility*. Pearson Education.

Christensen, C. M., Anthony, S. D., & Roth, E. A. (2004). *Seeing what's next: Using the theories of innovation to predict industry change*. Harvard Business Press.

Chung, L. H., & Gibbons, P. T. (1997). Corporate entrepreneurship: The roles of ideology and social capital. *Group and Organization Management*, 22(1), 10–30.

Cosh, A., & Hughes, A. (2000). *British enterprise in transition*. Department of Applied Economics, University of Cambridge.

Covin, J. G., & Slevin, D. P. (1991). A conceptual model of entrepreneurship as firm behavior. *Entrepreneurship Theory and Practice*, 16(1), 7–26.

Davis, D., Morris, M., & Allen, J. (1991). Perceived environmental turbulence and its effect on selected entrepreneurship, marketing, and organizational characteristics in industrial firms. *Journal of the Academy of Marketing Science*, 19, 43–51.

Deeds, D. L., & Hill, C. W. L. (1996). Strategic alliances and the rate of new product development: An empirical study of entrepreneurial biotechnology firms. *Journal of Business Venturing*, 11(1), 41–45.

Denison, D. R., & Mishra, A. K. (1995). Toward a theory of organizational culture and effectiveness. *Organization Science*, 6(2), 204–223.

Dess, G. G., Ireland, R. D., Zahra, S. A., Floyd, S. W., Janney, J. J., & Lane, P. J. (2003). Emerging issues in corporate entrepreneurship. *Journal of Management*, 29(3), 351–378.

Dornbusch, R., Park, Y. C., & Claessens, S. (2000). Contagion: Understanding how it spreads. *The World Bank Research Observer*, 15(2), 177–197.

Drucker, P. F. (1970). Entrepreneurship in business enterprise. *Journal of Business Policy*, 1(1), 3–12.

Drucker, P. F. (2006). *Classic Drucker: Essential wisdom of Peter Drucker from the pages of Harvard Business Review*. Harvard Business Press.

Dundon, T. (2002). Employer opposition and union avoidance in the UK. *Industrial Relations Journal*, 33(3), 234–245.

Eisenhardt, K. M., & Martin, J. A. (2000). Dynamic capabilities: What are they? *Strategic Management Journal*, 21(10), 1105–1121.

Floyd, S. W., & Wooldridge, B. (1999). Knowledge creation and social networks in corporate entrepreneurship: The renewal of organizational capability. *Entrepreneurship Theory and Practice*, 23(3), 123–144.

Frost, T. S., Birkinshaw, J. M., & Ensign, P. C. (2002). Centers of excellence in multinational corporations. *Strategic Management Journal*, 23(11), 997–1018.

Garand, D. J., & Fabi, B. (1991). Fondements conceptuels des pratiques de GRH en petites et moyennes entreprises (PME): Formalisation, vision entrepreneuriale et modèle contingentiel. A. BERNARD et al), 324–336.

Gatignon, H., & Xuereb, J. M. (1997). Strategic orientation of the firm and new product performance. *Journal of Marketing Research*, 34(1), 77–90.

Grant, A. M. (2008). The significance of task significance: Job performance effects, relational mechanisms, and boundary conditions. *Journal of Applied Psychology*, 93(1), 108.

Grupp, H. (1998). Foundations of the economics of innovation: Theory, measurement and practice. In *Foundations of the economics of innovation* (pp. 99–140). Edward Elgar Publishing.

Hall, L. A., & Bagchi-Sen, S. (2002). A study of R&D, innovation, and business performance in the Canadian biotechnology industry. *Technovation*, 22(4), 231–244.

Han, J. K., Kim, N., & Srivastava, R. K. (1998). Market orientation and organizational performance: Is innovation a missing link? *Journal of Marketing*, 62(4), 30–45.

Han, C., & Zhang, S. (2021). Multiple strategic orientations and strategic flexibility in product innovation. *European Research on Management and Business Economics*, 27(1), 100136.

Hills, G. E., & LaForge, R. W. (1992). Research at the marketing interface to advance entrepreneurship theory. *Entrepreneurship Theory and Practice*, 16(3), 33–60.

Hitt, M. A., Ireland, R. D., Camp, S. M., & Sexton, D. L. (2001). Strategic entrepreneurship: Entrepreneurial strategies for wealth creation. *Strategic Management Journal, 22*(6), 479–491.

Hitt, M. A., Nixon, R. D., Hoskisson, R. E., & Kochhar, R. (1999). Corporate entrepreneurship and cross-functional fertilization: Activation, process and disintegration of a new product design team. *Entrepreneurship Theory and Practice, 23*(3), 145–168.

Hornsby, J. S., & Kuratko, D. F. (1990). Human resource management in small business: Critical issues for the 1990's. *Journal of Small Business Management, 28*(3), 9.

Jo, G. S., Park, G., & Kang, J. (2016). Unravelling the link between technological M&A and innovation performance using the concept of relative absorptive capacity. *Asian Journal of Technology Innovation, 24*(1), 55–76.

Jung, C. S., & Lee, G. (2013). Goals, strategic planning, and performance in government agencies. *Public Management Review, 15*(6), 787–815.

Kanter, R. M. (1999). From spare change to real change: The social sector as beta site for business innovation. *Harvard Business Review, 77*(3), 122–123.

Katsikeas, C. S., Deng, S. L., & Wortzel, L. H. (1997). Perceived export success factors of small and medium-sized Canadian firms. *Journal of International Marketing, 5*(4), 53–72.

Kazanjian, R. K., Drazin, R., & Glynn, M. A. (2017). Implementing strategies for corporate entrepreneurship: A knowledge-based perspective. In M. A. Hitt, R. D. Ireland, S. M. Camp & D. L. Sexton (Eds.), *Strategic entrepreneurship: Creating a new mindset* (pp. 173–199), Wiley-Blackwell Publishing.

Keizer, J. A., Dijkstra, L., & Halman, J. I. (2002). Explaining innovative efforts of SMEs.: An exploratory survey among SMEs in the mechanical and electrical engineering sector in the Netherlands. *Technovation, 22*(1), 1–13.

Khavul, S., Peterson, M., Mullens, D., & Rasheed, A. A. (2010). Going global with innovations from emerging economies: Investment in customer support capabilities pays off. *Journal of International Marketing, 18*(4), 22–42.

Knight, G. (2000). Entrepreneurship and marketing strategy: The SME under globalization. *Journal of International Marketing, 8*(2), 12–32.

Knight, G. A., & Cavusgil, S. T. (2004). Innovation, organizational capabilities, and the born-global firm. *Journal of International Business Studies, 35*, 124–141.

Kuo, Y. C., Wu, Y. M., & Liu, Y. X. (2022). Identifying key factors for sustainable manufacturing and development. *Review of Integrative Business and Economics Research, 11*(1), 30–50.

Lee, C. Y., & Le, B. N. T. (2021). Technological diversification and firm performance: The contingency effects of independent directors and growth opportunity. *Review of Integrative Business and Economics Research, 10*, 53–69.

Lee, B. Y., & Nawata, K. (2021). Risky innovativeness: The role of myopic management. *Review of Integrative Business and Economics Research, 10*(3), 1–17.

Lee, S., Park, G., Yoon, B., & Park, J. (2010). Open innovation in SMEs – An intermediated network model. *Research Policy, 39*(2), 290–300.

Linder, J. C., Jarvenpaa, S., & Davenport, T. H. (2003). Toward an innovation sourcing strategy. *MIT Sloan Management Review, 44*(4), 43.

Liu, X., Lu, J., Filatotchev, I., Buck, T., & Wright, M. (2010). Returnee entrepreneurs, knowledge spillovers and innovation in high-tech firms in emerging economies. *Journal of International Business Studies, 41*, 1183–1197.

Ma, L., Zhang, X., Wang, G., & Zhang, G. (2021). How to build employees' relationship capital through different enterprise social media platform use: The moderating role of innovation culture. *Internet Research, 31*(5), 1823–1848.

Makumbe, W. (2022). The impact of organizational culture on employee creativity amongst Zimbabwean academics. *African Journal of Science, Technology, Innovation and Development, 14*(2), 523–531.

Mavondo, F., & Farrell, M. (2003). Cultural orientation: Its relationship with market orientation, innovation and organisational performance. *Management Decision, 41*(3), 241–249.

McDougall, P. P., & Oviatt, B. M. (2003). Some fundamental issues in international entrepreneurship. *Entrepreneurship Theory and Practice, 18*(27), 1–27.

McEvily, S. K., Eisenhardt, K. M., & Prescott, J. E. (2004). The global acquisition, leverage, and protection of technological competencies. *Strategic Management Journal, 25*(8), 713–722.

Ministry of SMEs and Startups. (2007). *Technology innovation system evaluation indicators.*

Moon, S. (2009). Medicines as global public goods: The governance of technological innovation in the new era of global health. *Global Health Governance, 2*(2), 1–23.

Moreno, A. M., & Casillas, J. C. (2008). Entrepreneurial orientation and growth of SMEs: A causal model. *Entrepreneurship Theory and Practice, 32*(3), 507–528.

Mosakowski, E. (1991). Organizational boundaries and economic performance: An empirical study of entrepreneurial computer firms. *Strategic Management Journal, 12*(2), 115–133.

Nonaka, I., & Takeuchi, H. (1995). *The knowledge creating* (Vol. 304).

O'Regan, N., Ghobadian, A., & Sims, M. (2006). Fast tracking innovation in manufacturing SMEs. *Technovation, 26*(2), 251–261.

Oshima, Y., & Toma, T. (2023). The product innovation process with the use of mediators for collaboration: The case of Japanese traditional local industry. *Review of Integrative Business and Economics Research, 12*(3), 50–69.

Pavitt, K., Robson, M., & Townsend, J. (1989). Technological accumulation, diversification and organisation in UK companies, 1945–1983. *Management Science, 35*(1), 81–99.

Prahalad, C. K., & Ramaswamy, V. (2003). The new frontier of experience innovation. *MIT Sloan Management Review.*

Raymond, L., & St-Pierre, J. (2010). R&D as a determinant of innovation in manufacturing SMEs: An attempt at empirical clarification. *Technovation, 30*(1), 48–56.

Rialp, A., Rialp, J., Urbano, D., & Vaillant, Y. (2005). The born-global phenomenon: A comparative case study research. *Journal of International Entrepreneurship, 3*, 133–171.

Rothwell, R. (1992). Successful industrial innovation: Critical factors for the 1990s. *R&D Management, 22*(3), 221–240.

Sackmann, S. A. (2011). Culture and performance. In N. M. Ashkanasy, C. P. M. Wilderom & M. F. Peterson (Eds.), *The handbook of organizational culture and climate* (Vol. 2, pp. 188–224), SAGE Publications.

Schein, E. H. (1985). Increasing organizational effectiveness through better human resource planning and development. *Readings in Human Resource Management, 376.*

Sexton, D. L., & Bowman, N. (1985). The entrepreneur: A capable executive and more. *Journal of Business Venturing, 1*(1), 129–140.

Siguaw, J. A., Simpson, P. M., & Enz, C. A. (2006). Conceptualizing innovation orientation: A framework for study and integration of innovation research. *Journal of Product Innovation Management, 23*(6), 556–574.

Simsek, Z. (2007). CEO tenure and organizational performance: An intervening model. *Strategic Management Journal, 28*(6), 653–662.

Song, Y. M., & Dyer, B. (1995). Innovation strategy and the R&D-marketing interface in Japanese firms: A contingency perspective. *IEEE Transactions on Engineering Management, 42*(4), 360–371.

Song, M., Dyer, B., & Thieme, R. J. (2006). Conflict management and innovation performance: An integrated contingency perspective. *Journal of the Academy of Marketing Science, 34*(3), 341–356.

Song, X. M., & Parry, M. E. (1996). What separates Japanese new product winners from losers. *Journal of Product Innovation Management: An International Publication of the Product Development & Management Association, 13*(5), 422–439.

Spence, M., & Crick, D. (2009). An exploratory study of Canadian international new venture firms' development in overseas markets. *Qualitative Market Research: An International Journal.*

Stevenson, H. H., & Gumpert, D. E. (1985). The heart of entrepreneurship. *Harvard Business Review, 63*(2), 85–94.

Stock, J. H., & Watson, M. W. (2002). Forecasting using principal components from a large number of predictors. *Journal of the American Statistical Association, 97*(460), 1167–1179.

Sul, H. K. (2002). *An exploratory model of the relationships among the external environment, entrepreneurial strategy, mechanistic-organic structure, and financial performance of restaurant franchisors from the perspective of franchisees.* Virginia Polytechnic Institute and State University.

Teece, D. J. (2007). Explicating dynamic capabilities: The nature and microfoundations of (sustainable) enterprise performance. *Strategic Management Journal, 28*(13), 1319–1350.

Verhaeghe, A., & Kfir, R. (2002). Managing innovation in a knowledge intensive technology organisation (KITO). *R&D Management, 32*(5), 409–417.

Vossen, R. W. (1998). Relative strengths and weaknesses of small firms in innovation. *International Small Business Journal, 16*(3), 88–94.

Wang, L., Zeng, T., & Li, C. (2022). Behavior decision of top management team and enterprise green technology innovation. *Journal of Cleaner Production, 367*, 133120.

Weerawardena, J. (2003). The role of marketing capability in innovation-based competitive strategy. *Journal of Strategic Marketing, 11*(1), 15–35.

Yam, R. C., Guan, J. C., Pun, K. F., & Tang, E. P. (2004). An audit of technological innovation capabilities in Chinese firms: Some empirical findings in Beijing, China. *Research Policy, 33*(8), 1123–1140.

Yang, M., Evans, S., Vladimirova, D., & Rana, P. (2017). Value uncaptured perspective for sustainable business model innovation. *Journal of Cleaner Production, 140*, 1794–1804.

Yoon, J. (2015). The evolution of South Korea's innovation system: Moving towards the triple helix model? *Scientometrics, 104*, 265–293.

Zahra, S. A., Ireland, R. D., & Hitt, M. A. (2000). International expansion by new venture firms: International diversity, mode of market entry, technological learning, and performance. *Academy of Management Journal, 43*(5), 925–950.

Zahra, S. A., & Nielsen, A. P. (2002). Sources of capabilities, integration and technology commercialization. *Strategic Management Journal, 23*(5), 377–398.

Zahra, S. A., Nielsen, A. P., & Bogner, W. C. (1999). Corporate entrepreneurship, knowledge, and competence development. *Entrepreneurship Theory and Practice, 23*(3), 169–189.

Zhou, L., Wu, W. P., & Luo, X. (2007). Internationalization and the performance of born-global SMEs: The mediating role of social networks. *Journal of International Business Studies, 38*, 673–690.

Zott, C. (2003). Dynamic capabilities and the emergence of intraindustry differential firm performance: Insights from a simulation study. *Strategic Management Journal, 24*(2), 97–125.

www.ingramcontent.com/pod-product-compliance
Lightning Source LLC
Jackson TN
JSHW011308171224
75586JS00004B/51